Henry Cowles

The Gospel and Epistles of John

Henry Cowles

The Gospel and Epistles of John

ISBN/EAN: 9783337714246

Printed in Europe, USA, Canada, Australia, Japan

Cover: Foto ©ninafisch / pixelio.de

More available books at **www.hansebooks.com**

THE GOSPEL

AND

EPISTLES OF JOHN:

With Notes,

CRITICAL, EXPLANATORY, AND PRACTICAL,

DESIGNED FOR BOTH PASTORS AND PEOPLE.

BY

REV. HENRY COWLES, D. D.

"The words that I speak unto you, they are spirit and they are life."—JESUS.

NEW YORK:
D. APPLETON & CO.,
549 & 551 BROADWAY.
1876.

Entered according to Act of Congress, in the year 1876, by
REV. HENRY COWLES, D. D.,
In the Office of the Librarian of Congress, at Washington, D. C.

PREFACE.

JOHN wrote his gospel for the twofold purpose—"that ye might believe that Jesus is the Christ, the Son of God; and that, believing, ye might have life through his name." The Christian commentator can have no other worthy object than to enter into the spirit and promote the purposes of his author.

In the present case he has no occasion to aspire to any thing higher, and can have no apology for any thing lower, or other. To *reveal Jesus to men,* so that, in the light of his words and of his deeds, they shall see him to be surely the promised Christ, the very Son of God, and therefore the Giver of life to morally dying souls—this is supreme. No object can be higher or nobler; none more vital to real salvation. To know Jesus as John reveals him is not only to know that he is sent of the Father; bears witness to the truth; suffered unto death as "the Lamb of God, taking away the sin of the world," but it is also to know his heart of love and sympathy, of fellowship with his people, and of most tender and confidential friendship.——It is the charm of John's writings that they bring Jesus impressively near to the heart, and beget a sense of personal acquaintance with the Lord. Under such apprehensions of Jesus, our love to him naturally becomes *intelligent* and therefore solid, enduring, and such as legitimately develops itself in joyous obedience.

In my Notes on John, my first aim has been *interpretation* —to unfold and illustrate the true and the whole sense of his words. The amount of labor expended upon passages has been in the compound ratio of their *difficulty* and of their relative *importance*. In this as in former volumes my plan presents not so much the processes of my investigations as the results, and not so much other men's opinions as my own.

A few passages involving vital issues, in which I could not be satisfied with the current and commonly received interpretations, have been treated with unusual fullness; *e. g.* (John 3: 5): "born of water and Spirit;" and (John 20: 23) on remitting or retaining other men's sins. Under a sense of their very high importance, I have sought to unfold thoroughly Christ's doctrinal discussions with the Jews (John 5 and 6); his views of their moral blindness and righteous doom, as in John 12: 37–41; the doctrine of the Holy Spirit; the scenes and the significance of Gethsemane and Calvary; the resurrection, also, and not least the true divinity of Christ in its relation to the trinity and unity of God.

In the way of practical application, I have aimed at little beyond *suggestion*. This field is naturally unlimited; my plan allows me only to indicate in few words where it lies, but not to range over it at will.

The Epistles of John have been subjoined as a natural appendix—the author's own application of the great facts of his gospel history. I trust this addition will not prove void of interest or of spiritual profit.

HENRY COWLES.

OBERLIN, O., *January* 28, 1876.

THE GOSPEL OF JOHN.

GENERAL INTRODUCTION.

I. THE AUTHOR.

THIS gospel history—the last in order of the four, and latest in date of composition—is, on the concurrent testimony of the best authorities, ascribed to the Apostle John. Noticeably he is spoken of in the book itself, not under his proper name *John*, but as "the disciple whom Jesus loved." (See 13: 23, and 19: 26, and 20: 2, and 21: 7, 20, 24.) The last of these verses indicates him as the author of this book.

The testimony in proof that John was the author falls naturally under two heads: The *external*, *i.e.* historical; and the *internal*.

The *external* comes to us in the earliest writings, more or less fragmentary, of the Christian age.

In sifting this testimony it should be borne in mind that oral tradition respecting the words and deeds of Jesus was earlier than the apostolic writings; and moreover that (according to Luke 1: 1-4) there were some written memoirs put in circulation by others than the apostles, in advance of theirs, at least in advance of Luke. In view of these facts, Meyer evinces commendable discrimination in omitting from his proofs of the genuineness of this gospel history sundry passages in writings now bearing the name of Barnabas or Ignatius (men nearest to the apostles), and a portion of what comes in Irenæus, on the ground partly of some doubt as to genuineness in the case of Ignatius, but more on the ground that the passages in question while they *may* perhaps have been taken from the writings of John, *may* also with equal probability have reached those writers by means of oral tradition. To make the proofs satisfactory, there should be some distinct reference to a written document like this gospel, and a somewhat exact quotation of its language.

With due regard to these principles we may name Papias * as perhaps the oldest witness, of whom Eusebius affirms that he used proofs from John's first epistle. It is conceded that this epistle and the gospel were written by the same John, so that testimony to the genuineness of one, makes with scarcely abated force for the genuineness of the other.

Of the same nature is the testimony of Polycarp † who quotes 1 John 4: 3; "For whosoever does not confess that Jesus Christ has come in the flesh is antichrist."

Justin Martyr ‡ (Apology I: 61) quotes from the conversation of Christ with Nicodemus (John 3: 5); "For Christ said, Except ye be born again, ye can not enter into the kingdom of heaven."——"The first power after God, the Father and Lord of all, is the Word who is also the Son;

---

* Bishop of Hierapolis in Phrygia, whom Irenæus describes thus: "An ancient man who was a hearer of John and a friend of Polycarp."

† Of Polycarp, who fell a martyr about A. D. 150, Irenæus his pupil, has this striking testimony (Irenæus II: 158, 159). Writing to Florinus, he says—"While I was yet a boy, I saw thee in Lower Asia with Polycarp. For I have a more vivid recollection of what occurred at that time than of recent events (inasmuch as the experiences of childhood, keeping pace with the growth of the soul, become incorporated with it), so that I can even describe the place where the blessed Polycarp used to sit and discourse; his general mode of life and personal appearance, together with the discourses which he delivered to the people; also how he would speak of his familiar intercourse with John and with the rest of those who had seen the Lord; and how he would call their words to remembrance. Whatsoever things he had heard from them respecting the Lord, both with regard to his miracles and his teachings, Polycarp, having thus received information from the eye-witnesses of the Word of life, would recount them all in harmony with the scriptures," etc.

‡ Justin, born at Sychem (Palestine); first a professional student and teacher of pagan philosophy; but after his conversion a laborious missionary of the gospel, labored among the churches of Asia Minor and also at Rome where, near the middle of the second century, he sealed his faith with his blood. Among his works (of great value) are two Apologies for Christianity, addressed to Roman Emperors, and a dialogue with Trypho a Jew, elaborating the argument from the Old Testament that Jesus was the Messiah.

and of him we will relate that he took flesh and became man." (Compare John 1: 1, 2, 14.) Justin's Apol. I: 32.

Tatian, a disciple of Justin, not only quoted from John's gospel but made up a "Diatessaron" (this word signifying *four in one*), the first effort known to us upon a harmony of the four gospels. This of course assumes the existence of the four in his time. He flourished about A. D. 170.

Athenagoras* evinces a familiar acquaintance with what John has said of the Logos, to which reference will be made in a special essay upon the relation of the Logos to the Trinity.

Meyer in his commentary (p. 14) remarks that the earliest of the Christian fathers who quotes John's gospel *by name* is Theophilus,† thus:—"Whence the holy scriptures and all the inspired men teach us, from among whom John writes: 'In the beginning was the Word,'" etc. This father also prepared a harmony of the four gospels.

The testimony of Irenæus ‡ is specially valuable—to the points that the apostles did not enter upon their great work of preaching the gospel to every creature, nor did they hand it down to men "in the scriptures to be the ground and pillar of their faith" until after they were filled with the Holy Ghost.

Concerning the gospel writers he specifies thus: "Matthew issued a written gospel among the Hebrews in their own dialect while Peter and Paul were preaching at Rome and laying the foundations of the church. After their departure [death], Mark, the disciple and interpreter of Peter, did also hand down to us in writing what had been preached by Peter. Luke also, the companion of Paul, recorded in a book the gospel preached by him. Afterwards John, the disciple of the Lord, who also had leaned upon his breast,

---

* Athenagoras, foremost among the fathers of the second century in the staple merits of an author, was a Christian philosopher of Athens, and wrote his Apology A. D. 177. His themes correspond with those of Justin—treated, however, more ably. His extant works are usually printed with Justin's.

† Theophilus, made bishop of Antioch in Syria, A. D. 168, wrote a commentary on the four gospels, not now extant.

‡ Irenæus, born in Asia Minor, trained under Polycarp and Papias, went as a missionary to Lyons and Vienne in France about A. D. 150; became bishop of Lyons A. D. 177; died a martyr's death A. D. 202. His great work against the heresies of his age stands among the choicest and most instructive relics of the second century.

did himself publish a gospel during his residence at Ephesus in Asia." (Irenæus I: 258, 259.)

Irenæus quotes often and largely from the gospel of John—for example thus: "John, the disciple of the Lord, desiring to put an end to all such doctrines [as those of the heretics referred to] commenced his teaching in the gospel thus: 'In the beginning was the Word,'" etc., quoting entire John 1: 1–5. (Irenæus I: 288.)

Curiously Irenæus sometimes gives scope to his fancy, as we may see in his argument from the nature of things as to the number four, that there must needs be four gospel histories; no more, no less; because (he says) there are four zones of the world in which we live and four principal winds; and the cherubim of John's Revelation had four faces, etc. (Vol. I. 293). We may accept his testimony to the fact that there were in his day four gospel histories extant, and four only, while we demur to his argument as to the reason why.

The external testimony to the early reception of John's gospel may be closed with the fact that all the prominent heretics of the second century (Marcion, the Valentinians, the Montanists, Cœlsus, etc.) recognized this book as not only extant, but of admitted authority among all Christians. (See Meyer, pp. 15, 16.)

Meyer suspends his citation of individual witnesses with this remark (p. 19): "By the end of the second century and from the beginning of the third, tradition in the church testifies so clearly and uniformly in favor of the gospel that there is no need of additional vouchers (*e. g.* Clement of Alexandria, Tertullian, Hippolytus, Origen, Dionysius, etc.). Eusebius (III: 25) places it among the homologoumena" [universally accepted].

The nature and force of this testimony will be readily seen if we consider that those Christian brethren who were most intimately associated with the Apostle John when he wrote this book and who first received it from his hands must have known beyond the possibility of mistake that he was the author. It should be borne in mind that the great body of Christians in those early ages appear to have appreciated very justly the value of inspired writings as compared with any thing whatever not inspired, and consequently, the critical responsibility resting upon themselves in this particular point of accrediting any document as the writing of apostles or their associates. It is on record that such men as Justin

Martyr (A. D. 140-160); Origen (A. D. 203-254); Jerome (A. D. 370-420), visited the churches of Asia Minor, of Rome, and of Palestine and Syria, to ascertain from those to whom the Epistles were addressed and among whom the gospel histories were first put in circulation, what books were written by accredited apostles or under their immediate supervision. Only on the basis of substantial testimony was any book admitted to the confidence of the churches as coming from inspired men. This was no less true of the gospel histories than of the Epistles, *e. g.* to Rome, Corinth, Ephesus. As in the case of these Epistles, those churches primarily addressed were the original witnesses, competent above all others to testify from whom they came, so in the case of the several gospel histories, those churches among whom they were first circulated, and for whom each severally was specially adapted and written, would be the primary authority as to their authorship. It deserves special notice that these four gospel histories bear internal marks of a very distinctive character. From such marks it appears that Matthew wrote primarily for Jewish readers, never pausing to explain what all Jews must understand, and quoting the Old Testament scriptures most abundantly, as might be expected of an author himself a Jew, writing to and for Jewish readers.——As to Mark, the tradition of those times witnesses that he had been intimately associated with Peter. Correspondingly the internal conditions of the book are met if we suppose it primarily written (like Peter's epistles) for "the strangers scattered abroad throughout Pontus, Galatia, Cappadocia, Asia, and Bithynia." The accurate memory of Peter as an eye-witness appears in the minute particulars given of the looks, actions, and manifest emotions of the chief actors—not to say also in the very full and honest account of Peter's denial of his Lord, and of his tears of bitter repentance.——Luke, it is well known, traveled and labored long with the Apostle Paul. Of Gentile origin himself, and conversant with Gentile churches, it was fitting that his gospel narrative should adapt itself as it does to their knowledge and wants. Luke's style stands highest in Greek culture, and most abounds in allusions to the current history of the Roman Empire. So it should if indeed he wrote primarily for those churches which Paul planted throughout most of the provinces of that great empire, and even in her very capital.——Of John it should be said that his explanations of Jewish usages; *e. g.* of their marriage customs (2: 6); of the Passover (2: 23, and

6 : 4); and of the national antipathy between Jews and Samaritans (4: 9) show plainly that he had in mind other readers than Jews in Judea. Suffice it to say that his internal marks harmonize most entirely with the testimony of early Christian writers that he wrote at Ephesus, and with special adaptation to the churches of Asia. Note the corresponding facts of his seven brief epistles to the seven churches of Asia, in Rev. 2 and 3. All those churches, therefore, must have known this aged apostle intimately. Receiving this gospel history from his hands, they were of all men the most important witnesses to his authorship. It is simply impossible that on this point they could be mistaken.

Thus the external, historical testimony justifies the conclusion that the author of this gospel was the Apostle John. No counter-testimony of any importance appears.

INTERNAL TESTIMONY.

1. The book throughout bears marks of having been written by that one of his disciples whom Jesus loved preëminently, who leaned on his bosom at supper, and enjoyed his intimate confidence. This disciple might be expected to remember best those words and deeds which form the staple of this book. The spirit of the book is in beautiful harmony with the spirit of the Apostle John as we may gather it from these incidental allusions.

2. The book corresponds admirably with the traditional notices of this apostle in his advanced years—affectionate, tender, earnest—whose spirit appears in his latest exhortation, "Little children, love one another."

3. The date of this gospel coincides with the great age of John. Every thing indicates that this gospel was written after the other three; and all history testifies that John long survived all the other apostles.

4. The style evinces much more skill and familiarity with the Greek tongue than the style of the Revelation—favoring the opinion that this gospel was written many, perhaps a score of years, subsequently to the prophetical book. (Tholuck and Meyer.)

5. Finally, no other man known to history, save John, was living in the age when this gospel history was written who was at all equal to its production. So Neander expresses himself with the strongest conviction (p. 6):

"It could have emanated from none other than that 'beloved disciple' upon whose soul the image of the Savior had left its deepest impress. So far from this gospel's having been written by a man of the second century (as some assert), we can not even imagine a man existing in that century so little affected by the contrarieties of his times and so far exalted above them. Could an age involved in perpetual contradictions; an age of religious materialism, anthropomorphism, and one-sided intellectualism, have given birth to a production like this, which bears the stamp of none of these deformities? How mighty must the man have been who, in *that* age, could produce from his own mind such an image of Christ as this! And this man too, in a period almost destitute of eminent minds, remained in total obscurity! Was it necessary for the master-spirit who felt in himself the capacity and the calling to accomplish the greatest achievement of his day, to resort to a pitiful trick to smuggle his ideas into circulation?"

PERSONAL HISTORY.

The Apostle John was the son of Zebedee and Salome; brother of the martyred James (Acts 12: 2); a fisherman by occupation, and resident on the shore of the Sea of Galilee, otherwise called Tiberias. The family was manifestly of some means. The fact that John was "known to the high Priest" (John 18: 15, 16) may have been due to his business relations with Jerusalem as the chief market; perhaps also, to his social and religious position among the leading men of Jerusalem.——Apparently Salome was a sister or sister-in-law of Mary, the mother of Jesus, for comparing the several enumerations of the women who from a distance witnessed the crucifixion, we have in John 19: 25, the mother of Jesus and "his mother's sister;" in Matt. 27: 56, "the mother of Zebedee's children;" and in Mark 15: 40, the specific name, "Salome." On this supposition John's relationship to Jesus may in part account for the intimate and tender sympathy between them.

DATE OF THIS GOSPEL.

It is very probable that John did not locate in Ephesus until after Paul's last interview with the elders of that church (Acts 20: 17–38), inasmuch as his presence, supposing him there at that time, could scarcely have failed of some notice in this narrative. Even Paul's second letter to Timothy, then at Ephesus (about A. D. 67), makes no allusion to the Apostle John as being there—not to say that John's presence there would have obviated the necessity of sending Timothy there at all. But the exigencies of those seven churches of Asia as they are brought to view in Rev. 2 and 3, may be supposed to have brought him there from Jerusalem, and the more so as the calamities impending over Jerusalem admonished not only the apostles, but all Christians to escape from the doomed city. Very definite historical testimony proves that John lived to a great age, and passed the closing years of his life with the churches of Asia Minor, at or near Ephesus. The fact that the first three gospel histories very minutely record while John entirely omits the prophetic discourse of Jesus with his disciples, foretelling the destruction of Jerusalem by the Romans and specifying the antecedent signs of this catastrophe (Matt. 24, and Mark 13, and Luke 21), may be accepted as proof that Matthew, Mark, and Luke wrote before the fall of the city, and John after. How long after, no existing data suffice to show with more than proximate precision. The most probable estimate assigns its date between A. D. 80 and 90.

The special aim and purpose of this gospel history deserve attention. After three gospel histories were already extant, what worthy object could call for a fourth?

Perhaps anticipating this question, John himself gave the answer which we find (chap. 20: 30, 31) in these words: "Many other signs truly did Jesus in the presence of his disciples, which are not written in this book. *But these are written that ye might believe that* Jesus is the Christ, the Son of God, and that, believing, ye might have life through his name." This seems to be very definite. His purpose was to prove to his readers that Jesus of Nazareth was truly the promised Messiah and indeed the Son of God; and further, to persuade them to faith in him as such in order that, believing, they might have life — the true gospel life of salvation — through his name. Thus, to prove the great gospel facts respecting Jesus, and to persuade men to accept him by cordial faith unto salvation, were the two coördinate aims of this gospel history.——If it be objected that this passage contemplates rather John's aim in his selection from Christ's miracles than his general purpose in the writing of his book, it may be fitly replied that a very considerable portion of the book hangs upon the miracles it records; that these were introduced, not as naked facts of history, barren of special pertinence and relations, but as the occasion of introducing those vastly important discussions with the Jews to which they gave rise, or with the no less broad purpose of showing forth the Messiah's glory to his disciples and friends. The author specifies the latter as the purpose of Jesus in the first recorded miracle (John 2: 11). The discussion with the Jews which grew out of the healing at Bethesda (John 5); out of the feeding of the five thousand (John 6); out of the healing of the man born blind (John 9); out of the raising of the dead Lazarus (John 11), are in point to show that the selection of precisely these from Christ's many miracles had for its ulterior object the proof of his claims to be the Messiah, and the setting forth of his glory as one "mighty to save."

In studying the purpose and aim of this gospel history as compared with the other three, we are met with a very considerable difference, not to say contrast, in its general character. Thus:—John omits what Matthew and Luke give in detail respecting the antecedents of the human birth of Jesus; the genealogy of Joseph and Mary; the angelic announcements, and the various incidents of his early history. On the other hand they all omit, but John gives, the antecedents on his divine side—how the divine "Word" was related to God, and ultimately "became flesh and dwelt among us."——In the line of historic facts John omits the temptation of Jesus in the wilderness, his transfiguration on the holy mount (though a personal witness), very many of his miracles, his agony in Gethsemane; and in the line of his instructions, John passes by the Sermon on the mount, his numerous parables, the prophetic announcements respecting the destruction of Jerusalem, etc., etc. But over against these he records matter which they all omit; *e. g.* the personal labors of Jesus with Nicodemus, with the woman of Samaria, with the man healed at the pool of Bethesda, with the man born blind, and his relations to the loved family at Bethany, and the raising of Lazarus; and especially the extended discussions with the hostile, captious Jews; also the full and free conversations and the remarkable prayer with his disciples during the evening preceding his arrest. Comprehensively we might say the three earlier gospel histories give the *moralities* of the Christian life; this of John, the *spiritualities*. Those unfold the moral law in its principles and applications; this, the law of the spiritual life—the relations of Jesus to his people as their bread of life, their "good Shepherd," their sympathizing Friend; and especially the doctrine of the Comforter—his mission and his work. The former are characterized by the Sermon on the mount, the royal law of love and its application to "my neighbor:" the latter, by the law of love to Christ and to the brethren, and the blessed fruits thereof.

With these points before us of broad distinction between John's and the three earlier gospel histories, it seems appropriate to ask—

Was this gospel history purposely made supplementary to the other three?

Beyond all question it *is* largely so; but was it made so of definite purpose—the others lying before him, and his mind being impressed with a sense of their deficiencies and of the importance of supplying them?——Or, did this gospel history become supplementary in a way mainly or altogether incidental, and without set purpose; *i. e.* as the result of having a somewhat different special aim before his mind, such as he has himself indicated, and by prosecuting it in a thoroughly independent way?——The latter seems to me most probable. There is at least no proof that John had the other gospel histories before him at the time of his writing. He makes no such allusion to them as we find in the Second Epistle of Peter (3: 15, 16) to the writing of his brother Paul, nor such as appear in Luke 1: 1, 2, to other gospel narratives. Yet, writing so long after the other three, it is *a priori* probable that John had known of their existence, and, moreover, had seen them, and had at least some general notion of their contents.——But on the other hand, if he wrote with those gospel histories before him, purposely to make his own supplementary to those, it is not easy to account for the discrepancies which he suffered to exist in some points between his history and theirs; as, for example, in the antecedents to the feeding of the five thousand. Why did he not either correct them if he thought them in error, or adjust his statement to theirs if he knew them to be correct? It is entirely manifest that John wrote in a perfectly independent way, adhering closely to his proposed object; selecting his matter and giving it shape, all for the precise ends which he had in view. He therefore stands before the world as an independent witness to the great facts both of the historic life and of the words of Jesus which he records. As such, his gospel is of priceless value. No estimate can exaggerate its importance or its living interest and vital bearings upon the inner life of his people.

Yet other points claim brief attention.

In circles of German criticism it has been gravely objected to the genuineness and authenticity of John's gospel history that its Messiah is *too unlike* the Messiah seen in the three antecedent gospels, and therefore can not have been the same personage, or at least can not have been drawn by the same divine inspiration.* As those critics accept the historic Messiah of the first three gospel histories, they claim to feel bound to reject the Messiah of John, and, consequently, the record itself.

This critical objection may be met as follows:

1. The points newly or more fully developed in John are in no respect *inconsistent* with the character and work of the Messiah as presented in the three antecedent gospels. Surely Matthew, Mark, and Luke have reported nothing of the Christ whose words and deeds they record which is inconsistent with his true divinity—nothing which precludes the doctrine that the personage named by John "the Logos"— existing from eternity with God, and really himself God— assumed, or in the phrase of John, "became" flesh, entered into a mysterious union with the Son of Mary, and became thus God manifest in the one man Jesus. For, observe, the Jesus Messiah of those first three gospels is sinless, so that on the moral side there can be nothing incompatible with his being really divine as well as human. He is, moreover, *all-wise;* he made no mistakes. He is all-powerful for any exercise of power which his mission called for. No miracle needful to his work was ever too stubborn for his arm. Thus we might expand this point indefinitely, to the preclusion of any, even the least possible inconsistency in supposing that the Messiah set before us in the first three gospels was really all that John represents him.

2. We have in the earlier gospels some remarkable foreshadowings of those great points which are the staple of what is most peculiar to John; *e. g.* in Matt. 11: 27, and 28: 18, and Luke 10: 22: "All things are delivered unto me of my Father" ["all power is given unto me in heaven and in earth"]; "and no man knoweth the Son but the Father, neither knoweth any man the Father save the Son, and he to whomsoever the Son will reveal him;" or as put by Luke, "No man knoweth who the Son is but the Father, and who

---

* As the objection is phrased in Olshausen (2: 288)—"The Savior as delineated in the fourth gospel appears a perfectly different person from that which he is described to be in the three other gospels."

the Father is but the Son," etc.——"All things delivered unto me;" "All power in heaven and in earth given to me:"——Who then is this "*me?*" Shall it be assumed that he is merely, only, a man, one of our own mortal race? ——Note further; this claim to have received from the Father the investiture of supreme control of the universe is backed up by the assertion of a somewhat in his nature unknown to all but the Father, and indeed that himself knows the Father as no other being in the universe can know him. How can these affirmations be true of any being lower than the Eternal Word who "was from the beginning with God," and who "was God?" Let it not, therefore, be said that the Divine Word, the Eternal Logos, is not distinctly foreshadowed in the words of Christ as recorded by Matthew and by Luke.

3. The points specially unfolded by John (though not by him alone and exclusively) are of exceeding vitality and importance, such as could in no manner be spared from the Christian system. It seems pertinent therefore to inquire briefly how it came to pass that they were not unfolded in their fullness by the earlier gospel historians, and why they should have been reserved (to such a degree) for John, and to a period so late?

My reply may be brought mainly under three heads:

(1) From the beginning it has been the divine policy—unquestionably and most obviously a wise one—that in shaping his written revelation to men there should be "*progress of doctrine.*" As in the history of all human science, so in the written revelation made to men of God and of his ways, the simpler elements come first in order, and so the mind is aided to rise by gradual stages of advance to the higher elements. This principle appears in the advance made by John upon the earlier gospel historians.

(2) According all honor and all efficiency to the wisdom of the inditing Spirit, we may yet attribute much that is peculiar in this gospel to what was in great measure special and peculiar in John himself. His mind was contemplative and loved to go into the deep things of God. His heart was affectionate, and for this reason entered into the deepest spiritual communion with Jesus. There was a reason in his inmost being why he, rather than any other one of the twelve, should lean on Jesus' bosom and be known as "the disciple whom Jesus loved." Hence he, more than any other one of the twelve, caught up, studied, and re-

membered those words in which Jesus spake of his relation to the Father, his pre-existent glory, and of his inexpressible love for his people. If we assume his personal relationship by blood to Jesus (as above noted), this fact may have had some bearing upon the very peculiar intimacy and freedom of affection and confidence which existed between them. To this may be added that the lapse of years, the mellowness of old age, and perhaps a careful and profound study of the earlier gospel histories may have combined to impress him with the importance of having the points which naturally interested him so deeply brought out in the greater fullness which we see in his gospel history.

(3.) Something may be attributed to what was external to his later life. His removal from Jerusalem to Ephesus—from Palestine to Asia Minor—transferred him from the atmosphere of Jewish to that of Grecian mind. It brought him into contact with new modes of thought, and we may also say probably with new and peculiar receptivities to truth. The Jews were the staunchest of Monotheists. It had been the work of ages to impress into the depths of Jewish thought—"*The Lord our God is one Lord.*" We find in this gospel history by John that they stumbled fatally over this offense—Jesus claiming to be equal with God. Somewhat as the result of ages of providential training, they could bear no modification of their monotheistic doctrine. In the Grecian mind as developed in Asia Minor and in Egyptian Alexandria, the case was far otherwise. The doctrine of emanation, applied to God, was no offense to them. There were some among them who held that the Supreme One might send forth from himself other beings of truly divine attributes, and had done so. This sect, currently known as "Gnostics," were, it is thought by many, in the eye of John when he wrote this gospel. It may be supposed that one inducement to write it was to set forth the true view as opposed to the subtle errors of the Gnostic sect.——Furthermore, it may be suggested that, in the capability of nice distinctions (one of the strong features of the Greek tongue), as well as in the acuteness of Grecian mind, and in the absence of foregoing prejudice, John might have seen special facilities and inducements for putting forth prominently the great points made in his gospel history. The way was providentially opened for the fuller development of the real doctrine of the Trinity, including the pre-existent divine person of Christ.

Another point it may not be amiss to discuss; for although it might not be thought of by those who make small account of the human element in inspiration but large account of the divine; yet it is wont to be an offense to those who on the other hand make chief account of the human and little or none of the divine.

The question is raised—Did John record these extended conversations of Jesus from memory, or from written documents made up at or near the time of their occurrence? How is the human thought and mind of John related to the facts he describes and the speeches he records? Were they given him by direct inspiration; or did he as a personal witness, seeing and hearing for himself, come to his knowledge under the normal laws of the human mind?

Let it be considered that according to our best knowledge, not far from half a century intervened between the historic events and the writing of the book. What can be said of John's remembering the events and the spoken words with accuracy for fifty years?

I suggest these points. The accurate and retentive remembrance of transactions seen and of spoken words heard, depends on several various conditions:

(*a*) It is partly a thing of original endowment, some minds being far more gifted in this respect than others.

(*b*) It is always a thing more or less of careful culture and practice. Training and use will work wonders. It should also be considered that before printing and before books came into current use, there was far greater demand for the culture of memory as to spoken words than there has been since.

(*c*) Very much will always depend on the *mind's interest* in the things seen or heard, and upon their being kept fresh before the mind by frequent repetition and by deep, absorbing reflection. We are by no means to assume that John dropped those deeds and words of Jesus from his mind through the lapse of those fifty intervening years. Rather it should be assumed that no day passed in which they were not in some aspects present to his thought and living in the deeps of his heart's emotions and affections, often repeated and impressed in his preaching and conversation.

(*d*) Something must be accorded to that well known law of mind by which, far into old age, the scenes of youth and the impressions made in the earliest years of life, abide in their freshness, while things and words of recent date fade out of memory.

(e) Though last not least, is the aid of " the Comforter." It was one of his promised functions—" He shall bring all things to your remembrance, whatsoever I have said unto you." We need not interpret this to imply any violation of the laws of the human mind. Under these laws there is ample scope for the effects promised. Verily there can never be any lack of resources in the Infinite Mind to reach the human mind which himself has made in his own image, with suggestions, quickened remembrance, sanctifying impressions.

In view of these points—all germain to the case—there need be no stumbling over the hypothesis that John recorded with sufficient accuracy for all the purposes of vital truth the events transacted and the words spoken a half century before he made the record which has come down to us.

GOSPEL OF JOHN.

CHAPTER I.

The author first introduces the great personage of his book by setting forth his true divinity, and especially his relations to God before he became manifest to men (vs. 1, 2). He was supreme and universal Creator (v. 3); the source and fountain of life and light to men (v. 4); albeit this light was strangely repelled by a benighted world (v. 5). Prominent among the subjects brought forward in this chapter is the mission of John the Baptist as a witness for Christ (vs. 6-8). Jesus was the true light of the world although so strangely repelled by his ancient people (vs. 9-11). Yet some did receive him, thus becoming sons of God by a birth truly from God (vs. 12, 13). The divine Word appeared in human form, revealing to men the glory of the Father (vs. 14, 18). Again the author reverts to the testimony of John the Baptist (v. 15), and enlarges upon the fullness of grace and truth which comes to men through Christ, other and greater than that which came through Moses (vs. 16, 17).——Priests and Levites are commissioned from Jerusalem to interrogate Jesus; his reply (vs. 19-28). John sees Jesus approaching and bears direct testimony that he is the Lamb of God and the Son of God (vs. 29-34). Two of John's disciples follow Jesus and invite others to him (vs. 35-42). Jesus finds and calls Philip and Philip introduces Nathaniel (vs. 43-45); what Jesus said to Nathaniel closes this chapter (vs. 46-51).

1. In the beginning was the Word, and the Word was with God, and the Word was God.

Who is meant by the "Word," is amply shown by the descriptive points presented in vs. 1-18, but especially in vs. 1-3, 14. The personage to whom this peculiar name is applied can be no other than the Christ, the Son of God with special reference to what he was *before* he became manifest to men in human flesh. This "Word," having been "with God" from eternity, himself really God, "became flesh and dwelt among us, and we beheld his glory." For, according to v. 1, *before* he thus became flesh, he existed even "from the beginning" and then was "with God and

(17)

was God." As further described (v. 18) he "was the only begotten Son;" was "in the bosom of the Father;" and having come forth before the world of mankind, declared or manifested God to them.

"In the beginning the word *was*"—existed. By the almost universal consent of critics, the phrase "in the beginning," signifies in the past eternity; before time; before the world was. The author must have thought of "the Word" as existing before this world or any part of the material universe came into being, for he affirms that "all things were made by him," and there was not the least occasion for saying that the Creator must have existed before he could create. Apparently John had in mind the first verse of Genesis; "In the beginning God created the heavens and the earth." We may infer this from his using equivalent words, and from his reference immediately to the creation of all things as done by the Logos.——If it be asked why John uses "In the beginning" to denote *in eternity past* I would answer: In the poverty of all human language to express the idea of past eternity, this phrase came to hand as the nearest approximation. In the beginning the Word was in being—not, came into being, but was already in being—before any thing else existed with which to compare it—before any epoch from which to date his existence; farther back than thought itself can travel—back of the remotest point reached by the boldest outgoings of human search—*there* was the eternal Word already in existence.

It should therefore be carefully remarked that John does not by any means attempt to fix the date when the "Word" began to exist, but only to help us conceive of his existence from eternity by saying that at the earliest point we can think of, the Word was already in existence.——It should be noted that the Greek word for "beginning"* is without the article. If John had referred to any well known beginning, to any definite recognized epoch as the point at which the Word came into being or even was in being, he would have used the article. Omitting it, he must mean that at first—at that intangible, ideal point which we may conceive of as the remotest point possible to human thought, then and there the Word existed.

"*The Word.*" Passing on from the inquiry *Who* was the Word? we meet the question—Why does John choose this Greek term *Logos*, as a name for the eternal Son of God?

To this question two answers have been given.

(*a*) That this name is chosen with an eye to its essential significance, *word* meaning that which conveys thought, which carries truth from mind to mind. With this may be coupled the antecedent usage of Scripture which associates power with spoken words as uttered by the Almighty.

(*b*) That the term "Logos" was chosen by John with special reference to existing or foregoing speculations in regard to the di-

* $\alpha\rho\chi\tilde{\eta}$.

vine being, *e. g.*, those of Plato the Grecian philosopher or of Philo the Jewish, coupled also perhaps with the usage of the Jewish Targums which in some cases translate the Hebrew terms for God by the circumlocution—"The Word of the Lord."

Instead of adopting either of these theories to the entire exclusion of the other, I prefer to attribute a measure of influence to both. The first named is altogether natural, and moreover is quite in harmony with the cast of John's mind—at once simple and profound. Hence he might think of the term *word* as the vehicle of thought—the medium for conveying truth from one mind to another. In this view the eternal Word is simply the revealer of God: his mission is the uttering forth to the apprehension of intelligent man, or more broadly, to the intelligence of all created minds the truth concerning God.——We notice that John makes this function of the Son every-where prominent. "No man hath seen God at any time; the only begotten Son *hath declared* him" (v. 18). "Truth came by Jesus Christ" (v. 17). Jesus himself makes this point emphatic: "I came into the world to bear witness to the truth" (John 18: 37).

Moreover let us not miss the great fact that in the Holy Scriptures God does honor to written words as the vehicle of truth in respect to himself. In the universe of matter God has made a lower revelation of himself: the higher comes through *words*, spoken in former times by the prophets; "in these last days by his Son" (Heb. 1: 1, 2). Abstractly therefore, yet most comprehensively, the Great Revealer himself may fitly be named the "Word."

That John rather than Matthew, Mark or Luke should originate this usage of the term "Word" may be due, not alone to his metaphysical cast of mind, but possibly in part to the fact that it fell to him as one of the gospel historians to record the verbal utterances of his Master. The other historians give his miracles; the great deeds that filled out his public life: John, far more than they, his spoken words—those extended discussions which he had with captious Jews, and his tender conversations with his beloved disciples.

Let it be noted also that while the term Word has naturally the primary sense of that which conveys thought—which carries truth from mind to mind, yet the Hebrew writers prior to John had associated with the spoken word of God the idea of *power*. "God *said*, Let there be light: and light was" (Gen. 1: 3). "He *spake*, and it was done; he commanded, and it stood fast" (Ps. 33: 9). "He commanded, and they were created" (Ps. 148: 5). "He sendeth forth his commandment upon earth; his *word* runneth very swiftly" (Ps. 147: 15, 18).——This accessory idea in the term logos made it still more appropriate for John's purpose.

It seems to me legitimate to sustain this view by appeal to John's analogous use of the terms "Life," "Light," "Truth." If it be objected that the term "word" denotes not the speaker but the thing spoken, so (it may be replied) does the term "life" denote properly the abstract entity and not its author and source; "light" is that by means of which we see and not the Light-bearer; the word "truth" denotes properly the abstract idea and not its Revealer, yet in almost the same breath John calls the Eternal Son first "the Word;" then the Life, the Light, the Truth. "The Life was the Light of men" (v. 4). "That was the true Light which is coming into the world" (v. 9). "For the Life was manifested, and we have seen and bear witness, and show unto you the Eternal Life who was with the Father, and was manifested unto us" (1 John 1: 2).——Here the argument is that this usage—the abstract term for the concrete—a name significant of what he does, applied to designate the Great Agent himself—is shown to be in harmony with John's cast of mind and habits of expression, and therefore goes far to sustain the theory that he gives the name *word* to the Eternal Son, in part at least because he came to men with the truth concerning God clothed in human speech.

Yet while I make chief account of this prime significance of the term "word" as the reason for John's use of it here, I see no occasion to rule out the other reason noticed above, viz: the fact that in the philosophical speculations of the Greeks and Jews as seen in Plato, Philo and in the apocryphal books ("Wisdom of Solomon" 9: 9-11, 17 and Ecclesiasticus 24), there had been an approximation toward this usage of the term "word," or its correlate, "wisdom." With an eye upon this usage, and with the purpose of correcting its misconceptions, and filling out more fully the great idea of which those philosophers had scarcely the germ, John may have defined and expanded the sense of this term Logos.

"The Word was *with God*." No just interpretation of this clause can drop below the implication of some sort of distinct personality. The preposition "with" does not indeed define the precise sense or give the exact measure of this personal distinction; but it certainly forbids absolute identity. The "Word" must therefore be somewhat different from and other than God—else he could not with propriety be said to be "with God." *

---

* The Greek student would notice that the preposition for *with* is not *meta* which would suggest companionship, intimate association; nor is it *sun* which would indicate a yet closer fellowship; but it is *pros*—the primary and usual sense of which is to be in front of, as when one thing is in the presence of or before another—suggesting therefore that the Logos is the visible manifestation of God; is that of God which is put forward and becomes patent, apprehensible, visible, to his creatures. Yet a few cases of New Testament usage are found in which pros is translated "with." Thus: "Are not his sisters all *with* us?" (Matt. 13: 56). "Are not his sisters here *with* us?" (Mark 6: 3). In these cases however pros might be taken in the sense—*before* us; in our presence. Also Mark 9: 19, "O faithless

"And the word was God"—not merely was godlike; not, was simply *divine* in the loose transcendental sense in which great men and their great thoughts and deeds are sometimes spoken of as divine. Nor in the opposite extreme does the phrase mean that the Word was *the God*—the only God; the God in the exclusive sense which should comprise within himself all there is of God. This exclusive sense would have been indicated by the Greek article if it had been used here. But standing without the article, the sense must be—was truly and essentially divine. The ancient exposition "very God" is felicitous, in the sense—nothing less than God, yet not excluding those other equally divine persons—the Father and the Spirit.*——Yet again; To translate, "was *the God*," meaning the *whole of God*, would nullify what John had just said—"was with God," for it would render such a fact impossible. Nor can we translate—The Word was a God—for this would imply an absolutely distinct being—another God—a statement revolting to the whole current of Scripture, both of the Old Testament and the New.

2. The same was in the beginning with God.

"The same was in the beginning with God."——"The same" —this very Logos; literally—this one; this personage.——Note that v. 2 brings together the first and second clauses of v. 1. In that verse John had said two things, viz: that the Word was *in the beginning;* and that the Word was *with God*. In v. 2 he affirms that the Word was with God in the beginning—*i. e.*, before the first act of creation; during the past eternity. Whatever the relation expressed by *with*, it was not a thing of time only; was not of recent occurrence or of transient duration, but had existed coeval with the existence of God. This point John makes emphatic by his perfectly explicit affirmation in this verse.——Moreover it is supposable that one object in repeating "was with God" may have been to guard the reader against the possible misapprehension above referred to, viz: supposing "the Word" to comprehend the whole Godhead.

3. All things were made by him; and without him was not any thing made that was made.

All things became existent—began to be—by him; and without his agency has nothing ever come into being. That the divine Word created the entire universe—has been *universal* Creator—is affirmed in the strongest possible language, first by the term "all;" second, by excluding all other creatorship—every other creative agency but his.

generation! how long shall I be *with* you?" *i. e.* going out and in before you. So 1 Cor. 16: 6, 7: "It may be that I will winter *with* you. I trust to tarry awhile *with* you" (*i. e.* in your society).

* For a more extended discussion of the divinity of Christ as related to the Trinity of the Godhead, see Excursus I in the Appendix.

It should be noted that although in this passage no allusion is made to any agency of the Father in creation, yet elsewhere in the New Testament his agency is brought to view, and that of the Son is represented as being mediate, executive: *e. g.* "In God who created all things *by* Jesus Christ" (Eph. 3: 9). "By whom (his Son) he (God) made the worlds" (Heb. 1: 2). We also find forms of statement entirely coincident with this of John, *e. g.* "For by him (the Son) were all things created that are in heaven and that are in earth; visible and invisible; whether they be thrones or dominions, or principalities or powers; all things were created by him and for him" (Col. 1: 16).——In yet another passage (1 Cor. 8: 6) the concurrent agency of the Father and of the Spirit is put in this form: "But to us there is but one God, the Father, of whom are all things and we in him; and one Lord Jesus Christ, by whom are all things and we by him." This passage from Paul has the metaphysical precision characteristic of his clear thought and nicely adjusted words.

If now the question be asked, Why did John at this point introduce the "Word" as Creator—a fact touched in this connection only in this one short verse and not referred to again; it may be answered:—(*a*) For the sake of the great fact itself:—(*b*) To confirm and enforce the idea of his true divinity: "He who built all things is God" (Heb. 3: 4).—(*c*) To give greater breadth to the conception of the Eternal Word as the Revealer of God. Naturally the Word should be thought of as the Messenger of God to men by his written revelation, being comprehensively the true *word* of God to men. But there is another grand department of God's revelation of himself—viz., that which is made *through the universe of matter*—here ascribed equally to the divine Son of God.—(*d*) Incidentally this verse augments the proof that John has before his mind the first words of Moses (Gen. 1: 1), in which God is introduced to mankind as the Creator of the heavens and the earth.

Comparing with each other the respective introductions to their several histories as given by Mathew and Luke on the one hand and by John on the other, we may note that while the two former put in the foreground the *human* birth and antecedents of Jesus, the latter gives first the divine antecedents of the Eternal Word who became flesh—*i. e.* came down to dwell as man among us. The former trace the genealogy of the man Jesus to Adam, Abraham, and David; the latter labors to carry us back to the position and relations of that exalted divine Personage who was in being before the world was, coexisting eternally with the Father, and really himself God. If the former sought to support the Messiahship of Jesus by showing that he was truly the Son of David, the latter sought equally to prove that Jesus is the Christ the Son of God (John 20: 31) "in order that believing" on such a Savior "we might have life through his name." Thus appropriately each author in the very manner and scope of his introduction foreshadows the drift of his book.

4. In him was life; and the life was the light of men.

"In him *is* life" [*is* rather than "was," on the best authorities]—the present tense implying that life is in him forevermore, and is not a transient, temporary endowment.——In him is life, moreover, not in the sense merely that he exists, but far beyond this—that he is the great and sole Life-giver—the infinite Fountain of Life.

Yet further we must ask—In what sense of the word "life?" ——This word being used here with no limitation whatever, we must interpret it in the absolutely universal sense—all life in the universe. Yet the context shows that John's thought is specially upon moral, spiritual life; for he proceeds to say, this life brings *light* to men—not sunlight to the eye of the body, but the light of God to human souls, that light which terminates in salvation as its end.——Following closely the course of John's thought—the laws of suggestion under which one thought follows another—we may assume that he passes from Creatorship which gives existence to matter and animal life to sentient beings, to this far higher function exercised upon a lost race dead in sin, which offers *life* in the rich and glorious sense of restoration to God, to hope and to bliss. He who first gave physical existence to all that is—vegetable or animal—advances to the analogous yet nobler function of breathing life into souls dead in moral ruin.

"This life was the light of men." It developed its power by means of truth—which shows that its action takes effect upon intelligent mind, not upon non-intelligent matter. For certainly "light" here must refer to mind—must be not sunlight upon the material eye, but the light of God upon darkened understandings. The subsequent context demands this spiritual sense of the word.——This light concerning God stands naturally correlated to the life which resurrects human souls from death in sin to reconciliation, peace, love, and blessedness in God.

5. And the light shineth in darkness; and the darkness comprehended it not.

Our translators should have followed the original and inserted the article before "darkness"—shineth in *the* darkness—the well known moral darkness of a fallen race.——As material light might be supposed to labor to pierce into the dense darkness [*e. g.* of a London fog] but meet only repulsion, so this precious light from heaven poured itself forth upon the darkness of benighted souls the world over, but alas! this darkness would not admit its heavenly rays.——"*Would* not" is the appropriate phrase in this case; for while in the material world light naturally penetrates and scatters away darkness, and we never think of darkness as making intentional or even natural opposition, it is entirely otherwise in the spiritual world. For here the very mischief—the real virus of darkness is its moral repugnance to Heaven's light—the alarming and guilty fact being that men love darkness rather than light, and therefore do not make light welcome—not even this glorious light from heaven, emanating from "the Father of lights," the very God of love.

6. There was a man sent from God, whose name *was* John.

7. The same came for a witness, to bear witness of the Light, that all *men* through him might believe.

8. He was not that Light, but *was sent* to bear witness of that Light.

This transition to John the Baptist may seem at first view abrupt. If so, a closer attention will show that the evangelist passes from the general statement in regard to the moral darkness of the race repelling the light of God, to particulars, to show the antecedent steps taken in the kind providence of God to secure a favorable reception for the Great Revealer of heavenly light when he should come.

"There was * a man," etc., we might paraphrase—It came to pass under the divine economy that a man was sent from God (after the manner of the old prophets) whose name was John. The specific and sole purpose of his divine mission was to bear witness to Jesus, the great Light about to appear from God, to the end that all men through him (*i. e.* through the influence of his antecedent teaching and testimony) might believe in Jesus when he should come. He was not that great Light of whom I have spoken, but was sent to prepare the way for his reception as the long promised Messiah. Thus the evangelist introduces John the Baptist.

9. *That* was the true Light, which lighteth every man that cometh into the world.

Here the writer would prove that Jesus (not John the Baptist) is the true—*i. e.* the real, genuine light from heaven. In v. 8 he had said that John was not that great Light but came to bear witness to him who was. Continuing the discrimination, he subjoins—"The true Light was that which, coming into the world, enlightens every man." The universality of his work is its token and identification. He came to bring the light of God, not to Jews alone; not to Jews and their proselytes; but to Jews and Gentiles without distinction; to all men of every race and clime. ——Critics differ on the point whether the phrase "coming into the world," is said of this "Light," or of "every man." Grammatically either is admissible. I incline to connect as above with the "Light," (Jesus Christ), because his coming into the world is a very prominent thought throughout this entire passage, kept constantly before the mind; while, on the other hand, connected with "every man," it seems altogether inept and purposeless. What does it add to the significance of the words "every man?"

---

* Greek, "Εγενετο," it came to pass.

Is there a tacit allusion to some men who do *not* "come into the world" and so fail of seeing this light? Does the writer make this a special point—that only those men who come into this world receive this light? This is scarcely supposable. But he does wish to impress the fact that Christ *came into this world*—from heaven to earth—on the grand mission of bringing down the light of God to all of every race who would receive it.——Moreover the Messiah had long been known as *the coming* one; "he that should come"—the word being the same as here. (Matt. 11: 3, and 21: 9, and Luke 7: 19, 20, and John 6: 14, and 11: 28, and 12: 13).

10. He was in the world, and the world was made by him, and the world knew him not.

11. He came unto his own, and his own received him not.

Note how the writer amplifies his subject, reiterates and rearranges his points, to express his amazement at the strange repulsion which this Light from heaven received. He actually came down into this very world in person: indeed the material world was his own creation, and moreover he gave all living men their very being; and yet these minds made intelligent by his own gift, would not know him. He came unto a people specially selected ages before to be his own, and even they did not (as a nation) receive him.*——The coming, specially in mind, is that of his incarnation rather than his antecedent manifestations to Israel through prophets or providential agencies.

12. But as many as received him, to them gave he power to become the sons of God, *even* to them that believe on his name:

13. Which were born, not of blood, nor of the will of the flesh, nor of the will of man, but of God.

While most of his originally chosen people rejected their Messiah a few received him by faith—a faith of the sort that both believes and loves—and so became "Sons of God." "*Power*" to become God's sons—in the sense of prerogative, high privilege. The power contemplated seems not to be a new moral ability by means of which alone the recipient could exercise saving faith, for the receiving of him by faith precedes in the order of nature this blessing of sonship toward God. To such as had received him, he gave this right or privilege.

"Who were born," (*i. e.* became sons of God) "not of blood

* The Greek reader would notice the difference of gender. He came unto his own *things* (τα ιδια, neuter), and his own people (οἱ ιδιοι, masculine) did not receive him. Israel considered as God's inheritance, the home of his sanctuary, is a *thing*—a possession, truly his own; the people acting as men on their personal moral responsibility, are persons, as the masculine gender implies.

(not by lineal descent from Abraham as the Jews of that day assumed)—not of the impulses of the flesh as in all human births; —not of any merely human willing or action, but of God, by virtue of his grace alone. The sonship of believers is all of God. Whoever will receive Christ by faith as his own personal Savior is adopted (or born) into the family of God as a son. The being born is simply and only being made sons of God. As many as receive Christ God receives into sonship—brethren of Christ.

14. And the Word was made flesh, and dwelt among us, (and we beheld his glory, the glory as of the only begotten of the Father,) full of grace and truth.

"The Word was made flesh"—the very phraseology suggesting the poverty of human language to express a truth so profoundly mysterious. For we must not think of any essential transformation of the Word into flesh of such sort as would convert Deity into humanity, though it may be admissible to suppose that the divinity subjected itself, under some law unknown to us, to the conditions of human flesh. The conditions and relations of this union between God and man are but partially revealed in the Scriptures and have never been fathomed by any human research. It seems safe to assume, because apparently revealed in Scripture, that this incarnation ("the Word became flesh") was the union of the divine Logos *with a whole man;* not to a human body only with no human soul; nor to the human soul only with no human body save in appearance or semblance; but the real divinity was united under laws and conditions not fully known to us, with a real and complete man.——There is no occasion to say—with humanity in the abstract, for such a conception only helps toward mysticism and obscurity—We may also assume as the result of this union on the negative side, that the man Jesus became thereby none the less a man—none the less subject to the incidents of normal humanity—the frailties, infirmities, fatigues, and sufferings, the demands for nutrition, sleep, and rest; the exposure to temptation, at least from the devil if not from the world and the flesh.— On the other hand, the divine Logos did not become in any respect less than divine by reason of this union. It did involve an obscuring of his divine glory, an *emptying of himself* as to this glory, as Paul puts it (Phil. 2: 7), yet manifestly only in the sense of what was apparent, and related to the form rather than the reality.

It is also clear that this union ensured a most intimate sympathy between the human and the divine in the person of Jesus, and indirectly a marvelous sympathy between Jesus and all his believing people toward whom he evermore bears himself as their Elder Brother—a relation which could not have been what it now is without the incarnation.——Of its great and precious results bearing upon the value of his atoning death, and of his mediation, ever living before the Father's throne; also upon the exaltation of his accepted brethren gathered home to the "many mansions" he has himself provided for them—it is not in place here to speak.

"And dwelt among us"—*tabernacled*, or dwelt in a tent among us, as the Greek word denotes, with manifest allusion to the visible glory which, under the old economy, dwelt in the thick darkness of the most holy place. Yet the divine glory though shaded was not entirely obscured, for we saw some forth-streaming rays thereof—"the glory as of the only-begotten of the Father." Interpreting to us the moral significance of this word "glory," he says, "full of grace and truth"—grace in the sense of kindness, love, favor; and " truth " comprehensively put for the revelations he was evermore making of God and of human duty.

The word "only-begotten" opens new questions, specially these two:—(a) Does it refer to the Logos—the divine nature of Christ; or to the man Jesus as born of the virgin Mary?——(b) If its reference be to the Logos, then we have the further question: Must the epithet be taken in its primary sense, involving actual birth into existence, and implying a derived and created being; or in its secondary sense—one best beloved, dearest to the heart?

As to this epithet " only-begotten," * the history of its N. T. usage is briefly this: It is used by John (1: 14, 18, and 3: 16, 18, and 1 John 4: 9), and by Luke (7: 12, and 8: 42, and 9: 38; also in Heb. 11: 17), which may be only another case of Luke's usage. Only John applies it to the person of Christ.——That he applies it rather to the divine person of Christ than to the human is strongly indicated in each case by the context, the "glory" spoken of (v. 14) being manifestly that of his pre-existent divine personality. His being from eternity in the bosom of the Father (v. 18) sustains the same reference. God's "giving his only begotten Son" (3: 16) naturally suggests the Logos rather than the man Jesus. So also in 1 John 4: 9; "In this was manifested the love of God because that God sent his only-begotten Son into the world that we might live through him."

(b.) Assuming then its special reference to the divine Logos, must we give the word its primary sense—*the only born*—excluding all other sons, yet involving the normal sense of bringing into being; or, ruling out the idea of derived existence as incompatible with his existing from eternity and with his being really God—(the very point which John affirmed in the outset) (1: 1),— may we limit its meaning to the secondary sense, viz, *best beloved?*

This secondary sense is a natural one, the special affection felt by the parent for an only son being an impulse and law of nature. It is moreover favored by the Hebrew usage of their corresponding word.†——Yet again, in view of the fact that John virtually foreclosed this primary sense of the epithet when he first introduced the Logos, affirming that he existed from eternity and was truly God, it seems plain that he could not gainsay those first solemn declarations by using the word " only-begotten " in a sense which involves derived existence.——Finally, the secondary sense

---

* Greek: μονογενης.   † יָחִיד

—best beloved—is in full harmony with the scope of the passages in John, e. g. "in the bosom of the Father;" "God so loved the world that he gave his Son," though most dearly loved, etc.

15. *John bare witness of him, and cried, saying, This was he of whom I spake, He that cometh after me is preferred before me; for he was before me.*

The Evangelist now adduces the testimony of John the Baptist, at whose feet he had been wont to sit. Hence the vividness of the picture, for the writer well remembered how the Baptist used to stand and cry aloud to the gathered multitudes. When he saw Jesus approaching he cried—This is he of whom I have often spoken as soon to come. Coming after me in point of time, he becomes before me in dignity and greatness, eclipses me with his superior glory, for (in his pre-existent divine nature) he existed before me, and therefore should take rank indefinitely above me. ——The reference to Christ's pre-existent divine nature in the words, "for he was before me," * seems unquestionable. The Baptist—last of the Old Testament prophets, and, on the authority of Jesus himself (Matt. 11 : 10, 11), greatest among them all—must be supposed to have understood the pre-existence of the expected Messiah not less clearly than Isaiah (6 : 1, and 40 : 3) and Daniel (7 : 13) and Malachi (3 : 1).——Note also the prophetic view of his father Zacharias (Luke 1: 16, 17, 76), who manifestly saw that John was to be the harbinger of the Messiah foretold by Isaiah and Malachi.

16. *And of his fullness have all we received, and grace for grace.*

The best textual authorities commence this verse not with "and" [*kai*], but with because [*oti*], indicating it as continuing the Evangelist's own words and closely connected with v. 14; v. 15 being a parenthesis. We saw the glory of the Divine Word when he appeared among us in human flesh, full of grace and truth, . . . because of his fullness [of grace and truth] have all we Christian believers received.——On the exact sense of the words "grace upon grace," the best commentators differ; some explaining them of the successive installments of grace given to believers—grace after grace, or grace upon grace—constant supplies to meet their ever recurring wants: while others would say—Christ gives to his people grace *like his own*, corresponding in its nature to that of which he has an infinite fullness. The latter construction well interprets the preposition "for" [*anti*]; is in harmony with the drift of thought; and evolves a most precious truth, viz., that Jesus gives to his people of the same grace of which he has such fullness—thus making them "partakers of his holiness."

* 'οτι πρωτος μου ην.

17. For the law was given by Moses, *but* grace and truth came by Jesus Christ.

The gift of grace through Jesus Christ is still further heightened by being placed in antithesis with the mission and work of Moses. Through him God gave the law, good in its time and place; and yet it was followed in the fullness of time by far richer manifestations of divine favor and of glorious truth.——There is no occasion to push this contrast to such an extreme as to make it imply that no grace and truth were revealed through Moses, or that no law came through Christ. The obvious sense is the true one;—the burden of the revelation by Moses was law; the fullness of Christ came in the line of grace and truth.

18. No man hath seen God at any time; the only begotten Son, which is in the bosom of the Father, he hath declared *him*.

The statement—"No man hath seen God at any time," will perhaps seem abrupt, until we trace the mental associations which suggested it. Do we not find these in the history of Moses, where we see his intense desire to behold the face of God, and have the response of the Lord which granted his prayer, subject however to large limitations (See Ex. 33: 12-23). No man during all the antecedent ages had come so near to seeing the face of God, yet the history shows how far he fell short of it.——Of course "to see one's face" expresses the deepest and truest possible apprehension of real character. The Psalmist said of the future life—"I shall behold thy face in righteousness." The present life affords no such experience.——" Hearing and learning" (John 6: 45, 46) indicate a lower grade of knowledge, made possible to men on earth through the teaching Spirit; but the perfect knowledge expressed by *seeing*, none save the Son has enjoyed. He whose relations to the Father were most endearing and his communion altogether perfect ["in the bosom of the Father"], having consequently known the Father perfectly, was competent to "declare him"—to set forth with all clearness, fullness and certainty, the deepest things of God.

19. And this is the record of John, when the Jews sent priests and Levites from Jerusalem to ask him, Who art thou?

20. And he confessed, and denied not; but confessed, I am not the Christ.

21. And they asked him, What then? Art thou Elias? And he saith, I am not. Art thou that Prophet? And he answered, No.

22. Then said they unto him, Who art thou? that we may give an answer to them that sent us. What sayest thou of thyself?

23. He said, I *am* the voice of one crying in the wilderness, Make straight the way of the Lord, as said the prophet Esaias.

This testimony of John the Baptist to himself and to Jesus may be regarded as *official*, given in reply to a special delegation, sent to him while prosecuting his work.——Jerusalem was the religious center of the nation. The Sanhedrim—the constituted religious authorities of the whole people—resided, or at least held their sessions, there. In the great movement produced by John's preaching, when there "went out to him Jerusalem and all Judea" (Matt. 3: 5), and even "many of the Pharisees and of the Sadducees" (Matt. 3: 7), the Sanhedrim could not be unaffected. Their official responsibilities and probably too their rational curiosity would suggest the deputation here spoken of. Apparently, there is no occasion to impute other than laudable motives in sending this embassy. It was both proper in itself and important to themselves and to the whole people that they should know who this great preacher might be. Was he the nation's long expected Messiah? This was naturally the first and main question. John answered it promptly and squarely in the negative. Was he Elijah?* The prophecy of Malachi (4: 5) had raised in some minds the expectation that Elijah would reappear from heaven. The true interpretation had been given by Zacharias, the father of John:—"He shall go before him [Jesus] *in the spirit and power* of Elias" (Luke 1: 17). That the prophetic eye of Malachi rested upon this John was repeatedly affirmed by Jesus himself (Matt. 11: 14 and 17; 10–13)——When John answered the second question—"Art thou Elias?" with an explicit denial, it must be assumed that he saw the sense in which they put the question and answered definitely *to that* sense of it—No; I am not Elias, literally returned from heaven. We need not suppose that John denied what his father had said, viz, that this son would go before Jesus, a second Elijah in his spirit and power. As to its words their question might have either of these two senses. John answered to the sense which he saw was in their thought—as he ought honestly to do.

Their next question—"Art thou that prophet?" is supposed by most critics to refer to the prophecy given through Moses (Deut. 18: 15, 18): "The Lord thy God shall raise up unto thee a Prophet from the midst of thee like unto me; unto him shall ye hearken," etc.——These questions repeated in various forms show that they were in earnest to ascertain whether this wonderful man had been at all fore-indicated in their own prophetic scriptures. It was reasonable that they should push this great inquiry. John seems to have accepted their questioning kindly. With no hesitation he proceeded to give them the true and full answer: "I am the voice of one crying in the wilderness, Make straight the way

---

* "Elias" is the Greek form of this Hebrew name.

of the Lord." Ye will find the prediction of this coming "voice" in the prophet Isaiah (40: 3). Matthew (3: 3) and Luke (3: 4) make the same explicit identification; while Mark (1: 2) simply says that this is "written in the prophets." There is good reason to suppose that Malachi (3: 1, and 4: 5, 6) followed the words of Isaiah and reaffirmed their application to the great forerunner of the Messiah.

Were the men of this delegation impressed by this straightforward, honest testimony to the coming Messiah and ready to implore this witness to lead them at once to their nation's great Redeemer? Alas! they were Pharisees, and their notions of greatness and glory were by no means met in the preaching, the spirit, the general appearance and bearing of this bold reprover of their sin.

24. And they which were sent were of the Pharisees.

25. And they asked him, and said unto him, Why baptizest thou then, if thou be not that Christ, nor Elias, neither that Prophet?

The Evangelist John suggests it as a significant fact that the men sent on this embassy were Pharisees; for none but they would have put and pressed the question—Why then dost thou baptize if thou art not the Christ, nor Elias, nor "that prophet?" The Pharisees were professionally and with full heart in charge over the whole domain of religious rites and ceremonial institutions.——Their question implies that they had some notions about baptism, its significance, and the authority to administer it; for they manifestly assume that either Christ, Elias, or "that prophet" might with propriety baptize—but no one of lower dignity than theirs.

Inquiring for the actual or supposable ideas of the Pharisees in regard to baptism, we find (1.) That the Mosaic ceremonial system abounded in ablutions, washings, (in the words of the writer to the Hebrews, "stood in diverse baptisms"—Eng. "washings,") all built on the analogy between physical cleanness and moral purity. No men could be more conversant and familiar with these things than the Pharisees.——(2.) In their own scriptures there occurred numerous references to the moral cleansing to be wrought by the Holy Spirit, symbolically indicated by washing, sprinkling and various references to fountains of water. We can see now that those passages in the Old Testament looked forward to the great moral work of the divine Spirit and bore within them the true significance of baptism. But how thoroughly the Pharisees of John's time understood those passages can not be fully known.——(3.) That proselytes from the Gentiles to Judaism were admitted by baptism is well attested by Jewish authorities, e. g. Maimonides and by the Jerusalem Talmud and the Babylonian. [See Smith's Bible Dictionary on "Baptism."]

With these facts before us, we may put the case thus: (*a.*) Baptism with water implied a confession of moral impurity and of the need of moral cleansing.——(*b.*) It involved in the subject of baptism the promise and covenant of a better life, coupled apparently with a measure of faith in gracious help from God.——(*c.*) Hence it would be legitimate for a great reformer, such as their expected Messiah, or Elias or " that Prophet," to baptize those who became his disciples, promising to follow him in the ways of a holy life. The Jews of that age expected their Messiah to institute a kingdom, and apparently did not object to his making baptism its rite of initiation. In the sense in which Paul says the Hebrew nation were " all baptized unto Moses in the cloud and in the sea " (1 Cor. 10: 2), all the followers of a great prophet, equal to or like unto Moses, might pledge themselves by baptism to become his disciples and to follow him in a new moral life.

26. John answered them, saying, I baptize with water: but there standeth one among you, whom ye know not.

27. He it is, who coming after me is preferred before me, whose shoe's latchet I am not worthy to unloose.

I understand John's answer thus: On your own principles it is proper for me to baptize. For though I am not myself the Christ, yet I am only a few days before him, laboring to prepare the people to welcome his advent and come penitently to his feet. Indeed, he is already standing among you, though ye know him not.——Moreover I baptize with water only: he, greater far in moral power than I, will baptize with the Holy Ghost (v. 33). On your own principles I am authorized to call the people to repentance, to take their pledge to accept the coming Messiah already so very near at hand, and to put this pledge in the expressive form of baptism by water. Even if there could be some question as to the propriety of such baptism when the Messiah's coming was remote, there can be none now that he is just at hand.——Moreover the baptism which I administer makes only the least possible account of their following *me* as their spiritual leader. It is the great and far more glorious Personage who comes after me to whom I direct every eye. As to myself I am not even worthy to untie his shoes. [This was deemed of all service most menial.]

28. These things were done in Bethabara beyond Jordan, where John was baptizing.

On the highest textual authority, the location of this scene is not Bethabara, but Bethany; yet not the Bethany on the Mount of Olives, but (to distinguish this from that) a place beyond the river Jordan. The place was doubtless small, obscure, in that wilderness region where John was preaching and baptizing. It seems to have sunk after this into oblivion. Origen, three hundred years later, could find no trace of the name Bethany, and therefore fixed upon Bethabara as the place—whence came (as is supposed) the change in some more recent copies of the text.

29. The next day John seeth Jesus coming unto him, and saith, Behold the Lamb of God, which taketh away the sin of the world!

The day following the interview with the priests and Levites from Jerusalem, John had an opportunity to identify Jesus and introduce him publicly to his own disciples. Seeing Jesus approaching, he cried aloud: "Behold the Lamb of God who taketh away the sin of the world." The Lamb *of* God, *i. e.* of his own providing, whose chief mission in coming to earth from heaven is to "take away the sin of the world." He does not say, Behold the world's Great Teacher; nor this—Behold Him whose spotless example is to enlighten and regenerate the race; nor even this—Behold your long expected King, for the kingdom of heaven, as ye have often heard from me, is even now at hand. Any one of these points he might have put forward into the foreground of this first announcement; but, passing them all, he seizes upon another, by far more central, prominent and comprehensive than either or all of these and announces him as the sacrificial Lamb who takes upon himself and bears away the sin of the world.

The definite reference in the words "*the Lamb*"—the well known, fore-indicated Lamb, raises the question, To what in particular does John refer? Is it to the Lamb of the Passover as typifying Christ and fulfilled in him? Or is it the daily morning and evening sacrifice; or may it refer to any one of the numerous sin or trespass offerings prescribed in the Mosaic ritual?
——We are relieved from discussing these supposable references by the entirely satisfactory evidence that John has his eye upon the Lamb spoken of in Isa. 51: 7—that Great Sufferer who was borne "as a lamb to the slaughter." For we know that John the Baptist was familiar with the book of Isaiah; he found his own mission and work foretold there as "the voice of one crying in the wilderness." There also he found the great, chief work of the Messiah—his specially characteristic work—delineated in clearest outline as he who "bore our griefs;" was "wounded for our transgressions;" upon whom the Lord "laid the iniquity of us all;" who was borne "as a Lamb to the slaughter," "dumb as a sheep before her shearers," never opening his mouth in self-vindication; who, in fine, "bore the sins of many and made intercession for the transgressors." This wonderfully graphic portrayal of the world's Great Sufferer and Sacrifice was most manifestly before the eye of John the Baptist, supplying to him those pregnant words with which he at once described and hailed the Coming One at this eventful hour, and introduced him to a waiting and expectant world.

As to the central, pivotal word in this announcement—"taking away,"* critics find in it two possible and apparently co-ordinate ideas: (*a*) Taking upon one's self to bear: (*b*) Bearing away, re-

---

*Greek, αιρων.

moving and taking out of the way; the latter, however, rather than the former being the most direct, natural, and necessary sense. But nothing forbids that we unite these two ideas in the one word, with the comprehensive result—Who *takes upon himself to bear and so does bear away* the sin of the world.—Thus John puts boldly in the foreground the sacrificial, atoning work of Jesus, the nation's Messiah.

If the question be raised whether "taking away the sin of the world" must not insure the salvation of the whole race, let these points of explanation and reply, briefly put, be considered, viz:— (1.) That in an announcement so concise as this, it were out of place to notice the limitations and conditions of this salvation; and (2.) That there is a vital sense in which Christ's atoning work was *for the world.*

The Evangelist John wrote (1 John 2: 2), "He is the propitiation for our sins, and not for ours only, but also for the sins of the whole world;" also, "We have seen and do testify that the Father sent the Son to be the Savior of the world" (1 John 4: 14); and Jesus himself said—"And I, if I be lifted up, will draw all men unto me" (John 12: 32). Plainly Christ's death for sinners made salvation possible for all the world. It brought the race out from a condition of universal condemnation into one where pardon was provided for and proffered to all. No more or other atoning blood was needful for the salvation of the wide world of sinners. God had so loved the world that he gave his Son to die for it. What each sinner must do for himself in order to appropriate this salvation and make it his own, it were not needful that John should include in this most brief announcement. That was left to be taught elsewhere. How needlessly, and sadly, and guiltfully many would fail of this salvation after it had been most adequately provided and most sincerely and warmly proffered, there was no need to say in this first proclamation by Christ's great Harbinger.

To those who have made themselves somewhat familiar with the fifty-third chapter of Isaiah and have studied the wonderful Personage described so graphically there; who have lingered (as many have) over that portrayal of the world's great, meek, yet glorious Sufferer; who have seen the very marrow of the whole Bible compressed into those few telling words, it must seem peculiarly felicitous that John the Baptist should seize the central idea of that chapter, and apply it to Jesus of Nazareth to identify him as the Messiah then already come. We might search the Bible through and through in vain for better words than those. If salvation for our race is through atoning blood, then these are of all possible words the most fitting to set forth a Savior slain. If life for the saved comes through the death of their Savior, then he can have no fitter description than this—"The Lamb of God who taketh away the sin of the world." If it were important that some great prophet should announce his coming into the world and his appearing before men as the world's Messiah, and then if it were also important that his announcement should put the central idea of his work in most graphic and unmistakable terms, then surely the end to be sought is well attained in these few but most forcible and expressive words.

30. *This is he of whom I said, After me cometh a man which is preferred before me; for he was before me.*

"Of whom I said"—as in vs. 15, 27. These are the very words in which his great testimony respecting Jesus as one about to come was usually expressed.

31. *And I knew him not: but that he should be made manifest to Israel, therefore am I come baptizing with water.*

32. *And John bare record, saying, I saw the Spirit descending from heaven like a dove, and it abode upon him.*

33. *And I knew him not: but he that sent me to baptize with water, the same said unto me, Upon whom thou shalt see the Spirit descending, and remaining on him, the same is he which baptizeth with the Holy Ghost.*

34. *And I saw, and bare record that this is the Son of God.*

Note here how emphatically the Baptist declares, twice repeated: "I knew him not"—till at his baptism he was pointed out, according to a prophetic pre-intimation, by the visible descent of the Holy Ghost in form as a dove, resting upon him.——But the narrative given by Matthew seems to imply that when Jesus came from Galilee to John to request baptism, John already knew him—it being there said that "John forbade him, saying, I have need to be baptized of thee, and comest thou to me?" To which Jesus replied, "Suffer it to be so now; for thus it becometh us to fulfill all righteousness." "Then he suffered him." This conversation manifestly preceded the baptism itself, and seems to show that John recognized Jesus as so much greater than himself that it was incongruous and inappropriate for himself to baptize him.

The explanation of this apparent contradiction turns upon knowing Christ in two different senses, a lower and a higher. In the lower sense John recognized Jesus before the scenes of his baptism, for he had heard of him; possibly had seen him, and had known many things about him. But the higher and more certain knowledge, the *definite and unmistakable certification from heaven*, John had not until that visible descent of the Holy Ghost upon him—the supernatural testimony from God himself. In view of this he might well say, I did not *know* him before. I had no knowledge of him worthy of the name—none equal to the emergency—no such positive certainty as I needed to have that Jesus was God's own Son, indorsed from the very heavens by the testimony of God himself.——Observe, moreover, that it was not for John's personal benefit alone that he needed this emphatic identification of Jesus as the Messiah. It was rather that this

Messiah "might be made manifest to Israel." For the sake of the whole people this testimony from the visible heavens was appropriate, not to say demanded.

With beautiful fitness it was the Spirit descending visibly and remaining upon him that pointed him out as he who should "baptize with the Holy Ghost." He to whom the Spirit was given "not by measure" (John 3:34), but in fullness above measure, was endowed with the prerogative of imparting the Spirit in blessed fullness to his people.

Note also here the words in which John bore his testimony to Jesus: "I saw and bare record that this is *the Son of God.*" Apparently this Sonship looks toward the incarnation, the words being used in the same sense as in Luke 1:35: "Therefore also that holy thing which shall be born of thee shall be called *The Son of God.*" The identification of Jesus before the Jewish nation should naturally contemplate his visible humanity rather than his pre-existent divinity. Their eyes saw the human form, and the thing they needed to know of him was that he was the incarnated Son of God.

35. Again the next day after, John stood, and two of his disciples;

36. And looking upon Jesus as he walked, he saith, Behold the Lamb of God!

37. And the two disciples heard him speak, and they followed Jesus.

38. Then Jesus turned, and saw them following, and saith unto them, What seek ye? They said unto him, Rabbi, (which is to say, being interpreted, Master,) where dwellest thou?

39. He saith unto them, Come and see. They came and saw where he dwelt, and abode with him that day: for it was about the tenth hour.

40. One of the two which heard John *speak*, and followed him, was Andrew, Simon Peter's brother.

The notices of time in the narrative portion of this chapter seem remarkable, especially when we consider the lapse of years (perhaps forty) between the events themselves and the writing of this record. The transactions of three successive days are mapped out (vs. 29-34; 35-42; 43-51). Eventful days were these in the life-history of the Evangelist John. He could not forget them.——John the Baptist was standing with two of his disciples; one said (v. 40) to be Andrew; the other we must assume to have been the Evangelist John, who never gives his own name. The Baptist, looking upon Jesus as he was walking about to and fro,* said again: "Behold the Lamb of God!"—omitting the

---

* Gr. περιπατουντι.

words "who taketh away the sin of the world," probably because they had been used before and would be suggested by the word "Lamb."——The remark was a hint to those two disciples to follow him. They at once understood and accepted it. Jesus saw them following; anticipated their purpose, and, as he is wont to do, met it promptly and most kindly: "What seek ye?"—My master, said they each; let me sit at thy feet and learn more of thee. Where is thy home that we may have leisure with thee? Jesus said, Come and see. Two more hours of the day remained. They went and abode with him through those hallowed hours.

41. He first findeth his own brother Simon, and saith unto him, We have found the Messias, which is, being interpreted, the Christ.

42. And he brought him to Jesus. And when Jesus beheld him, he said, Thou art Simon the son of Jona: thou shalt be called Cephas, which is by interpretation, A stone.

Those two hours of Andrew with Jesus had fixed his heart upon this new Master. What should he do next but find his own brother Simon to tell him the great discovery—We have found the Messiah; come at once and see him for yourself. You too must learn to know and love him.——He brought him to Jesus. Jesus saw in an instant all that Peter was to become in his group of disciples and in his founding of the new kingdom. Thou hast been called Simon; thou shalt have the surname of Cephas [Syriac] or Petros [Greek]—both words having the same significance—a stone or rock.——Such a prophetic foreshadowing ought to have impressed Simon, not so much with a sense of his importance and dignity as of his great and delicate responsibility.

The reader may also note that the author's explanation of the meaning of such words as "Messiah" and "Cephas" shows that he wrote originally for Gentile and not Jewish readers. No Jews of that age could need such interpretations.

43. The day following Jesus would go forth into Galilee, and findeth Philip, and saith unto him, Follow me.

44. Now Philip was of Bethsaida, the city of Andrew and Peter.

Jesus, about to leave the field of the Baptist's preaching and labors, and go back to his own home in Galilee, improved his opportunity to gather about him his chosen twelve. The first selected members of the apostolic group were taken from the school of John the Baptist—their preparatory school.——Philip being a townsman of Andrew and Peter, seems to have been drawn to Jesus by their influence.

45. Philip findeth Nathanael, and saith unto him, We have found him, of whom Moses in the law, and the prophets, did write, Jesus of Nazareth, the son of Joseph.

Philip had at least one personal friend—Nathanael; earnest and true-hearted. He forthwith seeks him to tell him the joyful news—"We" (several of us) "have found that wonderful Personage of whom Moses in the law, and the Prophets in their books, did write—Jesus of Nazareth, the Son of Joseph. Is not this good news?"

46. And Nathanael said unto him, Can there any good thing come out of Nazareth? Philip saith unto him, Come and see.

Nazareth was in bad repute. Recalling their manner of treating their own fellow-citizen [Jesus of Nazareth was such] as given by Luke (4: 16-30), we shall cease to wonder at their bad reputation. Nathanael's first feeling was surprise that one so great and good could possibly originate there. Fortunately for him, this slight prejudice readily gave way before appropriate evidence to the contrary. Philip said—Come and see what you will yourself think of this wonderful man.

47. Jesus saw Nathanael coming to him, and saith of him, Behold an Israelite indeed, in whom is no guile!

48. Nathanael saith unto him, Whence knowest thou me? Jesus answered and said unto him, Before that Philip called thee, when thou wast under the fig tree, I saw thee.

Jesus does not repel Nathanael for that slight prejudice, but promptly and openly recognizes his guileless, noble character. ——How camest thou to know me? said Nathanael. I saw thee under the fig-tree before Philip called thee.——That scene under the fig-tree must have been specially suggestive, with some more than ordinary bearing upon the pending issues; we can not otherwise account for this allusion to it. Taking into consideration the fact that good men found retirement for devout meditation and prayer under the shade and in the seclusion of gardens and their fruit-bearing trees, we may very naturally infer that Nathanael had been there engaged in prayer, the Lord moving upon his soul to prepare him for this revelation of Jesus to both his eye and heart. So God has his ways of preparing his people for eventful scenes.

49. Nathanael answered and saith unto him, Rabbi, thou art the Son of God; thou art the King of Israel.

Sure that no mortal eye could have seen him there under the fig-tree, he is at once convinced that Jesus saw with more than earthly vision, and therefore recognized him as the Great Searcher of hearts, the promised Son of God, the predicted King of Israel. If, as seems probable, Nathanael had been a disciple of John the Baptist, he would naturally apply to the Messiah the same descriptive title—"Son of God"—which his master had given (v. 34). The other name—"King of Israel"—came legitimately from the Old Testament prophecies, *e. g.* Zech. 9: 9, and Jer. 23: 5, and 30: 9, and Hos. 3: 5.

Who was this Nathanael, and what became of him? Does he appear under any other name in later gospel history?——The opinion is held somewhat extensively that Nathanael appears in the first three gospel histories under the name Bartholomew, and of course that he was one of the twelve. The main reasons for this opinion are these:——(1.) It was not uncommon for the same man to have two or more names; *e. g.* Thomas, Didymus; Simon, Cephas, Peter; Matthew, Levi, etc.——(2.) As Jesus was at that time making up the twelve known as his disciples, and as Nathanael appears here with all the essential qualifications, it is highly probable that he became one.——(3.) John nowhere gives the name Bartholomew, yet once elsewhere (21: 2) gives the name Nathanael as of Cana in Galilee and associated with the disciples.——(4.) But Matthew (10: 3), Mark (3: 18), and Luke (6: 14) give the name Bartholomew; never the name Nathanael. ——(5.) Noticeably these three authors in their respective lists of the twelve place Bartholomew immediately after Philip, precisely where we should expect to find Nathanael.——The combined force of all these considerations amounts to strong presumptive evidence for the identity of Nathanael and Bartholomew.

50. Jesus answered and said unto him, Because I said unto thee, I saw thee under the fig tree, believest thou? thou shalt see greater things than these.

51. And he saith unto him, Verily, verily, I say unto you, Hereafter ye shall see heaven open, and the angels of God ascending and descending upon the Son of man.

Commending his faith, Jesus promises that he shall see yet greater things, and proceeds (v. 51) to say what they should be. ——The best authorities omit the word for "hereafter," leaving it "Ye shall see," etc.——The just interpretation of the words— "Ye shall see heaven open, and the angels of God ascending and descending upon the Son of man," must assume a reference to the revelations of God made to Jacob in vision at Bethel. The import therefore should be essentially this:—God coming very near in most impressive manifestations; supernatural works not infrequent; angels coming and going as if a highway were opened and often traversed by angelic feet. If the vision at Bethel was verified in a series of answering facts throughout Jacob's life —double camps of angels at Mahanaim; the angel of the covenant wrestling with him at Peniel; manifest providences of God taking away his Joseph, but in due time restoring him again, a savior to Israel; how much more abundantly was heaven opened over the incarnate Son of man—angels coming down to minister to him after his great temptation, in the scenes of Gethsemane, and at the sepulcher. These demonstrations of a present God looking out as from an open heaven upon the earthly trials and work of his incarnate Son, should certainly suffice to confirm the faith of his trusting disciples. The earthly life of the incarnate Son of God could by no means lack such testimonials from the heavens above. On every principle of reason we should expect them.

It will be noticed that Jesus speaks of himself here as "the Son of man," while in this chapter John the Baptist (v. 34) and Nathanael (v. 49) concur in giving him the title—"Son of God." Why this diversity? Why does Jesus call himself "the Son of man," while his greatest prophet and his disciples all say "Son of God?"

The *facts of usage* in regard to these two designations—"Son of man" and "Son of God"—are striking and full of precious significance.

1. Usually and almost invariably Jesus calls himself—"*The Son of man.*" We may say he uses this name manifestly in preference to any other. He does not disclaim the title, "Son of God;" does not seem to object to it as used by others; never hints that it is in any wise inappropriate: but yet for some reason it is not the name of his choice for his own purposes.——In point for illustration are the passages Matt. 26: 63, 64, and Luke 22: 69, 70. On his trial before the Jewish Council the High Priest said—"I adjure thee, tell us whether thou be the Christ, the Son of God." Jesus answered—Thou hast said [expressing assent]; but adds in his own words; "Hereafter shall ye see the *Son of man*, sitting on the right hand of power and coming in the clouds of heaven." Here "Son of man" is for his own use the name of his choice.——As recorded by Luke, thus: "Hereafter shall the Son of man sit on the right hand of God." "Then said they all, Art thou then the Son of God? And he said unto them, Ye say that I am" [it is as ye have said]. Thus we see he does not choose the name "Son of God" for his own use; yet accepts it as entirely just when used by others.

2. Throughout the entire gospel history the disciples never call Jesus "The Son of man." The name which Jesus chooses for his use, they never have chosen for theirs. * We may perhaps find some adequate reason why they did not use the same name which Jesus so constantly prefers to use for himself.

3. With remarkable uniformity the disciples, and indeed all others save Jesus, use the name "Son of God."——The disciples use it in their most defined doctrinal statements—as we might say, in their most formal confessions of faith. Thus in that striking

---

* The case of Stephen (Acts 7: 56) looking into the open heavens and beholding there "the Son of man standing on the right hand of God," is only a partial exception, for Stephen was not one of the original disciples personally conversant with Jesus in the flesh, and moreover these words may be virtually quoted from the lips of Jesus as above, Matt. 26: 64.

conversation recorded by Matthew (16: 13–20) when Jesus asked his disciples—" Whom do men say that I, the Son of man, am?" they answered first as to the various opinions of the Jewish people—" Some say thou art John the Baptist, some Elias; and others Jeremias, or one of the prophets." But Jesus, seeking to draw out their own faith, made his question definite: " Whom say *ye* that I am?" Then Simon Peter—always prompt and foremost—answered: "Thou art the Christ, the Son of the living God." This confession of faith, Jesus approved warmly and emphatically.——The similar confession of Peter (John 6: 69) stands in the revised text of Tischendorf in these simple terms: " We have believed and have known that thou art the Holy One of God." As put by Martha (John 11: 27) thus: "I have believed [and still believe] that thou art the Christ, the Son of God, that should come into the world."

This name for Jesus is used by Satan in his temptation (Matt. 4: 3, and Luke 4: 3, 9); by demons (Matt. 8: 29, and Luke 4: 41, and 8: 28, and Mark 3: 11); by men under the awe of present miracles (Matt. 14: 33): " Of a truth thou art the Son of God: "—by the High Priest adjuring him to testify (Matt. 26: 63); by his revilers at the cross (Matt. 27: 40); and by the affrighted centurion at the scenes of his death (Matt. 27: 54, and Mark 15: 39). The standard passage, however, which definitely assigns the reason for this name, " Son of God," is Luke 1: 35—the words of the angel Gabriel to Mary: " The Holy Ghost shall come upon thee, and the power of the Highest shall overshadow thee; therefore also that holy thing which shall be born of thee shall be called " the Son of God."

4. Returning to speak more definitely of the usage of our Lord himself as to his significant names, note that he employs the title of his usual choice, " Son of man," with equal freedom, whether the scene suggests his humiliation or his glory. On the one hand, " the Son of man hath not where to lay his head" (Matt. 8: 20): on the other, " When the Son of man shall come in his glory and all the holy angels with him, then shall he sit upon the throne of his glory and before him shall be gathered all nations." "The Son of man shall come in the glory of his Father with his angels" (Matt. 16: 27, 28; also Matt. 9: 6, and 13: 41, and 24: 27, 30, and Mark 8: 38, etc., etc.)

5. The cases in which Jesus speaks of himself as "the Son of God " are not only few compared with those in which he calls himself " the Son of man," but are somewhat less direct, not being the subject of the verb, but put in remote cases. Of this sort are these: " Condemned because he hath not believed on the name of the only-begotten Son of God" (John 3: 18): " The dead shall hear the voice of the Son of God" (John 5: 25); To the man born blind— " Dost thou believe on the Son of God?" (John 9: 35); "Say ye of him whom the Father hath sent into the world, 'Thou blasphemest,' because I said, I am the Son of God?" (John 10: 36). " This sickness is not unto death but for the glory of God that the Son of God might be glorified thereby" (John 11: 4). These cases suffice to show that Jesus by no means disowns this title though

his far more frequent use of the name "Son of man," indicates his decided preference.

From this classification of the *facts* of New Testament usage, let us turn a moment to the further question as to the supposable reasons for the usage both of Jesus and of his disciples, and of its moral significance:

1. May it be supposed that Jesus said commonly "Son of man" as being less offensive to his enemies? We may notice that they never objected to his use of this name, and did not put it into their indictment against him; while they did emphatically object to his calling himself, "The Son of God." To their superficial eyes, the deep significance of the title, "The Son of man," may have been veiled, and its modesty may have disarmed their jealousy—as it certainly should.

2. This chosen title—"The Son of man"—manifestly looks toward the incarnation—the great fact of his earthly life. It must always suggest his human relations; and we can not forbear to say—suggest them as those of which he was *never ashamed*. Low as the race of man might be relatively to the Infinite and ever blessed God—exceeding far below the glory which the pre-existent Logos "had with the Father before the world was;" yet Jesus never sought to suppress, conceal or throw into the background the fact of his being born of woman into alliance with our unworthy race.

3. On the other hand, it is of the utmost consequence to hold in mind that this title, "The Son of man," always implied his pre-existent divinity. For he was no ordinary "Son of man," but par excellence, "*the* Son of man;" not *any* Son of man merely human; for this would nullify all its real significance. He stood forth alone in this grand distinction of his nature—that being eternally divine; from eternity "with God," and being really himself God, he yet "became flesh and dwelt among us;" was born of woman with no other father than God; and for this reason especially bore the name, "The Son of God;" while yet with reference to this human birth he assumed and ennobled the title "The Son of man." Thus this chosen title—"The Son of man"—always assumed and implied the pre-existent, pre-eminent glory of his divine nature, yet assumed it in no repulsive form, but with consummate modesty and humility—evermore with the bearing of ineffably tender love to his redeemed people as his brethren in the relationships of human flesh. As has been well said, the spirit of this chosen designation is put in the remark of the Evangelist John where he introduces the account of Jesus washing his disciples' feet. "Jesus, knowing that the Father had put all things into his hand, and that he was come from God and went to God, riseth from supper, and laid aside his garments; took a towel and girded himself"—to wash their feet. Fully aware of his own inherent and divinely recognized dignity of rank and glory; with those great facts of his past and of his future fully in his mind, he condescended to this service—most menial according to the notions of men—that he might leave to the world through

all its future ages this illustrious example. So every time he used of himself the name, "The Son of man," he meant it should breathe the same spirit of voluntary humiliation for love's sake—of willing sympathy with the lowliest for the sake of uplifting them toward purity and goodness and God.

4. In view of this sublime moral influence of the usage by our Lord of the title, "The Son of man," and also of its natural and forcible implication of his pre-existent divinity, it may at least be gravely questioned whether it is not really a higher title and one of more sublime significance than the other—"Son of God." This title—"The Son of God"—as interpreted by the angel Gabriel—while it starts with the divine, looks toward the human; suggests it; implies it: even as the title—"The Son of man" expresses the human side but assumes and implies the higher nature, the divine.

5. These considerations suffice to show why the title —"The Son of man" was inexpressibly pertinent, suggestive, precious as used by Jesus of himself, but altogether inept to be used of him by his disciples. Remarkably their sense of fitness recoiled utterly from using this title of their Lord. Was it not because they felt that its deeper implication of a pre-existent divinity was entirely inappropriate to their lips, and its beautiful humility and condescension as coming from his lips quite lost, not to say reversed, as falling from theirs?——On the other hand, the title, "The Son of God," was level to their position, involved the very assumption which it was becoming in them to make, and therefore became their standard designation.

CHAPTER II.

The topics of this chapter are—The marriage in Cana, and the miracle of water made wine (vs. 1-11); a short stay at Capernaum (v. 12); Jesus at the Passover in Jerusalem, purifying the temple (vs. 13-16), and what it suggested to his disciples (v. 17); the demand of the Jews for a sign to confirm his authority for assuming such control of the temple and the resulting conversations (vs. 18-22); the moral impression made by these first miracles and Christ's intuitive knowledge of men's hearts (vs. 23-25).

1. And the third day there was a marriage in Cana of Galilee; and the mother of Jesus was there:

2. And both Jesus was called, and his disciples, to the marriage.

"On the third day"—*i. e.* after the events of John 1: 43-51, which occurred when Jesus was about to leave the locality where

John the Baptist had been preaching and go back to his early home in Galilee. This is "Cana of Galilee" in distinction from another Cana named Josh. 19: 28, in the tribe of Ashur, far west toward Phenicia.*

The mother of Jesus was there before his arrival, coming apparently from her own home at Nazareth. It is every way probable that one or both of the parties in this marriage were near relatives to Mary. This will naturally account for her presence there, for her interest, and for her position of influence.——This family relationship would secure the invitation of Jesus. Five disciples, having so recently attached themselves to him, were now with him—thus unexpectedly swelling the number of guests at this humble wedding-feast—a fact which perhaps may account for the failure of the wine-supply.

3. And when they wanted wine, the mother of Jesus saith unto him, They have no wine.

4. Jesus saith unto her, Woman, what have I to do with thee? mine hour is not yet come.

5. His mother saith unto the servants, Whatsoever he saith unto you, do *it*.

The Sinaitic manuscript reads, v. 3: "And they had no wine, because the wine of the marriage was finished"—which is substantially adopted by Tischendorf. The sense is unchanged by this emendation, since both readings imply that a small stock had been provided, and (supposably by the unexpected increase of guests) exhausted.——The mother of Jesus, sympathizing keenly with the family in these straits, said to him; "They have no wine." His reply assumes that she looked to him for relief in this emergency, and probably for relief by miracle.——He answers, "What is there to me and to thee, woman?" *i. e.* What thoughts and purposes have we in common?——Much in the spirit of the remark made to his parents many years earlier: "Wist ye not that I must be about my Father's business?" (Luke 2: 49.) It seemed to him important to say even to one so much respected as his mother, that in his work as the Messiah— the incarnate Son of God—he must move in a plane of life and purpose far other than hers, and therefore he could not be controlled by her opinions, much less by her authority. He must judge for himself when his time for a miracle had come.——The case affords not the least countenance to the Romish doctrine of Mary's power as mediator with her son Jesus.——Yet note that the name he used—"Woman" (rather than mother)—was not disrespectful, for he used it again while hanging on the cross

---

* Dr. Robinson fully identified the Cana of this miracle, bearing the name of "Kana el Jelil" (*i. e.* of Galilee), "about N. ¼E. from Nazareth, and not far from three hours (nine miles) distant." Rob. Researches, pp. 204-208, First Edition.

(John 19: 26), where the spirit of his address is at the farthest possible remove from being disrespectful. But he did not say "Mother." After his public ministry began, he never (so far as is shown by the record) called her "mother"—another fact fatal to the Romish assumption.——His mother indicates no spirit of offense at his plain words; but, remarkably, seems to have taken some encouragement as to help toward her object, shown in her instructions to the servants to do any thing he might direct.

6. And there were set there six waterpots of stone, after the manner of the purifying of the Jews, containing two or three firkins apiece.

Personal cleanliness was one of the virtues of the Jews—made yet more sacred by their religion. Hence this provision in the household for large supplies of water, not improbably in this case an increased supply for the company expected.——As to the capacity of these vessels, the record is not quite definite—"two or three firkins apiece." Supposing them to average 2½, and the Greek word for "firkins" to indicate (as estimated) 8¾ gallons, then each water-pot would hold 21 gallons, and the six, 126 gallons, or about four barrels. In this estimate critical authorities substantially concur.

7. Jesus saith unto them, Fill the waterpots with water. And they filled them up to the brim.

8. And he saith unto them, Draw out now, and bare unto the governor of the feast. And they bare *it*.

The pots being filled entirely full of water, there could be no reasonable suspicion that wine was afterwards added.——The "governor of the feast" had the general direction of the entertainment and of its order.

9. When the ruler of the feast had tasted the water that was made wine, and knew not whence it was, (but the servants which drew the water knew,) the governor of the feast called the bridegroom,

10. And saith unto him, Every man at the beginning doth set forth good wine; and when men have well drunk, then that which is worse: *but* thou hast kept the good wine until now.

Not knowing the source of supply, and judging by the taste only, he pronounced it "good," and seemed surprised that it should have been reserved till near the close of the feast.

There has been much discussion of the Greek verb translated—"have well drunk," * some supposing it to mean, have drank rather freely, yet short of intoxication; while others give it the

* μεθυω.

sense—" have drank to intoxication." The cases of its New Testament usage give the sense "drunken" with entire uniformity, as the reader may see: Matt. 24: 49—" to drink with the *drunken;*" Acts 2: 15—" these are not *drunken* as ye suppose;" 1 Cor. 11: 21—" another is *drunken;*" 1 Thess. 5: 7—" are *drunken* in the night;" Rev. 17: 2, 6—" have been made *drunk* with the wine of her fornication;" "I saw the woman *drunken* with the blood of the saints," etc. The cognate verb bears the same sense in every case, viz, Luke 12: 45, and Eph. 5: 18, and 1 Thess. 5: 7. The principle that "usage gives law to language," would seem therefore to admit nothing less in this case than to have drunk quite freely, so that its effects are apparent.——The exigencies of the case where a word is used must be allowed a certain measure of influence in fixing its meaning there. In the case of a marriage-feast in rural Galilee, we should be shocked to read—" After the guests have made themselves drunk, then set before them poorer wine." Judicious criticism will therefore seek to give due weight to each of these considerations—the exigencies of the case on the one hand, and the usage of the staple word on the other, and will arrive at this medium result:—After the guests have drank to the point of apparent exhilaration, then give them wine of second-rate quality.——But the sense of this verb is not specially important for any supposed bearing upon the state of the guests at this feast in particular, inasmuch as the remark of the governor of the feast refers not to the condition of his company, but to the general custom of serving wine at festivals: Every man in the position I now hold, regulating the order of the entertainment, gives his guests the best wine first; the inferior grade afterwards when men have already drank enough, the reason for this usage being perhaps to lessen or remove the temptation to drink too much.

11. This beginning of miracles did Jesus in Cana of Galilee, and manifested forth his glory; and his disciples believed on him.

This was the first miracle wrought by Jesus, and consequently was the first step in this special manifestation of his divine glory. It answered its special object in confirming the faith of his new disciples.

Some general points made or suggested by the account of this first miracle should receive more special attention:

1. Its bearing against the idolatrous worship of the virgin Mary, and against prayer to her as mediator with her son Jesus, is most decisive. What could have been more so? It would seem that Jesus must have intended to suppress the first tendencies toward such reliance upon his mother and such homage to her.——As we might expect from such a man in such circumstances, Calvin hurls from this text the sternest denunciations against the then current Romanist folly and crime of Mary-worship.

2. The case bears a noble testimony of approbation and honor

to the marriage institution. Jesus purposely sanctioned marriage by his presence in company with his disciples, as one of the first public acts of his ministry. How could he have given this institution a more emphatic indorsement?

3. Must we not add also to this, that he recognized the propriety of a certain deference to the social usages of society, such as a joyous festival in connection with the marriage of friends? He not only attended this festival, but contributed miraculously to supply the deficiency of wine for the occasion. Perhaps he deemed it the more important to make his example clear and strong on this point because he would not give his sanction to the ascetic spirit which was current in his age among the Jewish Essenes, and which the life of John the Baptist might be supposed to favor.——The example of Jesus in this case is liable, no doubt, to abuse; yet this is no reason why it should not be accepted in its legitimate influence, sweetly hallowing the innocent joys of social life, and assuring us that our divine Father rejoices in the social enjoyments which he has himself provided for his children in the paths of virtue.

4. We must not pass this case without carefully considering its relations to the *cause of temperance*.——It is simply inevitable that this miracle should awaken the most intense interest for its real or supposed bearings on the temperance question, both among the advocates of free or moderate drinking, and the advocates of total abstinence. Did Jesus create by miracle a large quantity of alcoholic wine, to be drank by himself, his disciples, his mother, and the family relatives and friends? If so, why should not his example justify the use—at least, the *festive* use—of alcoholic wine as a beverage, and its indefinite manufacture for such use?

The following points will naturally be involved in this discussion:

(1.) It is an open question whether the wine made by this miracle was at all alcoholic. It might look like common wine and taste like it, without any alcohol whatever. There can be no positive proof of the presence of alcohol in this wine.——Yet inasmuch as it was called wine, with no intimation of any thing peculiar in it, it must, I think, be conceded as in a degree probable that it did not differ in this respect from the wine ordinarily used on such occasions. It is certain (judging from the record) that our Lord did not say in so many words—" I disapprove the use of wine that might cause drunkenness, and therefore have made this harmless in that respect."

(2.) As the governor of the feast called this wine " good," another debatable question will turn on the standard tests of " good wine." What kind of wine was then accounted " good;"—the new unfermented article, without alcohol; or the fermented, containing alcohol?

In favor of the former alternative it might be said—(*a*) That the Orientals prized most highly the first flowings of the juice of the grape, that which exuded under very slight pressure, and was entirely sweet—non-alcoholic.——(*b*) Kings, (*e. g.* in Egypt, Gen. 40: 11,) in a condition to command what was deemed the perfection of luxury, drank wine pressed from grape clusters before their eyes. Of course this wine was unfermented, and pure from alcohol.——(*c*) It is in evidence that the ancients had methods, analogous though inferior, to the modern process of canning, by which fermentation was prevented. I am not aware that it can be ascertained to what extent any of these methods were practiced in Galilee at the Christian era.

Yet all these considerations in favor of the theory that the wine accounted "good" in that age was unfermented, seem to me to be outweighed by the manifest implication in the Greek word here used (and in what is said here) that this "good wine" did exhilarate men perceptibly—so much that it was deemed expedient, after men had drunk of it somewhat freely, to exchange it for wine of inferior—*i. e.* less stimulating properties. Truth should be sought and evidence weighed with candor: hence I feel compelled to make this admission.

(3.) Most vital of all is the fact that the circumstances in the age of our Lord were so entirely different from what they are now that no inference can be drawn from his acts then to settle questions of duty now. Then, distilled liquors were unknown. Liquors adulterated with active poisons had not then as now filled and flooded all the channels of commerce until no purchaser can have the slightest assurance that what he buys under the name of wine has the first drop of grape-juice in it. The wines of Palestine in that age were not "enforced" as they often are now by the addition of alcohol. Of course there was not then as now a fearful inclined plane from fermented liquors (beer, cider, and wines) down to the countless forms of distilled spirits—a plane down which those who begin to slide are in infinite peril of the drunkard's doom. In our age the duty of abstinence from any beverage whatsoever containing alcohol rests mainly on the principle which the Great Apostle has well put and nobly honored: "If meat make my brother to offend" (stumble), "I will eat no meat while the world stands lest I make my brother stumble." The terrible logic of facts proves to us that any use of alcoholic beverages imperils the dearest welfare of men for this world and the next. Therefore let every friend of his race say—I will abstain entirely, and throw my influence solid against all such drinks. I do not need to raise the question whether drinks containing five or ten per cent. of alcohol are necessarily injurious to me. It suffices that I can live without them, and that my use of them would tempt somebody to his hurt—probably to his ruin. Therefore I can not bear the responsibility of ensnaring my brother to his ruin for the sake of even a luxurious indulgence. If the circumstances had been such in our Savior's time as they are now, there can not be the slightest question how he would have borne himself. He could not have fallen below Paul in his benevolent self-sacrifice for others' good. He could not have either made or drank alcoholic beverages. What he would have done with alcohol as a medicine it is of no consequence here to attempt to decide. But in the midst of such drinking usages as obtain to-day, and of such perils as those usages involve, and such fearful desolations as follow, it is simply impious to raise any question as to the path of Christian duty; or—which is the same thing—any question as to the example which our Lord would have put before the world if the world of his time had stood as to intoxicating drinks where it stands now.

But the question may be pressed—Did not Jesus *know* that alcohol would come in like a flood in this nineteenth century? Could he not anticipate every element in our present circumstances and give us example and instruction definitely adapted to them all?

I answer, There is no occasion to deny his perfect foreknowledge; but there is ground for saying that he lived and taught with definite adaptation to the generation then present, and not with like adaptation to generations eighteen centuries in the future. The examples and precepts of the Bible were always naturally and necessarily those of the times then present. As Jesus was to live but one life on earth, and as that must needs be with and before the men of his time, so he could shape his example only for the men of his generation, and his precepts must have a special adjustment to those times—applicable to other times, however, in so far as the circumstances were similar and the involved principles analogous; no farther. No other way of making up a Bible for the race was wisely practicable. It must have been addressed to the generation then living; written for them and adjusted to their circumstances; or it would have been nearly useless.—Besides; if we insist that it ought to be specially adjusted to the nineteenth century, why may not our remote posterity claim with equal force that it be adjusted to the nine hundredth century? Which of all the centuries down to the last shall have the preference?

But whether we can give truly all the reasons for the divine method in making up a Bible, (viz, the method of inspiring holy men to live each in his own age and to write each his own part for his own times severally,) this at least is true:—The Bible *is* written so and not otherwise. Jesus lived before his own generation—not before any other; set his example there, and not elsewhere; adjusted his life to those times, and not to any other times; and consequently never paused to say—"About so many hundred years from this day a process of making alcohol by distillation will be discovered, and by consequence the amount and variety of drunkard's drinks will be immensely increased; and then the use of fermented wines will come to sustain an entirely new relation to the public welfare," etc., etc. All this was destined to become true, and the divine mind doubtless foresaw it;—but what then? No such anticipatory instruction appears in the Bible. The *principles* that are to be applied to determine duty are there. The special circumstances to which they are to be applied are to be found by every man in his own century, amid his own personal surroundings.

The comments made by Dean Alford in his commentary on this miracle of the wine are so extraordinary that I can not forbear to quote and notice them.—He says: "The Lord here most effectually and once for all stamps with his condemnation that false system of moral reformation which would commence *by pledges to abstain from intoxicating liquors.* He pours out his bounty *for all;* and he vouchsafes his grace to *each* for guidance; and to endeavor to evade the work which he has appointed for every man by *refusing the bounty to save the trouble of seeking the grace* is an attempt which must ever end in degradation of the individual motives, and in social demoralization, whatever present apparent effects may follow its first promulgation."—These are Dean Alford's words: the italics for emphasis are his own.—I have read them over and over, each time with utter and painful amazement. What! Are there no drunkards' graves in England? While the rich are drinking wine, are not the poor led on by this example in high places to drink cheaper fermented and distilled liquors, till the curse of strong drink has fallen like the plague upon the whole land, with its desolations of poverty, pauperism, want, disease, premature death, crime, and eternal damnation? And are these evils so trivial that it would be absurd to suggest to those who fill high positions in England's society that they might well afford to deny themselves their wines for the sake of dissuading their less wealthy countrymen from all use of drinks that intoxicate? Is there no occasion in England for the martyr spirit of Paul—"If meat make my brother offend (stumble), I will eat no meat while the world stands?"——Moreover, have not wine and strong drink made many a sad wreck of life in families blest with every appliance for the best culture and the noblest fruits of Christian manhood? Do not the wine-drinking usages of England, defended by her highest influences in church and in state, cost too much?

But Dean Alford assumes that total abstinence is not only false in principle, but pernicious in its ultimate results. In his Christian philosophy, men should never try to shun temptation, but rather welcome it, only praying for grace accordingly.——Does he leave out of his version of the Lord's Prayer—"Lead me not into temptation"? Does he sneer at Paul for saying—"I keep my body under, lest I be a castaway"? Does he use honest words when he represents those who pledge themselves to total abstinence as "refusing the bounty to save the trouble of seeking the grace"? Is such an insinuation creditable to a distinguished commentator upon the gospel of Jesus Christ? Does he really believe that total abstinence from all that intoxicates, carried into practice from the highest ranks to the lowest throughout England, would "degrade individual character" and beget "social demoralization"? Has he yet to gain his first conception of the moral sublimity of self-denial for others' good?

12. After this he went down to Capernaum, he, and his mother, and his brethren, and his disciples; and they continued there not many days.

From Nazareth, where Jesus "had been brought up" (Luke 4: 16)—where his early life had been spent—the family seem to have removed ere this to Capernaum. To this family home, the entire group, including the disciples already called, came down from Cana; but as the Jews' Passover was near, the stay of Jesus and his disciples was short.——The precise site of Capernaum is still in dispute; the rival claimants being all in the plain of Genessaret, on the western shore of the Sea of Tiberias, otherwise called, of Galilee. See Smith's Dictionary, "Capernaum."

13. And the Jews' passover was at hand, and Jesus went up to Jerusalem,

14. And found in the temple those that sold oxen and sheep and doves, and the changers of money sitting:

15. And when he had made a scourge of small cords, he drove them all out of the temple, and the sheep, and the oxen; and poured out the changers' money, and overthrew the tables;

16. And said unto them that sold doves, Take these things hence; make not my Father's house a house of merchandise.

17. And his disciples remembered that it was written, The zeal of thine house hath eaten me up.

In calling this "the Jews' Passover," the writer shows that he wrote for readers other than Jews.——This Passover occurred not long after the baptism of Jesus and his entrance upon his public ministry; and consequently gives the first data from which to estimate its entire duration.

The supply of the various animals needed for sacrifice, and the exchange of foreign coin for the Jewish shekel in which the tribute for the temple service must be paid, created these branches of business—legitimate in themselves, but deserving stern rebuke for desecrating the sacred localities of the temple. Jesus boldly and nobly assumed the right to cleanse his Father's house of such defilement, and therefore drove out these traffickers and their animals in these memorable words: "Make not my Father's house a house of merchandise."——Was this "scourge of small cords" prepared for the tradesmen as well as for their animals? Perhaps not. The Greek words, closely translated, would read: "he drove out all, both the sheep and the cattle." The command—"Take these things hence," etc., was addressed to those that sold doves, for the doves could not be so well driven out with a scourge; perhaps it was said also for the other dealers.

This daring step impressed all parties. It suggested to his disciples the words of the Psalmist (Ps. 69: 10): "The zeal of thine house hath consumed me." It prompted the Jews to demand of him by what authority he acted, and how he supported his claim.

18. Then answered the Jews and said unto him, What sign shewest thou unto us, seeing that thou doest these things?

19. Jesus answered and said unto them, Destroy this temple, and in three days I will raise it up.

20. Then said the Jews, Forty and six years was this temple in building, and wilt thou rear it up in three days?

21. But he spake of the temple of his body.

The Jews rightly understood these words and acts of Jesus to involve the assumption of being the Messiah, or at least some extraordinary teacher sent of God; and therefore, not improperly, they demanded of him what "*sign*" (miraculous indorsement) he put before their eyes to justify himself for doing these things, viz, cleansing the temple.

The reply made by Jesus is every way memorable. He did not work a miracle on the spot before their eyes, as they perhaps expected and seem to have demanded. Jesus never wrought miracles *upon call*—in response to a special demand. His conscious quiet dignity of character forbade it. While he never fell below the point of giving *adequate* evidence of his Messiahship—all that could reasonably be asked for—he never descended to meet the caprices or the captious cavils of hostile spirits.——In the present case, his words—"Destroy this temple, and in three days I will raise it up"—come to us with the evangelist's own interpretation: "He spake of the temple of his body." I see not the least occasion to question the soundness of this interpretation, although many German commentators—perhaps half of those who are of the present century—have done so.——At the moment of this conversation the temple was before every mind; hence Jesus naturally takes from it his analogy. Noticeably the analogy between the Jewish temple under the old economy and the human body of God's people under the new became so familiar in the Christian age that Paul exclaims against the brethren at Corinth with amazement: "What! know ye not that your body is the temple of the Holy Ghost who is in you?" (1 Cor. 6: 19.) "Know ye not that ye are the temple of God, and that the Spirit of God dwelleth in you?" (I Cor. 3: 16.) In the old temple God dwelt in a visible radiance of glory. In the new he dwells by the light and glory of his Spirit.——There was the more reason why Jesus should assume that this analogy would be, or ought to be, intelligible to the Jews, because it had been foreshadowed in their own prophets, *e. g.* Zechariah (2: 5, 10): "For I, saith the Lord, will be the glory in the midst of her." "Sing and rejoice, O daughter of Zion, for lo, I come, and I will dwell in the midst of thee."——It is specially noticeable, however, that this sign given by Jesus was not immediately available; it did not bring out its great power until his actual death and resurrection. Then it became the standard and chief testimony to his divine Sonship. "This Jesus hath God raised up, whereof we all are witnesses" (Acts 2: 32). "If Christ be not risen, then is our preaching vain, and your faith is also vain" (1 Cor. 15: 14).

The Savior's policy seems to have been to bring out the evidence in support of his claims little by little as men might be prepared to receive it, reserving the most conclusive to the later stages of the progressive demonstration. On this policy his resurrection closes the argument from miracles triumphantly with its crowning glory:—"In three days I will raise it up"—and men shall know that Jesus was in very deed the Son of God. A method that should have reversed this order would have been impolitic—not to say impossible.

The Jews insisted that the words "this temple" in the mouth of Jesus must refer to their proud structure so long under the process of rebuilding by Herod the Great. Hence they replied—"Forty-six years was this temple in building; and wilt thou rear it up in three days?"——Herod sought the glory of splendid architecture. Too cruel and despotic to be in favor with the Jews, yet sorely needing their good-will because of his dependence on the Romans, he thought to ingratiate himself into favor by immensely lavish expenditures in rebuilding and adorning their temple. As the Jews would not trust him to tear down the old and build anew from the foundation, he was compelled to rebuild piecemeal by removing the old in small portions and replacing with new. Hence the process "long drawn out" might readily be made to span forty-six years. It was begun B.C. 20.*

22. When therefore he was risen from the dead, his disciples remembered that he had said this unto them; and they believed the Scripture, and the word which Jesus had said.

It is not clear that even the disciples fathomed the depth of his meaning at the time. But after he had risen from the dead, these words arose and lived again in their thought. We may suppose this was in fulfillment of the Savior's promise—"The Comforter shall bring all things to your remembrance whatsoever I have said unto you" (John 14: 26)—an illustrative case which shows that the Spirit not only brought back the words to memory, but (what is not only more but better) brought to their mind and heart their deep significance no less.

23. Now when he was in Jerusalem at the passover, in the feast *day*, many believed in his name, when they saw the miracles which he did.

24. But Jesus did not commit himself unto them, because he knew all *men*,

* See Smith's Bible Dictionary, "Herod."

25. And needed not that any should testify of man; for he knew what was in man.

This faith which rested on the miracles of Jesus alone was manifestly superficial, leaving the heart unchanged and unloving. Perhaps they were saying inwardly—This man might lead our nation to victory over the Romans. With such resources of power, what might he not do to aggrandize the house of David?——Perhaps the case may illustrate the natural imperfection of a belief which rests on miracles only—which goes not beyond the conviction of great power, and which limits its impression to the intellect, with no bearing on the heart.

Jesus knew their heart too well to commit himself to them. The Evangelist avails himself of this case to ascribe to Jesus that divine searching which goes to the bottom of all human hearts, before which no thought or unborn act can be hidden.

CHAPTER III.

This chapter is in two principal parts: vs. 1–21 narrate the night interview of Jesus with Nicodemus, and the extended discourse to which it gave occasion; vs. 22–36 bring Jesus once more near the scenes of John the Baptist's preaching, and give us the last testimony of the Baptist to Jesus and to his mission and doctrine. The locality of the former portion seems to have been at or near Jerusalem; that of the latter is definitely stated (v. 23).

1. There was a man of the Pharisees, named Nicodemus, a ruler of the Jews:

2. The same came to Jesus by night, and said unto him, Rabbi, we know that thou art a teacher come from God: for no man can do these miracles that thou doest, except God be with him.

The charm of a special interest gathers about these personal labors of Jesus with individuals, such as this conversation by night with Nicodemus, and that (chap. 4) with the woman of Samaria by Jacob's well. We see that Jesus entered warmly into gospel work to enlighten and save even one human soul; and that when he had but one hearer, he availed himself of his opportunity to give his instructions the more definite, and so more effective, adaptation.

In the first clause of v. 2, the corrected text, with the authority of the three oldest and most reliable manuscripts (S.V.A.) gives "*him*" in place of "*Jesus*": "The same came to *him* by night." This reading indicates a closer connection between the opening of this chapter and the close of the preceding, showing that Nicodemus is one of those men referred to (John 2: 23) who were impressed by the miracles of Jesus, but were still in great darkness on the vital points of salvation through his name.

Nicodemus was a Pharisee and a member of the Jewish Sanhedrim; is twice brought to light in John's subsequent history, viz; in 7: 50, and in 19: 39; in the former case protesting against the action of the council in condemning Jesus without a hearing: in the latter, bringing in his tribute (may we hope) of loving sympathy as well as respect for the Crucified One—"an hundred pounds of myrrh and aloes" with which to embalm the body. In both references John identifies him as the same who first "came to Jesus by night." We are left to infer that he came by night, not because of the pressure of other duties throughout the day so much as for a private interview that should not imperil his standing with his brethren of the Sanhedrim.

He accosts Jesus very respectfully—My Lord; my Teacher.—— "We know"—perhaps speaking the convictions of other candid men as well as his own—"that thou art a teacher come from God; for no man can do these miracles that thou doest except God be with him." Such miracles are wrought only by a power really superhuman, and therefore, if not even directly by God's hand, yet certainly *with his permission* given to superhuman agents. Consequently such miracles must be accepted as God's indorsement of the teacher's mission. Some critics disparage the concession—"Except God be with him"—as a very low and inadequate inference from the fact of miracles. I see no special force in this criticism. It lies equally against Peter as against Nicodemus (see Acts 10: 38): "How God anointed Jesus of Nazareth with the Holy Ghost and with power; who went about doing good and healing all that were oppressed with the devil; *for God was with him.*" That God should be "*with Jesus,*" proving his presence by miraculous powers, is the best and highest possible indorsement of his divine mission—the very sort of indorsement which should be rationally expected.——On these perfectly valid grounds, therefore, Nicodemus recognizes Jesus as a teacher sent from God, and comes to him to seek instruction in divine truth. Jesus proceeds at once to teach him what he most of all needed to learn.

3. Jesus answered and said unto him, Verily, verily, I say unto thee, Except a man be born again, he can not see the kingdom of God.

4. Nicodemus saith unto him, How can a man be born when he is old? can he enter the second time into his mother's womb, and be born?

"Jesus answered"—according to New Testament usage is, not necessarily answering a definite question, but may mean, taking up a subject suggested either by some previous remark or by the circumstances of the case.

If to some readers Jesus should seem to open the subject of the new birth abruptly, let it be considered—(*a*.) That Nicodemus, being apparently one of the class referred to (John 2: 23) had a certain faith in Jesus, yet a faith which precisely lacked what the new birth would supply. He believed in the power of Jesus to work miracles; accepted these miracles as indorsing his mission from God as a great teacher; yet came short of accepting Jesus with loving, trusting heart as his own personal Savior from sin.—(*b*.) These first words of Jesus will no longer seem abrupt and wanting in easy connection with pre-existing ideas if we bear in mind that Nicodemus as a well educated Jew had definite notions respecting "the kingdom of God"—definite though not in all respects correct, and in some great points fundamentally defective.——*He was familiar with the phrase.* This being a point of no small importance, let it be expanded so far at least as to suggest—(1.) That the Old Testament prophecies (in his own text-book) are full of it, four of the Messianic Psalms (*e. g.*) being built upon it (viz, the 2d, 45th, 72d and 110th); also a very large portion of all the Messianic prophecies in Jeremiah, Ezekiel, and Zechariah. They give us a king to reign after the model of David—so fully on his model that several give him the very name "David," in the sense of a second David.——(2.) That the entire phrase comes from Daniel (2: 44, and 7: 13, 14, 27): "The God of Heaven shall set up a kingdom which shall never be destroyed," etc.—hence called interchangeably, "kingdom of God" and "kingdom of heaven."——(3.) That John the Baptist made these words ring in the ears of all Judah and Jerusalem— "Repent; for the kingdom of heaven is at hand." Jesus began his preaching on the same key-note; from the same text—in the same sense.——(4.) The masses of the Jews were certainly familiar with the idea; else they would not have proposed to "take him by force to make him a king" (John 6: 15); would not have brought him into their city with all the regalia of a triumph, shouting (as put in John 12: 13, 15)—"Hosanna: Blessed is the King of Israel that cometh in the name of the Lord;" "Behold, thy King cometh." See the more full account, Matt. 21: 1–11, and Mark 11: 1–11, and Luke 19: 29–38—a scene so significant in the life-history of Jesus that each of the four evangelists has put it on record.——(5.) His murderers taunted him with having claimed to be "King of the Jews;"—and finally (6.)—The apostles honored him evermore as "Lord" and "King;" and most distinctly of all, the Revelator John gives high and most significant prominence to his kingdom and reign.—— Let these great facts suffice to show that Jews of average intelligence, like Nicodemus, must have been entirely familiar with the phrases "kingdom of God," or "of heaven."

Now let it be specially noted that Nicodemus had some vital things to learn about this kingdom, especially about the conditions of membership, *i. e.* of citizenship. As a Jew from the loins of Abraham, he had never thought of questioning his citizenship in this kingdom *by right of birth*. Was he not born a Jew? Was not his pedigree sanctioned and honored in the genealogies of his nation? Did any body ever question his place *by birth* in this expected kingdom of the Messiah who should "reign over the house of David forever"?

This, then, is his first fatal mistake. To make him a son and an heir in this kingdom, more is needed than the birth he thinks of. He must have a higher birth than that. So Jesus begins from this starting-point. Beyond all question he uses the figure of *birth* and speaks of being "*born*" for this kingdom because, in the mind of Nicodemus, his birth from the stock of Abraham gave him his credentials of membership in the kingdom of God.——Jesus, therefore, began with the solemn averment—"Verily, verily, I say unto thee, Except a man be born from above, he can not see the kingdom of God." The word which Jesus used * should certainly be translated, not "again," but *from above*. It means precisely this in its etymology, being a compound word, made from two others, one meaning *from;* the other *above*. In every other instance of its use in the New Testament, it means from above. †

Moreover, this sense is to be preferred as being more comprehensive, for it not only implies the sense, "again," the second birth, but points to the source of the power which brings the new birth.

If it be said—Nicodemus understood Jesus to mean, "born *again*," and therefore we must assume this to have been his meaning, it may be replied:—Nicodemus did not care to take issue on the primary idea—the source whence the new birth came; but seized upon the secondary one—born another time, by a new and second birth, and sought to push the absurdity of this birth in its literal sense. It is not by any means certain that Nicodemus failed to take the sense—*born from above*. It is more probable that he left that point unnoticed because he had nothing to say about that. Moreover, it is supposable that Nicodemus was not altogether honest. An excessive eagerness to involve his Rabbi in an absurdity may have blinded his mind to the point which Jesus sought to make prominent—the birth *from above*.

---

* "ανωθεν."

† The most illustrative cases are—John 3: 31: "He that cometh *from above* is above all;" John 19: 11: "Thou couldest have no power against me except it were given thee *from above;*" James 1: 17; "Every perfect gift is *from above* and cometh down from the Father of lights," etc. Also James 3: 15, 17: "This wisdom descendeth not *from above;*" "But the wisdom that is *from above*," etc.——The remaining cases, in the sense of what is higher in space or earlier in time, may be seen, Matt 27: 51; Mark 15: 38; Luke 1: 3; John 19: 23, and Acts 26: 5, and Gal. 4: 9. It will be seen that not one of all these cases will bear the sense of *again*.

To Nicodemus, himself an old man, the idea of being born over again as at the first, seemed most absurd. Is it strange that with this view of Christ's meaning he should exclaim—"How *can* it be?" Jesus will explain in due time.

But let us note here that the word "see" [*i. e.* the kingdom], while essentially synonymous with "enter into" in v. 5, and therefore involving membership and all its blessings—will naturally suggest that accurate and impressive knowledge which comes of vision—implying, therefore, that without the enlightening of the Spirit and the sense of divine things that comes with being born of the Spirit, no man will ever rightly and fully appreciate and know in his deep experience what this reign of Christ truly is.

5. Jesus answered, Verily, verily, I say unto thee, Except a man be born of water and *of* the Spirit, he can not enter into the kingdom of God.

6. That which is born of the flesh is flesh; and that which is born of the Spirit is spirit.

Jesus solemnly reaffirms the main points made in v. 3, yet reaffirms with explanatory modifications. We must note with the utmost care every point of change in this second speech.——(*a.*) The change from "seeing the kingdom" to "entering into the kingdom" can not be regarded as specially significant. If (as suggested above) "seeing" looked in a sort toward a deep thorough apprehension of its meaning, Jesus may have thought best to leave out that point and make his affirmation more simple, and so more emphatic, with the single point—*membership*.——(*b.*) But to change "born from above" to "born of water and Spirit" * was really an advance in the way of explanation. It brought in distinctly and by name what was only referred to before as to the source whence it came. Jesus teaches him that this new birth is wrought *by the Spirit*. In what sense *by water*, I reserve for subsequent discussion. As to the fact of the Spirit's agency in this birth, there is not the least ground for doubt or difference of opinion.——(*c.*) There is also a very vital point of explanation in v. 6. Jesus would say: You are thinking about that which is "born of the flesh"—of the human mother. That will of course be nothing but a human child, of mere flesh and blood like the parent. I am not speaking at all of such a birth. I speak of being "born of the Spirit" of God. That which is born thus of the Spirit will be a spiritual product—a soul with a new spiritual life; morally considered, a "new creature;" figuratively speaking, "a new heart and a new spirit" "put within."——This truth, vital far above all other truth pertaining to the conditions of membership in this kingdom, Jesus puts here, briefly indeed, but clearly as to its vital elements, and in manner with most impressive and solemn affirmation.

* εξ ἱδατος χαι πνευματος.

It remains to consider what is meant here by the word "water" in the phrase—"born of water and Spirit."

At the outset let me apprise the reader that more is depending upon the sense of this word "water" in this passage than may be at first thought apparent. In a statement from the lips of the Great Teacher, made under circumstances so impressive; in manner so terse and comprehensive, and bearing on a point so vital as the conditions of membership in his kingdom, every word may have—nay more, *must* have immense and telling significance. For we must ask, Are there here two agencies—one water, and the other Spirit; or only one—that of the Spirit? If two, are they both equally vital, both equally indispensable? Is being born of the Spirit sufficient without being born of water? Is being born of water sufficient without being born of the Spirit? What is the status of him who has been born of water only? What is his who, supposably, is born of the Spirit only, and not by water?——And yet again: Is the term "water," as used here, exactly equivalent to baptism? When Jesus says "water," does he mean baptism, and nothing more or less, so that water is nothing except as it is used in the proper mode of the ordinance of baptism? And does he imply that baptism with water carries with it the new birth by the Spirit? Or may it be that baptism has a function to perform quite distinct from that of the Spirit, and either equally essential or *not* equally essential to salvation?

Thus the questions over this word "water," branch out almost indefinitely. No intelligent Bible reader ought to satisfy himself without a very careful and thoroughly fundamental investigation of these points here in issue.

To facilitate progress we will take first this main question—one which in fact will mostly settle all the rest:—Is "water" here only another word for *baptism*, referring to that Christian ordinance, implying it, meaning it: or is it only a symbol of the Spirit's agency—significant of moral cleansing, and having, therefore, no reference to baptism as an external rite?

As preliminary to the discussion before us, let me remind the reader that Jesus has for his pupil a man of apparently fair candor [note how his candor appears in John 7: 51]—a real inquirer after truth (not a caviler); so that we must assume that Jesus aimed to enlighten his mind, and therefore would use words and phrases which Nicodemus might be expected to understand. Honest minds always talk for the sake of being understood; always choose their words and figures accordingly. Hence we are safe in assuming that Jesus adjusted his words to what he supposed Nicodemus knew, or at least might be supposed to know. That is, in addressing Nicodemus he really spake to that group of ideas and sentiments which lay in the mind of his hearer.

Coming now to the main discussion of the one point as put above, I note—

1. That Nicodemus is a *Jew;* therefore Jesus must talk as to

a Jew.——Moreover, Nicodemus is not only one of the Jewish people, but is a member of the highest Jewish council (the Sanhedrim), and therefore by profession a teacher—in the words of Christ, "*the* master [teacher] of Israel" (v. 10). As such the Old Testament was his text-book, and he might be presumed not only to understand that book fairly, but to be able to teach it to others. It is therefore all but certain that Jesus will teach him out of his own book; will assume that he ought to understand that, and will *not* assume that he ought to understand what that book had not taught.

2. This last named point is made the more certain because Jesus expresses his astonishment that Nicodemus, being the teacher of Israel, (*i. e.* one of the prominent, distinguished teachers,) should not know these things. In his view it was not only marvelous but unpardonable that a professed teacher of the Jewish scriptures should not comprehend the plainly taught things of his own book. We must therefore look for the usage of the term "water" in the Old Testament. As we meet it there, is it baptism, or is it simply a symbol of the Spirit's work? We will search this out shortly.

3. The first and most fundamental principle of interpretation being this—that "*usage gives law to language*," we are compelled to find this usage, and hence its behests, *in what precedes rather than what follows*. Therefore Jesus must have spoken according to the usage of the Old Testament rather than of the New, (the yet unwritten and unknown New,) for Nicodemus could not be supposed to understand the New, and Jesus, honestly aiming to teach him, must begin with making himself understood, and must therefore choose his words accordingly. Therefore we must interpret the words of Jesus from things previously known—not from things subsequently revealed; *i. e.* we must find the usage, which gives law to his language in the Old Testament—not in the New; in the teachings and symbols of the old economy, and not in the yet undeveloped institutions [*e. g.* baptism] and their explanations and analogies as brought out only in the later gospel age.

4. Again: As the phrase "kingdom of God" or "of heaven" comes from Old Testament prophecy, we might expect, or at least we might hope, to find the terms of membership there. We may at least say that as the kingdom itself is an Old Testament idea, expressed in Old Testament phrase, so should the conditions of admission, whether found in the Old Testament or the New, be expressed in terms familiar to a good student of the Old Testament scriptures.

5. Yet again: All the standard terms of the gospel system lie back in the Old Testament: so therefore should these terms "water and Spirit," in respect to regeneration. In the Old Testament we have repentance; we have faith, belief, trust; we have sacrifice for sins; redemption, reconciliation, pardon, righteousness, atonement; most surely then we have a right to look there

for the new heart and new Spirit, and for the true doctrine of the Holy Spirit of God, and also for the sense of "*water*" in this connection.

6. Still somewhat more definitely let it be said—The doctrine of the Spirit and of his work in regeneration is in the Old Testament as really as in the New, and "water" is spoken of in connection with the new heart as really there as in this conversation with Nicodemus. Every candid reader will see the propriety therefore of referring to the Old Testament for the true exposition of this word "water" in connection with the work of the Spirit in the new birth.

7. Advancing yet another step—a short one only—I remark that the customary, not to say the invariable, symbol under which the agency of the Spirit is illustrated in the Old Testament is "water." David has the idea in his fifty-first Psalm: "Wash me thoroughly from mine iniquity and cleanse me from my sin;" "Create in me a clean heart;" "Take not thy Holy Spirit from me." Isaiah has it in the form of gospel promise, first in symbol:—"I will pour water upon him that is thirsty, and floods upon the dry ground;"—then in the *thing* symbolized—"I will pour my Spirit upon thy seed and my blessing upon thine offspring;"—and "One shall say, I am the Lord's," etc. (Isa. 44: 3, 5).—— Joel has it (2: 28, 29): "I will pour out my Spirit" [*pour*, as if it were water] "upon all flesh"—a promise which Peter saw fulfilled incipiently on the day of Pentecost (Acts 2: 16-18).— In Zechariah the reader may consult chap. 13: 1, and 14: 8.

In Ezekiel we have the living water flowing forth from under the temple (47: 1-12)—but more significant than all the rest is the passage, Ezek. 36: 25-27: "Then will I sprinkle clean water upon you, and ye shall be clean; from all your filthiness and from all your idols will I cleanse you. A new heart also will I give you, and a new spirit will I put within you: and I will take away the stony heart out of your flesh, and I will give you a heart of flesh. And I will put my Spirit within you, and cause you to walk in my statutes, and ye shall keep my judgments and do them."

Here we have in one group all the leading ideas found in these words of Christ to Nicodemus:—first "*water*"—clean, cleansing water, sprinkled and cleansing from all moral filthiness; next, "the new heart and the new spirit" given—which is precisely regeneration; last, the recognition of "the Spirit of God" as the Supreme Agent whose work is set forth by the symbol of cleansing water, but which really gives the new heart and insures the new moral life: "I will put my Spirit within you, and cause you to walk in my statutes."

It admits of no reasonable doubt that Jesus had these words from Ezekiel definitely in mind when he said, "born of water and Spirit." In each passage—that in Ezekiel and this in Jesus to Nicodemus—we have the same three leading ideas, and in essentially the same order: water; the new heart or birth; God's Spirit, so that we may suppose Jesus to have almost said to his pupil—that "master in Israel"—"What! hast thou never read Ezekiel? Hast thou possibly forgotten what he said so clearly about 'clean water' to cleanse from all iniquity; 'a new heart and new spirit;' and all wrought by God's own Spirit put within the souls of men?"

Let me turn the reader's attention yet more definitely to this point, that Jesus uses the term "water" for a "catch-word," in the good sense common to some English Expositors—*i. e.* a suggestive word which will "catch" the hearer's ear and lead his mind into the desired line of thought. Thus the word "water" would naturally suggest to Nicodemus this very passage in Ezekiel—not to say also, numerous other Old Testament passages in which water symbolizes the Spirit's agency in the hearts of men.—— This explains sufficiently why Jesus puts "water" first in order; also why he names it once, and once only—*i. e.* not as being itself one of the agents in regeneration, but as suggesting the Old Testament passages which speak of the Spirit under the symbol of water.

Thus it seems to admit really of no question that Jesus, following Old Testament usage, speaks of water as a symbol of the Holy Spirit's renewing, heart-cleansing agency in regeneration.

8. But over against this, let it be carefully considered—*Baptism is not in the Old Testament at all*. The word in its Christian sense is not there. Therefore Jesus could not assume that Nicodemus ought to have found and learned it there. To have assumed this, and to have reproached Nicodemus for being "a master in Israel," and yet for not having learned from the Old Testament what was never there, is to make the rebuke recoil upon its author—the blessed Jesus! Whose heart does not exclaim, "God forbid!"

9 Yet further: It is entirely too early for Jesus to speak of Christian baptism. Christian baptism made very special account of the work of the Holy Ghost, for John the Baptist puts his baptism in contrast with it, saying—"I indeed baptize with water; but he that cometh after me shall baptize with the Holy Ghost."——At the time of this discourse with Nicodemus, the doctrine of the Spirit was but partially unfolded. No command had yet gone forth to "baptize into the name of the Father, and of the Son, and of the Holy Ghost." In fact this command which was legitimately the very institution of Christian baptism, dates only after Christ's resurrection.——Now, therefore, if it be said that Jesus used the words—"born of water and Spirit"—with reference to Christian baptism, Nicodemus might have replied—"Rabbi, even thy disciples have not heard yet of baptizing into the name of the Holy Ghost; how then dost thou reproach me for not understanding it?"——The reader will the more surely see the force of my argument here if he will consider that if "water" here means baptism, it must mean baptism *in its closest possible relations to the Holy Ghost and to his regenerating work*. To suppose otherwise is to rule out the great Christian element of

baptism; degrade it to a thing of mere water; and virtually subvert the whole gospel of salvation.——But to interpret baptism here of its special significance as related to the Holy Ghost is to interpret quite ahead of dates.

If it be objected that Jesus had already begun to baptize, even this objection is not altogether felicitous, for we are told that Jesus did not himself baptize, but passed it over to the hands of his disciples. This certainly does not look as if Jesus attached supreme importance to baptism—does not imply that he deemed it essential to admission into the kingdom of heaven, or that in his view the grace of regeneration came always with water-baptism, and never without it. If these had been his views, he could have spared no pains to make the administration impressively solemn; he could not have stood aloof personally from its administration and left it in the hands of novices—for such were his young disciples—at this time less than one year in his training school.

10. If in this passage "water" is interpreted to mean baptism, it springs upon us several questions of momentous bearing, e. g. Is baptism really vital to salvation, as truly so as being "born of the Spirit"? Is it vital by virtue of what is in itself, or only because of its relation to the Spirit? Does baptism certainly and necessarily involve the birth by the Spirit? If not, then what is the state of one born of water and *not* "born of the Spirit"? And again, what of him "born of the Spirit" and not "born of water"?——Now observe: under this interpretation these vital questions are sprung upon us and *then left utterly without solution*. Not a ray of light is thrown upon them. Jesus passes them all as if nobody could ever raise them or be troubled about them. But they will come up, and they must be met. If by "water" Jesus means baptism, he gives no light upon them whatever. All is left loose, indefinite, perplexing, bewildering, and the more solemnly in earnest we are to understand fully all the real conditions of salvation, the more agonizing becomes our perplexity.

Such results from interpreting this word "water" to mean baptism are utterly fatal to the interpretation which evolves and creates them. For this is never the way of God's teaching in the Bible—is never the way of Christ's opening the door into the kingdom of heaven. Woe to all honest inquirers after the way of salvation if it were!

The considerations already advanced are amply sufficient to prove that "water" is here only a symbol of the Spirit's cleansing agency, and has no reference to baptism as a visible, external rite. Several of them would be decisive alone, in their individual force; combined, they seem to me resistless.

11. But there are still other arguments; e. g. this: If Jesus meant baptism, and not water, why did he not say baptism? He might have used the word baptism as easily as the word water, and so have lifted his words above all the darkness of ambiguity and doubt.

12. Again: If he meant baptism, then he made *two* conditions of admission into the kingdom of God. But in v. 6 he seems to forget that there are two conditions, and speaks as if there were but one—being "born of the Spirit."

13. Yet again: If baptism be one of the conditions, distinct from the Spirit, then he assigns it the first place; puts it in the foreground: how then could he ignore it altogether throughout the remaining portion of this discourse, and indeed throughout all his future instructions? How can we account for it that Jesus never again brings up this doctrine to reassert or expound it; that never one of his disciples preached—never one of his apostles wrote—that men must be baptized or never enter into the kingdom of God?

It is hoped that these considerations, combining and massing their forces, will suffice to prove that "water" here is not baptism, but is only a symbol—borrowed from the Old Testament—of the cleansing, renewing agency of the Spirit in the new birth.

A word is perhaps due in reply to one single objection, put by those expositors who make large account of grammatical usage. They say that the figure known as "Hendiadys" (*i. e.* two words for one idea) by which the words "water and Spirit" come to mean the water or washing *of the Spirit*, is not well supported by Greek usage, and is therefore to be rejected in this passage.

My brief reply to this objection is that in this passage Jesus does not concern himself so much with Greek usage as with the usage of Ezekiel in his passage quoted above, about the "new heart." He spake with those words in his eye; says "water" because Ezekiel does, and Spirit because Ezekiel does; and puts the ideas represented by these words into their place in connection with the "new heart" because Ezekiel does, and because Nicodemus ought to understand these words and this sense of them. Hence we have not the least occasion to trouble ourselves over the question of Greek usage here. Old Testament usage in a case of this sort ought to be supreme.

Some of my readers will recall the fact without my aid—that the doctrine of "baptismal regeneration" rests upon this passage only, assuming that "water" here is baptism, and that regeneration goes with baptism, and not without it. Consequently infants, duly baptized, are therein regenerated. Some of the early Christian fathers wrote in this way of "baptismal regeneration"—"regeneration in the water of baptism," etc.

But if "water" is here only a symbol of the Spirit's cleansing, and is not baptism at all, then the whole doctrine of "baptismal regeneration" is a fancy only, and has no scriptural foundation. False interpretations of words found in the Bible have no more force than new words foisted into the Bible would have. The true sense of the words of Jesus is all that Jesus said. Any other supposed meaning which can not be legitimately put upon his words is utterly without his authority.

7. Marvel not that I said unto thee, Ye must be born again.

8. The wind bloweth where it listeth, and thou hearest the sound thereof, but canst not tell whence it cometh, and whither it goeth: so is every one that is born of the Spirit.

In the kindness and compassion of his heart Jesus fears that a sense of the marvelous, excited by what seemed strange and incomprehensible, is counteracting the moral impression of his words—"Ye must be born from above." Hence this caution; and hence also this analogy between the Spirit's agency and the gentle breeze—designed to suggest that mystery may overhang the philosophy of the commonest facts of human life. This analogy was the more suggestive because the same Greek word is used both for "Spirit" in the sense of the Heavenly Agent, and for "wind" as here said to blow—breathe gently—where it will. Of these gentle zephyrs you hear their sound (literally "their voice"), but they never report whence they come or whither they go. So there are untold, unrevealed things concerning the new birth by the Spirit. Do not doubt or in any wise disparage the glorious truth because some things about it lie shaded in mystery.

9. Nicodemus answered and said unto him, How can these things be?

Sad to say, Nicodemus is still snagged where he was before:— "*How* can these things be?" And how can I be born again if I can not understand it?

10. Jesus answered and said unto him, Art thou a master of Israel, and knowest not these things?

Is there in these words a slight under-tone of impatience, moving the Lord to this gentle rebuke—Art thou *the* professed teacher of spiritual things in Israel [the Greek has the article *the*]—one of the distinguished doctors of the law, and yet hast never read, or at least never understood what is so plainly said there of the "new heart and new spirit"—the work of the Spirit of God, symbolized by cleansing water?

11. Verily, verily, I say unto thee, We speak that we do know, and testify that we have seen; and ye receive not our witness.

12. If I have told you earthly things, and ye believe not, how shall ye believe, if I tell you *of* heavenly things?

13. And no man hath ascended up to heaven, but he that came down from heaven, *even* the Son of man which is in heaven.

In saying "we," Jesus may perhaps include with himself his

disciples, yet no special stress should be laid on the plural, for in vs. 12, 13, he speaks of himself only.

Jesus would say to Nicodemus—There are things in the great realm of divine truth which you must receive *upon testimony*. I know what I affirm; I testify only what I have myself seen: why should not you receive my testimony? Yet you refuse it.

In v. 12 "*If* I have told you," is equivalent to this: *Inasmuch* as I have—assuming that he has, and not making the supposition of what would be if he should. This usage of the word "if" is not infrequent in John.——This verse brings up the question—What things are spoken of as "earthly" and what as "heavenly"?——Some have answered: The former are things material; the latter are things spiritual. But this sense seems to me quite inept and not pertinent to the issues pending here.——Others have said: The "earthly" are things done here on the earth; the "heavenly" are done in heaven, or at least, their working forces originate there and come down from thence.——This explanation comes nearer to the truth, yet still falls short of it. I suggest that light on this subject may come from two quarters.——(*a.*) The "earthly things" are those which Jesus had told Nicodemus, yet which he would not believe; while the "heavenly" were those which Nicodemus demanded to know, but which Jesus implies that he would not believe if he were told them—probably would find even more stubbornly incredible because apparently more impossible. In the former class we may put the *fact* of the new birth and its absolute *necessity*; in the latter, the great question which so perplexed Nicodemus:—*How can it be?* How can it be done? The mystery of the Spirit's agency.——(*b.*) It is legitimate to fall back upon that Old Testament usage which speaks of things easy of apprehension as "earthly;" and of things difficult of apprehension as being "heavenly"—remote, too far away to be seen or learned by mortals. We find this usage first in Moses (Deut. 30: 11–14), but appearing again in Paul to the Romans (10: 6–10): "This commandment which I command thee this day is not hidden from thee, neither is it far off. It is not in heaven that thou shouldest say, Who shall go up for us to heaven and bring it unto us that we may hear it and do it? Neither is it beyond the sea that thou shouldest say, Who shall go over the sea for us and bring it unto us that we may hear it and do it? But the word is very nigh unto thee, in thy mouth and in thy heart, that thou mayest do it."—Paul applies this usage beautifully to the "righteousness of faith"—a thing so simple and so easily apprehended that no one need say in his heart—"Who shall go up into heaven for us to bring Christ down to us" that we may understand him? or who shall descend into the deep as if to bring up Christ from the shades below? "But what saith it? The word is nigh thee"—plain, simple, easy of apprehension:—for it is only to "confess with thy mouth the Lord Jesus, and believe in thy heart that God hath raised him from the dead; and thou shalt be saved."——Following this ancient Jewish usage we put into the class of "earthly things" the simple plain facts of the new birth which Jesus had announced—*e. g.* that it is wrought by the Spirit, his agency being symbolized as in the Old Testament by cleansing water; and that this morally new birth is the vital prerequisite for admission to the kingdom of heaven. We put into the class of "heavenly things" those laws of the Spirit's agency which no human ken has searched out, involved in the question—"*How* can these things be done?" and suggested by Jesus in his analogy of the Spirit to the winds that blow, but come, we know not whence, and go, we know not whither. These points Jesus did not propose to reveal, assured that Nicodemus would not believe these inasmuch as he hesitates to believe the far more plain and simple points already solemnly affirmed.

V. 13 follows by natural association from the usage of Moses and of Paul which speaks of "going up to heaven" to get knowledge that is too deep and vast to be found on earth. No man goes up to heaven to get this deep knowledge of the things of the new birth; but the Son of man comes down from heaven, and therefore is entirely competent to teach all the most abstruse things of the realm of truth.——The words—"The Son of man who is in heaven"—seem to recognize the relation of the Logos to the Father to be equivalent to his constantly abiding in heaven. Eternally with God, and indeed being in no respect less than God, he knows God and all the deepest things of the heavenly world, even as if he were dwelling forever there.*

14. And as Moses lifted up the serpent in the wilderness, even so must the Son of man be lifted up:

15. That whosoever believeth in him should not perish, but have eternal life.

By the delicate law of mental association of ideas, the lifting up of the serpent and the analogous lifting up of the Son of man upon the cross may have been suggested by the *ascending up* to heaven to get truth which is too far from human reach to be grasped below.

Let us note, moreover, that this allusion to Moses and the serpent in the wilderness is doubly pertinent in a discourse with Nicodemus, because it comes from his own text-book. There lay in it a most significant foreshadowing—first, of the lifting up of Jesus upon the cross; next, of the looking up to him by faith for life by every soul stung with conscious guilt, and verily lost under the doom of condemnation from God. The looking up to that uplifted serpent was in its nature, faith; the looking up to the Crucified One is definitely called *believing in him*, and is coupled with the promise, not of the life of the body for a few days or years longer as in the case of the serpent-bitten men, but with the prom-

---

* The old manuscripts (S. V.) omit the words—"who is in heaven." Tischendorf, however, retains them.

ise of *life eternal*—a life of restoration to God and of everlasting peace in his presence and favor.——Let it be noted that Christ's way of speaking of himself as to be "lifted up" (*i. e.* on the cross) seems to have made a deep impression on the mind of John. He remembered and put on record two other references to the same fact, in the same words: "Then said Jesus unto them, When ye have lifted up the Son of man, then shall ye know that I am he," etc. (John 8: 28). Also this: "And I, if I be lifted up, will draw all men unto me;" which John explains:—"This he said, signifying what death he should die" (John 12: 32, 33). ——Thus Jesus led Nicodemus along into the great things of the gospel system—the sacrificial death of the Son of man upon the cross, and the looking up to him thus crucified, as the world's Great Sufferer, who bore our sins in his own body on the tree—to look unto whom by faith is to live eternally.

We shall miss much of the beauty of these verses (14-21) if we overlook (as some readers do) the fact that we are still listening to Jesus in his night conversation with Nicodemus. How kindly and yet how briefly, in most comprehensive words, does Jesus lead his pupil on into the great elementary things of the gospel scheme! *

16. For God so loved the world, that he gave his only begotten Son, that whosoever believeth in him should not perish, but have everlasting life.

17. For God sent not his Son into the world to condemn the world; but that the world through him might be saved.

Moving forward in his discourse logically ("for"), his next point naturally is to trace this scheme of salvation for lost men to its source in the deep, eternal, absolutely *infinite* love of God for this lost world. If Nicodemus may be supposed to have understood to some extent the deep significance of "the Son of man lifted up" upon the cross—dying in torture that guilty men might have life by looking unto him, we might expect another exclamation like the former—"How can these things be!" Was ever such a sacrifice of dear life made for one's guilty enemies? And how is it possible that God should give up his Son to such a death? Anticipating this new marvel, Jesus by one word lets in a flood of light from heaven upon it: "For God *so loved* the world"—loved the world with love so pure, so unselfish, so self-sacrificing—that he gave up the only-begotten Son,† in order that no believer in

---

* In v. 15 the text corrected upon the authority of the Sinaitic and the Vatican, omits the words—"not perish, but"—reading the passage thus: "Whosoever believeth in him should have eternal life." It is supposable that they were introduced here by some copyist because he found them in v. 16.

† "*The* only-begotten Son" is the reading best supported.

him should perish, but every such one should have eternal life.*

In verse 17 we have a slight advance in the glorious gospel doctrine—the great purpose of God in sending his Son into this rebellious world being put in its negative side as well as its positive side. You might anticipate that the Great King, sending his royal Son into a revolted province, would commission him only to subdue and destroy; but so thinking, you would utterly misconceive the mission of the Son of God. For God did not send him to wield Heaven's exterminating thunders, nor to sit in righteous judgment unto eternal condemnation, but that the world through him might be saved. The world's salvation—not its damnation—was the declared purpose, the sublime design, of this wonderful mission.

We should wrest this scripture to our sore damage if we were to push it so that it should deny the doctrine, elsewhere revealed, of a *future judgment*, to be administered by "the Son of man." The two doctrines are in no respect self-conflicting. The first coming of Jesus is for salvation, the second for judgment. The first provides and offers a free salvation to all men whosoever will; the second brings before the "great white throne" of judgment the whole race of men to award their righteous doom to all those whom no mercy could save; whom no offers of pardon could move to accept it; whom no long-suffering and no beseechings of love have ever availed to bring to repentance and to faith in an offered Redeemer.

18. He that believeth on him is not condemned: but he that believeth not is condemned already, because he hath not believed in the name of the only begotten Son of God.

This verse expands more fully the thought of the last clause in v. 16—the truth that whoever believes in Christ shall have eternal life. So Jesus here puts first the case of the believer. He is not condemned but pardoned, and therefore saved. Then on the other side the case of him who *believes not:* he is condemned already because he does not believe in the name of the only-begotten Son of God.

Here the main point of inquiry exegetically will be brought out by the question—"Condemned already," for what sin? Is it *for the one sin of unbelief;* or for the sins *of his whole life*, for which no pardon has come, or can come while he will not believe in Jesus? Either of these views is in itself admissible—*i. e.* is true; but the scope of the passage seems to me to favor the former. Jesus seems to speak here as if in his thought the whole issue between saved

* In the last clause of each verse (15 and 16) "eternal" and "everlasting" (as in Matt. 25: 46) are used interchangeably to translate the same Greek word "*aiōnios*." It is unfortunate that regard to euphony should have led our translators to violate the best rule of translation—the same English word for its equivalent Greek.

and lost turned on the one point—believing or not believing in the name of the Son of God—every believer being saved; every unbeliever lost. Other sins besides this one of unbelief are comparatively of no account as bearing on the question of ultimate salvation, for all else can be forgiven; but the sin of unbelief in God's offered Son must of necessity be fatal to salvation, because it puts the soul beyond the pale of mercy; debars the sinner from the possibility of pardon; practically nullifies, as to the man who will not believe in Jesus, all that God in his great mercy has provided for human salvation.

If this exposition of the thought of Jesus in this passage be just, it will be readily seen that in his view every man's eternal destiny turns on the single point—gospel faith, or gospel unbelief. This point is lifted into a prominence which towers high above every thing else. It is not surprising therefore that he should proceed to show how unbelief roots itself vitally in the love of man's heart for sin, and, consequently, for the darkness which perverts his views of truth—as we shall see.

19. And this is the condemnation, that light is come into the world, and men loved darkness rather than light, because their deeds were evil.

20. For every one that doeth evil hateth the light, neither cometh to the light, lest his deeds should be reproved.

21. But he that doeth truth cometh to the light, that his deeds may be made manifest, that they are wrought in God.

Here gospel unbelief is traced philosophically to "evil deeds"—which if a man will justify and will not forsake, he must needs cover them as best he can *with darkness*. Hence he will love darkness rather than light. He comes to have a personal interest in darkness, since it is only by its help that he can make himself at all comfortable in sinning. It is the perpetual annoyance of sinners that God has made them with a moral sense which condemns sin—which insists upon witnessing against sin as wrong, base, unworthy of a moral being. This witnessing testimony of his own conscience the sinner must in some way withstand. How shall he do it? Shall he bribe the witness, or muzzle his lips, or mystify his points, or stop his own ears?——In the words before us, the Great Teacher treats the case with beautiful yet rich simplicity. Truth is light—truth being to the mind what light is to the body. This light of moral sort God has brought into the world. In his power of moral choices man has his option to come or not to come to this light. If he loves light, he comes; if he loves darkness rather, he hates the light and will not come. Of course he will love darkness if his deeds are deeds of darkness, such as can not bear the light. The philosophy of this is almost too simple to be made more plain by analysis or exposition. As long as a man proposes to continue in sin, he will vindicate his former sinning self so far as he can, and will labor to make his sins appear trivial, *i. e.* he will shut off the light, will dread its revelations; will hate it and will not come up to it lest it make his life and his soul unendurably odious.——On the other hand, if a man live up to his moral convictions;—in the words of Jesus, if he "doeth truth," then he will come to the light, and you may at once see that his doings are manifestly "*wrought in God*"—the deeds of a soul new-born to God with that birth which is by the Spirit.

The ultimate doctrine reached by this philosophy of gospel faith and unbelief is that both have their roots rather in the heart than in the head, since gospel faith wells up spontaneously in the heart that loves purity and truth; while gospel unbelief has its roots and impulses in cherished sin and in the darkness which brings the only comfort to a persistent sinner.——We reach essentially the same result when we say that repentance naturally goes before gospel faith, and impenitence as to sin begets gospel unbelief; for when a man turns against his former sinning self, he begins to welcome the light of truth; he gladly comes to it; gladly hails the help the gospel brings, and opens his soul to the peace and joy of Christ's salvation. But so long as any man persists in sin he keeps himself under the strongest temptation to justify sinning—for which the only available means are to shut off God's light, and to make a covenant with darkness.

When Christ said to Nicodemus (v. 19) "light is come into the world," we must suppose him to refer to his own coming from heaven to earth with the light of salvation; as said (1: 9) "This was the true light which coming into the world, enlightens every man." Thus Jesus would press it upon Nicodemus that the one supreme ground of condemnation—the great damning sin—is, repelling the light of heaven which the Son of God, becoming incarnate in human flesh, came to reveal.

Contemplating this conversation with Nicodemus as a whole, we are impressed with its simplicity, its directness, and the comprehensiveness with which Jesus puts before his pupil the vital truths of the gospel. With what concentration of truth and motive does he bring every thing to bear upon the one great point—believing on the name of the Son of God! We can almost see him throw his loving arms around the old man, saying with solemnly tender tone and flowing tears—If you will only break off your sins by righteousness; cease to love darkness for the sake of self-justification in evil ways, and thus open your soul to the light of God, and come in the spirit of a child to believe in that Son of God for pardon and life, how will your soul rest in the peace of God that passeth all understanding!

22. After these things came Jesus and his disciples into the land of Judea; and there he tarried with them, and baptized.

The second portion of this chapter, opening here, brings Jesus for the last time into contact with John the Baptist, and records the final testimony of the Baptist in behalf of Jesus as the Messiah.

If we inquire for the supposable reason why Jesus went from the city of Jerusalem into the country—Judea—to preach, we have it probably in the two facts—that the bigotry and pride of the Pharisees were most virulent and hostile in the city—less so in the country; and that John's preparatory work, preaching repentance and awakening expectation of a Savior near, had been by far most effective in the country. It was wise that Jesus availed himself of these preparatory labors of his Great Forerunner.

23. And John also was baptizing in Ænon near to Salim, because there was much water there: and they came, and were baptized.

John the Baptist was also baptizing at a point so near that his disciples were cognizant of the work Jesus was doing.

The precise locality of Ænon and Salim is still uncertain, the best authorities favoring either a point six miles south of Scythopolis (Bethshean), or a point some five miles north-east from Jerusalem—the latter corresponding best with the exigencies of the context. See Smith's Bible Dictionary on these words.—— Ænon signifies fountains, a place of copious springs. The Greek words translated "much water," may as fitly be translated, *many waters* or fountains, such as would supply the personal wants of a large concourse of people.

24. For John was not yet cast into prison.

The author assumes that his readers know the fact of John's imprisonment. Therefore he simply refers to it as not having yet occurred. The Baptist was still prosecuting his work.

25. Then there arose a question between *some* of John's disciples and the Jews about purifying.

26. And they came unto John, and said unto him, Rabbi, he that was with thee beyond Jordan, to whom thou barest witness, behold, the same baptizeth, and all *men* come to him.

All the better textual authorities say—not "the Jews," but *a Jew*, in the singular.——This "question about purifying" had reference obviously to baptism, that being the only thing in the context to which purifying can refer. But the precise shape of the question is not indicated. That the discussion resulted in sending John's disciples to their master to tell him what Jesus was doing in the way of baptizing multitudes favors the view that the dispute arose over the mutual relations of the two baptisms—that of John and that of Jesus. To John's disciples it may have seemed that Jesus was working in opposition to their master. Had his baptism any new significance, or only the same as that of John? If both signified essentially a spiritual purification, why should both be baptizing, each building up a distinct body of followers?——A feeling of dissatisfaction, akin to envy or jealousy, seems to underlie the message brought to John the Baptist by his disciples.

27. John answered and said, A man can receive nothing, except it be given him from heaven.

28. Ye yourselves bear me witness, that I said, I am not the Christ, but that I am sent before him.

29. He that hath the bride is the bridegroom: but the friend of the bridegroom, which standeth and heareth him, rejoiceth greatly because of the bridegroom's voice: this my joy therefore is fulfilled.

30. He must increase, but I *must* decrease.

Not the least tinge of envy is in the words or the heart of John because of the rising honor and growing success of Jesus. He begins his reply by saying, All spiritual success comes down to men from heaven. Therefore if God gives more to another than to me, who am I that I should complain?——Besides, ye know I never claimed to be the Messiah, but only that I was sent before him to prepare his way. As the bride belongs to the bridegroom, and not to the bridegroom's friend, so the church of God—all real converts—belong to Christ—not to me. My high mission is to wait on the bridegroom; hear his words of command; and promptly, joyfully obey them. This my joy is now complete. I work for *his* success—not for my own. It is enough for me if the multitudes throng around his feet. He must increase in influence and honor. I am to be thrown more and more into the shade, and my special followers must become, relatively to his, fewer in number.——There is moral grandeur in the hearty joy with which John accepts this overshadowing greatness of his Master, eclipsing his own popularity.

31. He that cometh from above is above all: he that is of the earth is earthly, and speaketh of the earth: he that cometh from heaven is above all.

32. And what he hath seen and heard, that he testifieth; and no man receiveth his testimony.

Jesus coming really from above, from heaven itself, must surely be above all others—higher in nature, in authority, in success. As to myself, I am only of the earth, and my teaching is of the earth, as compared and contrasted with that of my divine Master. ——The better textual authorities omit in v. 31 the last three words—"is above all"—and connect verses 31 and 32 on this wise: "He that cometh from heaven testifies what he hath seen and heard."——Yet, strange to say, almost no man—none with but few exceptions—receives his testimony.

33. He that hath received his testimony hath set to his seal that God is true.

There are some noble exceptions. He who does receive the testimony which accredits the Messiah, puts his seal to God's veracity—accepts the testimony of God as veritably true.

34. *For he whom God hath sent speaketh the words of God: for God giveth not the Spirit by measure unto him.*

The first clause is virtually a moral truism. He whom God sends and accredits will speak his words, being sent for no other purpose save to speak for God. He could not be indorsed by miracle if he did not speak truly for God. To him God gives his Spirit in unmeasured fullness—the special function and work of the Spirit as thought of here being the same which Jesus contemplates in his descriptive epithet—"The Spirit of truth" (John 14: 17, and 15: 26). Jesus being filled in the fullest measure by this truth-revealing Spirit, would surely speak the words of God.

35. *The Father loveth the Son, and hath given all things into his hand.*

Great truths are these, yet put in words most brief and expressive. The Father loveth the Son, especially for his pure, self-sacrificing benevolence; fully approves of his work of redemption; and has committed to him supreme power in heaven and earth for its execution.

36. *He that believeth on the Son hath everlasting life: and he that believeth not the Son shall not see life; but the wrath of God abideth on him.*

Peculiar solemnity is in these words, considered as the last recorded utterances of John the Baptist, whose life-mission it had been to preach repentance to Israel, and exhort his countrymen with mighty persuasion to turn from their sins that they might be ready to welcome their nation's Great Redeemer, soon to appear. At this point he sees this Redeemer already come—already preaching the gospel and ministering mercy to every penitent, waiting soul. Can he drop one last word of earnest, solemn testimony which may avail to press lost men forward to Jesus?—He has said that this Jesus came down from heaven, bearing the great seal of God, speaking words from God, filled with the Spirit beyond measure, loved of the Father, and invested from Him with all power: and now, to urge sinners with utmost pressure of motive, he proclaims—"He that believeth on the Son hath everlasting life"—blessedness that never ends; while "he that believeth not the Son shall not see life, but the wrath of God abideth on him." What could he have said more impressive; of vaster import; more appropriate for last words to be left vibrating in the ears of his generation when his own voice should be silenced by death?——This statement, let it be carefully noted, is strictly absolute and final; it denies unqualifiedly; no form of statement possible to human speech can be stronger. It shuts off all questions of limitation—as *e. g.* whether "everlasting" may not come to an end, and another and different sort of destiny follow. If the unbelieving sinner *shall not see life*, his die is cast beyond hope of reversing it. The blessedness of life with God, and with all the pure-hearted above, he can never enjoy.

Nor let it be said that he has still a refuge from the doom of eternal woe *in annihilation,* for according to this word of the Lord, "the wrath of God *abideth* on him"—remains and dwells upon him; and there the testimony of inspiration leaves him.—— Shall it be said that this abiding, ever-enduring wrath of God resting upon him does not prevent his dropping into non-existence? Why should men ascribe to God the absurdity of making his wrath abide forever upon nonentities? Do men change the eternal truth of God when they pervert his words—the plainest and most explicit words he can employ? Does it subserve any good purpose for sinners to wrest God's words to their own destruction?

CHAPTER IV.

Here is the conversation of Jesus with the woman of Samaria which opened the way for two days' successful gospel labor in her city and among her people (vs. 1–42); then the healing of a nobleman's son of Capernaum (vs. 43–54).

1. When therefore the Lord knew how the Pharisees had heard that Jesus made and baptized more disciples than John,
2. (Though Jesus himself baptized not, but his disciples,)
3. He left Judea, and departed again into Galilee.

Jesus went from Judea into Galilee to place himself for the time beyond the persecution which his great success in baptizing converts might excite. It had come to his knowledge that the Pharisees had heard that he was making more converts than even the Baptist had made, and he had reason to know that this would excite their jealousy and hate into fury. It was his policy to evade for a time, and so postpone, the outburst of this storm until he had trained his disciples; laid the foundations for great gospel work by his example and his preaching—in his own phrase, till he had "finished the personal work the Father had given him to do." Here we have the reasons why so large a portion of his miracles and teachings were in Galilee rather than in Judea.

The fact that Jesus himself did not administer baptism, but left it to his disciples, must be regarded as significant. This incidental mention of it manifests a like purpose, viz, to countervail an innate tendency in men to overestimate the value of the merely external and ritual things of religion. If Jesus had performed all the baptisms with his own hand; if the record had recited minutely the attendant circumstances—the solemn forms and ceremonies—the imposing display; the impression upon minds susceptible to the glory of the external would have been magic—and let us also say, fearfully perilous. To avoid this, Jesus adopted a method which bears its testimony through all the ages against overdoing the mere rites of religion, and against undue reliance upon the external matters of Christianity. He meant to show for all time that the efficacy of baptism lay not in the holy, consecrated hands administering it, but in the sincerity of the converts baptized; in "the answer of a good conscience toward God;" and in the power of the cleansing, sanctifying Spirit, signified under this symbol.

4. And he must needs go through Samaria.

5. Then cometh he to a city of Samaria, which is called Sychar, near to the parcel of ground that Jacob gave to his son Joseph.

6. Now Jacob's well was there. Jesus therefore, being wearied with *his* journey, sat thus on the well: *and* it was about the sixth hour.

"Sychar" is supposed to be the city of Sychem (otherwise Shechem)—this change of name by the Jews being designed for reproach, suggesting either falsehood as involved in idol-worship, or from another root, suggesting drunkenness. The city is remarkable for its proximity to Jacob's well, whose locality corresponds entirely with the sacred history of the patriarch, and is indorsed by unbroken tradition since the hour when Jesus sat there. It has been repeatedly visited and examined in modern times: was dug in solid rock, about nine feet in diameter and one hundred and five feet deep; was descended in part by steps—its depth of water varying, as measured at various times, from fifteen feet to five.——We have a probable reference to Jacob's gift of this piece of ground to Joseph in his dying benediction (Gen. 48: 22).
——The Orientals are wont to start their journeys with the early morning. A six hours' walk brought Jesus there wearied and worn, so that he seated himself by the well to rest and to wait his opportunity for a draught of water.

7. There cometh a woman of Samaria to draw water: Jesus saith unto her, Give me to drink.

8. (For his disciples were gone away unto the city to buy meat.)

9. Then saith the woman of Samaria unto him, How is it that thou, being a Jew, askest drink of me, which am a woman of Samaria? for the Jews have no dealings with the Samaritans.

While the disciples were gone into the city to buy food—an hour's absence—a woman of Samaria came up to this well for water—of course with the necessary means for drawing. Recognizing Jesus as a Jew, she is surprised that he should ask water to drink from a Samaritan, and even a Samaritan *woman*. In all Jews the caste feeling against Samaritans was intense, and by the laws of caste would manifest itself most intensely (though foolishly) in the point of drinking water from their hands.——John shows that he is writing, not for Jewish readers, who would need no explanation of this woman's surprise, but for Gentile readers—supposably of Asia Minor.——Jesus had no sympathy with this caste feeling of his countrymen. We may suppose he rather welcomed this opportunity to bear the testimony of his example and spirit squarely and totally against it.

10. Jesus answered and said unto her, If thou knewest the gift of God, and who it is that saith to thee, Give me to drink; thou wouldest have asked of him, and he would have given thee living water.

Skillfully, tenderly, impressively, Jesus leads the mind of this Samaritan woman into the great things of gospel salvation: "You think it strange that I ask you for a draught of water from this well. If you only knew the great gift of God to men, even his only-begotten Son who is now before you, you would have asked of him, and he would have given you living water."——Note with what inimitable modesty and beauty Jesus introduces himself as the Giver of the waters of life to perishing souls! Taking up the ever fresh and precious Old Testament usage of the term "waters" —*e. g.* "Ho every one that thirsteth, come ye to the waters"—he identifies himself as the long promised Savior whose mission to earth was to "seek and to save the lost."——"Living water"—not merely water from a living spring which never dries away, but *living* in a yet higher sense which Jesus himself will soon explain.

11. The woman saith unto him, Sir, thou hast nothing to draw with, and the well is deep: from whence then hast thou that living water?

12. Art thou greater than our father Jacob, which gave us the well, and drank thereof himself, and his children, and his cattle?

13. Jesus answered and said unto her, Whosoever drinketh of this water shall thirst again:

14. But whosoever drinketh of the water that I shall give him shall never thirst; but the water that I shall give him shall be in him a well of water springing up into everlasting life.

Slow to measure the full depth of the strange words, "living water," this woman discloses her perplexity :—"This well is deep, and thou hast nothing to draw with; how then canst thou get living water from it? And as for any other water than this, we know of none better. Art thou greater than our father Jacob who gave us this wonderful well the waters of which were good enough for him and his children? How is this that thou seemest to think of better water than this from our father Jacob?——These questions bring up the very point which Jesus wished to reach; his explanation is therefore ready: You drink from Jacob's well, and, good though the water be, you thirst again. But having drank of the water that I give, you never thirst again. It becomes within you a living fountain, and wells up unto eternal life. It becomes a self-perpetuating supply. It satisfies once and forever. You will never even desire any thing better. There is life in it for the very soul. It meets and fills the greatest, deepest wants of your being.——This is what Jesus meant by "living water;" his precious words contain the whole of this glorious, priceless truth;—but the woman of Samaria will need more help and more time to grasp these great thoughts as to the nature and the fullness of Christ's salvation.

15. The woman saith unto him, Sir, give me this water, that I thirst not, neither come hither to draw.

16. Jesus saith unto her, Go, call thy husband, and come hither.

17. The woman answered and said, I have no husband. Jesus said unto her, Thou hast well said, I have no husband.

18. For thou hast had five husbands; and he whom thou now hast is not thy husband: in that saidst thou truly.

One thing she can understand: If the water thus promised will quench her thirst for all time it must be a real treasure. She has had plenty of experience in the toil of coming under the sultry heats of noon to lift water from a hundred feet of depth, and she can see what a saving might be made with water that would supply itself and quench her thirst once for all. So she puts in her request for this new sort of water—of properties so strange.—The Master readily sees that he must lead her thought to deeper things, and therefore says, Go, call thy husband to come with you.—Her quasi-married life, she knew but too well, would not bear probing. Was it because she felt herself to be in a Presence which would pierce through all disguises, that she at once brought out the truth, "I have no husband," or did she, perhaps, suppose that this statement would foreclose all further inquiry? However this may have been, Jesus soon showed her that he knew her whole life-history. How much of crime may have lain in that history, running so rapidly through married life with five husbands, consecutive or otherwise, it was not important for the moral purposes of this story to disclose. The words of Jesus sufficed to show that he knew her whole life and her very heart. This was one of the impressions which the Master sought to make—one, but probably not the only one; for we must suppose that he meant also to awaken conviction of sin and suggest that she had ample occasion for penitence and pardon.

19. The woman saith unto him, Sir, I perceive that thou art a prophet.

20. Our fathers worshiped in this mountain; and ye say, that in Jerusalem is the place where men ought to worship.

This woman is frank to confess that her life has been truly told, and that this stranger must be a prophet. Still her thought does not readily turn toward her sinful life (as we may suppose the Master purposed and hoped); but rather, as human nature has often done before and since, drifted toward a theological controversy. Assuming as before that Jesus is a Jew, she brings up the old and long mooted issue between Jews and Samaritans as to the place of acceptable worship. Our fathers, said she, as you very well know, worshiped in this Mt. Gerizim: your people insist that men ought to worship in Jerusalem.——Did she propose to get his opinion on this question; or did she rather intend to suggest tacitly that, being a Jew, he would doubtless insist on his Jewish doctrine; while she, being a Samaritan, must be allowed to adhere to the doctrine of her fathers?

21. Jesus saith unto her, Woman, believe me, the hour cometh, when ye shall neither in this mountain, nor yet at Jerusalem, worship the Father.

22. Ye worship ye know not what: we know what we worship; for salvation is of the Jews.

23. But the hour cometh, and now is, when the true worshipers shall worship the Father in spirit and in truth: for the Father seeketh such to worship him.

24. God *is* a Spirit: and they that worship him must worship *him* in spirit and in truth.

This theological controversy, then already from four to seven hundred years old, had virtually run its course. So Jesus, instead of pronouncing upon it, as she probably expected, proceeded at once to supersede it by assuring her that all such questions as to the locality of ritual worship were ruled out of account as no longer of the least consequence. No matter whether men sacrifice on Gerizim or in Jerusalem, the hour has come when men may worship *anywhere* with equal acceptance before God, provided only they worship the Father in spirit and in truth. He seeks such worship. The homage of pure and loving hearts is accepted before him; the place where is no longer to be regarded. ——Moreover, ye Samaritans have had no sense of the Being ye have professed to worship; ye have sacrificed only to an unknown God. In this most vital respect, the Jews are entirely in advance of you, for the light of God abides with them, and from among them the Savior of the world is to come. A new era of light and truth breaks forth upon the world; old things are passing away; worship ceases to lie in sacrifices and ritualities. God makes himself known as a Spirit, and those who would worship him acceptably must give him their heart's homage in spirit and in truth. Thus the old Judæo-Samaritan issue is swept away and new light breaks forth.

25. The woman saith unto him, I know that Messias cometh, which is called Christ: when he is come, he will tell us all things.

26. Jesus saith unto her, I that speak unto thee am *he*.

The woman is borne onward by this new announcement. It suggests to her the ancient faith of her people—in some measure common to Samaritans and to Jews—"that Messias cometh," and that "when he shall come, he will tell us all things." The Samaritans, as is well known, had a version of the Pentateuch, differing only in few and slight particulars from the ancient Hebrew text. This, and this only, constituted their Old Testament scriptures. They have even to this day a copy of this Samaritan Pentateuch which (wrote Dr. Robinson * in 1838) "they professed was then 3460 years old, referring it to Abishua, the son of Phineas" (1 Chron. 6: 3, 4).——In this Pentateuch the Lord had said through Moses (Deut. 18: 15, 18), "I will raise them up a Prophet, like unto thee, and I will put my words in his mouth, and he shall speak unto them all that I shall command him." In the simple thought this corresponds closely with the brief words of this Samaritan woman—"When he is come, he will tell us all things;" so that we may safely assume that the great Messianic promise on which the Samaritan faith rested was this from Moses in Deuteronomy.—How must her ears have tingled when this stranger at the well announced—"I that speak unto thee am he"! Indeed; and has our Great Messiah, waited for through long ages, come at last! And these eyes have seen him!

27. And upon this came his disciples, and marveled that he talked with the woman: yet no man said, What seekest thou? or, Why talkest thou with her?

At this crisis in the conversation, the disciples came up from the city. They are surprised, not to say astonished, to find their Master talking with a Samaritan woman; but either through a sense of his personal dignity, or a half unconscious conviction of an unworthy prejudice on their part, not a man of them dared say—What can be thy object? or why shouldest thou talk with her? "Wisdom is justified of her children." Goodness and truth may sometimes in a sinning world like this seem strange, but will

---

* Robinson's Researches, Vol. III. 105.

always be their own vindication and command the homage of all honest minds. Hence the disciples, though startled at first, probably soon gave the Master their more profound respect.

28. The woman then left her waterpot, and went her way into the city, and saith to the men,

29. Come, see a man, which told me all things that ever I did: is not this the Christ?

30. Then they went out of the city, and came unto him.

Forgetting the water she came for, and even dropping her waterpot, the woman hasted away to the city with her good news. She hails the men from afar: "Come, see a man who has told me all things that ever I did: Is not this the Christ?" Did she tell them also how he said explicitly—"I that speak unto thee am he"? Very probably; but wisely she puts the argument before the assertion. She verily knew that this stranger had revealed to her the great—shall we say the *guilty*—secret of her life. He had shown her that he knew it all. She was therefore sure he must be far more than human. Moreover, must we not attribute her faith in him as the Messiah in no small part to the moral evidence that shone forth in his benignity, his manifest goodness of heart; his gentleness, and tenderness, and compassion; his marvelous interest in her welfare—so strange in the experience of a lone woman, from a despised race, engaged in a menial service, with not a thing to recommend her, save degradation, and want, and a poor human soul!——Her story, so earnestly told, so startling in its facts, seems to move the whole city. They follow her back to the scene and to the "Man."

31. In the meanwhile his disciples prayed him, saying, Master, eat.

32. But he said unto them, I have meat to eat that ye know not of.

33. Therefore said the disciples one to another, Hath any man brought him *aught* to eat?

34. Jesus saith unto them, My meat is to do the will of him that sent me, and to finish his work.

The disciples failed to appreciate how intently absorbed their Master had become in his labors for this woman and her people; or, we may perhaps suppose, thought that hunger and fatigue had demands which even this great spiritual crisis should not overrule. Accordingly, during the absence of the woman, they pressed him to eat. He replied, "I have meat to eat that ye know not of." Observe, they do not ask him to explain; do not say—"We do not understand what thou canst mean;" but they said in an under-tone one to another—Hath any man brought him food? Does any one know how or whence he has obtained bread?— Apparently there were limits to the familiarity which they felt to be admissible with their Master. There was more depth to his character than they had yet fathomed; a modest reserve on their part was therefore becoming.——In this case, as usual, Jesus knew their thought, and so proceeds to explain: "My meat is to do the will of him that sent me, and to finish his work." This is more to me than bread. In the crisis of a great harvest hour, men will forget the body through the unutterable yearnings and longings of the soul.

35. Say not ye, There are yet four months, and *then* cometh harvest? behold, I say unto you, Lift up your eyes, and look on the fields; for they are white already to harvest.

36. And he that reapeth receiveth wages, and gathereth fruit unto life eternal: that both he that soweth and he that reapeth may rejoice together.

37. And herein is that saying true, One soweth and another reapeth.

38. I sent you to reap that whereon ye bestowed no labor: other men labored, and ye are entered into their labors.

There are two slightly variant interpretations of the words— "Say ye not, There are yet four months and then cometh harvest?"—one assuming the words to be a proverbial expression, naturally on the lips of the sower as he looks onward from seeding to harvest; the other assuming that the disciples had been saying these words just then as they looked forth upon grain fields then green and full of promise. In either case it is held that Jesus made these words the text of his remarks onward to the end of v. 38.

The supposition of a proverb lacks support from known usage; and encounters grave difficulties from the fact that in Palestine the usual interval from the seed-time for grain to harvest is from five to six months, and not merely four.——Adopting therefore the latter construction of these pivotal words, we may paraphrase the passage on this wise: Were ye not just now saying as ye looked down these fertile valleys—Four months more and these fields now green will be waving with their yellow harvests? Behold, I say unto you, look down these valleys again; mark those thronging groups of men from the city, led on by the woman ye saw here at the well. Are ye aware how deeply their hearts are moved, how anxiously they are inquiring whether the Savior of the world has really come, and how ripe they are for a spiritual harvest? Now is the time for reaping and for the wages of fruit unto life eternal. Here you are spared the toil of sowing and the trial of waiting long months for the harvest hour. Should not such a harvest time as this charm even hungry men away from their bread?

39. And many of the Samaritans of that city believed on

him for the saying of the woman, which testified, He told me all that ever I did.

40. So when the Samaritans were come unto him, they besought him that he would tarry with them: and he abode there two days.

41. And many more believed because of his own word;

42. And said unto the woman, Now we believe, not because of thy saying: for we have heard *him* ourselves, and know that this is indeed the Christ, the Savior of the world.

The remainder of this narrative is put only in general statement. Many of the Samaritans from the city believed, on the basis of the woman's personal testimony. When they saw Jesus for themselves they begged him to come and stay with them. He went and abode there two days. In the result many more believed and said to this woman—We believe, not on the ground of your words, but of what we have seen and heard for ourselves. Now we know that this is indeed the Christ, the Savior of the world.

It is noticeable that no people in either Galilee or Judea seem to have embraced the gospel from the Savior's lips with equal readiness. Publicans and harlots enter the kingdom of heaven before proud Pharisees.——When, after the first persecution had driven the disciples out of Jerusalem, "Philip went down to Samaria and preached Christ unto them" (Acts 8: 5–8), "the people with one accord gave heed;" "and there was great joy in that city." Then the seed sown here by Jesus himself brought forth yet another glorious harvest.

Reviewing this story to gather up its marvelous points as they bear upon the labors and the life of the Great Master of Israel, let us note that these labors began, not with a vast congregation, but with a single individual; not upon a set appointment, but in a merely incidental, casual meeting; not when the Master was fresh and buoyant, but when weary and hungry with a six hours' walk; and note also that this one was not some distinguished gentleman, but an unknown woman, to be thought of as women are wont to be in Oriental society; not of high caste, but of low; not moving in the higher plane of social life, but apparently in the lowest; not a woman of previously unblemished reputation, but one whose record was at least doubtful, not to say suspicious. In short, the only point of attractiveness apparent to us in her case was that she was human—a soul to be saved or lost. To her Jesus addressed himself as we have seen, assiduously, discreetly, tenderly; he won her confidence by his benignity, kindness, and manifested interest in her true welfare, and pressed steadily toward the end he had in view, refusing to be diverted from it for even one moment to any side issue.——We admire his skill of approach; we love his spirit of inimitable goodness and condescension. Let us never forget that he has left us an example that we should walk in his steps. In our humble measure we may follow where he has so beautifully led the way, and if we can not do things as great, we may at least aspire through his grace to be equally loving, kind, and good.

43. *Now after two days he departed thence, and went into Galilee.*
44. *For Jesus himself testified, that a prophet hath no honor in his own country.*
45. *Then when he was come into Galilee, the Galileans received him, having seen all the things that he did at Jerusalem at the feast: for they also went unto the feast.*

The reasoning suggested by "for" (Gr. γαρ) in v. 44, has greatly perplexed critics. Assuming his own country to be Galilee, and that a man should naturally go where he could expect to receive the honor due him, they have said, How happens it that the reason assigned for his going into Galilee is that according to his own knowledge and frequent testimony, he could have no suitable honor there?——I have to suggest that some relief in this dilemma may come from the two following considerations:—(*a.*) That, comparing Samaria with Galilee, the former honored him as a prophet; the latter, only as a worker of miracles (v. 48). In Samaria, Jesus wrought no miracles, yet the people honored him as a great prophet. No such honor was accorded to him in his own country—Galilee.——(*b.*) It is supposable that Jesus had reasons for choosing to go for the time where he would have less honor rather than where he might have the greatest. Recurring to the points adduced in 4: 1–3, we see that he left Judea and went into Galilee because he was making disciples dangerously fast; because his popularity there might expose him too soon to the murderous rage of his enemies. For a similar reason it might be his choice to leave Samaria and go into Galilee, for no such reception awaited him in his own country as might prematurely excite the jealousy and wrath of the Pharisees and hasten their persecution to its deadly crisis.

The Galileans received him because they had seen his miracles in Jerusalem at the feast. (See 2: 23.)——The remark, "For they also went unto the feast," suggests again that the writer explains points which no Jewish reader would need to have explained, but of which remote Gentiles, *e. g.* those of Asia Minor, would need explanation.

46. *So Jesus came again into Cana of Galilee, where he made the water wine. And there was a certain nobleman, whose son was sick at Capernaum.*
47. *When he heard that Jesus was come out of Judea into Galilee, he went unto him, and besought him that he*

would come down, and heal his son: for he was at the point of death.

48. Then said Jesus unto him, Except ye see signs and wonders, ye will not believe.

49. The nobleman saith unto him, Sir, come down ere my child die.

50. Jesus saith unto him, Go thy way; thy son liveth. And the man believed the word that Jesus had spoken unto him, and he went his way.

51. And as he was now going down, his servants met him, and told *him*, saying, Thy son liveth.

52. Then inquired he of them the hour when he began to amend. And they said unto him, Yesterday at the seventh hour the fever left him.

53. So the father knew that *it was* at the same hour, in the which Jesus said unto him, Thy son liveth: and himself believed and his whole house.

54. This *is* again the second miracle *that* Jesus did, when he was come out of Judea into Galilea.

A "nobleman," of princely rank, but beyond this fact, indicated by the Greek term,* nothing is known of him. His son lay at the point of death in Capernaum. The father met Jesus in Cana and besought him to come down and heal his son. This request brought to the mind of Jesus the moral dullness of the Galilean people, which could be moved to faith by nothing short of miracle. Whether Jesus intended this remark to bear directly upon this nobleman does not appear. It at least fell short of a prompt consent to go. But the nobleman was thoroughly in earnest and would not be put aside. His urgency evinced his faith in both the power and the love of Jesus—a case which Jesus could not refuse to meet. Hence the reply was decisive: "Go thy way, thy son liveth." The man believed this word, and moved on homeward joyfully. It was the next day that his servant met him to say that his son was doing well. He inquired from what hour, and found it to be the moment when Jesus gave him that word of promise and life. On the joyful testimony of this miracle, himself and all his house believed.

We may note the striking variety *in the manner* in which Jesus performed miracles. Sometimes he wrought, as here, at a distance, but usually in his presence; sometimes he imposed hands; sometimes imparted the gift through the touch of his garments; sometimes in silence, and at other times after crying aloud as in one case, "Lazarus, come forth." Restricted to no set forms, apparently adopting the widest range of variety for the very purpose of heightening the evidence of real miracle, yet always care-

---

* βασιλικος.

ful to shape these great works so as to inspire faith in his divine person, and to reveal the deep love and compassion of his heart, his miracles reach the perfection of testimony (in this line) to his Messiahship, and evermore couple with this testimony the most precious illustrations of his spiritual power for the saving of human souls from death in sin to life in God. We look with admiration upon the wise economy of spiritual forces and the wealth of great truth illustrated which was secured by the miracles of the Son of God.

CHAPTER V.

The wonderful words of Jesus recorded in this chapter were occasioned by the miracle at the pool of Bethesda, and the captious hostility of the Jews because Jesus bade the restored cripple take up his bed and walk upon the Sabbath.

The facts of the case stand in verses 1–16; the reply of Jesus, remarkable for its unbroken continuity, for its pungency, its moral force, its boldness, and its astounding revelations, fills out vs. 17–47.

1. **After this there was a feast of the Jews; and Jesus went up to Jerusalem.**

The discussion of the question, *What feast?* has been vigorous and long protracted, without as yet reaching any general agreement among critics. Special importance attaches to this question because of its bearing upon the duration of Christ's public ministry. The data for this question are in this gospel of John—and, more specifically, in the notices he gives us of the several Passovers that occurred between his baptism and his death. Of these, three are fully defined, viz. (1) John 2: 13, 23, supposed to have been about six months after his baptism; (2) John 6: 4; (3) John 12: 1, and 13: 1, at which last his ministry closed with his death. If now this doubtful reference (John 5: 1) be a fourth, we have a ministry of three and a half years; but if this be some other than a Passover feast, his ministry is apparently reduced to two years and a half. Hence the special importance of this question.

The discussion has narrowed the question mainly to the one issue between the feast of *Purim* in the month Adar—the last of the Jewish year, and the *Passover*, which would be in the first month.

One point of some importance is the omission or insertion of the Greek article. Did John write—"a feast," or "*the* feast"? Unfortunately this point is in dispute with the testimony for and against the article nearly balanced—perhaps slightly preponderating against. The Sinaitic, however, gives the article, and Tischendorf admits it, but Alford, Meyer, and Tholuck reject it. The article, admitted, would favor the theory of the Passover.—— It makes against Purim that it did not convene the Jews *en masse* at Jerusalem. They rather kept it in their several villages over the whole country. But here are the multitudes together (v. 13). Also that this was not a specially religious festival, but rather one of hilarity and feasting in commemoration of victory over Haman and his party in the days of Esther. It is asked with no little force—Would Jesus be likely to go up to Jerusalem to attend this feast there?——Yet again: This feast is not described as being that of Purim. But John is wont to describe those feasts that might need description, *e. g.* the feast of tabernacles (7:2); and the feast of dedication, dating from the times of Antiochus (John 10:22). A feast of the Jews with no descriptive epithet or name is most likely to be the one best known of all—the Passover.—— It is thought to make somewhat against the Passover that in other references to this feast, John names it definitely. Why, it is asked, should he not in this case? The proper reply is that this argument bears with yet greater force against any and every other feast of the Jews, and therefore throws its weight in favor of the Passover.

It is also urged very earnestly that assuming this to be the Passover, there is too much unoccupied time between this one and that of John 6:4. But who can tell how many of Christ's deeds and words may be unrecorded? No one of the four histories claims to be exhaustive.——In my view, the strongest circumstance in favor of the shorter ministry ($2\frac{1}{2}$ years), is the virulence of his enemies. Is it probable that they were frustrated and kept in check through three and half years?

This synopsis of the arguments, *pro* and *con*, is by no means exhaustive. I incline to the Passover theory, but recognize the difficulties and uncertainties of the problem, and honor the great names arrayed on the other side. I doubt if the question can ever be determined with entire certainty.

2. Now there is at Jerusalem by the sheep *market* a pool, which is called in the Hebrew tongue Bethesda, having five porches.

3. In these lay a great multitude of impotent folk, of blind, halt, withered, waiting for the moving of the water.

4. For an angel went down at a certain season into the pool, and troubled the water: whosoever then first after the troubling of the water stepped in was made whole of whatsoever disease he had.

In this passage the best textual authorities omit from v. 3, the words—"waiting for the moving of the water," and also v. 4 entire. The three most ancient manuscripts (the Sinaitic, Vatican, and Alexandrian) omit the last clause of v. 3; the Sinaitic and Vatican omit v. 4 altogether, while the Alexandrian has instead of it—"An angel of the Lord washed at a certain season." Hence the best modern critics disallow the original authority of these passages. They suppose that the waters of this pool were medicinal and intermittent—both these facts depending upon natural and not supernatural causes; but that this healing virtue as well as the intermittent flow came to be associated in the popular mind with angelic agency, and that this tradition was ultimately embodied in the text as in our received version.——It is supposable that the first flow after an intermission would be more highly charged with medicinal gases, and hence the popular belief might have had some basis of fact—viz, that the first man to bathe in the pool when the water came freshly in would be healed.

This pool obtained the name "Bethesda"—House of mercy—from the circumstance that so many poor objects of compassion found relief in its waters. Consequently, there lay around it a great multitude suffering under various ills, biding their time for the hour of healing.

5. And a certain man was there, which had an infirmity thirty and eight years.

6. When Jesus saw him lie, and knew that he had been now a long time *in that case*, he saith unto him, Wilt thou be made whole?

7. The impotent man answered him, Sir, I have no man, when the water is troubled, to put me into the pool: but while I am coming, another steppeth down before me.

Among them was one, a paralytic, almost powerless, who had been under this infirmity thirty-eight years. Was there still a flickering hope in his stricken heart? He might as well be there as anywhere, dim as the last ray of hope in his soul seems to have been. Jesus knew he had been long in this sad case. Is it strange that his compassions were moved, and that, unasked, he came forward to accost him—"Dost thou wish—art thou willing—to be made whole?"——Observe here that in the words used by Jesus, "wilt" is not the English future tense, but is a verb of willing, of purpose inspired by real desire. Art thou waiting and longing for the soundness and strength of a whole man?——He replies—I am here, friendless and alone, with none to help me into this pool at the favored moment; while I am crawling slowly forward, another, less crippled than I, steps in before me, and I miss it every time.——This was his answer to the point of being willing to be healed:—"Indeed I am; I have done my best never so long—sick at heart over my perpetual disappointment."

8. Jesus saith unto him, Rise, take up thy bed, and walk.

9. And immediately the man was made whole, and took up his bed, and walked: and on the same day was the sabbath.

With the words, "Rise, take up thy bed and walk"—a new power courses through his long crippled frame; a new energy comes to his will; and ere he has time for a second thought, he springs to his feet, seizes his pallet and begins to walk—a new man! Ah, indeed; this is the power of Jesus; thus it became manifest that "in him is life." So the new life toward God of souls new-born through faith in Jesus found a rich and truly wonderful illustration.

It happened that the day of this healing was the Sabbath. On this fact hinged the furious, bigoted assault made upon Jesus by the Jews.

10. The Jews therefore said unto him that was cured, It is the sabbath day: it is not lawful for thee to carry *thy* bed.

11. He answered them, He that made me whole, the same said unto me, Take up thy bed, and walk.

12. Then asked they him, What man is that which said unto thee, Take up thy bed, and walk?

13. And he that was healed wist not who it was: for Jesus had conveyed himself away, a multitude being in *that* place.

The words, "The Jews," as used by John in such a connection denote the adherents of the Sanhedrim—the party, mostly Pharisees, who were by position the spiritual leaders of the Jewish people. There was a class of "common people," quite distinct from these "Jews" (so called) who "heard Jesus gladly."—— " They said to him that was cured "—for they knew him as such—knew that he had been, through an average life-time, a miserable, helpless cripple, till now, all suddenly, he is before them a healed and sound man. Do they rejoice with him in sympathy and love? Do they invite him into their temple to render his thank-offering to God there? Do they ask—Who is he that spake thy palsied body into this new and wonderful life?—Not a word of all this. No; but they assail him rudely for carrying his cot—perhaps every thing he can call his own on earth—on the Sabbath.—— He answers according to the simple truth: "The man who made me whole bade me take up my bed and walk." They ask him who it was, not that cured him—for that seems in their eye a matter quite indifferent—but who it was that ordered him to carry his bed on the Sabbath.——At first the man could not tell; it was a stranger, and he suddenly disappeared, to escape the notice of the multitude.——We fear this healed man did not fix a grateful, tearful eye upon his benefactor—did not rush to his feet to pour out his thanksgivings there for the first great mercy of his life. Certainly his record is less fair on this point than we could wish.

14. Afterward Jesus findeth him in the temple, and said

unto him, Behold, thou art made whole: sin no more, lest a worse thing come unto thee.

15. The man departed, and told the Jews that it was Jesus, which had made him whole.

Afterward Jesus met him "in the temple." We may hope he was there for a grateful purpose. It was the fit place for him.——The words of Jesus—"Sin no more, lest a worse thing come unto thee"—seem to imply that sin had brought on him that fearful malady of his life; and that more sin of similar sort would bring on a relapse into a state more dreadful still. There are abuses of the human body—sins, they deserve to be called—which entail swift and appalling retribution. Let men mark them and take warning! It is at least supposable that Jesus saw in this healed man but too much proclivity still toward his old paths of self-destruction.

This man has now learned that his benefactor is Jesus, and seems to have lost no time in reporting the fact to the Jews.—— Was he under moral obligation to report this? Was it kind in him toward his best earthly Friend? Did he not know that they sought this information for a malicious purpose?——We hear of this healed man no more, and are left to infer that there was very little of moral stamina, or of wholesome, lovable character, or of real gratitude, in him. So many weary years of sinning and of suffering may have given him but the least possible moral culture, bringing out almost nothing worthy of love or esteem, so that Jesus may have been moved to heal him solely through pity for a great sinner and sufferer. We will not overlook the fact that on this supposition of the case, the character of Jesus shines out with peculiar brilliancy and beauty.

16. And therefore did the Jews persecute Jesus, and sought to slay him, because he had done these things on the Sabbath day.

Now the Jews have a case of crime against Jesus. They have testimony which in their view will convict him of violating the Sabbath. For the laws of Moses forbade the bearing of burdens on the sacred day (Jer. 17: 21, 22, 27, and Neh. 13: 15); and Jesus had bidden a man rise and carry his bed on the Sabbath. They are now ready for measures against his life.

Such unreasoning, virulent hatred seems in every aspect astounding. Did they see no love and kindness in this healing of a miserable paralytic, thirty-eight years before their eyes a helpless sufferer? Did they see no *power* in it which should have awed them into reverence, and forced them to ask—What manner of man is this who bids a life-long paralytic "rise and walk;" and he rises in their sight, a whole man? How can we account for it that facts like these fell powerless upon their hardened souls?—— It is very much easier to adjust this case to the well known laws of depraved human nature than to justify it to reason. To these

Jews, their religion was bread and honor—all their living. But, the soul of their religion being practically extinct, its body—the merely external form—required the more careful adornment. When religion has nothing but an outside, the utmost possible must be made of this. Hence their rigid, extreme construction of the law of the Sabbath. Farrar (Life of Christ, p. 175) speaks of "the wretched formalistic inferences of their forged traditions as having gravely decided that on the Sabbath a nailed shoe might not be worn because it was a burden, but an unnailed shoe might be worn; that a person might go out with two shoes on, but not with one only; that one man might carry a loaf of bread but that two men might not carry it between them, and so forth to the utmost limit of tyrannous absurdity."——Naturally these Jews lacked all sympathy with Christ. Worse still; they malignly hated him. His whole life and spirit were a silent but terrible rebuke: his uttered words were unendurably scorching. They must be rid of this man and of his influence, or their religion and themselves must go down hopelessly and forever. Hence they seize eagerly upon this charge—"He has broken the Sabbath," and they intend to treat it as a capital crime punishable with death.

17. But Jesus answered them, My Father worketh hitherto, and I work.

This answer fully justifies the remark elsewhere on record—"Never man spake like this man." All suddenly Jesus plants himself upon the highest ground possible. He enters into no small discussion over the details of Sabbath prohibition, into no minor questions of legal interpretation. He does not urge in defense that this violation of the Sabbath was rather apparent than real; that it was a very trivial matter; that no harm was done; no true worship interrupted, and nothing done that could militate against the sacredness of the day. He does not attempt to show that this healing was an act of mercy; that it was kindness to the man to allow him to take away all the little property he had in the world; that such a case of healing might properly be attested before the people by this manifestation of restored strength. Nothing of this sort is thought of. On the contrary Jesus rises at once to the dignity of the Son of God—authorized therefore to do what his Father had ever done and was still doing. My Father whose example of rest from creative work laid the foundation for the Sabbath command has never rested from his spiritual work for the souls of men. In this he has been laboring ever since the creation of the world, and is laboring in it still. I am only doing the same. This work of saving the souls of men knows no law of Sabbath rest. Walking therefore in the steps of my Father I have broken no law; my work has the sanction of the highest authority in the universe.——This was indeed taking the case out of their jurisdiction. If Jesus had a right to say what he did, they would touch him at their peril. So doing they would come into collision with the Infinite Son of God.

18. Therefore the Jews sought the more to kill him, because he not only had broken the sabbath, but said also that God was his Father, making himself equal with God.

With their view of the case, their course is by no means surprising.——In addition to the first charge—Sabbath-breaking—they have now another—blasphemy—for he has said that God was *his own* Father (so the best textual authorities)—thus "making himself equal with God." The argument in the reply of Jesus did unquestionably assume a substantial equality with God. It claimed for Jesus such a sonship as made it right for him to do what his Father was doing, and right, because his Father did it. Because God wrought with unresting labor for the salvation of human souls, therefore Jesus his Son might and ought to do the same, and no law of Sabbath observance could restrain him from this, as no law to this effect could reach his Infinite Father. The Jews therefore can not be accused of misinterpreting his words. In those words Jesus had put himself on an equality with God in dignity, in the point of being above the Mosaic law of the Sabbath, and of having the right to do all that his Father was doing.

19. Then answered Jesus and said unto them, Verily, verily, I say unto you, The Son can do nothing of himself, but what he seeth the Father do: for what things soever he doeth, these also doeth the Son likewise.

20. For the Father loveth the Son, and sheweth him all things that himself doeth: and he will show him greater works than these, that ye may marvel.

The case is fairly opened, and Jesus proceeds to define more fully his relation of sonship to God and its consequent powers, responsibilities, and duties. Observe, he did not reply—You misunderstand me; I by no means arrogate to myself equality with God; I would not be understood to put my defense on that footing. This, he does *not* say; but on the contrary, with most solemn asseveration he declares—The Son does nothing of his own motion: originates no plans; strikes out into no schemes of his own, but simply follows the example of his Father. The Father in the truly parental spirit loves the Son, and, therefore, kindly shows him all that himself is doing in order to make this law of his Son's life evermore plain and perfect; and will go on to yet greater works than ye have yet seen at which ye will marvel. But all will follow the same law—the Father making his own work the example and guide for his Son.

The discussion in this chapter leads us into the profound relations between the Son and the Father. Some readers will perhaps raise the question—In what precise sense does Jesus speak of himself as "*the Son*"?——On this question we must choose between three possible (or supposable) alternatives: (*a.*) As the divine Logos—the Eternal Word—simply and only, with no reference to a human nature: (*b.*) As human only—the mere Man of Nazareth, born of Mary: (*c.*) Or as not only born of woman, but as having no father other than God—being therefore the divine Logos in mysterious union with the babe of Bethlehem.——Of these three, we must doubtless accept the latter as being the only alternative which is in harmony with the inspired statements, Matt. 1: 18, 20–23, and Luke 1: 35: and (what is not less decisive) the only one which corresponds with the views given us in our author John, in his expressive language, "The Word was made flesh, and dwelt among us; and we beheld his glory—the glory as of the only begotten of the Father" (John 1: 14). This then is definitely the sense in which Jesus speaks of himself in these discussions as "*the Son.*" *

21. For as the Father raiseth up the dead, and quickeneth *them*; even so the Son quickeneth whom he will.

The key to the main thought of the passage (vs. 21–29) lies in this verse, turning essentially on the point.—In what sense is the Father said here to raise up the dead?—Premising that the choice

---

* Dean Alford, commenting on the word "*can*" (v. 19)—"The Son *can* do nothing of himself" (Greek, (δύναται), indulges in metaphysical discussion of the point whether this be a *natural* or a *moral* impossibility, and concludes by deciding for a natural and necessary and against a moral agency of the Son. He says—"Jesus here states that he can not work any but the works of God—*can not* by this very relationship to the Father, by the very nature and necessity of the case;—the ἀφ'ἑαυτοῦ ('of himself') being an impossible supposition, and purposely set to express one. The Son *can not work of himself* because he *is* the Son; his very person pre-supposes the Father's will and counsel as *his* will and counsel, and his perfect knowledge of that will and counsel. And this because every *creature* may abuse its freedom and may will contrary to God; but the Son, standing in essential unity with God can not, even when become man, commit sin—break the Sabbath—for his whole being and work is in and of God."

Underlying these speculations are two assumptions which vitiate their value; viz. (*a.*) That the will of the Son is not only harmonious with the will of the Father, but absolutely and necessarily *identical*, not distinguishable even in thought.——This is wholly at variance with the drift of these passages;—"The Father loveth the Son;" "The Son doeth whatsoever he seeth the Father do;" "As the Father raiseth up the dead, etc., so the Son quickeneth whom he will."——What could imply distinct, moral personality and a distinct (not identical) moral activity if these words do not?

(*b.*) That the highest supposable excellence is the product of *necessity* not of *freedom*—which is equivalent to saying that the effects of the law of gravitation are infinitely praiseworthy; but that the free-hearted, voluntary love and obedience of a morally responsible *mind* are simply dangerous and not to be thought of as in essence morally excellent.

5

must lie between raising up dead bodies from their graves and raising dead souls to new life, I suggest that in addition to what may be gathered from the subsequent context, there are two other legitimate sources of evidence on this question:—viz: (*a.*) The facts out of which this discussion arose, together with the discussion itself thus far.——(*b.*) The usage of the Old Testament. (*a.*) Let it be remembered that this discussion arose from the case of quickening power which went forth with the words, "Rise: walk;"—a case much more directly suggestive of the morally quickening energy which renews men's souls than of that power which is (in the great future day) to raise dead bodies. That the former rather than the latter was before the mind of Jesus seems clear from the words—"My Father worketh hitherto"—for this working was rather the saving of men's souls than the raising of their bodies.——(*b.*) Old Testament usage is in point because this discussion is had with Jews to whom those writings were at once familiar and classic. They had a recognized authority, and commanded a professed respect. It must certainly be assumed that these words were intended to be intelligible to all honest-minded Jews, and hence with the highest probability would be in harmony with Old Testament usage.——Now the Old Testament gives some well-defined cases of the spiritual, *i. e.* figurative sense of resurrection; *e. g.* Isa. 26: 14, 19 and Ezek. 37: 1–12. On the other hand, in its literal sense—raising the body from its grave, the word resurrection occurs in the Old Testament but rarely.——These considerations strongly favor the sense in our passage of raising *dead souls* to life.

The same conclusion is strongly supported by the limitations as to the application of this resurrection power of the Son—"quickeneth whom he will;" for when he raises the dead from their graves, there are no such limitations: "*all* shall hear his voice and come forth."——Moreover, this construction is put beyond all doubt in v. 24—the passing from death unto life being conditioned there upon hearing the words of Jesus and believing on the Father as having sent him.

22. For the Father judgeth no man, but hath committed all judgment unto the Son:

23. That all *men* should honor the Son, even as they honor the Father. He that honoreth not the Son honoreth not the Father which hath sent him.

The logical connection throughout vs. 20–22, expressed in our version by "for" (Greek γαρ) should be carefully noticed. This discourse is a chain of reasoning, every point bearing upon the relation of the Son to the Father as worthy of equal honor, and as amply justified therefore in his great work on the Sabbath.

"Hath committed all judgment unto the Son"—suggests the question whether the reference be specially to the final judgment, subsequent to the general resurrection; or, more comprehensively, to the entire administration of the divine moral government of our world, not to say of the moral universe. The latter view is favored by this comprehensive language—"*all* judgment;" also by the more specific reference (v. 27) to the "authority to execute judgment"—which seems to look particularly to that of the last day. In the comprehensive sense—administering "*all* judgment"—Jesus determines the conditions of pardon and who has fulfilled them; the control of the entire scheme of earthly probation, discipline, preliminary retribution (as in the present world); every thing that comes under the head of the executive administration of God's moral government both in the present life; at the final judgment; and throughout the realms of eternal retribution.

The reason for committing all judgment in this broad sense to the Son is given plainly;—"that all should honor the Son even as they honor the Father." Any earthly king who should entrust such responsibilities to his son would be likely to do it for this definite purpose. In this case not to honor the Son equally with the Father is to dishonor the Father, since it would disregard his avowed purpose; would be construed to impugn his wisdom; would contemn his authority.

We can not fail to see how forcibly all this bears upon the great argument of Jesus with the Jews in vindication of himself for healing the impotent man and bidding him carry his bed on the Sabbath.——Nor can we fail to see its incidental bearing as proof of his true divinity—none the less forcible for being *incidental*—an assumption underlying the entire argument,

24. Verily, verily, I say unto you, He that heareth my word, and believeth on him that sent me, hath everlasting life, and shall not come into condemnation; but is passed from death unto life.

If we have correctly the sense of the words "all judgment" in v. 22, we may find here the development of some of its ground principles, particularly the conditions on which men pass from death unto life. Hearing the words of Jesus attentively and obediently; believing, not merely on me [Jesus] but on "him that sent me"—*i. e.* believing on me *as* one sent by the Father and fully commissioned to the work of Savior and Judge—"he hath everlasting life," a life that shall begin here in the new heart and morally changed life, and shall hold on unto everlasting life in the blessedness of the redeemed. He shall no more come into condemnation—there being "no condemnation to them that are in Christ Jesus" (Rom. 8: 1). This man has passed from a state of death, condemnation, in sin, unto life in God and his infinite favor.

25. Verily, verily, I say unto you, The hour is coming, and now is, when the dead shall hear the voice of the Son of God: and they that hear shall live.

With solemn asseveration as one announcing a most momentous truth—"verily, verily"—Jesus declares that even now dead souls are hearing the voice of the Son of God, and so hearing are passing from death into life. We can scarcely miss the reference in this phraseology to the voice which sent life thrilling through the bodily organs of the powerless man at the pool of Bethesda. So, new life shall breathe through the souls of those who listen with faith and obedience to the voice of Jesus calling them to him.——The hour is coming when the numbers saved to new life shall be greatly augmented: even now the work is gloriously begun.*

26. For as the Father hath life in himself; so hath he given to the Son to have life in himself;
27. And hath given him authority to execute judgment also, because he is the Son of man.

Life is here more than existence—the main stress of the idea in fact goes beyond that to the life-imparting power. As the Father has in himself the power of imparting life, so has he given this power in full measure to the Son. And also "authority to execute judgment," in the broad sense of the words in v. 22; yet perhaps with a drifting toward the more specific sense which is so fully implied in vs. 28, 29. This is specially the *execution* of judgment; not only the judicial decision of the highest tribunal but the carrying of that decision into effect in the final awards of destiny according to deeds done.

"Because he is the Son of man."† The fact of the incarnation is made the reason for committing all judgment to Jesus and especially, the final judgment of the race. Having loved this fallen world so deeply, so tenderly, that he could consent to assume our very nature and suffer in it even unto death, who throughout all the universe will ever doubt his compassion, his pity, his heart to save whosoever will meet his revealed conditions and put himself within the possible reach of mercy? With infinite confidence will all the intelligent universe trust him for ever to administer the final judgment in the truest sympathy for our race and never with undue severity—inflicting never one pang of

---

* The Sinaitic manuscript omits the clause "and now is." Other authorities with great unanimity sustain it. It is supposable that the clause was omitted to make the passage conform to v. 28. But Jesus doubtless intended a contrast between that verse and this. In this, the process is already begun: in that it waits for the blast of the final trump of God.

† In the Greek text the word "Son" lacks the article. But New Testament usage gives other similar cases of its omission; *e.g.* Matt. 14: 33, and 27: 43, and Luke 1: 35, and John 19: 7. The sense remains essentially the same if we translate—"Because he is a Son of man"—really human; truly incarnated into the race.

suffering in excess of what justice must demand. That he will care tenderly for those who love and trust him, who shall ever doubt? O, how will he gather them under his sheltering wing and hold their souls sweetly calm and joyful under the blast of the great trump of doom, amid the opening of countless graves, the waking of the dead of all the ages, and the wreck of worlds!
——Moreover, how fitting that Jesus should sit in judgment on those who heard his calls of mercy only to refuse them, or (as the case may be) to repel them with scorn; who *would* not believe on his name, but in their freedom *chose* their lot among the neglecters of this great salvation! How impressive before the moral universe that the same voice which once called so tenderly, "Come unto me for life"—should, in the great final day, proclaim with infinite majesty and irreproachable righteousness—" Depart from me, ye cursed!"
Moreover, the entire moral universe will see that Jesus richly deserves this honor of administering and executing the final doom of every one of the human race.

28. Marvel not at this: for the hour is coming, in the which all that are in the graves shall hear his voice,

29. And shall come forth: they that have done good, unto the resurrection of life; and they that have done evil, unto the resurrection of damnation.

"Marvel not at this" which I have been saying—the word "this" referring more naturally to things said before than after. Let it not surprise you that the Father hath given me power to speak dead souls to life, *for* He hath given me the power to bring dead bodies from their graves.
" For the hour is coming"—somewhere in the future; it is not said where.—Observe, Jesus does not add—"And now is"—for this form of resurrection is not yet. "In which all that are in their graves"—a description entirely definite and unambiguous. He does not say as in v. 25, "the dead"—a term which when plainly distinguished from "those in their graves" describes not bodies but souls, spiritually dead, who pass from this death into life through hearing the Savior's word and believing.——" Shall hear his voice"—keeps up the analogy with v. 25,—the word "voice" in both cases involving some allusion to that voice which said, "Rise and walk."——That this resurrection is *universal*, extending to all the race, is shown not only in the words, " all that are in their graves," but in the specification of the two great and only classes—" those that have done good " and " those that have done evil." The former rise with a " resurrection unto life "— not merely existence but blessedness; the latter, to a resurrection followed by damnation.—The same truth is taught by Jesus more in detail in Matt. 25: 31–46.

30. I can of mine own self do nothing: as I hear, I judge:

and my judgment is just; because I seek not mine own will, but the will of the Father which hath sent me.

Here the great question exegetically is whether this hearing and judging refer specially to the final judgment, or, in their broadest possible application, to the whole moral administration conducted by Jesus. The latter view must be taken, especially because Jesus uses the present tense, implying that this hearing and judging were then in progress; and because his argument with the Jews demands this broad application.

Jesus rests his claim to righteous impartiality upon his absolute freedom from selfishness. He seeks only the Father's will, seeking that supremely, and therefore judges with perfect equity.

31. If I bear witness of myself, my witness is not true.

32. There is another that beareth witness of me; and I know that the witness which he witnesseth of me is true.

The original Greek makes the contrast strong between "I" and "another" as witnesses by writing out "ego" and by the location of "αλλος"—[another]. If I were the only witness to myself; if the Father did not indorse and sustain my claim, it would justly fall to the ground. But "another" is my witness, even God.— "And *ye* know"—the reading *ye* being better sustained than "I." Jesus appeals to the convictions of their reason—*ye* know that the testimony which God the Father bears to me must be true.

33. Ye sent unto John, and he bare witness unto the truth.

34. But I receive not testimony from man: but these things I say, that ye might be saved.

35. He was a burning and a shining light: and ye were willing for a season to rejoice in his light.

"Ye sent unto John"—as recorded above, 1: 19-28. He testified to me with most entire truthfulness. But I do not rely chiefly or specially upon the testimony of any man. I refer to John the Baptist only in the hope of carrying your convictions and thus saving your souls. He brought from heaven a brilliant light; for a season ye seemed to rejoice in that light.—They knew very well that it was for a brief season only; for though John called their attention most earnestly and emphatically to the Greater One to come after him, yet when they came to know this Greater One, they repelled and rejected him.

John was a light—*i. e.*—a lamp; not the sun. He burned and shone, not with original but with borrowed light: "a light illuminated, not illuminating"—said Augustine.——John "*was*," not is; for at the time of this conversation he had been cast into prison, or perhaps had gone to the executioner's block.

36. But I have greater witness than *that* of John: for the works which the Father hath given me to finish, the same

works that I do, bear witness of me, that the Father hath sent me.

37. And the Father himself, which hath sent me, hath borne witness of me. Ye have neither heard his voice at any time, nor seen his shape.

38. And ye have not his word abiding in you: for whom he hath sent, him ye believe not.

Greater witness than any from John came through the miracles which he wrought by virtue of his connection with the Father, and which were the Father's own indorsement of his mission.

Apart from these miracles was yet another form of testimony from the Father (v. 37). What was this other form?—Not, as some have supposed, the audible voice, heard by a few at the baptism of Jesus, or that heard by yet fewer at his transfiguration, for manifestations of this sort seem intentionally excluded: "Ye have neither heard his voice, nor seen his shape." Nor does there seem to be any authority for supposing a reference here to God's voice to man's inner consciousness—the witness of the Spirit. Nothing in the passage itself or in the context favors this view.—— It remains to find this new testimony in God's revealed word—the Old Testament Scriptures. We are sustained in this finding by what immediately follows—"And ye have not his word abiding in you." God has given you in the Scriptures most decisive testimony to the Messiah, all which (Jesus implies) has been fulfilled in myself; but alas! as to you this is unavailing, because God's revealed word does not *abide in you;* its power is not felt in your souls. And the proof of this is that ye do not—will not—believe in him whom God has sent. There could be no stronger proof than this.

39. Search the Scriptures; for in them ye think ye have eternal life: and they are they which testify of me.

40. And ye will not come to me, that ye might have life.

The original Greek—"Search the scriptures"—may be either indicative or imperative; the statement of a fact, or the injunction of a duty. Commentators are sharply, perhaps almost equally divided in opinion between these alternatives.——The indicative would run thus:—Ye search the scriptures, making great account of them, supposing that ye have eternal life in them even in your way of studying and obeying them. Yet they are my special witnesses (so the Greek puts it; they are *the* witnesses for me)— a fact ye are too blind to see. Ye will not—choose not to—come to me for life.——But as imperative, thus: The Father bears witness to me in your own sacred scriptures; but this word of the Father ye have not abiding in you. Let me exhort, yea command you to search those scriptures, as ye in conscience and self-consistency ought to do, for ye suppose that in them ye have eternal life, and they testify abundantly of me. Ye would see this testimony if your eye were clear and your heart honest. But alas! "ye will not come to me that ye may have life." The settled purpose of your obdurate heart is wholly against coming to me.

In my view the imperative should have the preference as being more in harmony with facts, and in a moral point of view, more forcible.

41. I receive not honor from men.
42. But I know you, that ye have not the love of God in you.

"I receive not honor," etc., strikes by contrast at the root of their obdurate rejection of Jesus—the contrast being brought out in v. 44. I am not, like yourselves, poisoned morally by a depraved ambition for the glory that comes from men. But I know your heart; ye have no love of God in you. Your love runs wholly toward the honor that comes from men. The first great precept of your law (Deut. 6: 4, 5) enjoins love supreme, with all the heart, to God. Here is the fatal lack in your souls.

43. I am come in my Father's name, and ye receive me not: if another shall come in his own name, him ye will receive.

Yet how utterly inconsistent and unreasonable! Ye are looking with extreme and even passionate eagerness, for some great Coming One who may bring salvation to Israel. I come in my Father's name, yet ye will not receive me. Despite of the Father's indorsement by miracles, and by the testimony of your own scriptures, sustaining my claims, ye yet reject me. But if some other shall come in his own name, ye will readily receive him—a statement borne out remarkably in the subsequent history of the Jewish people. The number of false Christs who did appear in the ages subsequent was legion. Many of them drew immense throngs of followers.——The moral explanation of this fact is simple. Jesus was too pure and the leaders of Jewish thought too corrupt to admit of the least practical sympathy. There could be only collision and repellency between the meek, spotless Jesus, and the bigoted, covetous, self-seeking, sanctimonious Pharisees. The silent rebuke of his example and spirit stung them: his words of rebuke were daggers to their proud hearts.

44. How can ye believe, which receive honor one of another, and seek not the honor that *cometh* from God only?

These few words reveal the root and mainspring of their unbelief in Jesus. They sought, they loved, the honor that came from one another: they neither cared for nor sought the honor which came from God only. They built themselves up by means of mutual admiration. They honored each other according as they were valiant, and mighty, and fierce in opposing Jesus. Under the power of this master-passion, how could they possibly believe in Jesus? How could any sort or amount of evidence get into their mind, force conviction upon their souls, and command the homage of their heart? That man must have read human nature most superficially who has not learned the power of an overmastering passion to blind the mind to evidence, and make the heart as adamant against the voice of either reason or conscience.——But if they had sought the honor that cometh from God, the whole course of their thought and heart would have been reversed. For, would they not then have honored the Infinite Son of God? Would they not have accepted the miracles as God's voice through the realm of nature, and their own accredited scriptures as another voice from God, witnessing to his predicted Son?

45. Do not think that I will accuse you to the Father: there is *one* that accuseth you, *even* Moses, in whom ye trust.

46. For had ye believed Moses, ye would have believed me: for he wrote of me.

47. But if ye believe not his writings, how shall ye believe my words?

Jesus would not put himself forward as accusing them to the Father. We must take his words in this comparative sense: It is not so much myself as Moses who accuses you. I came, not to condemn but to save. But the same Moses in whom ye trust and in whose name ye glory as your Great Lawgiver, your model patriarch, your highest ideal of a Teacher sent from God—he accuses you. If ye had truly believed him, ye would have believed me, for he wrote of me; described me; foretold my coming, my character, my work. But since ye do not believe his writings, how can ye believe my words? Their professed admiration of Moses is thus shown to have been utterly fallacious—a mere delusion.

Thus closes this wonderful discourse. In the high stand-point of its defense against the charge of Sabbath desecration; in the calm and solemn majesty of its tone; in the conscious dignity with which Jesus set forth his relation to the Father; in the pertinence and moral force of his presentation of himself, first as giving spiritual life to spiritually dead souls; and next, as one day to give life from the dead to all who are in their graves—revealing himself thus as the Infinite Arbiter of all human destiny, the Great Judge of quick and dead—this discourse has no parallel in human language.

How was it received by the Jewish elders? They were thinking they had him at their mercy under the double charge of Sabbath-breaking and blasphemy; how must they have been astonished at his defense: I have violated the Sabbath only as my divine Father does; I work only as he works; he shows me all that he is doing; I follow his example; I can not do otherwise than fulfill the mission he has assigned me. I raise dead souls into life new and divine, even as he does; and ere long " the dead in their graves shall hear my voice and come forth "—to their eternal reward.——Thus while they thought to arraign him at their tribunal, they found themselves the culprits and Jesus their final judge!——Were they not utterly incredulous? Did they not repel every point in these statements which, admitted as true, would have been fearfully appalling? No doubt we must for the most part assume this. Jesus assumed it, and therefore went on to sustain his claims by appealing to the testimony of John; to the indorsement which the Father had given him by miracles, and Moses by his prophetic writings. He spake to them calmly, but with most searching scrutiny and appalling truthfulness, of the reason why they could not believe; of that passion for the honor coming from men which made them utterly blind and dead to the claims of the Son of God. He said—"I know you that ye have not the love of God in you." I know you that though ye applaud Moses, ye will not believe his writings in their witness for me. I know, alas! but too well that ye simply *will not* come to me that ye may have life. Solemnly and yet sadly we must suppose Jesus pointed these rebukes and bore this painful testimony. What more could he do?

Perhaps the inquiry will spring up in some minds: Why did not Jesus drop off the outer vail of his weak humanity, and stand out before their eyes in all the majesty of the transfiguration, or of that other scene of his unvailed glories before him of Patmos —" his eyes as a flame of fire;" " his face as the sun shineth in its strength;" " his voice as the sound of many waters"? Then, like the ancient seer, they might have " fallen at his feet as dead." But it is not the wisdom of God to work the scheme of human probation in this way. To overwhelm is not to convince. To appall is not to persuade. The freest moral activities of human souls must be provided for, because it is only by their normal working that radical changes in moral character are wrought. If searching truth—tenderly, solemnly, pungently pressed upon the human understanding and conscience—proves unavailing, all effort is hopeless; nothing else can be effective; and men must be left where Jesus was compelled to leave the great body of those Jewish councilmen—to the infatuation, blindness, and moral death of their own free and persistent choice.

CHAPTER VI.

The historical events of this chapter and the remarkable discourse to which they gave occasion hinge upon the feeding of five thousand men on the eastern shore of the Sea of Tiberias. The account of this miracle fills (vs. 1–14); the less public miracle of walking upon the sea occurred during the succeeding night (vs. 15–21); the multitude follow him to Capernaum the next day (vs. 22–25); after which the ensuing conversation presenting Jesus as the "bread of life," fills out the chapter (26–71).

1. After these things Jesus went over the sea of Galilee, which is *the sea* of Tiberias.

2. And a great multitude followed him, because they saw his miracles which he did on them that were diseased.

The events of this chapter seem to have followed those of chapter 5 at no long interval.——" Went over the Sea of Galilee," *i. e.* from the western side where lay the Galilean homes of Jesus (Nazareth and Capernaum) to the eastern shore near which were the plain where Jesus fed the five thousand and the mountain where he sat with his disciples.

This great multitude were following him, not, like the Samaritans, because they saw in him the long expected prophet of Israel, but because their curiosity and interest were excited by his miracles of healing.

3. And Jesus went up into a mountain, and there he sat with his disciples.

4. And the passover, a feast of the Jews, was nigh.

Comparing this narrative with that given by Matthew (in 14: 13–21); by Mark (in 6: 30–44); and by Luke (in 9: 10–17), we find that Jesus had just heard of the murder of John the Baptist, and that the disciples had but recently returned from their first missionary tour "through the towns, preaching the gospel and healing every-where." The inquisitive people were thronging upon him; thrilling events had been transpiring; it was a time therefore both for physical rest, and yet more, for instruction and meditation. The disciples needed a quiet and restful sitting at the feet of their Master.

That "the Passover was nigh" seems to be noticed here to account for the great multitude of people seeking for Jesus. Some may have gathered here for their journey to Jerusalem; others, living more remote, may have tarried here a season on their way.

5. When Jesus then lifted up *his* eyes, and saw a great company come unto him, he saith unto Philip, Whence shall we buy bread, that these may eat?

6. And this he said to prove him: for he himself knew what he would do.

7. Philip answered him, Two hundred pennyworth of bread is not sufficient for them, that every one of them may take a little.

8. One of his disciples, Andrew, Simon Peter's brother, saith unto him,

9. There is a lad here, which hath five barley loaves, and two small fishes: but what are they among so many?

10. And Jesus said, Make the men sit down. Now there was much grass in the place. So the men sat down, in number about five thousand.

11. And Jesus took the loaves; and when he had given thanks, he distributed to the disciples, and the disciples to them that were set down; and likewise of the fishes as much as they would.

12. When they were filled, he said unto his disciples, Gather up the fragments that remain, that nothing be lost.

13. Therefore they gathered *them* together, and filled twelve baskets with the fragments of the five barley loaves, which remained over and above unto them that had eaten.

This miracle is the only one recorded by each of the four evangelists.——Some have thought it the same as that recorded, Matt. 15: 32-39 and Mark 8: 1-10. This latter is similar in its nature—a miraculous increase of food; but is too unlike in most of the details to admit the supposition of identity. For in this latter the people had been with Jesus, mostly fasting, three days; the bread to begin with was seven loaves (not five); the fishes not "two" but a "few;" the fragments that remained were seven baskets, not twelve. The people in this latter miracle came, "divers of them, from far"—apparently Gentiles; while in the first miracle they were Jews, looking toward the feast at Jerusalem. Moreover it is scarcely supposable that the same historian would give two accounts of the same miracle—whether with or without variations.

Comparing John's narrative of this miracle with that given by the other three evangelists, there is apparent discrepancy on the point of the immediate antecedents—specially on the question who made the first suggestion of their need of food and of the possible means of supply. The other three—often called "the synoptists"—concur in saying that the first suggestion came from the disciples. "They came to Jesus, saying, This is a desert place, and the time is now past; send the multitude away, that they may go into the villages and buy themselves victuals," etc. In John's narrative the first suggestion named came from Jesus himself: "He saith unto Philip, Whence shall we buy bread that these may eat?"

In view of this apparent discrepancy, many have impugned the accuracy of the gospel historians, and have thought it a very grave and damaging allegation.

On this point I suggest——(*a*.) That John does not deny what the other three assert on the point of the first suggestion, viz, that it came from the disciples. For ought that John relates, the disciples may have called the attention of Jesus to this matter *before* he spoke to Philip as in v. 5. Admitting this, the supposed discrepancy mainly if not wholly vanishes. The difference between the first three and John is chiefly in regard to the omission or insertion of the several points—the first three omitting things which John records, and John omitting things which they record. But this is exceedingly far from being a stubborn and damaging discrepancy.——(*b*.) The minuteness of John's narrative in giving the names of Philip and of Andrew evinces an accurate memory and entitles his statements to confidence.—— (*c*.) But finally, these points are of very minor importance, and the diversity in these four narratives on points so trivial, even if it did involve slight discrepancies, should by no means weaken our confidence in their entire truthfulness as to all the vital matters of the history. Supreme attention to the things that are vital will often involve a relative inattention to points unimportant. So long as the human mind is less than infinite, this law will surely find some scope; an absorbing interest in the things of chief concern will withdraw attention from the small and incidental points so that slight inaccuracies as to them will become the common law.——If over against this remark it be said that inspiration, if real, ought to bring in the infinite mind and thus secure perfect accuracy in all points however minute, I answer— When Inspiration speaks through human lips and pens, its style partakes of the human channel through which it flows. Be the philosophy of this fact what it may, the fact itself is every-where obvious and therefore simply undeniable.

In this narrative the points requiring verbal explanation are few. V. 6 explains the reason of the question put to Philip, viz: to call his attention to the difficult problem of feeding so many men, and to see what he had to say of it.—Not that Jesus needed any helpful suggestions, for he had already decided what he would do. Philip estimates the amount of bread requisite for a moderate supply at "two hundred penny-worth." As the best standard of money value the world over and through all the ages of human history is the amount of day labor it represents, we find our best measure in the New Testament fact that wages then ruled at a penny a day. Two hundred days' work would earn this amount of bread.——The other evangelists state that the men were seated on the grass by hundreds and by fifties—a method which made enumeration easy and reasonably correct.——The "baskets" which received the fragments were the common traveling baskets of that age, adapted to carry provisions for a journey.

As to the special nature and the moral value of this miracle, let it be noted——(*a.*) It thoroughly precluded deception. Five thousand hungry men are very certain to know beyond mistake whether or not they have been honestly fed and their stomachs really satisfied.——(*b.*) The people had no conceivable inducement to connive at deception. So far as appears they would have detected and exposed a fraud (if there had been any) as indignantly as any modern skeptic, living then, would have done.—— (*c.*) This feeding made all the impression upon the people which a real miracle could have made, for we see that they were ready to "take Jesus by force to make him their king." Some of them followed him the next day over to the other side of the lake as men thoroughly convinced that this was surely "that great Prophet who should come into the world" (v. 14.)——(*d.*) The service of waiting upon this vast company would naturally impress the miracle forcibly upon the disciples. No wonder they never forgat it. No wonder that the record of it has found place in each one of the gospel histories.-——(*e.*) The order to save all the fragments that remained would perpetuate the impression of the scene, and be withal a wholesome lesson in economy—not to say also, would obviate a possible abuse of this miracle in the shape of a feeling that henceforth they were sure of perpetual plenty and might afford to waste.——(*f.*) And finally, this bountiful supply is beautifully typical of the fullness of spiritual bread in our Father's house—"bread enough and to spare"—so that never a man need to suffer from hunger (Luke 15: 17), miserable prodigal though he may have been.

14. Then those men, when they had seen the miracle that Jesus did, said, This is of a truth that Prophet that should come into the world.

15. When Jesus therefore perceived that they would come and take him by force, to make him a king, he departed again into a mountain himself alone.

Does this reference to "the Prophet that should come into the world" look specially to Deut. 18: 15, 18? Apparently so; and yet their thought to make him their king suggests that they saw in him their nation's Messiah, and applied to him, not that one prediction only, but the great body of Old Testament prophecy. Restive under the Roman yoke, ever aspiring to national independence and greatness, nothing could be more congenial to their ambition than a king of their own who should lift their nation at once to power and glory.——But with this feeling of theirs, Jesus had not the least sympathy. To yield to their notion would have been to abandon the purpose for which he had come into the world: would have fired into flame the hardly suppressed ambition of even his disciples; and must have prostrated all his efforts for the spiritual regeneration of Israel.

16. And when even was *now* come, his disciples went down unto the sea,

17. And entered into a ship, and went over the sea toward Capernaum. And it was now dark, and Jesus was not come to them.

18. And the sea arose by reason of a great wind that blew.

19. So when they had rowed about five and twenty or thirty furlongs, they see Jesus walking on the sea, and drawing nigh unto the ship: and they were afraid.

20. But he saith unto them, It is I; be not afraid.

21. Then they willingly received him into the ship: and immediately the ship was at the land whither they went.

The scenes of this eventful night, briefly sketched here, appear more fully in Matthew (14: 22–33); also in Mark (6: 45–52), but are omitted in Luke. The circumstances in full were these:—that Jesus sent the disciples back by water without him, remaining himself to dismiss the people; then went up into the mountain to pray, and when evening had come was there alone; that a fearful wind-storm fell upon the lake—a head-wind to the toiling disciples and their crew; that they had made only some three or four miles of their voyage—scarcely more than half across, when, far on toward morning, Jesus appeared, walking on the surging billows; that they saw the strange sight, thought it a phantom, and "cried out for fear;" that then the sweet and well known voice fell on their ear—"Be of good cheer, it is I: be not afraid:"—to which words, their most impulsive man, Peter, responded: "Lord, if it be thou, bid me come to thee on the water." "Come," said Jesus: and forth from the ship Peter sallies, managing apparently to get on well so long as his eye was upon Jesus; but dropping his eye to the tossing waves, and struck by the stiff blasts, a tremulous fear came over him, and, beginning to sink, he cried, "Lord, save me;" whereupon Jesus put forth his hand, caught and saved him;—with however the gentle rebuke—"O thou of little faith, wherefore didst thou doubt?" According to John the disciples were now *wishing* to take him into the ship, and presently the ship was in the haven they sought. Mark omits these circumstances respecting Peter (why?) saying however that Jesus seemed about to pass by them, but, hearing their cry of fear and alarm, came up to them into the ship.—— Remarkably in referring to the moral impressions of the scene upon the disciples, Matthew gives prominence to their joyous testimony to his divine sonship;—"They worshiped him, saying, Of a truth thou art the Son of God;" while Mark says, "They were sore amazed in themselves and wondered; for they considered not the miracle of the loaves; for their heart was hardened." Thus Matthew testifies that their faith was refreshed and specially manifested; while Mark seems to have been impressed by their moral dullness and unbelief in not appreciating the force of the recent miracle. Shall we explain this apparent discrepancy by supposing that the moral attitude of the twelve was not a unit—a part of them being described by Matthew; another part by Mark?——It is hard for us to conceive how such a scene could have failed to be sweetly and most deeply impressive upon them all.

22. The day following, when the people, which stood on the other side of the sea, saw that there was none other boat there, save that one whereinto his disciples were entered, and that Jesus went not with his disciples into the boat, but *that* his disciples were gone away alone;

23. Howbeit there came other boats from Tiberias nigh unto the place where they did eat bread, after that the Lord had given thanks:

24. When the people therefore saw that Jesus was not there, neither his disciples, they also took shipping, and came to Capernaum, seeking for Jesus.

25. And when they had found him on the other side of the sea, they said unto him, Rabbi, when camest thou hither?

It seems that the efforts of the Master to send the five thousand away to their homes or onward in their journey, were not altogether successful. Some of them at least are soon on hand again, carefully noting that the disciples were sent on board ship to cross the lake alone (without their Master), and in the only boat which lay in sight. Other boats came up, however, during the night, driven over perhaps by the same wind-storm against which the disciples contended during that fearful night. Entirely uncertain where Jesus might be, they entered these boats and crossed over to Capernaum, seeking for Jesus, their first question on finding him being naturally this:—"Rabbi, how camest thou hither?"— Did they ever learn that he *walked* over those surging billows? He took no pains to exhibit or in any way disclose this miracle, but turns his thoughts and theirs to their low and unworthy aims in seeking him, and to the far nobler aims they should have had— as we shall see.

26. Jesus answered them and said, Verily, verily, I say unto you, Ye seek me, not because ye saw the miracles, but because ye did eat of the loaves, and were filled.

27. Labor not for the meat which perisheth, but for that meat which endureth unto everlasting life, which the Son of man shall give unto you: for him hath God the Father sealed.

They had been fed by miracle, yet it was not the miracle but the feeding that had impressed them and that drew them on after him. Strangely they failed to accept the miracle in its true intent and for its real value; they did not—perhaps rather *would not*—see in it the Father's indorsement of his Son as the Infinite Fountain of life to dying men. This great and fatal failure on their part prompted the exhortation—"Labor not for bread that perishes, but for that which endures unto everlasting life"— such as the Son of man gives you; for him hath the Father commissioned, indorsed, and set apart for this very service, sealing his credentials by miracles, as ye should have seen.—— "Meat"—not flesh but food; and here better in the special sense—bread—as in the subsequent context—"the bread of life."

The laws of thought by which Jesus reached the figure here— "the bread of life"—are at once obvious and beautiful. Common bread had been multiplied by Jesus for the feeding of the five thousand; they had eaten it and were filled; and were now with no little labor following after him for more. Jesus says to them—There is other and better bread than what ye seek— bread that both satisfies and endures—the latter point, in the case of the bread as in the case of the water commended to the woman of Samaria—being the distinctive test. This bread endures unto and naturally ensures everlasting life. It brings into human souls the very life of God. It is the mission of his Son to give it. Ye are seeking of me only bread that perishes; the thing ye should seek of me is the bread that endures and gives life forever.

28. Then said they unto him, What shall we do, that we might work the works of God?

29. Jesus answered and said unto them, This is the work of God, that ye believe on him whom he hath sent.

Our translators would have indicated the course of thought better, if following the original Greek, they had put it—"*Work* not for the meat that perishes" (v. 27); and "What shall we do that we may *work* the works of God?" (v. 28). The Jews took up the identical word which Jesus had used, inquiring,—What is the *work* which thou wouldest enjoin? What *work* is this which God requires?—To this Jesus replies, "This is the work" God enjoins—"that ye believe on him whom he hath sent." The one great work which God expects of you is *faith in his Son.*—— To Jews, toilsomely working out their salvation (as they supposed) by external works of meritorious righteousness, it was supremely pertinent and fitting to say—Faith in Jesus is the one comprehensive work required by God. Here was an Infinite Savior. To accept him in true faith was then and is evermore the one condition of salvation.

30. They said therefore unto him, What sign showest thou then, that we may see, and believe thee? what dost thou work?

31. Our fathers did eat manna in the desert; as it is written, He gave them bread from heaven to eat.

"The Jews (said Paul, 1 Cor. 1: 22) require a sign"—evermore demanding, never satisfied with the miracles exhibited before them. Only the evening before, five thousand of them had been fed to the full on five loaves and two small fishes; and still they demand more *sign*—as if Jesus had never given them any reliable sign of his divine mission! "That we may see and believe thee"—as if they were entirely ready to believe if only they could have the appropriate evidence. "What dost thou work?" has the tone of sheer insult when construed in the light of the miracle then fresh as the scenes of yesterday. How weakly and wickedly they assume that the miracle they had just seen should go for nothing! Perhaps they had some preconceived notions as to the sign that Jesus in their view ought to give; and unless they could bring him to their idea would accept nothing.

The Jews first suggested the manna which their fathers ate in the desert—an illustration which Jesus subsequently resumed twice (vs. 49, 58). We may suppose the course of their thought to have been on this wise:—He bids us work for bread that endures unto everlasting life, and speaks of giving it to us himself and of coming down from heaven, sealed of God. But our fathers had bread from heaven, and yet it did not endure unto everlasting life. Would he pretend to have any thing better than that? So the woman of Samaria could not see how Jesus could have any better water than that of Jacob's well.

The reference—"it is written"—is to Ps. 78: 24, 25, where in poetic imagery God is said to have "given them of the corn [bread] of heaven." The manna actually fell with the dew from the lower heavens—the atmosphere above them; and more than this,—God's hand was so signally in it that with striking propriety, it could be said to have come down from his abode—heaven.

32. Then Jesus said unto them, Verily, verily, I say unto you, Moses gave you not that bread from heaven; but my Father giveth you the true bread from heaven.

33. For the bread of God is he which cometh down from heaven, and giveth life unto the world.

Jesus speaks, not according to the license of poetry but to the precision of prosaic fact. That manna-bread Moses did not send down from the true—the real heaven; but my Father (said Jesus) gives to men blessings most worthy to be called the true bread from heaven. Jesus then advances to the yet higher idea—that this bread from heaven is a real, living *person* who comes down from heaven and gives life to the world. Apparently in this form of statement, Jesus fell slightly short of saying—It is I myself.

34. Then said they unto him, Lord, evermore give us this bread.

Here is the woman of Samaria repeating herself. As she said (John 4: 15)—"Give me this water that I thirst not;" so under their first impulse these Jews said; "Lord, evermore give us this bread." Alas, that they should have so poorly understood their own words!

35. And Jesus said unto them, I am the bread of life: he that cometh to me shall never hunger; and he that believeth on me shall never thirst.

Jesus here advances to the further point of identifying this person—"he who cometh down from heaven"—with himself:—"I am the bread of life."———This bread is to be tested and known by its effects. Like the water described to the woman of Samaria, it forever satisfies; it meets the great moral want in man's soul—meets it perfectly once and forever.———Yet one other truth lies in this first wonderful statement; viz., "Coming to Jesus" is the true sense of eating this bread of life. He that comes to Jesus does in that act eat this life-giving bread; just as believing on him is equivalent to drinking the waters of life. Who drinks shall never thirst more.

36. But I said unto you, That ye also have seen me, and believe not.

Some preachers would have caught up the words—"Lord, evermore give us this bread"—as proof of conversion. Jesus goes deeper; knows his men better; seeks rather to *make* real converts than to count them. He may repel some; he must deal with them faithfully.—As I have told you before, so now again:—ye have seen me and have not believed. Ye have not lived up to your light. This bread of life has been before you, offered freely—and ye *would not take it.*———Let them not deceive themselves. If they will, it shall not be through any lack of faithful, pointed instruction from the world's great model preacher.

37. All that the Father giveth me shall come to me; and him that cometh to me I will in nowise cast out.

It behooves us to study these words and the analogous passage (vs. 44, 45) very carefully and withal thoroughly.———Jesus intimates that he does not expect *all men* to come to him for life, but only all whom the Father hath given to him.———Pausing a moment over this fact as developed in vs. 36–45, I suggest these three inquiries:—(1.) *Why,* may we suppose, did Jesus put this truth before these Jews in this form?—(2.) How are those who are "given by the Father to the Son" described and to be known?—(3.) How is this doctrine guarded against abuse—especially the abuse of discouraging sinners from coming to Christ?

To the first point I answer suggestively—Perhaps because those Jews with extremest self-righteousness claimed to be the chosen and specially favored people of God, and because they gloried in this claim. Jesus therefore may have sought to show them that this claim was utterly groundless.—If ye were indeed God's chosen people, how surely ye would receive and honor his Son; how certainly would ye be taught of God and come in solid masses to hear the words of his Son and to welcome from his hand the bread and the waters of life.—The intended effect of these statements may therefore have been to show these Jews that they entirely misconceived their own moral attitude toward the Father.——(2.) On the second point (above named) we may know *who* are given to Jesus by the Father, for all such will come to him. Their *coming* identifies them.——(3.) No rational ground is afforded for abusing the doctrine as here put, for no matter who comes to Jesus, he shall in nowise be cast out. Let no sinner be deterred by the fear that he is not one of those who are "given to Jesus" by the Father. Let him settle that question in his own favor by coming to Jesus at once—coming with all his heart—coming, not as worthy but as invited and as made welcome. This assurance—the coming one never cast out—was put by the Master in the very best place possible.

38. For I came down from heaven, not to do mine own will, but the will of him that sent me.

39. And this is the Father's will which hath sent me, that of all which he hath given me I should lose nothing, but should raise it up again at the last day.

40. And this is the will of him that sent me, that every one which seeth the Son, and believeth on him, may have everlasting life: and I will raise him up at the last day.

The logic expressed by "for" (v. 38) should refer specially to the last clause of the verse preceding rather than to the first, for it should look to what Jesus does and not to what the Father does; thus: I will never cast out, but will surely save to the uttermost all who come to me; *for* I came down from heaven to do not my will but his; and his will is that I should save and never cast out those whom he has given me.——This will of the Father is expanded and reiterated in most striking words (vs. 39, 40).——Let the reader note carefully in what points these verses are the same and in what they differ. They are the same in that they both define the will of the Father in sending Jesus—especially that he should save every one of a certain defined class, losing none, but saving them all unto everlasting life, even unto the raising them up, saved soul and body, at the last day. On the other hand they differ in this one respect, viz., that the class referred to are described in one verse as given to Jesus by the Father; in the other, as seeing the Son and believing on him. That is, the first puts forward into the foreground the agency of God; the second, the agency of man. That the class is in each case identically the same can not be doubted. They may be described in either of these two ways—either as given by the Father to the Son; or as seeing the Son and believing in him. Each fact and both are descriptive and serve equally well to identify. The former fact (may we not say) insures the latter; and yet insures it in a way which by no means interferes with human agency—much less supersedes it.

The certainty of ultimate salvation for all who fall within these descriptive terms—"Given by the Father to the Son;" "Seeing Jesus and believing on him"—is the main point specially affirmed here. I see not how any human language could be more explicit and decisive to this point of certainty than what we read here.*

41. The Jews then murmured at him, because he said, I am the bread which came down from heaven.

42. And they said, Is not this Jesus, the son of Joseph, whose father and mother we know? how is it then that he saith, I came down from heaven?

The Jews murmured at him, complaining, objecting, repelling —not what he had said of the Father's agency in giving him those who should come to him; but more fundamentally because he claimed to have come down from heaven—the bread of life for men. They said—Do we not know all about this Jesus? Have we not seen both his father and his mother? How then can he say—"I came down from heaven"?——The evidence of his miracles they seem to have thrown out utterly: the purity of his life, and the inimitable perfection of his teachings, fell powerless on their souls. Possibly they had some notions of their own as to the manner in which their Messiah ought to come down from heaven—supposably, in a blaze of glory; a chariot of fire; or with the peal of the archangel's trump: but if God would not adjust his methods to their ideas, they were too self-conceited to conform their views to his.

43. Jesus therefore answered and said unto them, Murmur not among yourselves.

44. No man can come to me, except the Father which hath sent me draw him: and I will raise him up at the last day.

45. It is written in the prophets, And they shall be all taught of God. Every man therefore that hath heard, and hath learned of the Father, cometh unto me.

---

*The use in v. 39 of the neuter ("it" and also "all" in the Greek) is noticeable—apparently designed to indicate the entire body—the mass as a whole.

The best manuscripts differ from our received text (vs. 39, 40) in placing the word "Father" not in v. 39, but in v. 40; thus: In v. 39, "This is the will of him that sent me;" but, v. 40; "This is the will of my Father." The difference has no bearing on the meaning of the verses. The same may be said of an immense number of the various readings of the New Testament text.

46. Not that any man hath seen the Father, save he which is of God, he hath seen the Father.

In tones of blended tenderness and decision, we may suppose Jesus besought them *not* to give place to murmurs among themselves.——The declaration, "No man can come to me except the Father who hath sent me draw him," gives the negative side, corresponding to the positive as put in v. 37. There he had said, All who are so given shall come; here, None can come except those who are drawn by the Father. In the last clause of v. 45, the same point made in v. 37 is put again, adjusted in phrase to the context: All who have heard and learned of the Father come to me.——The points of chief practical importance here lie under the question—Is this inability ("*can not come*") moral or physical—that of the will, or that of proper incapacity, want of power? So also secondly: Is this "drawing" of the sort which moves matter, or of the sort which moves free, intelligent minds? Does it act, like creative power, to *produce* faculties; or, like persuasive power, to *induce* the desired moral activity? The distinction is a broad one, easily apprehended and exceedingly important to be understood.

As bearing on the *nature* of this inability, whether moral or physical, I suggest:——(*a*) That if physical, it could involve no blame for not coming. Physical incapacity to walk exempts from all blame for not walking. One so intelligent as Jesus, and withal so far from making unreasonable requisitions, could never have blamed the Jews for not coming to him if really they had no ability—no capacity to come.——(*b*) The thing they needed was to be *drawn* of God. But the very idea of drawing implies that they had the power and lacked only the inducement, the persuasion —which is equivalent to saying that they were entirely able if only they had chosen to do so.——(*c*) Yet more conclusive is the explanation of this drawing which Jesus himself subjoins, viz., that it consists in being "taught of God." So v. 45 shows decisively. But being taught applies only to intelligent mind; not here to unintelligent matter. It contemplates moral action under the power of truth, and not any change wrought by creative energy or by force applied to matter. If a man can not come without being drawn, and the drawing consists in being taught of God, we come to the root of the difficulty when we raise the question—*Why* can not men be "taught of God"? *Why* do they not receive his instruction, and why do they not obey it? Plainly, not for want of mental capacity; not because of idiocy; not by reason of any *can not* which takes away blameworthiness; not for any incapacity which lies beyond the range of their voluntary control. "Ye *will not* come to me that ye may have life," tells the simple and the whole truth in the case.

V. 46 seems designed to guard the Jews against supposing that the "being taught of God" of which he spake (quoting from Isa. 54: 13) implied seeing him. No one had seen the Father save the Son who came down from heaven—a state in which he was near God.*

47. Verily, verily, I say unto you, He that believeth on me hath everlasting life.
48. I am that bread of life.
49. Your fathers did eat manna in the wilderness, and are dead.
50. This is the bread which cometh down from heaven, that a man may eat thereof, and not die.

In the usual form of solemn emphasis with which Jesus is wont to propound new and momentous truths, he declares—"He that believeth hath everlasting life: I am that bread of life."—— There is more force (he would say to those Jews) in your own allusion to the manna than yourselves altogether apprehended. Your fathers did indeed eat manna in the wilderness, and died— died, alas! but too soon; died, many at least of them, before their time. But all unlike that manna-bread is this which came from the real heaven, of which it will be universally and forever true that whoever eats of it shall not die.

51. I am the living bread which came down from heaven: if any man eat of this bread, he shall live for ever: and the bread that I will give is my flesh, which I will give for the life of the world.

"I am the living" (in the sense of life-giving) "bread." The whole course of thought demands the sense *life-giving*.——The better text in the middle clause is—not "*this* bread;" but *my* bread.——In the last clause we have yet another advance in the figure. Having said repeatedly—"I am the bread of life," he here advances to the more definite statement—"The bread that I will give is *my flesh*, which I will give for the life of the world." The true and full significance of these words should be carefully studied. They are reiterated and somewhat explained below.

52. The Jews therefore strove among themselves, saying, How can this man give us *his* flesh to eat?
53. Then Jesus said unto them, Verily, verily, I say unto you, Except ye eat the flesh of the Son of man, and drink his blood, ye have no life in you.
54. Whoso eateth my flesh, and drinketh my blood, hath eternal life; and I will raise him up at the last day.
55. For my flesh is meat indeed, and my blood is drink indeed.

* Greek, παρα του θεου. The more approved reading makes the last clause—" he hath seen God."

56. He that eateth my flesh, and drinketh my blood, dwelleth in me, and I in him.

57. As the living Father hath sent me, and I live by the Father; so he that eateth me, even he shall live by me.

58. This is that bread which came down from heaven: not as your fathers did eat manna, and are dead: he that eateth of this bread shall live for ever.

59. These things said he in the synagogue, as he taught in Capernaum.

This advanced doctrine sprung a fresh debate among the Jews; they could not understand how this man could "give them his flesh to eat."——Jesus replies—not retracting a word he had said; not toning down his strong language, but reaffirming and expanding with some explanatory statements: Ye *must* absolutely eat the flesh of the Son of man, and drink his blood, or ye can have no life in you. Every man who thus eats and drinks has eternal life, and I will raise him up, saved, at the last day—every such man, and no other. For my flesh is real food for human souls— the food that restores and gives enduring life to souls dead in sin. Then vs. 56, 57, add somewhat in the nature of explanation. "Dwelling in me and I in him" involves and expresses the most intimate relationship—a perfect communion and fellowship. Let it be also carefully noted that these words must rule out the whole realm of *matter*—must exclude all reference to flesh and body in the material sense as to be eaten literally. For if "I in him" means that the flesh of Jesus passes by being eaten and digested, into the flesh, the real body of his people; then, on the other hand, "dwelling in me" must also mean that the flesh of the believer goes in like manner into the material body of Christ. Why not?——We are therefore driven from the material to the spiritual sense of this figure.——To the same construction we are brought also by v. 57, which gives the analogy between Christ's relation to his Father, and the relation of his people to himself.

"As I live" (said Jesus) "by the Father," drawing my life from the Father—so "he that eateth me shall live by me." But the life which Jesus draws from the Father can not for a moment be thought of as in any sort the product of material bread—is not the sort of life in which our bodies are sustained by digesting bread.——Let it also be noted that Jesus subsequently affirms this construction (v. 63) in the words:—"It is the Spirit that quickeneth" (giveth life); "the flesh profiteth nothing." I have never meant to say that the flesh of my body giveth life to those that eat it in the same sense in which bread sustains life in human bodies. No; I am thinking only of the truth I teach, the sense of the words I speak—as giving life to human souls.

In pressing the figure of himself as the bread of life, to the extent of eating his flesh and drinking his blood, Jesus must (it would seem) have had reference to his sacrificial death on the cross. His own institution—the holy supper—warrants this construction of his words in this chapter. He meant to lead the thought of his disciples forward to that atoning death, and to teach them that his power to give spiritual life to their souls came in a measure through his laying down his life as the Lamb of Sacrifice. It was in this point of view that his *blood* as well as his *flesh* enters into the redemption of his people.——May we not also assume a pushing forward of the analogy of digestion as an agency for the material life of the body, to illustrate the agency whereby Jesus brings spiritual life to human souls? In this spiritual realm his flesh and blood are represented (v. 63) by "the words I speak unto you which are spirit and life." Words, inwardly digested, feed the soul, as bread properly digested, feeds the body. The spiritual power of the ordinance of the supper is altogether of the same sort—not the bread eaten feeding the body, but the truth suggested and illustrated feeding the soul.

A freshened sense of the importance of a thorough and clear exposition of this chapter comes over me as I read the comments of such a critic as Dean Alford. He maintains strenuously that these words of Christ can not take effect—that Christ can not become the bread of life to his people, so that the sense of these words shall be realized in Christian experience *until after his resurrection*, because it is Christ's *resurrection body*, and that only which his people eat. These are Alford's words: "His (Christ's) flesh is the glorified substance of his resurrection body, now at the right hand of God." "It is then *in his resurrection form only* that his flesh can be eaten and be living food for living men." "It is *only through or after the death of the Lord* that by any propriety of language his flesh could be said to be eaten." [The italics in the above quotations are his.]——Again: "To eat the flesh of Christ is *to realize in our inner life the mystery of his body now in heaven—to digest and assimilate our own portion in that body.*"——So of the blood. His view as to both the flesh and the blood of Christ he brings out in this remarkable statement:—"The eating of his flesh and drinking of his blood import the making to ourselves and the using, as *objectively real*, those two great truths of our redemption in Him of which our faith *subjectively* convinces us."——And as if to carry his mysticism to its perfection, he maintains elaborately that the world [kosmos] is to have life through Christ's body, and says—"The very existence of all the created world is owing to and held together by that resurrection body of the Lord." [But was not the world created quite a while *before* the resurrection body of the Lord came into being?]

Now let the reader inquire soberly, What can be the meaning of all this? Is it that Christ's resurrection body is to be eaten as men eat the flesh of animals for dinner? If so, when and where? Is it here and now? or only after we have our resurrection bodies? If here and now, is this eating a fact cognizant to our senses, or even to our consciousness? When Christ's resurrection body is eaten and digested by the believer, does the portion of that body, so eaten and digested, cease to be a part of Christ's body, and become a constituent portion of the saint's body? And again—Is this eating of Christ's resurrection body an essential condition of salvation? If so, how were the ancient saints saved who lived and died before Christ's resurrection?—— Does not this whole system of Alford's utterly ignore those qualifying, explanatory words of Jesus—"It is the Spirit that quickeneth; the flesh profiteth nothing. The *words* that I speak unto you, they are spirit and they are life" (v. 63)? Does it not also violate and render nugatory the analogy (put in v. 57) between Christ's living by the Father and the believer's living by Christ? Is it not absurd and revolting to our common sense to assume a material or physical *eating* as the mode by which Christ derives life from the Father?

This entire scheme of interpretation put forward by Dean Alford, I must regard as mystical in the bad and dangerous sense, as entirely misleading, and as exclusive of the true and wholesome sense of Christ's words.

Far more simple, more sensible, more scriptural in every bearing, is this construction (as above given), viz: That the bread, miraculously multiplied for five thousand men, suggested to the Jews the manna of the desert. Following out this suggestion Jesus said—That bread was not from the real heaven; it did not impart enduring life; those who ate it died fearfully soon. I give you the real bread from heaven. I am the bread of life. Receiving me by faith ye live forever. And to make the analogy more forcible he pushes it yet further;—My flesh I give for the life of the world. Men must eat my flesh and drink my blood to gain eternal life—said with an eye to his sacrificial death as providing the means and agencies for the life of man. Dying he made atonement for sin, and thus made pardon possible and salvation sure to all who believe. His death, moreover, evolved the great moral forces which reach men's hearts and subdue them to penitence, gratitude, and love.——The bread and wine of the supper set forth in symbol the precise significance of these verses.——This construction of "eating the flesh of the Son of man" is sustained against all other constructions, and especially against the mystical one of Alford, by the explanations and analogies supplied by Jesus himself, as in vs. 56, 57, 63. No rule of interpretation is more reasonable or more imperative than this—that Jesus should be allowed to interpret his own words; and that we are bound to take his interpretation.

60. Many therefore of his disciples, when they had heard *this*, said, This is a hard saying; who can hear it?

61. When Jesus knew in himself that his disciples murmured at it, he said unto them, Doth this offend you?

62. *What* and if ye shall see the Son of man ascend up where he was before?

63. It is the Spirit that quickeneth; the flesh profiteth nothing: the words that I speak unto you, *they* are spirit, and *they* are life.

Some who had previously been regarded as his disciples stumbled at these teachings and murmured. "This," said they, "is a *hard* saying"—hard in the sense of repulsive, unacceptable, such as we can not receive.——What was precisely the point upon which they stumbled? Was it that he said—"No man can come to me except the Father draw him"? There is nothing in this chapter which indicates offense at this.——Was it what he said of "eating his flesh"? This was one of the hard sayings over which the Jews strove among themselves, as appears v. 52. And this seems to have been the head and front of the offense. It involved a Messiah suffering and dying—not as they construed it, conquering, reigning; and therefore it ran counter to all their cherished notions of their nation's Deliverer. His work as thus set forth made no account of the worldly greatness they aspired to, but utmost account of that spiritual life, in purity and love, for which they had no aspirations. Hence they said in their hearts—We are disappointed in this man; he meets none of our cherished hopes; why should we follow him longer? Jesus said (v. 64) that they "believed not"—*i. e.* did not accept him as the promised Messiah.

In v. 62 the Greek, literally translated, would read—"If then ye should see the Son of man ascend where he was before"—leaving the real question, *What then?* to be supplied. The bearing of this is plain. The visible ascension of Jesus to the Father was ere long to take place; some human eyes would see it: What would ye think of it if it should transpire before your very eyes? This future fact would carry with it a certain power of demonstration. Our Lord fitly refers to it in this way as one of the proofs yet to be revealed of his real Messiahship.

Suddenly dropping that point, he seeks (v. 63) to remove the offense from before them by turning their minds from their gross literalism to the just view of what he had said as to eating his flesh. It is only the spirit—not at all the flesh—which gives men real life, and by which I become to men "the bread of life." It is in the words I speak—not in the literal flesh supposably eaten by human teeth—that this power of life for men resides.

It deserves remark here that this figure of "eating" (as applied to Christ's flesh) was far more in harmony with Jewish than with modern ideas and usage, and therefore more readily intelligible to them than to us. They could say (as in Jer. 15: 16) "Thy words were found, and I did eat them;" or (Ezek. 3: 1) "Son of man, eat that thou findest; eat this roll;" also (Isa. 55: 1) "Come ye, buy and *eat;* yea come, buy wine and milk without money and without price." "The wicked eat the fruit of their own way," etc.

64. *But there are some of you that believe not. For Jesus knew from the beginning who they were that believed not, and who should betray him.*

65. *And he said, Therefore said I unto you, that no man can come unto me, except it were given unto him of my Father.*

Jesus saw in their heart the root of all this trouble—the true occasion of this sad stumbling. There were some among his professed disciples who did not heartily believe on him. Some, we know not how many, seem to have followed him up to this hour, but left him here. It was with an eye to their case that Jesus had said (as above)—"No man can come to me except it were given unto him of my Father." These apostates had not been "taught of God;" they had never sought—had never accepted the teaching that comes from God through the Spirit. Their supposed conversion had been *without God*, no hand of God being in it. Their motive and spirit had been wholly of the earth, earthy.

66. *From that time many of his disciples went back, and walked no more with him.*

67. *Then said Jesus unto the twelve, Will ye also go away?*

68. *Then Simon Peter answered him, Lord, to whom shall we go? thou hast the words of eternal life.*

69. *And we believe and are sure that thou art that Christ, the Son of the living God.*

Was it because *so many* turned back at this point that Jesus said—as if feeling almost utterly forsaken—"Will ye also go away?" Or was it rather to draw out from them this grateful testimony to their fidelity?——Be this as it may, Simon Peter is always prompt and ready. Go away from Thee? Go where? To whom else could we go, or should we? "Thou hast the words of eternal life." There can be no higher Teacher—none better. Thy words are unto life eternal. We accept—we love them. We want no other.——Moreover, "we *know thee*."——Peter's words according to the best text were—"We have believed and have known that Thou art the Holy One of God." The reading in our English Bible is supposed to have come from Matt. 16: 16—the transcriber assuming that Peter must have used the same expression here as there.——The coincidence of this language with that of the demoniac as in Mark 1: 24 and Luke 4: 34 is remarkable. ——The Sinaitic and Vatican manuscripts concur in this reading—"the Holy One of God"—beautifully brief and expressive.

70. *Jesus answered them, Have not I chosen you twelve, and one of you is a devil?*

71. He spake of Judas Iscariot *the son* of Simon: for he it was that should betray him, being one of the twelve.

Even of you, "one is a devil"—said of Judas Iscariot, the traitor whose heart was bare before the eye of Jesus. "A devil," in the sense of being a ready instrument for Satan's work; temptible, and sure when the occasion came, to fall before Satan's temptation and betray his master.

If the question be raised—*Why* did Jesus choose one Judas into the number of the twelve? we may not see all the reasons, yet we may perhaps conjecture some of them. We may at least suggest that the testimony of this traitor—"I have betrayed innocent blood"—served to supplement and fill out to perfection the proof that Jesus was honest and sincere. Judas had been with him in his daily life, present in his consultations; conversant with his most secret plans, so that if there had been another side to his character—an inner side known only to his chosen associates—here was the man to divulge it—a man who had not merely the ability but every inducement, in order to justify his treason to himself and to mankind. In the hour of crisis not a word had he to say in self-justification—not a word of testimony against Jesus to give the court and the prosecution who were seeking testimony with untiring zeal; but on the contrary, stung with remorse, he cried, "I have sinned in that I have betrayed the innocent blood!"

Moreover inasmuch as very many, not to say most of the local churches of Christ will have one or more members of the character of Judas, there may lie in this fact a reason why Jesus should submit to the trials of such a condition, that his people through all time might see that he was tempted in all points as we are, and knows how to sympathize with and succor his people in every need.

CHAPTER VII.

The conversations and scenes of this chapter occurred in the temple in Jerusalem at the feast of tabernacles. First is the discussion between himself and his lineal brethren as to his going up to the feast (vs. 1–10); then the general inquiry among the Jews as to his character and claims (vs. 10–13); his teachings in the temple and the discussion which followed (vs. 14–20); renewed discussion over the healing of the impotent man at Bethesda (vs. 21–24): persecution excited afresh by the men of Jerusalem (vs. 25–31): officers are deputed to arrest him and the ensuing conversation (vs. 32–36); the public announcement by Jesus on the great day of the feast and the diverse opinions among the people (vs. 37–44); the officers failing to arrest him make their official returns and a fierce debate ensues (vs. 45–52).

1. After these things Jesus walked in Galilee: for he would not walk in Jewry, because the Jews sought to kill him.

2. Now the Jews' feast of tabernacles was at hand.

3. His brethren therefore said unto him, Depart hence, and go into Judea, that thy disciples also may see the works that thou doest.

4. For *there is* no man *that* doeth any thing in secret, and he himself seeketh to be known openly. If thou do these things, shew thyself to the world.

5. For neither did his brethren believe in him.

"Walked"—traversing the country from place to place as the Greek word implies, preaching and healing.——"Jewry"—another name for Judea which is the Greek word here. No reason appears for using this word rather than Judea unless it be to indicate it as the special residence of Jews.——Jesus knew that the Jews were incensed against him, plotting his death; and shaped his movements accordingly.——At this point in his ministry his lineal brethren had not believed in him as the nation's Messiah. They professed not to understand why he should be so retiring and so averse to publicity. "Go up," said they, to Jerusalem; perform miracles in the presence of the people who are willing to hear thy instructions; for surely, one who claims to be the nation's Messiah, and whose business therefore it should be to make himself known, ought not to work only in secret.——They seem to imply that this policy must disparage his claims. The historian (v. 5) accounts for their words by saying that as yet they did not believe on him.

6. Then Jesus said unto them, My time is not yet come: but your time is always ready.

7. The world can not hate you; but me it hateth, because I testify of it, that the works thereof are evil.

8. Go ye up unto this feast: I go not up yet unto this feast; for my time is not yet full come.

9. When he had said these words unto them, he abode *still* in Galilee.

10. But when his brethren were gone up, then went he also up unto the feast, not openly, but as it were in secret.

My time for the publicity you insist upon is not yet; I know my work and its obstacles; I understand what wisdom and prudence demand. Ye have no occasion for such caution; ye have never incurred the hatred of bad men by faithfully rebuking their sins.

At first view it may appear to some readers that Jesus fell short of entire frankness, not to say truth with these brethren in first saying—"I go not up to this feast;" and afterwards in going. Must this be regarded as duplicity?—On this point let it be noted: —(*a.*) Jesus did not say, I am not going at all; but I am not going *now*—using the present tense. He left it an open question whether he should go at some later time if it should seem to him best.——— (*b.*) It is supposable that his eye was specially upon the public manner of going up which his brethren advised; and that therefore he meant to say—I can not go in the way ye recommend and demand. If I go it must be in a much more private way—as the historian is careful to say (v. 10) that he actually went.———(*c.*) May it not be said that a remarkable consciousness of integrity is manifest both in the words of Jesus and in the fidelity of the historian—in that the statements are so unguarded, as if there were no fear or thought that any one would suspect duplicity. There is no studied attempt to avoid the appearance of it.

11. Then the Jews sought him at the feast, and said, Where is he?

12. And there was much murmuring among the people concerning him: for some said, He is a good man: others said, Nay; but he deceiveth the people.

13. Howbeit no man spake openly of him for fear of the Jews.

The public mind was profoundly moved with the question of the claims of Jesus.———This "murmuring" was not in the sense of complaining, fault-finding; but rather of whispering, talking in an under-tone. It contemplates the talk as heard by a listener— a buzzing sound. Those men feared to speak openly lest they should incur the suspicion or the wrath of the Jewish leaders— already furious against Jesus.———The "Jews" in such a connection are the members of their Great Council with the leading Scribes and Pharisees in their sympathy.———Noticeably, the primary and pivotal question was that of moral character—Is he a good man; or is he a deceiver of the people? For if Jesus were a thoroughly good man with none but honest intentions, he must be the long promised Messiah; since it was not even supposable that he was himself mistaken as to his being sent of God, taught of God, and indorsed of God by receiving from him the miracle-working power.

14. Now about the midst of the feast Jesus went up into the temple and taught.

15. And the Jews marveled, saying, How knoweth this man letters, having never learned?

16. Jesus answered them, and said, My doctrine is not mine, but his that sent me.

17. If any man will do his will, he shall know of the doctrine, whether it be of God, or *whether* I speak of myself.

18. He that speaketh of himself seeketh his own glory: but he that seeketh his glory that sent him, the same is true, and no unrighteousness is in him.

This feast was held eight days, half of which had past before Jesus appeared in the temple. His time had come for a more open manifestation of himself and of his claims.—"The Jews "— the same parties as above (v. 13) marveled at his knowledge of their scriptures, for they knew he had not been trained in their schools—had never sat at the feet of their Gamaliels. They could not comprehend how one could get so much knowledge of this sort anywhere else.——It is highly probable that this discourse was mainly an exposition of the Old Testament Scriptures, especially of the prophecies concerning the Messiah like that in the synagogue at Nazareth (Luke 4: 16–22). For the time had then come for such a discourse in the temple, and this supposition well accounts for their expressed surprise at his knowledge of their books— ["grammata"].——Jesus replies; What I teach is not original with me but comes from him who sent me. These prophecies which I have been expounding are God's own words; all I teach comes from him. This answers your question—How knoweth this man the things of our Scriptures?

"If a man will do his will" (as given in our English) is too tame and weak. The word "will" in the phrase "will do" is not a future tense but a verb—full of force; if one *has a will* to do God's pleasure, if he sets his heart upon it and solemnly purposes to do all God's known will and nothing else or other, then God will teach him concerning me and my doctrine whether it be from God, or whether I speak out of my own heart only, with no message from God. This is the old doctrine;—"The meek will he guide in judgment; the meek will he teach his way" (Ps. 25: 9). The docile and obedient God loves to lead on into all truth. He sends his Spirit on this very mission, to do this very work.——This principle gives the great secret of learning the truth of God. It shows what attitude of mind and state of heart toward God will insure his divine guidance, and consequently, lead into all vitally important truth.——In the phrase (v. 17, 18) "speaketh of himself"— "*of*" is not in the sense of *concerning* but rather—*out of*—out of his own heart as opposed to speaking what is given him by and from God. If Jesus had spoken so it would have been seeking his own glory, whereas in fact he sought only the glory of God who sent him and thus proved himself a true man and no impostor.

19. Did not Moses give you the law, and *yet* none of you keepeth the law? Why go ye about to kill me?

20. The people answered and said, Thou hast a devil: who goeth about to kill thee?

Christ's appeal in this way to Moses and the law was specially pertinent to them because they gloried in being his professed followers—above all other students or teachers of his law. But Jesus puts it to their conscience—"None of you keepeth the law"—for that law describes myself as the great prophet to be sent of God; yet ye not only reject me but seek my life.——The people answer— "Thou hast a devil." They did not say diabolos, as is said of Judas (6: 70), but "daimonion"—a demon spirit, which they meant to say *possessed* him—perhaps in their view the real author of the words he spoke and of the deeds he wrought. Could the infatuation of moral blindness farther go?——"Who goeth about to kill thee"? as if they were supremely innocent of any such purpose and had never heard even a whisper thereof! Apparently they did not see the way open yet to strike and therefore deliberately *lied* to keep dark for yet a season longer.

21. Jesus answered and said unto them, I have done one work, and ye all marvel.

22. Moses therefore gave unto you circumcision; (not because it is of Moses, but of the fathers;) and ye on the sabbath day circumcise a man.

23. If a man on the sabbath day receive circumcision, that the law of Moses should not be broken; are ye angry at me, because I have made a man every whit whole on the sabbath day?

24. Judge not according to the appearance, but judge righteous judgment.

The "one work" referred to was the healing of the impotent man at the pool of Bethesda, which, it should be remembered, occurred at Jerusalem, as also the long discourse which ensued (as in John 5). Here Jesus resumes that discussion with a fresh argument, viz, that the law of circumcision, which like the Sabbath was older than Moses, required the infant to be circumcised on its eighth day, and this was done even though the day was the Sabbath. Should they then be angry at him for making a man entirely whole on the Sabbath? Was the sacredness of the day more violated by what he had done than by what they were often doing in the act of circumcision? Was not healing a poor cripple as good a work and as needful as the circumcision of a babe eight days old? "Judge not" (says he) upon the merely surface view, but according to intrinsic righteousness.

25. Then said some of them of Jerusalem, Is not this he, whom they seek to kill?

26. But, lo, he speaketh boldly, and they say nothing unto him. Do the rulers know indeed that this is the very Christ?

"The men of Jerusalem" lead off, more virulent against Jesus than any others. Living at the central, focal point of Pharisaism, they had (as they felt it) more and deeper interests at stake than any other Jews.———Is not this the man, said they, who has been found worthy of death for both Sabbath breaking and blasphemy? (John 5: 18). Why do they let him go on thus in bold and public speech misleading the people? Do the rulers know that this is the very Christ? Of course this, in their thought, is an impossible supposition, put only for effect. It amounts to a challenge to those rulers to repel the taunt and clear themselves of the suspicion of being disciples of the supposed Nazarene.

27. Howbeit we know this man whence he is: but when Christ cometh, no man knoweth whence he is.

28. Then cried Jesus in the temple as he taught, saying, Ye both know me, and ye know whence I am: and I am not come of myself, but he that sent me is true, whom ye know not.

29. But I know him; for I am from him, and he hath sent me.

It does not appear on what ground they assumed that the Messiah must come from some unknown quarter. In fact the prophecy of Micah (5: 2) had indicated his birth-place very definitely—Bethlehem. Yet it is not certain that they knew of his birth there.———In saying—"Ye know me and know whence I am," Jesus, no doubt, meant to rebut their argument against his Messiahship—viz, that his origin was unknown. He meant to say—Ye know enough of me and of my mission from God to demand your belief. Your skepticism has no valid foundation. Your plea—We do not know his credentials—is false and unavailing. Ye know I have not come of my own motion. Ye know I am sent of God, though ye are far from knowing God in the deep spiritual sense in which I know him.

30. Then they sought to take him: but no man laid hands on him, because his hour was not yet come.

31. And many of the people believed on him, and said, When Christ cometh, will he do more miracles than these which this *man* hath done?

Infuriated by such plain rebuke and such exposure of their fallacies, they sought to seize him. Precisely how they were prevented is not apparent. Perhaps the masses were not ripe for it and would not sustain or even permit his violent arrest. This is made probable by the remark that "many of the people then believed on him." With much good sense they reasoned that the real Messiah should not be expected to work more miracles than this man had wrought.

32. The Pharisees heard that the people murmured such things concerning him; and the Pharisees and the chief priests sent officers to take him.

33. Then said Jesus unto them, Yet a little while am I with you, and *then* I go unto him that sent me.

34. Ye shall seek me, and shall not find *me:* and where I am, *thither* ye cannot come.

35. Then said the Jews among themselves, Whither will he go, that we shall not find him? will he go unto the dispersed among the Gentiles, and teach the Gentiles?

36. What *manner of* saying is this that he said, Ye shall seek me, and shall not find *me:* and where I am, *thither* ye cannot come?

The Pharisees heard of this talking in under-tone among the people, and forthwith commissioned a band of officers to arrest him.——The manner in which Jesus met them is characteristic. With quiet yet solemn, impressive dignity; unawed by their authority; fearless of their violence; he said—"I have a little longer yet to remain among you; all your threats of violence and attempts at arrest will not shorten this hour. When my time comes, I shall go to him that sent me, and ye will seek me then in vain."——The spirit of these words appears again in what Jesus said to Pilate; "Thou couldest have no power at all against me except it were given thee from above; therefore he that delivered me unto thee hath the greater sin" (John 19: 11). I am under the care of Almighty God; ye can do nothing more or worse than his wisdom permits. He will soon take me safely to himself; your wrath against me will be utterly futile.——In their speculations as to the sense of his words, they scornfully taunt him with perhaps thinking of going abroad to preach to Gentiles and to Jews exiled in other lands among despised outsiders. Yet they could not quite fathom his meaning to their own satisfaction. His words would lie heavy and hard upon their souls. Could it be that this man was really as safe under God's care as he seemed?

37. In the last day, that great *day* of the feast, Jesus stood and cried, saying, If any man thirst, let him come unto me, and drink.

38. He that believeth on me, as the Scripture hath said, out of his belly shall flow rivers of living water.

39. (But this spake he of the Spirit, which they that believe on him should receive: for the Holy Ghost was not yet *given*; because that Jesus was not yet glorified.)

It is generally held that this last and great day of the feast was the eighth, and that this proclamation of Jesus may have been suggested by the Jewish custom of having water borne on that day in joyful procession from the pool of Siloam and poured out before the Lord. Some, however, hold that the water was not brought in at this time, yet that even this failure may have been suggestive—as if Jesus would say to the expectant, waiting, but disappointed people—Look rather to me! If any man thirst, let him *come unto me*—not go to the waters of Siloam—and in me find the true waters of life. However the case may be as to Jewish usage on this last great day, there can be no question that Jesus had his eye somewhat upon the words of ancient Scripture— "With joy shall ye draw water out of the wells of salvation" (Isa. 12: 3); "I will pour water on him that is thirsty and floods upon the dry ground." . . . . . "I will pour my Spirit upon thy seed and my blessing upon thy offspring" (Isa. 44: 3); "Ho, every one that thirsteth; come ye to the waters" (Isa. 55: 1)—with passages of kindred import in Joel and Zechariah (Joel 2: 28, 29, and 3: 18; Zech. 13: 1 and 14: 8).

In regard to the specific reference in v. 38—"As the scripture hath said"—we fail to find precisely these words in the Old Testament scriptures. Yet taking into view the New Testament usage by which the human body is spoken of as "the temple of the Holy Ghost," we find the symbol naturally corresponding to the Savior's words in Ezekiel 47: 1-12, where rivers of living water flow out from under the spiritual figurative temple. As this passage in Ezekiel beyond a doubt looks toward the effusions of the Spirit in the gospel age, it seems to meet the conditions of our Savior's allusion—"As the scripture hath said, *out* of his belly shall flow rivers of living water." The historian (John) seems aware that these words of Jesus (vs. 37, 38) might be obscure, especially to his contemplated Gentile readers—less familiar than Jews with the Old Testament prophetic scriptures (as above quoted), and therefore subjoins the explanation in v. 39, viz. that Jesus referred to the gift of the Spirit, then shortly to be shed forth abundantly, as Isaiah, Joel, and Zechariah had foretold. He makes it a special point that this gift of the Spirit in its extraordinary fullness was yet *future* though near; "not yet given, because that Jesus was not yet glorified." The scriptures show clearly that this being "glorified" involved his resurrection from the dead, and referred specially to his ascension in his risen body, and his public exaltation to the throne of heaven in equal honor with the Father—"high above all principalities and powers in the heavenly places" (Eph. 1: 20, 21). The apostles are joyfully emphatic on the point of this exaltation, and of its being followed at once by the signal outpouring of the Spirit. Earliest in time is Peter's testimony on the day of Pentecost: "This Jesus hath God raised up;" "Being therefore by the right hand of God exalted, and having received of the Father the promise of the Holy Ghost, he hath shed forth this which ye now see and hear" (Acts 2: 33). Compare also Acts 5: 31.

In this connection let us recall the remarkably full instructions respecting the mission and work of "the Spirit of truth"—the Comforter—which Jesus gave his disciples on the evening before his arrest—as in John 14: 16-18, and 15: 26, and 16: 7-15. In view of the fullness and richness of these words, they might seem almost a new revelation.——Luke is definite on the point that Jesus in repeating the promise of this gift from the Father bade his disciples "tarry in Jerusalem till they were endued with power from on high" (Luke 24: 49, and Acts 1: 4, 8). Obeying this command, they waited and prayed—"all continuing with one accord in prayer and supplication" "until the day of Pentecost had fully come;" then "a sound from heaven as of a rushing mighty wind" gave token of the Spirit's coming.

As to the divine philosophy of this arrangement—the *reason why* this great gift of the Spirit—delayed through all the ages before the Messiah came; kept in waiting till after his earthly ministry had been finished, and his death on the cross had transpired, and up to the very point of his ascension and enthronement in the highest heavens;—we can not mistake widely in its solution.——On the earthward side of the case, it was fitting that the great facts and truths which the teaching Spirit would make mighty through his power for the salvation of lost men should be *out*—patent—ready to be witnessed unto by his chosen apostles, before the great work of the Spirit should commence. As the age of the world, beginning with Christ's advent and fully inaugurated at his ascension, was to be pre-eminently the dispensation of the Spirit, it was well it should open with impressive manifestations, at once illustrative of his nature, and inspiring to God's people through all the onward centuries.

On the heavenward side it may not be amiss to consider that Jesus as incarnate had not been seen in heaven—manifest to the view of its glorious hierarchies of angels and seraphim before. It was fit that his coming should be a marked event—that his inauguration should be (may we say) an high day in the heavenly world—that infinite honor should be conferred on him who throughout his earthly life had been "despised of men"—a glorious testimony to the loving appreciation in which he was held by the Infinite Father.

The great gift of the Spirit at this eventful hour witnesseth that this was the highest favor Jesus chose to ask, more dear to his heart than all others. It came before the universe as the Father's indorsement of the scheme of salvation to which the Son was fully committed: it testified that henceforth the whole Deity—every perfection and power of the Triune God—Father, Son, and Spirit—are at one in working for this sublime consummation—the redemption of the world to Christ. It was deserved honor to the Mighty Conqueror who had vanquished Satan and all his powers of darkness. The scene suggested to Paul the Roman triumph which the Senate of Rome was wont to grant to her grandest conquerors when they returned to her proud capital with the spoils of vanquished nations. With this triumph in his eye as an illustration, he wrote—"When he [Jesus] ascended up on high, he led his captives captive," *i. e.* gracing his triumphal march as he entered the glorious city of God; and "gave gifts to men"—rewards of honor to his valiant and faithful soldiers.

These gifts Paul enumerates—"Apostles, prophets, evangelists, pastors, teachers"—"for the perfecting of the saints," etc.—all to be specially imbued with gifts of the Spirit. (Eph. 4: 8-12).—— When the incarnate Son took his place visibly on the throne of heaven to administer the reign of grace over this fallen but redeemed world, it was supremely appropriate to signalize the opening of his administration by very special effusions of the Spirit. The hosts of the heavenly world were then able to understand the grounds and reasons of this honor paid to the Son, and of this power lodged in his hands.

Returning to contemplate the words in vs. 37, 38, as part of the human history of the man of Nazareth, let us think of their bearing upon a question we often ask—Did Jesus place himself before the thousands of his countrymen as truly their promised Messiah?——The records of his public life speak of him mostly as being in remote Galilee, traversing cities and villages, healing the sick; casting out devils; teaching his disciples; occasionally, yet rarely, drawing about him and after him large crowds of people;—but not often in Jerusalem, and only on few occasions becoming conspicuous at the great annual festivals of the nation. But in this chapter we see him in the temple on the great day of their most joyous festival; the thousands of Israel are gathered there; and his time has fully come to announce himself as their Redeemer and Messiah. "*He stood and cried;*" taking his stand conspicuously in the presence of the multitude, he lifted up his voice as one who had an important message to proclaim, and a right to be heard; and then and there, in words chosen from their well known prophetic scriptures, he declared— I come to fulfill in myself those munificent promises. I come to give the waters of salvation to every thirsty and believing soul. If any man thirsts, let him come unto me and drink. The waters I give shall be an unfailing fountain in his soul; a well of water springing up unto everlasting life; "rivers of living water," flowing out in blessings to others if so they will—never to fail.—— What better words could he have spoken to place himself before the people as their own Messiah? What one feature in the scene could be changed or what new feature added to make the whole more impressive, more majestic, more tender, and yet more sublime?

40. Many of the people therefore, when they heard this saying, said, Of a truth this is the Prophet.

41. Others said, This is the Christ. But some said, Shall Christ come out of Galilee?

42. Hath not the Scripture said, That Christ cometh of the seed of David, and out of the town of Bethlehem, where David was?

43. So there was a division among the people because of him.

Naturally the people were impressed. Probably the officers, with writ of arrest in hand, were within hearing, awed by the majesty and touched by the tenderness of this strange man and message, to say—"Never man spake like this man." Of the people some declared—This must be the great prophet; others, This is the Christ; while yet others stumbled over his supposed Galilean origin, inasmuch as the prophet Micah had distinctly located the birth of their nation's Deliverer in Bethlehem—the second David coming from the same town as the first.

44. And some of them would have taken him, but no man laid hands on him.

"Some would have taken him."—Strangely dead to the sweetness and glory of these words of life; repelled by the purity and goodness which made their own moral ugliness unendurable: but they were too few to carry their measures against the greater number who admired and sustained;—so that no man laid hands on him. It is plain that in a fair field, when Jesus spake in sweetness and majesty before the people, he had the hearts of too many to permit the small and malignant minority to resort to violence. Hence the necessity of treachery and betrayal in order to arrest him in the absence of the multitude.

45. Then came the officers to the chief priests and Pharisees; and they said unto them, Why have ye not brought him?

46. The officers answered, Never man spake like this man.

The officers commissioned to arrest him return their writ—the service it required being impracticable.
"Why did ye not bring the culprit before us?"
"Never man spake like this man." Did they mean to say—We can not find it in our hearts to touch him? Or only this: The people will not let us? Perhaps, nay probably, both. The officers make no further reply.

47. Then answered them the Pharisees, Are ye also deceived?

48. Have any of the rulers or of the Pharisees believed on him?

49. But this people who knoweth not the law are cursed.

The Pharisees seem to have supposed that they were led away—"deceived" they call it—by the words and the manner of Jesus. Assuming moreover that their officers must have been influenced by the opinions of others (some men can never think of any other influence), they push their question;—"Have any of the great men, whose opinions are of any value, believed on him?" Ye can not be so senseless as to care for the notions of the common people—the mere rabble who know nothing of the law—

miscreants, all; "accursed." Hard words these, to use of the common people; but they indicate the self-conceit and moral infatuation that reigned in the bosoms of the Pharisees who constituted the Great Sanhedrim.

50. Nicodemus saith unto them, (he that came to Jesus by night, being one of them,)
51. Doth our law judge *any* man, before it hear him, and know what he doeth?

One man—one honest man—was there; the same Nicodemus of whom we have heard before. He quietly suggests that their law did not judge any man until it had heard him in his own defense,* and learned from his own lips what he was doing or had done. This principle, always grandly equitable—an honor to any system of jurisprudence—he suggested should be applied in the present case.——Nicodemus deserves our respect for this dignified interposition. Perhaps he was not sufficiently resolute and firm; and perhaps he was. At least he made his point forcibly.

As to the true text in v. 50, modern critics quite unanimously reject "by night;" Tischendorf with the Sinaitic omits the entire clause—"He that came to Jesus by night;" while Meyer would have it—"Who came to him before." All accept the words—"Who was one of them." These variations have no doctrinal importance.

52. They answered and said unto him, Art thou also of Galilee? Search, and look: for out of Galilee ariseth no prophet.

They put the question, "Art thou also of Galilee?" with the same Greek interrogative which Nicodemus used—"Doth our law judge," etc.?—both questions implying the expectation of a negative answer. The Pharisees would say—We know thou art not a Galilean by birth; but can it be possible that thou art in sympathy with this Galilean? Wouldest thou take sides with that outlandish people against the holy city and the holy people of thine own country?——Look carefully into this case. No great prophet ever did or can come out of Galilee. Probably they would have said—If God should discriminate thus against his own holy city and people by sending the Messiah through Galilean blood and parent-

---

* The words of the law referred to are of this sort: "I charged your judges, saying; Hear the causes between your brethren, and judge righteously between every man and his neighbor," etc. "Ye shall not respect persons in judgment, but ye shall hear the small as well as the great," etc. (Deut. 1: 16, 17). "If a false witness rise up against any man to testify against him that which is wrong, then *both the men* between whom the controversy is shall stand before the Lord, before the priest and the judges which shall be in those days; and the judge shall make diligent inquisition," etc. (Deut. 19: 16-18).

age, away with him!—Bigotry is always blind; bigotry strong and fierce as theirs was doubly so; for in the first place God did raise up some old prophets from Galilee, *e. g.* Jonah certainly (2 Kings 14: 25), and in the spirit of it Elijah also, and perhaps others whose birth-place is not recorded: and in the second place, Jesus was not born in Galilee, but in Bethlehem-Judah—as they should have known.

53. *And every man went unto his own house.*

This verse belongs with the disputed portion of chap. 8.—viz. vs. 1–11. It naturally precedes 8: 1, and stands or falls with it.

CHAPTER VIII.

The opening of this chapter springs a new and truly grave question;—viz. as to the genuineness of the passage respecting the woman said to have been taken in adultery—(v. 1–11). [The question involves also the last v. of chap. 7.]

The objections to its genuineness are certainly very strong; in the view of the ablest and most thorough critics, decisive. Substantially the objections, external and internal, are as follows.

I. The external.

1. Of the four oldest and most important manuscripts, the Vatican and Sinaitic omit precisely these verses. The Alexandrian and the Codex Ephrem omit this passage and somewhat more; viz. the former from John 6: 50 to 8: 12, and the latter from 7: 13 to 8: 34. But the relative size of the space wanting seems to prove that this passage was never in those manuscripts.—2. The oldest and best manuscript which does contain this passage—that of Beza gives it with very considerable diversity from the received text. —3. A large number of manuscripts dating from the ninth to the twelfth century contain it, yet with very great variations—a fact which goes strongly against the genuineness of the passage. It should be noted also that a number of those which contain the passage in substance, locate it, not here, but at the close of Luke 21.—4. The balance of testimony from the church fathers bears against its genuineness.*—5. It is wanting in the most ancient manuscripts and editions of the Syriac and Coptic; but appears in the Itala—the oldest Latin version.

Thus it will be seen that the balance of external evidence is strongly against the genuineness of this passage.

II. As to the internal evidence:

---

* It is at least not named by Origen, Apollinaris, Theodore of Mopsuestia, Cyril, Chrysostom, Basil, Tertullian, Cyprian. [Tholuck].

(1.) There is strong objection to this as its original and natural place, because it breaks the connection of thought, and has no logical or other relation with what precedes or follows.——(2.) It also contains quite a number of words, forms of expression and connective particles, which are foreign from the usage of John, and therefore strongly against the theory of his being the author.

In answer to the question—How came the passage here? and has it any historical authority whatever?—the hypothesis which receives most favor is that, in substance, it is historically true; that it was handed down through several centuries by tradition; and at length admitted into a number of the later manuscripts. This hypothesis accounts for the diversity of text where it appears at all, and for its ultimate admission into our received version.

The passage is rejected as *not* genuine by Tischendorf, Meyer, Tholuck, Olshausen and Alford. Ellicott holds somewhat decidedly that it was not written by John; Farrar has "no shadow of doubt that the incident really happened, even if the form in which it is preserved to us is by no means indisputably genuine."

From v. 12 onward, we have an animated discussion between Jesus and the captious, hostile Pharisees;—Jesus presents himself as the light of the world; his opponents question his testimony (vs. 12–20): Jesus repeats his previous declaration as to going away whither they could not come, and meets their question—"Who art thou?" (vs. 21–30): A remark by Jesus to certain young converts—"If ye continue in my word, the truth shall make you free"—stirred up his opponents to aver that they were Abraham's children and never in bondage (v. 31–33), but Jesus declares that they were in bondage to the devil, were *his* children and doing his work (vs. 34–47). The Jews retort, charging Jesus with being a Samaritan and possessed with a devil (vs. 48–53), to which Jesus makes his final reply, affirming himself to have been before Abraham was. They take up stones to stone him as their only adequate reply, but he escapes their vengeance (vs. 54–59).

1. Jesus went unto the mount of Olives.

2. And early in the morning he came again into the temple, and all the people came unto him; and he sat down, and taught them.

3. And the scribes and Pharisees brought unto him a woman taken in adultery; and when they had set her in the midst,

4. They say unto him, Master, this woman was taken in adultery, in the very act.

5. Now Moses in the law commanded us, that such should be stoned: but what sayest thou?

6. This they said, tempting him, that they might have to accuse him. But Jesus stooped down, and with *his* finger wrote on the ground, *as though he heard them not.*

7. So when they continued asking him, he lifted up himself, and said unto them, He that is without sin among you, let him first cast a stone at her.

8. And again he stooped down, and wrote on the ground.

9. And they which heard *it*, being convicted by *their own* conscience, went out one by one, beginning at the eldest, *even* unto the last: and Jesus was left alone, and the woman standing in the midst.

10. When Jesus had lifted up himself, and saw none but the woman, he said unto her, Woman, where are those thine accusers? hath no man condemned thee?

11. She said, No man, Lord. And Jesus said unto her, Neither do I condemn thee : go, and sin no more.

In so far as the inspired authority of this passage becomes doubtful will its interpretation lose both interest and importance. In my view it has only a modified, weakened demand upon us for exposition of its meaning, or for defense of the course of our Lord *as here presented.* A few words must suffice.

The great questions have been these:

(*a.*) Was the allegation against this woman true or false?

(*b.*) *In what way* did the scribes hope to tempt Jesus, and find means to accuse him?

(*c.*) *Of what* were they convicted by their own conscience, and *why* did they withdraw?

(*d.*) On what ground did Jesus refuse to condemn this woman?

(*e.*) What moral lessons (if any) are taught here?

Taking these questions in their order, I suggest as to the first:

(*a.*) That the allegation is probably to be taken as true because it would be too hazardous to make if false; would react severely upon false accusers; and because Jesus seems to imply tacitly that she had sinned—*i. e.* in the respect charged.

· (*b.*) It may be supposed that they hoped to entangle him in the dilemma between condemn and acquit, inasmuch as to condemn would put him in collision with the Roman civil authorities, then in the ascendant, although to the Jewish courts irksome and odious; while to acquit would put him in antagonism against Moses.——Or, on the supposition that the case has no relations to the Roman authorities, it is generally admitted that the law of Moses against adultery had become mostly inoperative, public feeling and usage being against it. Hence to condemn would bring Jesus into odium before the people; to acquit, would expose him to the charge of dishonoring Moses and the ancient law.

(*c.*) Convicted of malicious designs against Jesus, and perhaps of being personally guilty of the very crime charged against this woman. According to history the Rabbis of that age were in this respect flagrant offenders.

(*d.*) Apparently on the ground of having no jurisdiction in the case. The prosecution had disappeared. There remained no case before him. There was not the least occasion therefore for him to pass judgment upon the wisdom or authority of the law of Moses; or upon the innocence or guilt of this woman, even on the yet doubtful supposition that *under any circumstances* he would become a court of justice for a criminal prosecution.—— Consequently he did not decide (as some have supposed) that men —themselves in sin—ought never to administer civil law—*i. e.* ought never to condemn others while in some sense more or less guilty themselves. Nor did he decide that a criminal who gives evidence of penitence is therefore and on that ground to be discharged as not guilty.——It should be very carefully noted that civil jurisdiction is one thing; a merely moral jurisdiction quite another;—that Jesus was among men, not as a civil magistrate— not a court of justice under civil government; but as a teacher of moral truth, dealing with the human heart and conscience as an individual and not as a public magistrate.

(*e.*) As to the moral lessons of this passage, I am mainly impressed with the obvious fact that Jesus aimed at only moral results. At these he did aim; at once wisely, earnestly, and successfully. Toward his accusers who sought to ensnare him, his words and no less his manner were fraught with scorching rebuke, laying bare to their own eye the malignity of their heart and the rottenness of their professions. There is scarcely another case on record in which his assailants so manifestly quailed and recoiled from before him. Rarely, if ever, did they so feel the power of his kindness and compassion toward the erring, put in contrast with their own heartless severity and shameless hypocrisy.

Then as toward this woman—cruelly sinned against in the manner of her exposure, yet having sinned under circumstances, we know not whether more or less aggravated, his bearing was marked by thoughtful compassion, adapted as best it could be to lead her to repentance. Having no responsibilities as a civil magistrate, to what should he turn his attention and direct his efforts, but this—to reclaim her from a life of sin and shame, and to save her soul?——The example of Jesus in this respect should stand before his followers as, in spirit at least, supremely worthy of imitation. It was never intended to bear upon the question of civil law, or the duty of civil magistrates to enforce wholesome law. Jesus was not acting in any such capacity. He gave no opinion, left no example, bearing upon civil jurisprudence. But upon the moral and spiritual duties of all good men and women toward the fallen, it reads us lessons at once wholesome, wise, and heavenly.

12. Then spake Jesus again unto them, saying, I am the light of the world: he that followeth me shall not walk in darkness, but shall have the light of life.

"Spake again"—resuming the discourse which closed John 7:

44. Another chapter or section of this discourse stands in vs. 21–30 below.——"I am the light of the world"—in point of moral instruction what the sun is for the material light. The light I shed illumines the path of all those who follow me. They shall have "the light of life"—all needed light to guide them unto eternal life.——Some critics suppose that the words—"I am the light"—were suggested to Jesus by the great chandeliers of the temple which were lit up during some at least of the evenings of this feast. While the people were admiring and enjoying their brilliant light, Jesus would say—In the true and far higher sense, I am the light of the whole world.——Such reference is perhaps supposable; but we may fitly remember that Jesus had used this figure long before, even in the sermon on the mount (Matt. 5: 14–16), and that John also had spoken of Jesus (1: 4–9) as "the light," "the true light," etc.

13. The Pharisees therefore said unto him, Thou bearest record of thyself; thy record is not true.

14. Jesus answered and said unto them, Though I bear record of myself, *yet* my record is true: for I know whence I came, and whither I go; but ye can not tell whence I come, and whither I go.

"Bearest record" translates the Greek verb for *testify*. They mean to say that Jesus was his own and his only witness; and they imply that any impostor could do as much; that any mere pretender might be expected to make out a good story for himself.——Jesus replies: It is appropriate that I should testify of myself. My testimony of myself is true because I know whence I came and whither I go. I know with infinite certainty that I came forth from God my Father, and shall soon return to him again—things of which you can have no such conscious knowledge. And nothing can be more obvious than that the real Messiah—he who was anointed and sent forth from God—must have this perfect consciousness of his mission, and therefore by virtue of his own nature must be the first and best witness of his own Messiahship.

15. Ye judge after the flesh; I judge no man.

16. And yet if I judge, my judgment is true: for I am not alone, but I and the Father that sent me.

17. It is also written in your law, that the testimony of two men is true.

18. I am one that bear witness of myself, and the Father that sent me beareth witness of me.

"Judge after the flesh," is in tacit contrast with judging after the spirit, and involves imperfection, frailty, error. Jesus may in this case have thought of their carnal views of the Messiah and his kingdom; of their fleshly and false notions which perpetually perverted their ideas of himself and his work.——"I judge no man," so—*i. e.* as ye judge me. Or his thought may have been—"I judge no man *now*; my mission to the world at this time is not to judge, but to save. Yet it must be conceded that the context does not specially favor this supposed reference to passing judgment upon human character and destiny. The course of thought is rather upon judging as to his personal claims to be the Messiah. So far as I do testify ("judge") of myself, my testimony is true, for I am not alone: the Father who sent me bears witness of me; and by your own law, the testimony of two witnesses is conclusive. (See Deut. 17: 5 and 19: 15).

19. Then said they unto him, Where is thy Father? Jesus answered, Ye neither know me, nor my Father: if ye had known me, ye should have known my Father also.

20. These words spake Jesus in the treasury, as he taught in the temple: and no man laid hands on him; for his hour was not yet come.

The keenest insult was purposely couched under the question, "Where is thy Father?" The question utterly ignored his claim to be the Son of God:—You talk much about your Father; what do you mean?—Where is that Father?——Their notions on this point are brought out (John 6: 42); "They said, Is not this Jesus, the son of Joseph, whose father and mother we know?"—— It is to this attitude of their mind that Jesus replies: "Ye neither know me nor my Father: if ye had known me, ye should have known my Father also."

The "treasury" was a precinct of the temple in which gifts, brought for the temple service, were deposited. (See Mark 12: 41).——"No man laid hands on him"—all his enemies being restrained by some agency of God's providence: perhaps the presence and demonstrations of too many friends ready to protect him. The fact that ultimately his enemies were compelled to hire a traitor to guide them to his place of retirement that they might arrest him in the absence of the multitude, favors this explanation.

21. Then said Jesus again unto them, I go my way, and ye shall seek me, and shall die in your sins: whither I go ye can not come.

22. Then said the Jews, Will he kill himself? because he saith, Whither I go, ye can not come.

23. And he said unto them, Ye are from beneath; I am from above: ye are of this world; I am not of this world.

24. I said therefore unto you, that ye shall die in your sins: for if ye believe not that I am *he*, ye shall die in your sins.

"I go my way, on my mission. We must part company forever, since ye *will* not follow me, and I can neither go nor stay with you."——"Ye shall seek me"—in the day of your calamity, when it shall be all too late!——It is better to apply these words to their individual and personal rather than national relations to Christ. What is true of all sinners must be true likewise of those individual men. Rejecting Jesus, they will sooner or later come to sorrow; will feel their want of a Savior and would fain seek him—if then it could be of any avail.——"Shall die in your sins"—or in the expressive form of the Greek—"In your sin, ye shall die!" In your one, all-comprehensive, and fatal sin of unbelief, ye must die forever! With mournful and solemn emphasis we must suppose these words fell from those blessed lips, suggested by the contrast between his future and theirs—himself going so soon to dwell with the Father in blessedness perfect and eternal; they "going to their own place" to meet the doom of the guilty and the lost! "Whither I go ye can not come;" my home is no home for you; with spirit utterly uncongenial—of character totally unlike—under the sternest of all necessities, ye *must go* to an abode and to a destiny far other than mine.

The Jews said—"Will he kill himself" to get beyond our reach? For they saw in his words—perhaps in his tone and manner—that he thought of death as parting them asunder. But did they, at this stage of their persecution, surmise that he would go, not by suicide, but by their own murderous hand? Wicked men, led on by Satan, are not always aware how far they may be pushed on in wickedness.—The Jews had a special abhorrence of suicide, yet did not shrink from imputing it (supposably) to Jesus.

The thought of Jesus was upon the contrast between them and himself; "Ye are from beneath; I am from above:" ye are from Satan—his pupils, followers, servants: I came down from my Father. "Ye are of this world," acting upon its principles; imbued with its spirit; obeying its behests—in all which I have not the least sympathy. It was for this reason that I said unto you, "Ye shall die in your sins." There can be no other result of such a character and such a life as yours.——"If ye believe not that *I am*"—this is the precise translation and sense of the Greek:—if ye believe not in me as the unchangeable "*I am*"—said (as it seems) with reference to the name of the revealing God, given to Moses at the bush (Ex. 3: 14). We find the same Greek word in vs. 28 and 58 below;—"When ye have lifted up the Son of man, then shall ye know that *I am*"—*i. e.* that I am truly divine—the very Son of God. "Before Abraham was, *I am;*"—my eternal being was moving on its career of existence long before Abraham lived.——In the passage before us (v. 24) the literal translation impresses me as far more significant and forcible than that of the English version—"I am he." It will seem so, I judge, to most readers unless they take the word "*he*" in the sense which appears in some Old Testament passages (*e. g.* Deut. 32: 39 and Isa. 41: 4 and 48: 12) where the Hebrew pronoun for *he* is put with a peculiar emphasis for the name of God.

Is it not supposable that this was in the mind of the English translators?

25. Then said they unto him, Who art thou? And Jesus saith unto them, Even *the same* that I said unto you from the beginning.

The spirit of this question (made by the Greek word τις) seems to be—What *kind* of a being or person art thou? What dost thou pretend to be?——The answer has been explained variously by able critics; some giving it—What I told you at the beginning; while some would put these same words in the interrogative form—*What* have I told you, etc.? others thus: Fundamentally, comprehensively, what I have said; or thus: Essentially what my words show; estimate what I am by what I say; or what I have said *all along*, from the very first. These shades of difference are of no great account in the general discussion.

26. I have many things to say and to judge of you: but he that sent me is true; and I speak to the world those things which I have heard of him.

27. They understood not that he spake to them of the Father.

Ye ask me who I am. I have already said much in answer to that question. I could say much more, and much in rebuke and condemnation of your unbelief: but, obstinate as your unbelief is, he who sent me is true, and all his words sent through me to the world are true. I speak those truthful words and none other. ——Such seems to be the drift and connection of thought in v. 26.——Yet even then they failed to see that he spake of God the Father.

28. Then said Jesus unto them, When ye have lifted up the Son of man, then shall ye know that I am *he*, and *that* I do nothing of myself; but as my Father hath taught me, I speak these things.

29. And he that sent me is with me: the Father hath not left me alone; for I do always those things that please him.

30. As he spake these words, many believed on him.

"Lifted up the Son of man"—signifying by what death he should die at their hand. (See the phrase repeated and explained in John 12: 32, 33). At his death and thereafter, new and more impressive proofs would appear of his true Messiahship. Amid the scenes of the crucifixion, some would cry out, "Verily, this was the Son of God" (Matt. 27: 54, and Mark 15: 39). His resurrection would bring yet other confirmations of his mission from heaven. The descent of the Spirit would bear home these new testimonies to many hearts.——The points then to be shown (as here put) were his divine nature; his mission from God; his unselfish fidelity to his trust; that the Father stood by him, indorsing, approving, sustaining, with his manifested love. It was the joy of this "man of sorrows," that though rejected and forsaken of men, he was neither rejected nor forsaken of the Father.

At this stage of the discussion, the historian pauses to say that "many believed on him." Was it that this allusion to his death was tenderly effective; that these views of his relation to the Father seemed to them just and convincing? Yet it should be said—Many critics, assuming that the rest of this chapter refers to these same believers, explain away their belief as being entirely superficial and transient. We must (in the sequel) inquire whether this assumption is justified.

31. Then said Jesus to those Jews which believed on him, If ye continue in my word, *then* are ye my disciples indeed;

32. And ye shall know the truth, and the truth shall make you free.

Turning to these professed believers, Jesus admonishes them to *continue in his word*, with docility and loving obedience. So should they know the truth more and more, and this truth would redeem their souls from the dominion of sin—make them *free* in the high and glorious sense of spiritual emancipation from the slavery of sinful passion. The admonition assumes danger in their case lest they might be drawn away from him so as to reject his word and come under their old bondage to sin.

33. They answered him, We be Abraham's seed, and were never in bondage to any man: how sayest thou, Ye shall be made free?

Here the first question is—Who are included under the word "*they?*" Must we answer—The converts just before spoken of as "believing on him"? Some commentators assume this; but (as it seems to me) against the probabilities of the case. There is no necessity for identifying these respondents with the believing Jews spoken of in v. 31. In scriptural usage, the antecedent to the pronoun can not always be determined by proximity; we must not always take the nearest word for the true antecedent. The sacred writers give their readers large scope for the use of their good sense (*e. g.* Isa. 37: 36, last part; also Psa. 7: 11, 12). Old Testament usage is remarkably controlled by this principle of common sense. It should not surprise us to find more or less of the same usage pervading the New.

Jesus had said to those that believed—"The truth shall make you free"—to be slaves no longer. Thereupon those who had been debating with Jesus in hostile, prejudiced mood, throughout this chapter, are offended at his implying that they were not free men but slaves; and therefore they repel the implied charge:—

Do not insinuate that we are slaves. "We are children of Abraham, and have never been in bondage to any man." What can you mean by saying—"Ye shall be made free"?——Those Jews took pride not only in being the children of Abraham, but in their national and personal liberty—never in fealty to any human power. It was at that very time a hotly contested question whether, and to what extent, if any, they were under the jurisdiction of Rome.

34. Jesus answered them, Verily, verily, I say unto you, Whosoever committeth sin is the servant of sin.

35. And the servant abideth not in the house for ever: *but* the Son abideth ever.

36. If the Son therefore shall make you free, ye shall be free indeed.

Jesus neither thought of nor much cared for freedom in the political sense. Going far deeper than that, he insists that *every sinner is a slave*. In committing sin he yields to a master; he surrenders himself to do the will of the devil; his own lusts overpower his better judgment and reason. He is absolutely in bondage—a bondage at once tyrannous, terrible, humiliating, disgraceful. Then, recurring to the figure of servitude [slavery] he contrasts the state of the slave in the household with that of the son. The slave has no permanent home there; no rights of home; may be ejected at any time; at best (if a Jew) serves out his time in six years—if of Gentile birth, in fifty—and goes. The son is the heir, and is at home there with no limit of time. If now the Son of man gives you the rights of freemen in God's house ye are indeed free—not otherwise.

37. I know that ye are Abraham's seed; but ye seek to kill me, because my word hath no place in you.

38. I speak that which I have seen with my Father: and ye do that which ye have seen with your father.

39. They answered and said unto him, Abraham is our father. Jesus saith unto them, If ye were Abraham's children, ye would do the works of Abraham.

40. But now ye seek to kill me, a man that hath told you the truth, which I have heard of God: this did not Abraham.

Jesus admits that they are the "*seed*," but denies that they are "*children*" of Abraham.* They were unquestionably born in his lineage, but, as unquestionably, were aliens in spirit and character; utterly far from being children of Abraham in the sense of bearing his image and inheriting his virtues.——Ye

---

* He says they are "σπερμα," but not "τεκνα."

seek to kill me because I tell you the truth which I have heard from God. Abraham never did any thing like this—never could have done it. Abraham was eminently "the friend of God" (2 Chron. 20: 7, and Isa. 41: 8, and James 2: 23) obedient to every command, of unshaken faith in every promise. In every point they were totally unlike Abraham—children of another father; men of entirely opposite character.

Of course these words cut into their pride and self-conceit with unsparing faithfulness.

41. Ye do the deeds of your father. Then said they to him, We be not born of fornication; we have one Father, *even* God.

42. Jesus said unto them, If God were your Father, ye would love me: for I proceeded forth and came from God; neither came I of myself, but he sent me.

43. Why do ye not understand my speech? *even* because ye can not hear my word.

44. Ye are of *your* father the devil, and the lusts of your father ye will do: he was a murderer from the beginning, and abode not in the truth, because there is no truth in him. When he speaketh a lie, he speaketh of his own: for he is a liar, and the father of it.

45. And because I tell *you* the truth, ye believe me not.

To men making so much account as these Jews did of parentage, it was both pertinent and forcible to speak of them as children of him whose spirit they inherited and whose deeds they were reproducing. So Jesus said, "Ye do the deeds of your father," showing whose children ye are by the sort of deeds ye are doing. Sharply resenting this remark they declared themselves born in honest matrimony, and said they had but one Father, viz, God. But here they were persecuting with mortal hatred God's only and well-beloved Son—proof enough that they had no ground whatever for assuming themselves to be children of God. If God were your Father and ye were his dutiful, loving children, ye would love me—not hate me without cause and with spirit so malignant.

In v. 43 the exact thought seems to be—Why do ye not understand my plain words? Because ye can not hear—in the sense of can not *bear* my doctrine—the substance of the truth I teach.

As those malicious Jews with murder in their heart had boldly declared that their one Father was God, Jesus responded with like plainness of speech:—"Ye are of your father the devil, and the lusts of your father ye will to do"—do with the will—the real choice and purpose of your souls. From the beginning of the race—from the age of Eve and of Cain,—he was a murderer, and *stood* not in the truth; his moral status was never there but always in the moral opposite of truth—in lies. There was never any truth in him—no love for truth—no speaking of truth. Speaking lies is but uttering his own heart, for he is a liar and the father of it—the lie. Pregnant with falsehood, he naturally brings forth lies; they are his legitimate offspring. In this sense he is "the father of lies."——Those Jews claimed to be children of Abraham in the sense of inheriting his virtues. Precisely in this sense Jesus declared that they were children of the devil, for they inherited his spirit of falsehood and lies. It was because they had no natural sympathy with truth that they could not and would not believe Jesus and his truthful words.

46. Which of you convinceth me of sin? And if I say the truth, why do ye not believe me?

47. He that is of God heareth God's words: ye therefore hear *them* not, because ye are not of God.

They had held Jesus guilty, but without convicting him of any crime or falsehood whatever. They had simply *assumed* him guilty without proof; and this because they hated his just rebukes of their sin.——If I say the truth (and ye can not deny that I do), why do ye not believe me?——He proceeds to answer his own question:—The words I bring to you are words of God. If ye were of God, his children, in sympathy with his Spirit, ye would hear and receive these words. This explains your conduct. Ye hear not my words because ye are not in harmony with God— with his Spirit and his truth.

48. Then answered the Jews, and said unto him, Say we not well that thou art a Samaritan, and hast a devil?

Irked and stung by such truth-telling, heart-revealing words, they turn again upon him to taunt him with being a Samaritan—one of the most odious epithets they could think of—one which the Jews customarily applied to outcasts from their people. Perhaps they had some allusion to the fact that Jesus had associated with Samaritans and made converts from among them.——They also seek to vilify him and break the force of every thing he had said, by the charge—(made before; John 7: 20): "Thou hast a devil." The same thing appears again (John 10: 20): "Many of them said—He hath a devil and is mad; why hear ye him?" He is only a maniac, insane; probably they meant to imply—not morally responsible for the incoherent, irrational words he utters. At least, they meant—a man whose words were of not the least account, being void of sense and truthfulness.——As above (7: 20) the word here used for "devil" is not diabolos but daimonion— demon; the current doctrine of the age being that these demons entered into the human body, and displacing the rational mind, took possession—speaking through human lips and controlling all the activities of the man. This charge, therefore, so far as it was believed, broke the moral force of every word Jesus might utter.——Their question as put here—" Say we not well that thou hast a devil?" not only suggests that they had said this before, but assumes with unblushing boldness that they had said this "*well*"—with good reason; on valid grounds. How could the cool impudence and the moral hardihood of the basest depravity go farther?

49. Jesus answered, I have not a devil; but I honor my Father, and ye do dishonor me.

50. And I seek not mine own glory: there is one that seeketh and judgeth.

The charge of being a Samaritan Jesus passes unnoticed; the other charge—that of being possessed with a devil—he meets with a square denial. It was too vital in its bearings, not to be repelled.——In his next words Jesus seems to fall back upon the convictions of his deepest consciousness;—I *know* that I honor my Father; I *know* that the words I have spoken and the deeds I have done have sprung from supreme devotion to his service and glory. They might blind their eyes to the evidence of this; the fact lived in his own deep consciousness—his consolation under the keenest reproaches; his joy under the bitterest failures.—— I honor my Father; but ye give me only *dishonor*, scorn, shame. The thought seems to be suggested by the contrast.——I say not this because I selfishly aspire after personal glory: It is not because it smites down some idol in my heart that I shrink from the scorn ye heap on me. It is enough for me that my Father smiles his approbation. This is what he intimates—"There *is* One that seeketh" my glory and "judgeth" between me and my vilifiers. I can well afford to await his judgment.

51. Verily, verily, I say unto you, If a man keep my saying, he shall never see death.

In the discourses of our Lord the words—"Verily, verily,"—always imply an advance to some new point of special importance.——If we look inquiringly for the law of mental association which suggested this announcement, may we not find it in this line of thought:—Ye repel my words with scorn and baffle my utmost endeavors to lead you into truth and back to God. I look with unutterable sorrow upon the ruin of eternal death which lies but one step before you: therefore let me say solemnly and tenderly, one word more:—If any man of you all shall keep my saying—accept my doctrine with loving heart and abide therein— "he shall never see death." Such a connection of thought does justice to the love of his heart for the vilest; to his compassion over the men who were soon to become his murderers. O, how gladly would he have plucked even one soul from among them out of the open jaws of death!

52. Then said the Jews unto him, Now we know that thou hast a devil. Abraham is dead, and the prophets; and thou

sayest, If a man keep my saying, he shall never taste of death.

53. Art thou greater than our father Abraham, which is dead? and the prophets are dead: whom makest thou thyself?

More unwilling than unable to take in the high, spiritual sense of these words of Jesus, they seem glad to find in them another proof (as they would pretend) of his insanity—an impostor holding forth that whoever would keep his saying should never die! "What!" they would say; Dost thou pretend to be greater than our father Abraham, who yet—good man as he was—had to die; and all the prophets met death in their time; whom dost thou pretend to be?

54. Jesus answered, If I honor myself, my honor is nothing: it is my Father that honoreth me; of whom ye say, that he is your God:

55. Yet ye have not known him; but I know him: and if I should say, I know him not, I shall be a liar like unto you; but I know him, and keep his saying.

If my words were those of high, fulsome, vain pretension, they should justly go for nothing. It is my Father—not myself—that honors me. Of him ye say, he is your God. (Would there were truth in your claim—but there is not!) Ye have not known the true God in any right sense at all. But I know him; this I must maintain as the cardinal point in my testimony before the world. I know God; he is my Father; he sent me from heaven; I come to bring his words of truth and mercy to perishing men. If I should say with you that I know him not, then I should belie my own deepest convictions, and should be a liar like yourselves.——Thus Jesus puts the great issue between himself and these hostile, maligning Jews.

56. Your father Abraham rejoiced to see my day: and he saw *it*, and was glad.

Your father Abraham, all unlike yourselves, appreciated my work; leaped for joy that he might "see my day"—not my *person*, which would have been a yet more glorious vision—but my "day;" its general outline, purpose, work and results. The knowledge of your nation's Messiah which ye despise, he longed to attain, though he could hope for it only in an inferior measure. He did attain that and rejoiced therein with great joy. So much for the application of this case of Abraham to rebuke at once their contempt of him and their self-conceited assumption of being the children of Abraham.

What is said here of Abraham's vision of Christ, seems to imply two distinct stages: first, he was exhilarated with the hope

or prospect of seeing it; next, his hopes were realized in at least some good measure: he saw and exulted with joy.——Were these in fact two distinct stages of revelation to him—the former less full and the latter more: or was the former only the traditional views of the far-future Deliverer which came down from the first promise made to Adam—somewhat dimly hinted also to Noah?
——This is at least supposable, and, if accepted, would seem to show how good men in those times were animated with bright hopes of a day far better than the world of their age had seen.

Still another supposition has found some favor, viz: that the second stage of his vision—"he saw and was glad"—was not of that prophetic sort which came of old to saints yet in the flesh; but of that higher sort which saints receive in glory—such knowledge as Moses and Elijah may have rejoiced in before they met Jesus on the mount of transfiguration, and which may have suggested themes for that wonderful conversation.——In choosing between these two theories, it should be considered that Abraham actually had successive prophetic visions, and certainly visions very much in advance of what had come down to him by tradition from the fathers, so that there is no violence to known facts in the supposition that the "seeing" and "gladness" pertained to his latest visions in the flesh.——Further, the supposition of a reference to knowledge reached after death should not be accepted without some real demand for it, inasmuch as the scriptures are not wont to give intimations on this subject.

57. Then said the Jews unto him, Thou art not yet fifty years old, and hast thou seen Abraham?

How camest thou to know so much about Abraham? Surely thou hast never seen him.——The reason why they named fifty years, is supposed to be that this was an average limit to human life. May it not have been suggested by his apparent age: judging from your appearance you must be short of fifty.——The prophet Isaiah said of him, "His visage was so marred more than any man, and his form than the sons of men" (Isa. 52: 14); and his disciples were reminded on one occasion of the *consuming* zeal of their Master for which they found expression in words of scripture—"The zeal of thine house hath eaten me up" (John 2: 17); so that possibly he had the appearance of more years than he had actually seen.

58. Jesus said unto them, Verily, verily, I say unto you, Before Abraham was, I am.

No fair construction of these words can make them mean less than this: *I existed before Abraham was born.* My life is not to be limited within fifty human years. Ye have no just views of my person while ye restrict my existence within this limitation. Long before Abraham was born my divine person was " with God "—the real "*I am,*" eternally self-existent. This must be the sense of these words of Jesus. Those who accept the doctrine of the Logos as taught in John 1: 1–14, can have no difficulty with this statement.

59. *Then took they up stones to cast at him: but Jesus hid himself, and went out of the temple, going through the midst of them, and so passed by.*

This last declaration brought the conversation to its crisis. His adversaries, in a frenzy of excitement, began to gather stones to hurl upon him. Jesus suddenly withdrew—and so this scene closed.

The thoughtful reader of this chapter must be impressed with the hopeless moral hardihood of these captious Jews. The efforts of Jesus to convict their consciences of sin, to lead them into truth, and to bring them to a docile, honest faith in himself, were utterly powerless as toward these results. Every fresh point in his progressive argument only maddened them the more. When they reached the point where they could say, "Thou hast a devil," there must have been, it would seem, an end of hope in their case.——We have no further occasion to wonder that they rushed madly on to plot and to take his life; or that the nation, following such religious leaders, waxed more and more corrupt, infatuated and desperate in guilt, till the judgments of heaven fell on their city and nation, and "there was no remedy."

CHAPTER IX.

This chapter has unity, presenting one event and one only—the healing of a man born blind, with the discussion which it occasioned.

1. *And as Jesus passed by, he saw a man which was blind from his birth.*
2. *And his disciples asked him, saying, Master, who did sin, this man or his parents, that he was born blind?*
3. *Jesus answered, Neither hath this man sinned, nor his parents: but that the works of God should be made manifest in him.*

That this entire scene occurred on a Sabbath is shown in v. 14; but whether on the same day with the discussion recorded 3: 12–59 is in dispute among commentators; some holding it to have been on the same day; others, on the Sabbath next succeeding.——Accustomed to sit near the temple to beg his living, this man probably pled the fact of having been born blind. This raised the question among the disciples *whose* sin was punished in this case of congenital blindness.* Was it the sin of the man himself, or the sin of his parents? They assumed it must be *somebody's* sin. How could it be for *his* sin before he was born: and how could it be just to punish him for the sin of his parents? Here was a hard problem. They bring it to their Master. He answers—Neither of your alternatives meets the case. This blindness was permitted of God for the purpose of manifesting his works to men.

4. I must work the works of him that sent me, while it is day: the night cometh, when no man can work.

5. As long as I am in the world, I am the light of the world.

Manifestly Jesus thinks of such *works* as he spake of in John 5: 17: "My Father *worketh* hitherto, and I work." He is sent into this world to do such works of mercy as those done by the Father. Now another occasion occurring, he must improve it. ——"While it is day"—the time for work. He saw that his night drew near—a night of no more *work* here and now, of this sort.——"I am the light of the world"—said with his thought upon the opening of sightless eyes—first in the physical sense; then in the far higher spiritual sense in which he unseals eyes blinded by life-long sin.

6. When he had thus spoken, he spat on the ground, and made clay of the spittle, and he anointed the eyes of the blind man with the clay,

7. And said unto him, Go, wash in the pool of Siloam, (which is by interpretation, Sent.) He went his way, therefore, and washed, and came seeing.

In this miracle, the things required of the blind man to do can not be supposed to have had the least natural influence. Neither the saliva, the clay, or the washing, could have had any agency or virtue in giving vision to eyes that had never seen. The obedience and the faith which it implied were no doubt conditions in the spiritual realm, without which Jesus would not have wrought the miracle.——We may notice in the miracles wrought by Jesus a wide range of diversity in the method of operation—the manner and the circumstances; and the antecedent conditions. All the reasons for this diversity we may not be sure of discerning; some of them we can probably understand. One stereotyped method

---

* The precise import of their question is—Who did sin, this man or his parents, that, as a punishment, he *must needs be* born blind? They assumed it to be a necessity under the moral connection between sin and suffering.

would have greatly lessened their moral power as miracles. Diversity augments their moral force. It goes strongly against any supposition of collusion or deception. Moreover, Jesus seems in most cases to have had an eye to a good moral impression upon the subject of the miracle or his friends.

The pool of Siloam was in the south-east part of the city—a beautiful fountain of pure and sweet water. The word Siloam came from a Hebrew root, having the meaning, "sent." No other reason appears for this allusion to the meaning of the name except the coincidence between this command and this significance.——The blind beggar obeyed promptly and came back seeing.

8. The neighbors therefore, and they which before had seen him that he was blind, said, Is not this he that sat and begged?

9. Some said, This is he: others *said*, He is like him: *but* he said, I am *he*.

10. Therefore said they unto him, How were thine eyes opened?

11. He answered and said, A man that is called Jesus made clay and anointed mine eyes, and said unto me, Go to the pool of Siloam, and wash: and I went and washed, and I received sight.

12. Then said they unto him, Where is he? He said, I know not.

This story tells with great simplicity the surprise, the inquiries, and the circumstances of the case as developed among the neighbors and those who had known him from birth. It appears that Jesus performed this miracle with no pains to make himself known, and then disappeared; so that when this blind man came back with seeing eyes, Jesus had gone, he knew not whither.

13. They brought to the Pharisees him that aforetime was blind.

14. And it was the sabbath day when Jesus made the clay, and opened his eyes.

15. Then again the Pharisees also asked him how he had received his sight. He said unto them, He put clay upon mine eyes, and I washed, and do see.

16. Therefore said some of the Pharisees, This man is not of God, because he keepeth not the sabbath day. Others said, How can a man that is a sinner do such miracles. And there was a division among them.

They bring the restored man and his case before the Pharisees. An important fact in the case comes to light here;—It was *done* on *the Sabbath*. Jesus could not have forgotten the fierce persecution he had suffered once before for performing a similar miracle on the Sabbath (John 5), yet he seems to have taken no pains to avoid exciting like prejudice and persecution again. He was right in performing works of mercy and power on the Sabbath, and he purposed to maintain his position, with no parade and no needless provocation, yet with firmness and decision.——The Pharisees examine the man, demanding and receiving his straight-forward account of his restoration to sight. Some of them at once prejudged Jesus: he could not be a man of God because he did not keep the Sabbath—*according to their notions*. And they were entirely too bigoted to allow the thought that possibly their notions of Sabbath-keeping were not of God. Some among them said very sensibly—"How can a man that is a sinner draw upon the Almighty for power to work such a miracle?" "If I regard iniquity in my heart, the Lord will not hear me"—makes an appeal to the good sense of men which no candid mind can resist.

17. They say unto the blind man again, What sayest thou of him, that he hath opened thine eyes? He said, He is a prophet.

Very appropriately they ask him of restored sight what he thinks of the man who gave him eyes to see. His good sense answered promptly—"He is a prophet." He remembered that his Old Testament scriptures spake of miracles somewhat like this, done by the Lord's ancient prophets.——This man appears throughout the narrative to have had excellent good sense, and withal firmness and independence of character, worthy of high commendation. He has a much better record than the man healed at the pool of Bethesda on that other Sabbath.

18. But the Jews did not believe concerning him, that he had been blind, and received his sight, until they called the parents of him that had received his sight.

19. And they asked them, saying, Is this your son, who ye say was born blind? How then doth he now see?

20. His parents answered them and said, We know that this is our son, and that he was born blind:

21. But by what means he now seeth, we know not; or who hath opened his eyes, we know not: he is of age; ask him: he shall speak for himself.

22. These *words* spake his parents, because they feared the Jews: for the Jews had agreed already, that if any man did confess that he was Christ, he should be put out of the synagogue.

23. Therefore said his parents, He is of age; ask him.

We can have no great respect for incredulity so unreasonable and so manifestly begotten of prejudice and hate; yet in this case it powerfully subserved the interests of truth. They happened to live just when stubborn skepticism, no matter how wicked, unreasonable and gratuitous, would yet turn to most excellent account for all future time. The skeptics of all after ages might afford to thank these unbelieving Jews for sifting the evidence of this miracle and rejecting every thing short of moral demonstration.—— They must have the identity of this man proved by the testimony of the father who begat him and of the mother who bare him. Very well. We may be glad they demanded this testimony—and got it. They did not like to be satisfied with even this testimony; but really they could doubt that point no longer.——The parents were timidly afraid of losing caste with the Jewish authorities, and seem not to have been much affected with gratitude to the stranger for the great blessing he had brought to their son.

24. Then again called they the man that was blind, and said unto him, Give God the praise: we know that this man is a sinner.

"Give God the praise," coming from their lips, meant—Do *not* give the praise to this man who is a sinner. We know this man to be a sinner because, according to our notions of the day, he breaks the Sabbath. Of course they know that their notions are right. Men supremely bigoted always know this. *How* this wicked man could work such a miracle, they perhaps tried to think was no concern of theirs. It seemed a very religious way to dispose of this case, to tell the restored man to give the praise to God.——A slightly different view of their meaning in the words—"Give glory to God," is at least supposable, viz. that they used them as Joshua used similar words to Achan (Josh. 7: 19); Honor the Omniscient God by confessing your sin; telling the whole truth; acknowledging that such a sinner as Jesus never could have wrought this miracle as you say.——This construction supposes them to have been supremely bigoted and overbearing— as they actually were.

25. He answered and said, Whether he be a sinner *or no*, I know not: one thing I know, that, whereas I was blind, now I see.

This restored man knows nothing of the antecedents of his benefactor; does not at this stage of the discussion claim to be profound (as they claim to be) in his philosophy as to the miracle-working power of a sinner; and does not feel called upon (just now) to advance any opinion on that point. But as to the fact of having been honestly blind all his previous life and of now seeing, he is ready to testify. So much he *knows*, and no browbeating shall stop his mouth to the effect of shutting off this testimony.——All the world (unless those bigoted Jews be an exception) have admired his grit, his honest love of truth, and his fearlessness in maintaining it.

26. Then said they to him again, What did he to thee? how opened he thine eyes?

27. He answered them, I have told you already, and ye did not hear: wherefore would ye hear *it* again? will ye also be his disciples?

28. Then they reviled him, and said, Thou art his disciple; but we are Moses' disciples.

29. We know that God spake unto Moses: *as for this fellow, we know not from whence he is.*

Oh, if they could only find some flaw in this testimony—if they could only get over this great solid fact, looking them so calmly, yet uncomfortably in the face! Is there not some way to explain it without admitting miraculous power? This pinch has troubled many thousand skeptics from that day to this. It is a comfort to all honest, truth-loving souls to see that the battle with skepticism as to the facts of the case was fought out bravely while the scenes were all yet fresh, the original witnesses living, and fortunately, the very parties in the fight.——It is not perhaps strange that this honest-hearted man who had told the story over quite a good many times—in the same way, to the same purport every time—should have his patience a little tried by the strain brought upon it. Perhaps it seemed to him to reflect somewhat upon his veracity. I have told you all about it once and again, and ye did not hear; ye seem not to accept and believe what I said: why should ye wish to hear it over again? Do ye think of becoming his disciples?——This last word was perhaps a little sharp. They felt insulted, and retorted with reviling.——It is perhaps supposable that the question—Do ye wish to become his disciples? was put in good faith, in this sense:—Are ye pushing these inquiries in the spirit of an honest regard for truth, prepared, if ye find the evidence satisfactory, to admit his mission from God, and place yourselves at his feet as disciples? If so, his position was noble; his regard for truth, sublime.——Their claim to be disciples of Moses had an eye to their sanctimonious regard for the Sabbath-law which came to them through Moses. Moses was a good man; they know that. It can not be wrong, they think, to stand up for Moses and his Sabbath-law; but as for this man, they can not speak of him with too much scorn. They neither know or wish to know any thing of him.

30. The man answered and said unto them, Why herein is a marvelous thing, that ye know not from whence he is, and *yet* he hath opened mine eyes.

31. Now we know that God heareth not sinners: but if any man be a worshiper of God, and doeth his will, him he heareth.

32. Since the world began was it not heard that any man opened the eyes of one that was born blind.

33. If this man were not of God, he could do nothing.

The restored man waxes bold, and plies the logic of his strong common sense vigorously. What shall be thought of it, for * here is a strange fact—that ye should not know whence this man is, and yet he hath opened my eyes! How happens it that ye should know nothing of a man possessed of such powers. This ignorance is not much to your credit. But look ye into the nature of this case. It is entirely certain that God does not hear the prayer of sinners; but if one be a worshiper of God and a doer of his will, God will hear his prayer, and may help him work a miracle. The man who gave me eyes *must have had* help from God. There is no weak spot in this reasoning. No mere man, unaided of God, has ever since the world began, opened eyes born sightless. If this man were not of God, he would be utterly powerless for such a miracle.

34. They answered and said unto him, Thou wast altogether born in sins, and dost thou teach us? And they cast him out.

Bigotry had swamped their common sense—not to say also common honesty. Having never a word to answer to this logic or to the facts and principles that were underlying it, they throw it in this man's face that his eyeless birth proved him a worthless sinner, not fit to be regarded by such holy men as themselves. They put themselves upon their dignity as not to be taught by such a sinner—and cast him out of the synagogue!——Did they feel easier in conscience after this? Such men make but the least possible account of conscience. It was perhaps a momentary relief to get out of their way a man whose testimony to facts was so very annoying, and whose honest reasoning upon those facts it was so impossible for them to meet.

35. Jesus heard that they had cast him out; and when he had found him, he said unto him, Dost thou believe on the Son of God?

36. He answered and said, Who is he, Lord, that I might believe on him?

37. And Jesus said unto him, Thou hast both seen him, and it is he that talketh with thee.

---

* Greek writers sometimes begin a sentence with γαρ (for), leaving some brief expression to be supplied, as here; What shall I make of this—*for* it is indeed wonderful that *ye*—such men as ye are—who ought to know all the eminently great and good men of your time should not know a man so good and so great as to be able to open eyes that never saw before!

38. And he said, Lord, I believe. And he worshiped him.

A charming sequel. The man who had borne himself so nobly need not be cast down in spirit—for Jesus is near and will give him his own sympathy. A mind so honest, a spirit so brave for the truth and so candid, is not far from the kingdom of God. Jesus soon found him—found him ready to inquire—"Who is the Son of God that I may believe on him?" and to say—"Lord, I believe."——We hear of this man no more.

39. And Jesus said, For judgment I am come into this world, that they which see not might see; and that they which see might be made blind.

The case suggested to Jesus this comprehensive remark as to the moral results of his mission to this world—that the not-seeing (like this man blind from birth) might have sight restored: and that men, blessed with all needful vision but abusing their blessings, should be judicially blinded. Naturally the blind man's case became suggestive of what takes place in the moral realm of human hearts and consciences under the light of revealed truth:—one class—long sitting in moral darkness—brought forth into light: another class, favored above others with the light-bearing word of God, yet resisting its demands, and blinding their eyes to its pure teachings, are doomed in judgment to the blindness they have cherished, and are given over to their own chosen infatuation. The world is full of cases illustrating this contrast. For such judgment has Jesus come into this world; such are every-where the fruits of his coming.

40. And *some* of the Pharisees which were with him heard these words, and said unto him, Are we blind also?

41. Jesus said unto them, If ye were blind, ye should have no sin: but now ye say, We see; therefore your sin remaineth.

Some of the Pharisees, hearing this remark, said—Dost thou mean that for us? Wouldest thou insult us by the insinuation that we are blind?—Jesus answers: If ye were really blind, having no knowledge of God and duty, ye would have no sin: but now that ye say, We see;—now that in fact ye have had ample means of moral light, and might have been wise unto salvation, your sin *abides*—is upon you and is to be, forever! "Ye knew your duty, but ye did it not." No other form of sin is so surely damning! What can save those men whom all the light and truth of God fail to save, and serve only to heighten and aggravate their guilt?

CHAPTER X.

This chapter is closely related in *thought* and in *time* to the two preceding. It seems to have been suggested by the case of the Pharisees—then the recognized spiritual leaders of the covenant people, but altogether apostate from God—blind leaders of blind men. To the fold of God's people they were as thieves and robbers who get in by scaling the walls, "climbing up some other way." They did not enter legitimately through the door.
——This line of thought led Jesus to speak of himself as the *door* of the sheep-fold—a figure which to a considerable extent obtains through vs. 1–10. The conception of Jesus as also "the *Shepherd*" appears in vs. 2–5, but especially in vs. 11–18, and 26–30. The resulting division of sentiment among his hearers comes to view (vs. 19–21). This discussion seems to have been resumed at the subsequent feast of dedication (v. 22 and onward). In this discussion the words of Jesus—"I and the Father are one" —revived the charge of blasphemy, under which they again attempt to stone him. Jesus defends his declaration—I am the Son of God—from the Old Testament scriptures (vs. 34–36), and appeals again to his miracles (vs. 37, 38); escapes a violent arrest, and repairs to the locality where John at first baptized (vs. 39–42).

1. Verily, verily, I say unto you, He that entereth not by the door into the sheep-fold, but climbeth up some other way, the same is a thief and a robber.
2. But he that entereth in by the door is the shepherd of the sheep.

In studying the figurative imagery with which this chapter opens; the *door* of the sheep-fold; the porter; the shepherd; the thieves and robbers;—it is wise to seek in a docile spirit for the real meaning of Christ's words, and to guard ourselves against being hypercritical in demanding congruity of figure throughout. What if the figurative conception should change— first presenting Jesus as the *door;* and afterward as the "Shepherd"? The sense is still clear. In some aspects he is the door; in others, the shepherd.

A sheep-fold is an inclosure, with walls and a door. The owner is supposed to employ and control the porter, and also, the shepherd; or perhaps, as in the application of the figure here, he may fill all these offices himself. He is lord of the fold and of the flock; and of course has command of the door of entrance.——"Thieves and robbers" scale the walls; get in as they can, "some other way." By this they may be known. Of course they have no rights there; and none but bad intentions.

3. To him the porter openeth; and the sheep hear his

voice: and he calleth his own sheep by name, and leadeth them out.

4. And when he putteth forth his own sheep, he goeth before them, and the sheep follow him: for they know his voice.

5. And a stranger will they not follow, but will flee from him; for they know not the voice of strangers.

6. This parable spake Jesus unto them; but they understood not what things they were which he spake unto them.

The porter opens the door to the real shepherd; the sheep hear his call, recognize his voice. "He calleth them *by name*"—a remarkable fact in Oriental husbandry, that in a flock of hundreds or thousands, each individual sheep has its name; knows it, and is known by it. So Christ's sheep are never so numerous that he will not know each one's individual name—each one's peculiarities, personal character, talents, fitnesses, weak and temptible points, exposures and demands for his sympathy and care. A positive personal communion of mind, thought, sympathy, and love, is constantly active between Jesus the Shepherd and every one of his sheep. They severally know him; he personally knows each one of them. He can call each one by name, and lead him out from the fold into the pasture grounds that will best meet his wants.

"When he putteth forth all his own" (so the most approved text reads), "he goeth before them, and the sheep follow him; for they know his voice"—the usages of shepherd life being in every point applicable most beautifully to the spiritual nurture and care of his people as exercised by Jesus their Shepherd. As sheep will not follow a stranger whose voice is unfamiliar, the people of Christ may learn to know the voice of their good Shepherd, so as, with quick and sure perception, to detect every strange voice and refuse to follow it. How well for them to make and maintain this definite personal acquaintance with Christ, so that they surely know his from every misleading voice!——These words of Jesus give us the true theory of the Christian life. Let it be ours to reduce this theory into our living and undeviating practice.——This "parable,"—not precisely in the same sense as this English word has in the other evangelists—nor is John's Greek word the same as theirs. John's word means only in general a figurative illustration—as may be seen also in 16: 25, 29. V. 6 raises the question—*To whom* was this parable spoken? *Who* did not understand it? Is this said of his own people, or of the Jews? Probably the latter, as we might infer from v. 19, and as might be inferred also from its having been apparently suggested (as above said) by the case of the apostate Pharisees, breaking into God's fold and acting the thief and the robber. It is not specially strange that they did not readily understand an illustration which bore with just severity against themselves and cut so deep into their self-conceit.

7. Then said Jesus unto them again, Verily, verily, I say unto you, I am the door of the sheep.

8. All that ever came before me are thieves and robbers; but the sheep did not hear them.

As they did not take his meaning readily, he proceeds to speak yet more plainly. Commencing with his emphatic "Verily, verily," he declares, "I am the door of the sheep." I own this fold; I keep the door and have the care of this flock. "All that ever came before me"—*e. g.* Satan scaling the walls of the garden of Eden; and all his servants from that time to this—are thieves and robbers.——There is no need to press these words, "All that ever came before me," so as to include the patriarchs and prophets—Abraham, Moses, David, Isaiah—whom God certainly used as his own shepherds in their time and sphere. His thought is not upon them, but first (it would seem) upon Satan himself, and thence onward upon all his instruments and helpers. ——"The sheep did not hear them" states the general fact; or, as hinted above, the *theory* of the Christian life, under which Christ's people are to know and follow his voice, and neither know nor follow the voice of strangers.

9. I am the door: by me if any man enter in, he shall be saved, and shall go in and out, and find pasture.

10. The thief cometh not, but for to steal, and to kill, and to destroy: I am come that they might have life, and that they might have *it* more abundantly.

The striking, not to say interesting thing in these verses, is the facility with which the speaker passes from figurative to literal terms. Here is a sheep-fold with its "door." The door is Jesus himself. It is a "man" who enters in through this door; and so entering, he is "*saved*" as the souls of men are saved; yet the figure returns again. He "goes in and out" of this sheep-fold as sheep are wont to do, night and morning, and he "finds *pasture*"—such grass as is good for sheep. But no reader need miss the sentiment—at once beautiful and forcible—the Christian soul lives on Christ; is fed and guarded, kept and made peaceful, safe and quiet as the trustful lambs under the faithful care of their kind shepherd.——All unlike the good shepherd and the faithful door-keeper comes the thief into the fold, with no object but to steal, kill, and destroy; reckless of the shepherd's rights of property—reckless of the comfort and even of the life of the sheep.——What is he but an *enemy*—a destroyer!——The case suggests how sorely Jesus must have been tried, grieved and fired with indignation against the Pharisees who had climbed into his sheep-fold only to steal and to kill, murdering human souls instead of leading them into paths of life!——Jesus puts his own purpose and work in the sharpest contrast with theirs: "I am come that they may have life" and may live well—with a life at once healthful, vigorous, enduring and full of joy. How expressive are these blessed words! How full of truth is the spiritual reality which they represent!

11. I am the good shepherd: the good shepherd giveth his life for the sheep.

12. But he that is a hireling, and not the shepherd, whose own the sheep are not, seeth the wolf coming, and leaveth the sheep, and fleeth; and the wolf catcheth them, and scattereth the sheep.

13. The hireling fleeth, because he is a hireling, and careth not for the sheep.

These exquisitely precious words—"I am the good shepherd"—lead our thought first to the admirable fitness of the figure, considered as originating in Oriental lands, based on the charming relations as there seen of the shepherd to his flock, in which we have care and sympathy on the one side, met with never faltering trust and never flagging obedience on the other—begetting fellowship and companionship never to be intermitted by day or by night, in summer or in winter, in sunshine or in storm—the relations of want and supply reaching to food and to shelter, to help in weakness, to succor in trouble, to protection against enemies—indeed to every possible aid which interest can prompt or affection demand. The people of Christ have found comfort and quickening in this similitude—Christ the good shepherd, and themselves the sheep of his fold—ever since David embalmed his Christian experience in his sweet twenty-third psalm: "The Lord is my shepherd; I shall not want."

But further: these words of Jesus should carry us back to those prophetic scriptures which had put the Messiah in contrast with the false and vile shepherds who had assumed to control the flock of God, but, in fact, only to make it waste and desolate. Such contrast is rather implied than distinctly expressed in Isa. 40: 11: "He shall feed his flock like a shepherd; he shall gather the lambs with his arm and carry them in his bosom, and shall gently lead those that are with young." The description is beautiful; the tenderness and sympathy inimitably fine, and to all suffering Christian souls, full of hope and consolation.——In Ezek. 34, we have no lack of strong points of contrast, such as give force to the words—"I am *the* good shepherd"—the well known shepherd of your prophetic scriptures whose mission was specially promised; whose work was put in sharp contrast even there with the evil shepherds who served none but themselves, and only cursed the flock.——"Son of man, prophesy against the shepherds of Israel; Woe be to the shepherds of Israel that do feed themselves! Ye eat the fat and ye clothe you with the wool; ye kill them that are fed; but ye feed not the flock." Therefore God arises in majesty for the relief of his flock and for retribution on their destroyers, saying: "Therefore will I save my flock, and they shall no more be a prey. . . And I will set up one shepherd over them, and he shall feed them, even my servant David: he shall feed them, and he shall be their shepherd; and I the Lord will be their God, and my servant David a prince among them; I the Lord have spoken it" (Ezek. 34: 2, 3, 22–24).——Zech. 11 also develops in very graphic style the relations of Jesus as the good shepherd to those who during his earthly life were acting the part of thieves and robbers to his fold.

Over against the good shepherd, we have here another character—at least one put under another figure. Thus far in the discourse, the enemy is a thief and a robber, breaking into the fold over its inclosing walls; but the new character is an "hireling," and not the shepherd. He neither owns, loves, nor cares for the sheep. He cares only for his wages. Seeing the wolf coming, he does not face the foe and fight, to save his flock, but runs. The wolf catches some, and scatters the rest. Nothing less than a heart-felt interest in the flock will make the shepherd brave in peril, and if need be self-sacrificing for their good. The good shepherd puts himself in strong contrast with the hireling; and more than suggests that his under-shepherds should be like himself—true and even fearlessly brave to protect the sheep.

14. I am the good shepherd, and know my *sheep*, and am known of mine.

15. As the Father knoweth me, even so know I the Father: and I lay down my life for the sheep.

At the point where the contrast would seem to require "I *care for* my sheep," we have instead, the word "*know*"—"I know mine and mine know me" (the best manuscripts have it). But the word "know" came ultimately and very pertinently up to the full idea which the contrast leads us to expect here. For, intimate personal acquaintance begets sympathy and love, so that the Hebrews were wont to use the verb *know* in the sense of loving, *caring for*. Jesus knows every believing, trustful soul—knows each one perfectly; never fails to note and feel every sorrow, every want, every outgoing toward himself of love, gratitude, trust;—and this all-embracing knowledge begets love and watchful care.——"They know me" also—*know* in a like full, minute, comprehensive sense—a sense which begets love and trust.——Moreover, let it be noted that v. 15 stands in very close connection with v. 14—closer in the Greek than in our English—of this sort: "I know mine and mine know me, even as the Father knows me and I know the Father." The analogy between Jesus and his people on the one hand and between Jesus and his Father on the other is the point made here, expressed in both cases by the comprehensive word *know*—this word involving not merely knowledge, acquaintance; but the love, the sympathy and mutual interest which intimate acquaintance is wont to beget.

16. And other sheep I have, which are not of this fold: them also I must bring, and they shall hear my voice; and there shall be one fold, *and* one shepherd.

The "other sheep not of this fold" are without doubt Gentiles. "Not of this fold" because the "fold" thus far since Abraham had included only the covenant people. If any Gentiles were brought in, they came as proselytes and were reckoned as of the same fold. But the time is near for a new order of things. Others in great numbers are to be brought into the fold of Jesus, hearing his voice and obeying his call. So shall there be one *flock* (more true to the Greek than "fold"), for the idea of inclosure is slightly modified. The church is thenceforward rather a flock than a fold.

17. Therefore doth my Father love me, because I lay down my life, that I might take it again.

18. No man taketh it from me, but I lay it down of myself. I have power to lay it down, and I have power to take it again. This commandment have I received of my Father.

Twice already in this discourse had Jesus spoken of laying down his life for his sheep (vs. 11, 15). Here he resumes this thought to say yet more concerning it.——Two points deserve special notice:—(*a.*) That the Father approves the sacrifice even to death of his Son. He loves his Son because he is free-hearted to make this sacrifice. We may infer from this that the Father is perfectly in sympathy with the scheme of atonement in which the death of Christ was the great central fact. He had "so loved the world as to give up his only begotten Son" to meet this death. In his view the prize to be won was worth this cost.——(*b.*) Jesus was to lay down his life—not as a failure in his enterprise; not as a warrior falls in battle, the cause of his country falling with him; but—unlike any human analogy—was to lay down his life with his own consent and with power to take it again. The death of Jesus contemplated a glorious resurrection—a rising to a higher life and to a mightier power.——"This commandment have I received of my Father"—in the sense that this was in the plan or scheme. Jesus was to lay down his life, but also to take it again—soon, gloriously—to reach thereby the sublime results of salvation to a lost world and of infinite honor and glory to God.

19. There was a division therefore again among the Jews for these sayings.

20. And many of them said, He hath a devil and is mad; why hear ye him?

21. Others said, These are not the words of him that hath a devil. Can a devil open the eyes of the blind?

As usual, the words of Jesus stir the Jewish mind profoundly, but affect various men variously. Some, here as elsewhere—now as before—say: "He hath a demon and is mad"—language which shows that in their view some forms of demoniacal possession produced insanity—yet whether in his case they supposed it of such sort as to vacate personal responsibility does not appear with certainty. Their inference in this case was that a man so possessed could say nothing of value; was not fit to be heard. How far this was an honest conviction, or on the other hand, how far it came under that law of mind by which "the wish is father to the thought," we are left to infer from the character of the men.——Others, with more and better reason, said—His words are too full of good sense and wisdom and love to come from a demon spirit within him. And besides, think of what he has done before all the people. Can a demon open blind eyes? *Would* he if he could? Have ye ever known such a case? Can ye suppose a demon to have either the power or the will to do such a miracle?——Thus folly and wisdom were in sharp discussion. There were some men of sense living in those days; and unfortunately some men, high in religious place and power, whose speech was by no means very sensible.

22. And it was at Jerusalem the feast of the dedication, and it was winter.

23. And Jesus walked in the temple in Solomon's porch.

Appropriately a new chapter should commence here. The time, the occasion, and naturally the theme, have entirely changed. Since the opening of chapter 7, the events have gathered close about the feast of tabernacles, in the Jewish seventh month. Here we are set forward not far from three months, to the latter part of the month Chisleu, corresponding to our Christmas (Dec. 25). "The feast of dedication" was in progress at Jerusalem—a feast which celebrated the cleansing and re-dedication of the temple after it had been profaned by Antiochus Epiphanes and its customary sacrifices suspended three and a half years.* It was winter—the rainy season of Palestine; therefore Jesus did not teach in the fore-court in the open air, but in the eastern porch of the fore-court of the Gentiles which had continued to stand at the destruction of Solomon's temple by the Chaldeans. Being thus a relic of Solomon's building, it fitly retained his name.——Jesus was walking to and fro when the conversation here narrated took place.

24. Then came the Jews round about him, and said unto him, How long dost thou make us to doubt? If thou be the Christ, tell us plainly.

* See 1 Mac. 4: 41–59 and 2 Mac. 10: 1–8 and Josephus Antiq. 12: 7, 7.)

To the Greek verb translated—"make us to doubt," some critics, closely following its normal significance, give the sense—*lift up; excite* our minds; keep us in this unnatural fever of expectation. But the context is decisive for the meaning—hold us in suspense; keep our minds strained upon the doubts of the case.
——If thou be the Christ, tell us in plain words, publicly spoken.
——This complaining tone tacitly assumes that Jesus has been in fault, while they—poor unfortunate men—are not only innocent, but abused. They would, forsooth, be very glad to know something certain. It is painful to be kept thus in suspense!

25. Jesus answered them, I told you, and ye believed not: the works that I do in my Father's name, they bear witness of me.

26. But ye believe not, because ye are not of my sheep, as I said unto you.

Very appropriately Jesus answers—Your complaints are entirely gratuitous. I have told you already, but ye would not believe. I have not only declared myself to be your nation's Messiah—the Coming One foretold by your prophets in your own scriptures, but I have wrought miracles in my Father's name which have been his witness to me. Still ye have neither believed my word nor my miracles. "Ye believe not because ye are not of my sheep." The last clause—"As I said unto you" is omitted in the Vatican and Sinaitic manuscripts. Tischendorf also omits; but Alford, Tholuck, Meyer, and others, retain them because not far from three months had transpired since the discourse in the temple (John 10: 1-18) to which he refers, the text of which was—"I am the good Shepherd;" "my sheep hear my voice," etc. Some of his hearers on this occasion may not have been present there, though obviously many of them were.

27. My sheep hear my voice, and I know them, and they follow me:

28. And I give unto them eternal life; and they shall never perish, neither shall any *man* pluck them out of my hand.

29. My Father, which gave *them* me, is greater than all; and no *man* is able to pluck *them* out of my Father's hand.

30. I and *my* Father are one.

Those who are really my sheep are not troubled with the doubts which you claim to feel. They know my voice; I know them; they follow me. That peculiar relation of shepherd to flock is fully, beautifully developed between myself and my people. Hence they are surely mine forever: I give them life—not transient life, but life eternal. They shall by no means ever perish ·[the Greek is very strong]; no one shall ever pluck them from my hand. My Father also is pledged, for He gave them to me, and no one has power to pluck them from the Father's hand.*———"I and the Father are one." (The approved text has, not "my" but *the* Father).———The peculiar accuracy and force of the Greek language are developed in these words. With the help of a special form for the first person plural of the verb, they are able to say—"I and the Father *we* are one."

This text has been pressed into service for the metaphysics of theology to prove that the Father and the Son are one *in essence*, and not merely in sympathy, purpose, and work. Whatever may be true as to unity of essence in the case of the Logos and the Father, the argument as made from this passage is materially weakened by these two considerations:—(*a*.) That the context demands nothing beyond unity of sympathy, purpose, and work. If the passage teaches any thing beyond this, it must be by an inference of this sort, viz. a unity of purpose and of operation must assume and imply unity of essence.———Perhaps we are scarcely competent to establish such an inference.———(*b*.) It is by no means certain that the speaker, Jesus—the "I" of this passage—is precisely equivalent to the Logos. Should it not rather be assumed that the speaker here is the "Word made flesh, dwelling among us," and manifesting his glory before human eyes? In this view of the case, is it logical to assume that all which is true of the Logos as existing antecedent to his incarnation, can be affirmed (as to *essence*) after the incarnation—*i. e.* of the Son of man when the human was present equally with the divine, in these words and deeds?

Another controverted theological point has brought vs. 28, 29, into requisition—viz. that of the final perseverance unto salvation of all the truly converted.———This is not the place for extended theological discussion. A few words may be due in the interests of exposition, interpretation.

To break the force of these verses as proof texts for the final perseverance of all real converts, it is urged that for aught said here, saints may *tear themselves* away from Christ and so perish —nothing being affirmed here except that no violence *from without* shall pluck them from Jesus' hand.

To this it may be replied; (*a*.) The form of these assertions adjusts itself to the figure before the mind—that of sheep and their shepherd. Now it is not even supposable that sheep *tear themselves* from their shepherd. The nature of the sheep utterly forbids this. To suppose it would be in revolting violation of the genius and nature of the figure of sheep and shepherd. The only danger conceivable in the case of sheep is that they perish from wolves attacking, or from thieves and robbers breaking into the fold. The affirmation is therefore purposely made as strong and absolute as the nature of the figure admits. What more need

---

* The Sinaitic and Vatican give it, not *my* Father, but *the* Father. Tischendorf and Alford follow their authority. The sense is not materially affected by the change.

we ask?——(*b.*) "Shall never perish" guaranties against both violence from without and apostasy from within.——(*c.*) Other declarations of scripture are pointed especially against the danger of lapsing through impulses from within;—*e. g.* "Confident of this very thing, that He who hath begun a good work in you will perform it until the day of Jesus Christ" (Phil. i: 6). "Kept by the power of God through faith unto salvation" (1 Pet. 1: 5).
——(*d.*) Query: Is not the real question this—Whether Jesus, the good Shepherd, is *able* to take care of his own sheep so that they shall not fail of ultimate salvation? Are his resources of power through his providence, his word, his manifested presence, and his Spirit—all combined, adequate to this result? In making the affirmations before us in these verses, did he duly consider that the beings given to him of the Father to be saved ("sheep" they are in the figure, but men, human beings, in the thing figuratively represented), have a moral nature—a free will, and are therefore to be influenced, not so much by physical force as by moral considerations, adapted to free, intelligent mind? For it must be conceded, I think, that if Jesus made these declarations in full view of the nature of the beings to be saved, there can be no reason to question that he understands his work, and is equal to its accomplishment.

31. Then the Jews took up stones again to stone him.

32. Jesus answered them, Many good works have I shewed you from my Father; for which of those works do ye stone me?

33. The Jews answered him, saying, For a good work we stone thee not; but for blasphemy; and because that thou, being a man, makest thyself God.

Note how quietly—shall we not say also shrewdly—Jesus assumes that he had wrought no other than good works—none at all that were bad. But had he not a perfect right to make this assumption? It served only to put the actual case on its real merits. Those Jews were proposing to stone him for some of his good works, or good words;—fitly therefore does Jesus ask—for *which?* Let them think which. It may open their eyes to their mistake, or shall we not rather say—to their *crime?*——They answer; Not for any good work, but for blasphemy—the blasphemy of making thyself God when thou art so manifestly a man.—— They understood—at least they claimed to understand—his words—"I and the Father—we are one"—to be equivalent to making himself God. Prosecutors are under great temptation to make up a strong case.

34. Jesus answered them, Is it not written in your law, I said, Ye are gods?

35. If he called them gods, unto whom the word of God came, and the Scripture can not be broken;

36. Say ye of him, whom the Father hath sanctified, and sent into the world, Thou blasphemest; because I said, I am the Son of God?

For many reasons, but especially for its bearings upon the views which Jesus himself held respecting his own divine nature, this passage should be examined with the utmost candor and care. ——Jesus had said, "I and the Father—we are one." This was equivalent to calling himself "the Son of God" in a very special and peculiar sense. Upon the testimony of these words the Jews charged him with blasphemy in that, being a man, he made himself God. What answer did Jesus make to this charge? He appealed to their law, and specifically to Psalm 82: 1, 6, which passage, moreover, refers to Exodus 21: 6, and 22: 8, 9, 28. In these passages from Exodus civil judges are called Elohim—one of the names of God. The English Bible, however, translates the word "judges." But in Psalms 82, the same word in the same sense is twice translated "gods." The reason for applying this word "Elohim" to civil judges we may suppose to have been that they were acting in the place of God, in his behalf administering his law; also that the original, etymological sense made it appropriate—the *high* ones—elevated to high responsibility over their fellow-men. It may be added that this name for God admits of a wider range of application than any other one of his various names—it being used for angels (Ps. 8: 6), and in the singular number for the gods of the heathen (Isa. 44: 10, 15, and 45: 20, and 46: 6). (See my Notes on Ps. 82). So much should be said as to the words quoted by Jesus from the Old Testament— "I said, Ye are Gods."

Here we have to meet the question—What is the nature of this self-defense of Jesus? What is his argument and what are its legitimate bearings?

Two suppositions have been made:—(*a*.) That Jesus puts his own case on the precise footing of the Jewish civil magistrate, inferring that if those magistrates were called "gods" in their law and there was no blasphemy in giving them this name of God, no charge of blasphemy could lie against him for calling himself the Son of God. They were called "gods" because the word of God came to them—"word" in the sense of commission, delegating authority to act as judges; including also, perhaps, the laws they were to execute and all needful instructions as to the processes of civil trial, etc.——Now if Jesus puts himself under the wing (so to speak) of this Old Testament usage in speaking of civil judges, virtually pleading that under such a sanction he might at least speak of himself as the Son of God without blasphemy, we have one theory of his defense—one which, apparently, makes no claim on his part to real divinity.

(*b*.) Another construction of his argument is supposable; viz: That Jesus does not by any means tone down his claims as to his person and work to the grade of those Old Testament judges;

does not assume an exact analogy between himself and those judges; but makes an argument of this sort: "If he called them gods who were only civil judges, *how much more* may I, being not merely one "to whom the word of God came," but being from eternity the *very Word* of God—myself "sanctified" [set apart] of the Father "and sent into the world" as his Supreme Vicegerent, to administer his moral realm as Judge and Lord of all—how much more may I with propriety speak of myself as the Son of God?——In this view of it, his appeal to the Old Testament is made because those Jews held their ancient scriptures in the highest regard and even reverence, and because, an argument drawn from their usage would have more force than any thing else he could possibly adduce.

This latter construction seems to me unquestionably the true one. The phrase—"unto whom the word of God came" seems chosen of design for the purpose of suggesting the inference as put above—*How much more* may he who comes from the Father as the very Word himself be called the Son of God.——Then, moreover, a strong point of difference between himself and those ancient judges lies in the descriptive points as to himself—"Him whom the Father hath sanctified and sent into the world." This description purposely lifts Jesus entirely above the grade of those ancient judges who yet were called "gods."——These considerations combine to sustain the latter of the constructions named above, and to show therefore that no argument adverse to the true divinity of Christ (in his own view of himself) can be drawn from this answer made to the Jews.

37. If I do not the works of my Father, believe me not.
38. But if I do, though ye believe not me, believe the works; that ye may know, and believe, that, the Father *is* in me, and I in him.

"The works of my Father" must be taken here substantially as where first used by Jesus (John 5: 17), "My Father *worketh* hitherto, and I work." I am working as he works; doing the same things, in the same spirit, for the same ends. These works were primarily his miracles of mercy and of power, done in the Father's name; in a sense, by means of the Father's power and specially as an indorsement of the mission of his Son. Jesus says—If I have not performed such miracles, believe me not. If I have performed such, then, though ye reject the testimony of my word, yet ye must accept the testimony of these works—God's own testimony to his Son.

In the latter part of v. 38, some of the most reliable manuscripts give us—not "know" and "believe," but know and *understand*. The difference in sense is (as often) of small account.

39. Therefore they sought again to take him; but he escaped out of their hand,

40. And went away again beyond Jordan into the place where John at first baptized; and there he abode.

Another ebullition of rage and another escape of their intended victim. The time for his arrest had not yet come.——His choice of the region where John the Baptist began his work was made (supposably) on two main grounds: Its quiet retirement far from Jerusalem and the fiery Pharisaic zealots who frequented that city; and also, the preparation for his labors which naturally resulted from the antecedent labors of John.

41. And many resorted unto him, and said, John did no miracle: but all things that John spake of this man were true.

42. And many believed on him there.

This must be the man of whom John speaks as to come after him. He fills out the description given of him by our great Teacher of righteousness. Besides, he works miracles as our teacher John did not. Thus many of the people there believed on Jesus.

———◦◦❀◦◦———

CHAPTER XI.

The central fact of this chapter is the raising of Lazarus from the grave. The story is told in full detail, with some of its results.

1. Now a certain *man* was sick, *named* Lazarus, of Bethany, the town of Mary and her sister Martha.

2. (It was *that* Mary which anointed the Lord with ointment, and wiped his feet with her hair, whose brother Lazarus was sick.)

First the historian identifies the man Lazarus. He was of Bethany—not the Bethany where John the Baptist preached (John 1: 28), but that Bethany which lay just over the summit of the Mount of Olives, east of Jerusalem; fifteen furlongs (v. 18) —one and seven-eighth miles—distant. This was a "*town*," in the sense of a small unwalled village in the country, and was known as the residence of Mary and her sister Martha—the sick man Lazarus being their brother. There being in the circle of Jesus' special friends several of the name Mary, this one is identified as the same who (John 12: 1-3) "anointed the Lord with ointment."
——According to Jewish tradition—more or less reliable—Martha was now a widow, her husband, Simon the leper, having deceased.

It is more to our purpose and more reliable that the family were in easy circumstances; that this was one of the dear, peaceful homes of the man of Nazareth; that Martha delighted to minister to his personal wants; while Mary delighted not less to sit at his feet and drink in his blessed words.——The sisters come to view in Luke 10: 38–42, and also again in John 12: 1–3.

3. *Therefore his sister sent unto him, saying, Lord, behold, he whom thou lovest is sick.*

4. *When Jesus heard that, he said, This sickness is not unto death, but for the glory of God, that the Son of God might be glorified thereby.*

Why should they not send to their dear sympathizing friend, if only for the sake of his sympathy? But they had known so many sick ones restored by his power, that they fondly hoped he might work such a miracle upon their only brother.——This first reply of Jesus foreshadowed the ultimate result with deeper significance than the hearers of it at first apprehended.——This sickness is not unto his final death, for I purpose to raise him from death, that the glory of the Father and of the Son may be made manifest thereby. Jesus was accustomed to speak of his miracles as "manifesting forth his glory." (John 2: 11, and 11: 40.)

5. *Now Jesus loved Martha, and her sister, and Lazarus.*

6. *When he had heard therefore that he was sick, he abode two days still in the same place where he was.*

7. *Then after that saith he to his disciples, Let us go into Judea again.*

The writer seems purposely to bring together these two facts—the love of Jesus for this family, and yet his delay of two days before he set off to visit them upon their very urgent call. He had a reason for this delay. The writer leaves us to think what it might be.

8. *His disciples say unto him, Master, the Jews of late sought to stone thee; and goest thou thither again?*

9. *Jesus answered, Are there not twelve hours in the day? If any man walk in the day, he stumbleth not, because he seeth the light of this world.*

10. *But if a man walk in the night, he stumbleth, because there is no light in him.*

Sensitive to the danger of their Master after the several cases of attempted violence to his person which had alarmed them, it is not strange that they gently protested against his going again so near Jerusalem.——The reply of Jesus imports that he should go fearlessly where his life-work lay, and should expect to work his twelve hours of daylight through without stumbling.

11. These things said he: and after that he saith unto them, Our friend Lazarus sleepeth; but I go, that I may wake him out of sleep.

12. Then said his disciples, Lord, if he sleep, he shall do well.

13. Howbeit Jesus spake of his death: but they thought that he had spoken of taking of rest in sleep.

Here for the second time (see the first case in Matt. 9: 24, or Mark 5: 39, or Luke 8: 52)—Jesus spoke of death as a sleep—a usage in respect to God's children which has long since become established—suggestive of whatever is most sweet, peaceful, blessed, and ultimately restoring in the highest sense:

"Asleep in Jesus—peaceful rest,
Whose waking is supremely blest."

To the disciples this usage was yet unfamiliar; so they thought that sleep in the case of this patient might be a favorable symptom.

14. Then said Jesus unto them plainly, Lazarus is dead.

15. And I am glad for your sakes that I was not there, to the intent ye may believe; nevertheless let us go unto him.

16. Then said Thomas, which is called Didymus, unto his fellow disciples, Let us also go, that we may die with him.

Their misapprehension brought out the explanation in plain terms—"Lazarus is dead." For your sake I am glad, since it prepares the way for a manifestation of my power which should confirm your faith in me.

The meaning of Thomas in his remark to his fellow disciples turns upon the reference of the last words—"him." Does he mean, let us go and die with *him*—Lazarus—as intimate friends sometimes feel when a dear one dies: Let me die also and go with him; or is it rather, Let us go with our Master, and if he must die by the violence of his enemies, let us share the same fate and rejoice to die with him?——The latter is the more rational and therefore probable—a pleasing testimony to the loving fidelity of at least one of the chosen twelve.

17. Then when Jesus came, he found that he had *lain* in the grave four days already.

18. Now Bethany was nigh unto Jerusalem, about fifteen furlongs off:

19. And many of the Jews came to Martha and Mary, to comfort them concerning their brother.

Of these four days, the messenger sent may have mostly occupied one (the distance being about twenty miles); two were passed in the delay before setting off (v. 6); and a fourth in the journey of the Savior with his disciples. This would show that Lazarus died soon after the messenger started; also that, as usual in the climate of Palestine, interment in the sepulcher followed very soon after death.——The high social position of this family and their endearing qualities had drawn around them numerous friends, of whom many came to minister whatever comfort their sympathy and condolence might afford.

20. Then Martha, as soon as she heard that Jesus was coming, went and met him: but Mary sat *still* in the house.

21. Then said Martha unto Jesus, Lord, if thou hadst been here, my brother had not died.

22. But I know, that even now, whatsoever thou wilt ask of God, God will give *it* thee.

Martha, impulsive and warm-hearted, rushed out to meet Jesus when she heard of his approach. Thoughtful Mary still sat musing, waiting. When Martha and Jesus met, she seems to have been the first to speak, giving expression to the cherished hope of both herself and her sister, that if Jesus had only been there; if he could by haste have reached them in time, her brother need not have died. It had long been settled in her mind that Jesus could heal the sick. In fact, she goes yet a little farther. Jesus is a man of prayer—as she has had frequent occasion to know. She hints her half-cherished hope that if he were to give himself to prayer in the present emergency, something—she can not well surmise what—more perhaps than she dared to hope—might yet be done.

23. Jesus saith unto her, Thy brother shall rise again.

24. Martha saith unto him, I know that he shall rise again in the resurrection at the last day.

25. Jesus said unto her, I am the resurrection, and the life: he that believeth in me, though he were dead, yet shall he live:

26. And whosoever liveth and believeth in me shall never die. Believest thou this?

27. She saith unto him, Yea, Lord: I believe that thou art the Christ, the Son of God, which should come into the world.

Remarkably Jesus advances by stages of progress toward disclosing the great purpose of his heart. First, "Thy brother shall rise again." He did not say *when*; did not intimate distinctly that it should be on that very day.——Martha replied, I know that—if thy meaning be only that he shall rise when all the dead shall come forth from their graves at the last day. Thou hast taught us that before. (John 5: 28, 29.) Whether this were a commonly received doctrine of the Jews, other than those taught by Christ, can not be inferred with certainty from this confession of her faith by Martha, for she may have learned it from Jesus only.——Then Jesus resumed his answer in those wonderful words, so characteristically brief and pregnant with meaning: "*I am the resurrection and the life;*" the power of raising the dead and of all real life resides in me. "He that believeth in me, though dead, shall yet live" in the resurrection to immortal life. Also, the man now living who believes in me shall never die—the second death—the death eternal. These words seem to take their special form and meaning from the case of Lazarus, then present to his mind, and to bear relations to both the body and the soul—to both natural death and immortal life—thus: "He that believeth in me, though dead"—*as Lazarus now is*—shall yet live (as I am about to raise him to life); and whosoever is not dead (as Lazarus is now), but is living, if he believes in me, shall never die in the great and fearful sense of death eternal. Whether one is now dead or now living, faith in me will surely save him from the second death, and ensure to him the resurrection of the body and eternal life. This exposition accounts for the antithesis between "Though he were dead," on the one side, and "Whosoever liveth," on the other. True faith in Jesus will save each class unto eternal life.

When Martha is asked—"Believest thou this?" she answers as one not entirely sure that she had his full meaning, and therefore puts her confession of faith in her own words: "I believe that thou art the Christ, the Son of God"—the One long promised to come into the world. I believe this, and she would imply (probably) all else that is involved in being the Christ, the Son of God and the long promised Messiah.

28. And when she had so said, she went her way, and called Mary her sister secretly, saying, The Master is come, and calleth for thee.

29. As soon as she heard *that*, she arose quickly, and came unto him.

30. Now Jesus was not yet come into the town, but was in that place where Martha met him.

31. The Jews then which were with her in the house, and comforted her, when they saw Mary, that she rose up hastily and went out, followed her, saying, She goeth unto the grave to weep there.

32. Then when Mary was come where Jesus was, and saw him, she fell down at his feet. saying unto him, Lord, if thou hadst been here, my brother had not died.

"Called her *secretly*," we may suppose, for fear of the Jews; it being well understood to be unsafe for Jesus to appear in public among the Jews in and near Jerusalem.

Mary, whose modesty or contemplative spirit had restrained

her from going out uninvited to meet Jesus, now moves most promptly upon his invitation. Remarkably, Jesus still remained where Martha had left him—shall we suppose—resting from the fatigues of his journey, or choosing not to advance to the house till he better understood the state of things there, especially as to the Jews, hostile to himself; or perhaps because he chose to see Mary also alone.—But some, at least, of the Jews followed Mary, supposing she was going to the grave—a very natural supposition, this usage being common in Palestine. In consequence of thus following Mary, a considerable number of them were present at the raising of Lazarus.——We may notice that Mary's first words to Jesus—falling at his feet—were the very same as those said by Martha when she met him (v. 21), showing that their views on this point were the same—the result supposably of their conversation on the subject. So far their faith in Jesus had borne them before they met him.

33. When Jesus therefore saw her weeping, and the Jews also weeping which came with her, he groaned in the spirit, and was troubled,

34. And said, Where have ye laid him? They say unto him, Lord, come and see.

35. Jesus wept.

36. Then said the Jews, Behold how he loved him!

On the part of Jesus these were tears of sympathy, purely and only. For there was no occasion to deplore the fate of Lazarus, or to mourn over the purposed result of his death, viz. the raising of him from death which Jesus fully purposed and was about to do. This grand event would avail to the glory of God and to untold consolations to God's people down through the ages by virtue of its palpable demonstration of the great fact of resurrection from the grave. It was therefore not for these things that Jesus wept, but because he felt so tenderly the appeal to his sympathies. His very heart was sympathy. So the historian puts it:—"When Jesus saw Mary weeping and the Jews also—her friends, weeping," his own bosom swelled with emotion. "He groaned in spirit"—our English version has it; but legitimately the Greek word means he made efforts to restrain and keep under due control the deep tides of his sympathetic feeling; he "*troubled himself*"—(so the Greek); the effort to command his emotions produced deep agitation. Did he think also of like scenes of grief, suggested by this, which his all-embracing eye might take in around myriads of dying beds and open graves, where the tenderest of human ties are sundered and hearts are torn and bleeding? Did there come up before his view these keenest pains of our mortal life—these bitter fruits of sin and death as seen in this dying world?——But we quite fail to do justice to this scene unless we give emphasis to the point that our Jesus as seen here is thoroughly, not to say, intensely *human*. His sympathies are those of our own human nature. We know this, for we have all felt them. We feel in our own bosom the deep sorrow we see manifested in other human bosoms. The tears of other eyes bring tears to our own. We may not be able to tell why; we do not stop to reason why; we know they come. Jesus wept because he saw Mary weeping. In the broader view of the results in this case as they lay before the mind of Jesus he might see much to relieve this sorrow; but still his sympathies for Mary were touched none the less. It was human; it came of his human range of view; it testified to his sympathizing human heart;—and herein lies its never-dying charm and consolation for his suffering people. It is consoling to think that our Jesus appreciates and does not rebuke these sorrows of our smitten hearts; that he sees the tears that fall and knows the pangs of bereavement: has wept himself over such scenes, and is "the same yesterday, to-day, and forever." Even the Jews who had known little personally of Jesus before, were impressed by this manifestation of sympathetic sorrow;—"Behold, how he loved him!" Such an impression should naturally have had the effect to conciliate their feelings toward Jesus—perhaps prepared the way for some of them (at least) to believe on him.

37. And some of them said, Could not this man, which opened the eyes of the blind, have caused that even this man should not have died?

Even some of these Jewish friends of the family suggest that one who could open the eyes of a man born blind might have saved the life of Lazarus if he had been present in season.— The miracle upon the blind man occurred in Jerusalem and appears to have been known to many. The two cases in which Jesus had restored the dead to life, viz. the daughter of Jairus (Luke 8: 49-56) and the son of the widow of Nain (Luke 7: 11-16 and Mark 5: 35-42) were located in remote Galilee, and perhaps were not generally known to the residents in Jerusalem. We might naturally expect, however, that the dear friends in this Bethany household would have heard of those cases of the really dead restored to life by their Lord.

38. Jesus therefore again groaning in himself cometh to the grave. It was a cave, and a stone lay upon it.

39. Jesus said, Take ye away the stone. Martha, the sister of him that was dead, saith unto him, Lord, by this time he stinketh: for he *hath* been dead four days.

40. Jesus saith unto her, Said I not unto thee, that, if thou wouldest believe, thou shouldest see the glory of God?

With sympathetic grief still unabated Jesus approaches the grave. As was the custom in Palestine, this was not a grave dug in the earth in our modern style, but an excavation in rock—more nearly the modern tomb. A stone closed and secured the entrance. Jesus bade the bystanders remove the stone. He might have applied his miraculous power to remove it, but he never made useless displays of this power; never applied it where ordinary human agencies were adequate.

The words of Martha make it almost certain that up to this moment she has not been thinking of her brother's resurrection as near. Would it not be offensive to open that sepulcher—for decomposition must have commenced? She shows at least that she supposed him to be really dead. There can be no stronger proof, scientifically considered, of absolute death than decomposition of the body.——Moreover, though it may seem scarcely worth the mention, her simple-hearted remark shows that this was no farce—no contrived scheme to get up a sham miracle for effect.——Was it a gentle hint to Martha that she had been slow of heart to take in the sense of his words, when Jesus reminded her how he had said, "If thou wilt believe, thou shalt see the glory of God?" We do not find precisely these words on record, but their sentiment was involved in the first words of the Lord (v. 4) which may be supposed to have been sent as his message to the afflicted sisters, and was perhaps virtually implied in v. 25; "He that believeth in me, though he were dead, yet shall he live." But nothing forbids the supposition that Jesus said these very words to Martha, though the historian did not record them.

41. Then they took away the stone *from the place* where the dead was laid. And Jesus lifted up *his* eyes, and said, Father, I thank thee that thou hast heard me.

42. And I knew that thou hearest me always: but because of the people which stand by I said *it*, that they may believe that thou hast sent me.

43. And when he thus had spoken, he cried with a loud voice, Lazarus, come forth.

44. And he that was dead came forth, bound hand and foot with grave clothes; and his face was bound about with a napkin. Jesus saith unto them, Loose him, and let him go.

The prayer before the summons—"Come forth"—was specially designed to show the people standing by that Jesus wrought the miracle by virtue of his relation to the Father—*i. e.* as man rather than simply and only as God. That, as the Messiah, God's Son, incarnated in human flesh—he was sent from God to men; was teaching men as one from God; was fulfilling all the functions of his great mission from heaven as one sent of God and indorsed by miracles wrought by the power of God—these were the very points which Jesus sought to make clear and prominent before the Jewish mind. Hence the fitness of this audible prayer.

Note the confidence in the Father which this prayer breathes.

I know (the *I* emphatic); I know past all doubt that thou hearest me. It is not for my sake, therefore—not that I may have some fresh or additional proof that thou hearest my prayer; but that the people standing by might have the proof they need—"that *they* may believe that thou hast sent me."——Then with loud voice that all the people might hear—loud also (we may perhaps suppose) as a suggestive pre-intimation of that final peal of the archangel's trump which shall wake all the sleeping dead and burst myriads of human sepulchers—Jesus cried: "Lazarus, come forth!"——The words were few; but oh, how majestic they seem! How impressive upon those who stood listening to the prayer, and looking toward the open sepulcher with intense eagerness for the possible results! And what shall we say of the emotions of Martha and Mary when with their own eyes they saw their dear and only brother actually coming forth at this command, swathed in his grave clothes, his face bound with a napkin! That is our own brother, living again! And this is what is meant by the resurrection from the dead! So Jesus *can* raise his believing people from their graves in his own time, and so he will!

It may aid our conceptions of the value of Jesus as a Friend to ask just here what Martha and Mary must have thought of him as their friend in their great need? They had known him somewhat before; but never before as now. It has been sometimes said that we measure the worth of a friend on this twofold scale; one side graduating the *sympathy* that is born of love; the other, the *power* which is available for help in need. With these standards in our mind, let us think how wonderfully Jesus revealed himself to the sisters in this emergency! Was ever human sympathy more tender and pure than his? What sweet confidence in his love it must have begotten in their bosoms!—— And then, on the other side, there was power to help—it were idle to wish it were greater. What more can our human weakness ever need? How safe we may feel under the wing of such a friend! The dear sisters at Bethany will remember these testimonies to the value of such a friend as Jesus to the end of their days. We hope they rendered many a song of thanksgiving all along their after pilgrimage of trials and griefs.——And is not their Jesus also our own?—as true, and quick, and tender in his sympathies with us as with them? as mighty to save in our weakness as in theirs?

45. Then many of the Jews which came to Mary, and had seen the things which Jesus did, believed on him.

46. But some of them went their ways to the Pharisees, and told them what things Jesus had done.

The moral power of this miracle was immense. Many of those Jews who were present believed in Jesus at once. Yet not all—for some turned away to report the case to the Pharisees.

Yet even there it still appears that the power of this miracle was very great; scarce any one ever wrought by Jesus was more so. It brought matters at once to a great crisis in the Jewish Sanhedrim—as the historian proceeds to say. It led the chief priests to consult how they might get Lazarus out of their way, because so many Jews were brought by his resurrection to believe on Jesus (12: 10, 11). And it moved the people to honor him with that triumphal march into Jerusalem which is recorded by all the Evangelists, but only by John ascribed to the impression made by this miracle (12: 17, 18).

47. Then gathered the chief priests and the Pharisees a council, and said, What do we? for this man doeth many miracles.

48. If we let him thus alone, all *men* will believe on him; and the Romans shall come and take away both our place and nation.

Notice here that Christ's enemies make not the least attempt to dispute the reality of his "many miracles." Their reasonings as to the policy to be pursued, and also the policy itself, rest on these two assumptions: (1.) That the miracles are real; (2.) That the masses of the people *believe them to be real*, so that he became, in their notion, a dangerous man to the nation on this special account. "If we let him alone, all men will believe on him."——But why do they fear that the Romans will come upon them?——We can not vouch for the entire honesty of their professed fears; but the pretense, the doctrine put forth (honestly or otherwise), was that he claimed to be a king; that his kingdom was so far "of this world" that it would come into collision with the jurisdiction of Rome, and bring down her vengeance upon the Jewish nation. This, they said, would take away their "place"—in the sense probably of exterminating them from their country; and their "nation" then of course—in the sense of putting an end to their nationality.——It was in harmony with these notions of theirs that the indictment which they emblazoned on his cross was—"*This is Jesus, the King of the Jews;*" and also that before Pilate Jesus met this charge by declaring—"My kingdom is not of this world" (John 18: 36).

We must not overlook the fearful retribution which fell, some forty years subsequently, upon Jerusalem, and the whole nation by the hand of this Roman power—fell not because they "let Jesus alone," but because they seized and murdered him; not because his kingdom brought down the wrath of Rome, but because their own corruption, depravity, crime, brought down on them the wrath of God; not because they were too feeble to withstand the sweep of Roman ambition and conquest, but because they lifted their voice to God, saying, "His blood be on us and on our children" (Matt. 27: 25), and God answered—Let it be as ye have said!

49. And one of them, *named* Caiaphas, being the high priest that same year, said unto them, Ye know nothing at all,

50. Nor consider that it is expedient for us, that one man should die for the people, and that the whole nation perish not.

51. And this spake he not of himself: but being high priest that year, he prophesied that Jesus should die for that nation;

52. And not for that nation only, but that also he should gather together in one the children of God that were scattered abroad.

The animus of this speech by Caiaphas went to tone their convictions up to the necessity of sacrificing the life of one man, though he were innocent and good, for the sake of saving the nation. If we let him live and go on, our nation is ruined. It is expedient therefore that we take his life so that the nation may be saved. He marvels that they do not see this:—"Ye know nothing at all" if ye do not see it; for what can be more certain?——Such were the human thoughts of this high-priest, and this *his* meaning as intended by himself, and understood by the council. But we notice that in the view of the Evangelist, his words were shaped—not "of himself" alone, but of God, above and beyond any thought of his—so as to become a *prophecy*—signifying that it was deemed of God expedient that Jesus should die—not for the nation of Jews only, but for the world—not with the result of scattering the Jews into every land under heaven (as the council had suggested, v. 48) but rather, of gathering into one vast brotherhood the children of God from all lands of the earth—all the believing and redeemed—into the one spiritual kingdom of the glorious Lord of all. The phraseology in the last part of v. 52—"gather together in one," etc., seems designedly put in contrast with the words of the council in v. 48—"take away our place and nation."

As to the possibility of such unconscious prophecy from the lips of the high priest, there can not be the least question that John believed in it; nor is there any room to question that his construction of the words has the sanction of the Spirit under whose inspiration he wrote. There is no shadow of authority for assuming that this was merely a private opinion of his, never suggested or sanctioned by the divine Spirit.——That it is possible for God to shape the words of a bad man to express a prophetic truth of which he had no thought, I see no reason to doubt. The historian suggests that his being "high priest that year" gave occasion to subsidizing his lips (so to speak) for the utterance of this prophecy. Under the ancient regime God was wont to speak sometimes through those (officially) sacred lips.

53. Then from that day forth they took counsel together for to put him to death.

From that day the policy of murder was fixed and only waited its opportunity.

54. Jesus therefore walked no more openly among the Jews; but went thence unto a country near to the wilderness, into a city called Ephraim, and there continued with his disciples.

This place of retreat—Ephraim—is supposed to be identical with Ophrah—about twenty miles north of Jerusalem (See Ellicott, p. 240).

55. And the Jews' passover was nigh at hand: and many went out of the country up to Jerusalem before the passover, to purify themselves.

56. Then sought they for Jesus, and spake among themselves, as they stood in the temple, What think ye, that he will not come to the feast?

57. Now both the chief priests and the Pharisees had given a commandment, that, if any man knew where he were, he should shew *it*, that they might take him.

The last Passover—the one during which Jesus suffered on the cross—is now at hand. In the group of those who came up early to the holy city, the question was anxiously put—Will Jesus come?—showing that the public mind was intensely moved by his miracles and by his teaching. This question awakened the deeper feeling because it had become generally known that the council had issued an order for his arrest, commanding all loyal citizens to inform the authorities where he might be that they might take him. Thus the great crisis was hastening on.

CHAPTER XII.

This chapter groups together several miscellaneous points: the supper at Bethany at which Mary anointed the feet of Jesus and the revelation made there of the character of Judas (vs. 1-8); the interest among the people to see Lazarus and the plots of the chief priests against his life (vs. 9-11); the great triumphal entry into Jerusalem (12-18) which excited the rage of the Pharisees yet the more (v. 19). The desire of certain Greeks to see Jesus (vs. 20-22) leads him to speak of the great crisis of his life then just at hand and its bearings upon his friends (vs. 23-26) and upon himself (vs. 27–33); the nice question whether according to the Scriptures Christ should abide forever (v. 34), and the indirect reply of the Master (vs. 35, 36). The historian finds the prevalent unbelief of the Jews foretold in Isaiah (vs. 37–41); speaks of the weak, ineffective faith of some chief rulers (42, 43), and gives the concluding comments of Jesus (vs. 44–50).

1. Then Jesus six days before the passover came to Bethany, where Lazarus was which had been dead, whom he raised from the dead.

2. There they made him a supper; and Martha served: but Lazarus was one of them that sat at the table with him.

3. Then took Mary a pound of ointment of spikenard, very costly, and anointed the feet of Jesus, and wiped his feet with her hair: and the house was filled with the odor of the ointment.

While many of the people came up to Jerusalem in advance of this Passover (11: 55), Jesus also came at least as far as Bethany six days before it commenced. This social supper made for him was an expression of grateful interest for the raising of Lazarus, and an opportunity for the special friends of the family to meet both Jesus and Lazarus.——Matthew and Mark speak of this feast as being "at the house of Simon the leper" (Matt. 26: 6 and Mark 14: 3)—a statement not necessarily inconsistent with John inasmuch as Simon may have been a neighbor and intimate friend where Martha's habit and nature of "serving" (see Luke 10: 40) found scope. Lazarus sat with Jesus, they being the two distinguished guests of the occasion. Mary's work was specially the service of love—with a pound of most fragrant, pure and costly ointment, to anoint the feet of Jesus and to wipe those sacred feet with her hair. Service done to the feet in Oriental life was, as we might expect, menial, and for this reason well expressed her deep humility and her yet deeper love. Was there any thing involving cost or personal humiliation she would not joyfully do for this dear honored Friend?——We love her for this spirit, and wish ourselves might have more of it.——As to the manner of applying this ointment, Matthew and Mark concur in saying—"poured it down on his head"—which may be true since she might have poured it upon both his head and his feet; or, if poured upon the head, it may have flowed down to the feet. Matthew adds—"In that she hath poured this ointment *on my body*, she did it for my burial" (26: 12). As fragrant odor was one object and the quantity was large, no discrepancy in the statements can be complained of.

4. Then saith one of his disciples, Judas Iscariot, Simon's son, which should betray him,

5. Why was not this ointment sold for three hundred pence, and given to the poor?

6. This he said, not that he cared for the poor; but because he was a thief, and had the bag, and bare what was put therein.

Judas Iscariot did not like this. John, more outspoken as to Judas than the other gospel historians, not only fastens this fault-finding upon Judas, but discloses his heart-motive. Whereas, Matthew (26: 8) speaks of "the disciples" as having indignation and saying—"To what purpose is this waste?" and Mark says (14: 4)—"There were *some* that had indignation within themselves," John is entirely definite in attributing the complaint to Judas;—"Why was not this ointment sold for three hundred pence and given to the poor?"——This was (we may suppose) the first suggestion, and, seeming to some others at first view plausible, they may have too easily concurred. But John gives Judas no credit for sympathy with the poor. Being the treasurer of the company and a thief, it was for his convenience to have the bag well filled. Had he been known to be a thief before? John assumes this. Arrant hypocrite!—that he should ask this money in behalf of the poor, yet with no better purpose at heart than to steal it! Such a man could be mean and wicked enough to betray his Master for money!

As to the estimated value—"three hundred pence"—we may remember that "two hundred penny worth of bread" was the estimate for supplying five thousand men with their supper. Hence this amount would provide more than a few meals of bread for the poor. But such a manifestation of overflowing love and gratitude to Jesus was even better than this.

7. Then said Jesus, Let her alone: against the day of my burying hath she kept this.

8. For the poor always ye have with you; but me ye have not always.

Was Mary disconcerted amid the murmurs sprung around this table by the rebuke from Judas Iscariot? Did the thought perhaps begin to trouble her that possibly her love had carried her too far? If so, Jesus came kindly and in good time to her relief:—"Let her alone;" spare those cruel criticisms; not a word of them is just. As reported by Matthew and by Mark, Jesus said—"Why trouble ye her? She hath wrought a good work on me. She hath done what she could. She is come beforehand to anoint my body to the burying."——Was she so far in advance of the disciples in her understanding of Christ's prophetic words that she was already forecasting his death and had it in mind that while she could, she would give his body its last obsequies? Or was this anointing anticipative of the burial only in the thought and plan of God?*——Jesus would not disparage the

* In the last clause of v. 7 some of the best textual authorities (the Sinaitic and Vatican, whom Tischendorf and Alford follow)

giving of alms to the poor. But he intimates—Ye will always have opportunity for such alms: there will be but one opportunity for this anointing of my body for its grave—but one for such an expression of grateful sympathy and self-sacrificing love.

9. Much people of the Jews therefore knew that he was there: and they came not for Jesus' sake only, but that they might see Lazarus also, whom he had raised from the dead.

Through the wise arrangements of God's providence, many Jews from Jerusalem were present at the raising of Lazarus. The startling news must have reached many others in the great city. Consequently, this family-supper, which was an outgrowth of that event then recent, had drawn together a large company, curious not only to see and honor Jesus, but also to see Lazarus who so lately had been four days in the state of the dead.——Curious, were they? Did they ask him what he could tell them of that unknown world? Did they come hoping to hear words such as had never fallen from human lips before?——Whether the lips of Lazarus were sealed; whether the things he saw were simply "unspeakable"—such as it were not possible for man to utter (2 Cor. 12: 4)—we are not told; but not a word from his lips passed into this historic record. Our historian John has given us no light as to the supposable testimony of this man from the realms of the dead.

10. But the chief priests consulted that they might put Lazarus also to death;

11. Because that by reason of him many of the Jews went away, and believed on Jesus.

All this awakened interest in Jesus of Nazareth and this conviction of his true Messiahship which was pervading the public mind were excessively annoying to the chief priests. Lazarus in their view has become a dangerous man. If it were expedient that Jesus should die for the nation's good, it must be equally expedient to take off Lazarus. Therefore they came not reluctantly to the conclusion that he too must die. No scruples of conscience, no recoil from the crime of murder, must be allowed to stand in their way.

12. On the next day much people that were come to the feast, when they heard that Jesus was coming to Jerusalem,

13. Took branches of palm trees, and went forth to meet

give it—"That she may keep it unto the day of my entombment"—in this sense (we may suppose)—"Let her alone:" it is noble in her thought and heart "that she should keep this against the day of my burial."——The sense is not changed materially by this modification of the text.

him, and cried, Hosanna: Blessed *is* the King of Israel that cometh in the name of the Lord.

14. And Jesus, when he had found a young ass, sat thereon; as it is written,

15. Fear not, daughter of Sion: behold, thy King cometh, sitting on an ass's colt.

16. These things understood not his disciples at the first: but when Jesus was glorified, then remembered they that these things were written of him, and *that* they had done these things unto him.

17. The people therefore that was with him when he called Lazarus out of his grave, and raised him from the dead, bare record.

18. For this cause the people also met him, for that they heard that he had done this miracle.

Here one of the most remarkable and most public events in the entire recorded history of Jesus comes before us in its historical and logical place. We are shown when and how it came to pass, and why the people gathered about him in such crowds to do him homage as Sion's Great King. The people that were with him when he summoned Lazarus from his grave had been bearing their testimony to that deed. Moved by this testimony yet other crowds of people met him "because they heard that he had done this miracle."——John omits many of the particulars of this triumphal entry into the great city—supposably because the three earlier historians had given them so fully, or possibly because those details were somewhat aside from the main purpose of his book. Thus while Matthew and Mark describe, John omits, how Jesus and the disciples obtained the young ass on which he rode; how they got the owner's consent; how the people spread, not palm-branches only, but their garments along the way he went; how the whole city was moved and rushed to the scene inquiring—Who is this? and were answered—"This is Jesus the Prophet, of Nazareth in Galilee." It is even more remarkable that he omits certain matters recorded by Luke only—*e. g.* that some of the Pharisees from among the multitude were bold enough to say to Jesus himself—"Master, rebuke thy disciples"—as if this scene were all too noisy and rude for their holy city!—To whom Jesus made answer—"I tell you that if these should hold their peace the stones would immediately cry out."——Another circumstance, recorded by Luke only, we are moved to ask how such a man as John could possibly omit; viz: that when he was come near, probably descending the Mount of Olives at a point where the whole city lay open to his view, "he beheld the city and *wept over it,* saying, If thou hadst known, even thou, at least in this thy day, the things that belong to thy peace!—but now they are hidden from thine eyes!——Ah indeed, a conqueror in triumph and yet in tears! Jesus, at the point of his highest earthly honor, testifying how little he thought of the pageant of display and how deeply he felt for the souls of his hopelessly hardened and desperately infatuated enemies. Never elsewhere so near the point of being suitably inaugurated as the nation's glorious Messiah, yet heart-burdened even to tears over the suicidal madness of those who "would not have this man to reign over them"! Where, other than here, have the records of royalty in its triumphs evinced such compassion for the guilty—such tears for traitors in arms!——We are thankful that Luke did not omit this record: how it happened that John left it out is scarcely within the reach of conjecture. The silences of Scripture are sometimes more remarkable than its utterances.——At this point it naturally occurs to ask how the first three evangelists could have come so near to the great facts respecting Lazarus and yet not touch them. They tell us of the feast gotten up in honor of the leading parties—Jesus and Lazarus;—but they quite omit to speak of its relation to the raising of Lazarus; leave out every one of the three honored names of the Bethany household—Mary, Martha, Lazarus; tell us of the anointing of Jesus with the precious ointment, but speak of her who acted Mary's part only as "a woman." As said already, they give us the triumphal entry with ample detail, but not a word to indicate that it had any connection with the raising of Lazarus. Was not this great event sufficiently prominent, sublime, yea also tenderly impressive and potent in its bearings upon the violent death of their Lord, to entitle it to some notice in their histories?

For myself I see no explanation of these facts so plausible as that which finds it in the *respective dates* of the writing of these books. The first three were (supposably) written before the death of Lazarus; the fourth, after. While Lazarus yet lived, the notoriety which the inspired record of these facts would give him might be painful to a modest man, or provocative to an idle curiosity in others; possibly annoying to his quiet, if not even dangerous to his life. In these aspects of the case we may see the wisdom of delaying one of the four gospel histories so long after the occurrence of its great events.

Returning from these side questions to our main subject, we note that each of the four historians, except Luke, finds in this triumphal riding into Jerusalem a fulfillment of prophecy—that of Zech. 9: 9, 10. John, and he only, adds (as we should expect from him) that though the disciples did not dream at the time that they were fulfilling prophecy, it all came to them afterward what time the Holy Ghost began to "bring all things to their remembrance" which Jesus had said and done to them and they to him, and to put them in the sunlight of prophecy and of their relations to God's great scheme of salvation. It then became both comment and illustration of what Jesus had said of that particular function of the Comforter (John 14: 26).

This triumphal entry must be regarded as one of the extraordinary events in the wonderful history of Jesus of Nazareth. This is the only event which has in any measure the aspect of display. Here only did Jesus allow himself to assume the air and manner of a king, advancing to his capitol to take possession of his throne. It is plain that the time had then come for a great change of policy in some points; for whereas Jesus had usually sought retirement rather than publicity, and had avoided what might expose him very seriously to the murderous designs of the chief priests, he here shrinks from no publicity and seems to fear nothing from the madness of his enemies. There had been a time when a great multitude were ready to "take him by force to make him a king;" then he was not ready. Over and over again he slipped away from threatened assault or arrest: now he seems to feel that his time has come, and the policy of fearlessness in duty with any exposure is in order. Consequently events are shaping themselves rapidly for the great crisis.

19. The Pharisees therefore said among themselves, Perceive ye how ye prevail nothing? behold, the world is gone after him.

See how the Pharisees are stirred up. They were powerless to stop this vast procession; powerless to hush the voices that were making the welkin ring with their Hosannas; but they could meet in secret conclave and stir up each other's zeal to fury against the Nazarene, and plot his death. "The world (said they) is gone after him." They could not stop the world from going; they saw the scepter of their power over the people in danger of dropping from their hand; they must make way with this hated—this dangerous man.

20. And there were certain Greeks among them that came up to worship at the feast:
21. The same came therefore to Philip, which was of Bethsaida of Galilee, and desired him, saying, Sir, we would see Jesus.
22. Philip cometh and telleth Andrew: and again Andrew and Philip tell Jesus.

This visit from certain Greeks—proselytes from the Gentiles, we must suppose—stands here as a story begun, but suddenly left unfinished. We learn very particularly how they obtained their introduction, and that for some unexplained reason they wished to see Jesus. The introduction came naturally through Philip, who was himself of Bethsaida in Galilee, and probably an old acquaintance. But whether they did see Jesus, and if so, what they said to him, or he to them, remains untold. For, the remarks that follow (v. 23 and onward) seem rather addressed to those disciples who came and told Jesus, than to these Gentile strangers, since they appear to assume a long previous acquaintance with his teachings and history. It would seem therefore that this visit of these Greeks is noticed by the historian only because it became to the mind of Jesus specially *suggestive*. It brought up a train of reflections upon the near approaching crisis in his life-work. These men, said he to himself, are moved to seek a personal introduction to me. Are they aware how far my earthly career is already run, how near 1 am to the great crisis; and how critical the hour must be for those who are willing to be known as my adherents? But his course of thought, suggested by their request for an interview, will appear in the sequel.

23. And Jesus answered them, saying, The hour is come, that the Son of man should be glorified.

24. Verily, verily, I say unto you, Except a corn of wheat fall into the ground and die, it abideth alone: but if it die, it bringeth forth much fruit.

25. He that loveth his life shall lose it; and he that hateth his life in this world shall keep it unto life eternal.

26. If any man serve me, let him follow me; and where I am, there shall also my servant be: if any man serve me, him will *my* Father honor.

"Glorified"—*i. e.*, through death and the resurrection and ascension to the highest heavens, and to the highest dominion there—all which were to follow soon. The analogy in the vegetable kingdom to illustrate this change from weakness to power is at once patent and beautiful. A grain of seed-wheat, kept dry, remains itself and itself only; but, laid in the warm, moist bosom of its mother earth, it dies; yet dying, it soon rises again to verdure, fruitage, glory. So is the resurrection of all the righteous dead; so specially would be the death of Jesus and its resulting consequences.——This case seems to have suggested the related analogy which appears in the Christian life. He who lives for himself only, makes an utter failure of life: working only to save his life, he will surely lose it. On the contrary, he who lives *as if* he hated his life in this world—who lays himself—his life-power and all there is of himself—on the altar of Jesus for other's good, he keeps and saves himself unto life eternal. It is the great Christian paradox. Give thy life away if thou wouldest save it forever. In niggardliness and the tightest selfishness, labor to make the utmost for thy little single self; so shalt thou surely lose thy soul—thy all. The force and beauty of these principles are heightened by their twofold application, *i. e.*, both to Jesus and to his believing people.——Onward in v. 26, the course of the Savior's thought seems to be on this wise: Such self-sacrifice; such a launching forth upon self-abnegation; such disregard of dear life—are not according to the common impulses of human nature. Men will need some powerful motive for it. Therefore let me point the way and suggest the reward. As to the way: "If any man serve me, let him follow me." I ask no more of him than I have done and suffered myself. "Where I am, there shall my servant also be"—which ought to be reward and inducement enough for all who love me. "If any man serve me, him will my Father honor"—and what higher reward should mortal man desire?

27. Now is my soul troubled; and what shall I say? Father, save me from this hour: but for this cause came I unto this hour.

28. Father, glorify thy name. Then came there a voice from heaven, *saying*, I have both glorified *it*, and will glorify *it* again.

29. The people therefore that stood by, and heard *it*, said that it thundered: others said, An angel spake to him.

30. Jesus answered and said, This voice came not because of me, but for your sakes.

The approaching crisis, involving self-sacrifice even unto death, seems here to rush upon his soul in most vivid forethought. As Gethsemane was Calvary in anticipation, this is Gethsemane before its time—the same in kind, though less in degree and in duration. We can not know how often such scenes of poignant grief and heart-trial in anticipation of the dread hour may have occurred in the experience of Jesus. We know only that they come of our frail human nature, and in the case of Jesus are to be ascribed to his human nature only—not at all to his divine. Historically, only John refers to this scene, while he and he only passes in silence the apparently more protracted scenes in the garden. The other three historians have described Gethsemane with considerable fullness (Matt. 26: 36–46; Mark 14: 32–42; Luke 22: 39–46).——"Now is my soul troubled"—agitated, tossed with anxious, fearful forebodings, not unmixed with perplexities, indicated by the question—"What shall I say?" What shall I pray for?——The middle clause of v. 27 ("Father, save me from this hour") is read in some texts interrogatively; in others, affirmatively; the former in this sense: Shall I pray, "Father, save me from this hour?" Nay, because I have come to this hour for the very purpose of enduring these agonies—of drinking this cup of sorrows.——The affirmative construction makes the middle clause itself a prayer—"Father, save me from this hour;" yet supposes the suppliant to check himself suddenly with the thought: I may not insist on this, because I came to this hour in order to meet its woes.——The ultimate thought is substantially the same on either construction. In favor of the affirmative construction it may be said: (*a*) The Greek text gives no indication of an interrogative. (*b*) The more full expression of feeling in Gethsemane certainly has prayer equivalent to—"Save me from this hour"—in the words: "If it be possible, let this cup pass from me;" "He prayed that if it were possible, the hour might pass from him;" "Father, all things are possible unto thee: take away this cup from me; nevertheless, not what I will, but what thou wilt."

In this case the prayer upon which his agitated soul settled down at length was—"Father, glorify thy name." To this a voice from heaven brought answer, audible at least to his ear: I have glorified it; I will glorify it again.——Of the bystanders, some, hearing a sound which seemed to them inarticulate, mistook it for thunder; others thought it the voice of an angel. Such utterances sent down from heaven will be heard intelligently by those to whom they are specially spoken; not always by all others present. In the case of Saul of Tarsus, the apparently discrepant accounts (Acts 9: 7, and 22: 9) are best harmonized on the supposition that while Saul heard the words, his attendants heard only inarticulate sounds, and failed to get the words spoken. Speculations on this point are of small importance; yet obviously much will depend on the receptivity of the hearer. Failure to catch the words may be due to perturbation.——In the present case the voice came in no whispering tones, but in solemn majesty; perhaps through angelic ministration. Jesus remarked that the voice came not for his satisfaction but for theirs.

31. Now is the judgment of this world: now shall the prince of this world be cast out.

32. And I, if I be lifted up from the earth, will draw all *men* unto me.

33. This he said, signifying what death he should die.

The course of our Savior's thought here taken in its connection is grand, sublime. From extreme depression, agitation, intense forecasting of woes to be endured, from which human heart and flesh recoil, he rises through prayer—the prayer of deep submission and devotion to the Father's will—to the assurance of glorious triumph. He sees the crisis of this world's great conflict close at hand. He sees his great antagonist, the Prince of this world, fallen, cast out, dethroned, despoiled. Of his death on the cross, indicated here as being "lifted from the earth," he foresees that it will itself beget an attractive power which will draw men to himself in love and homage. The first effect of being thus "lifted up," will be to him simply torture, heart-darkness, his cup filled with woes; but the after effects will be the drawing of men away from Satan unto himself, the casting out of his chief antagonist —the great usurper—and the firm enthronement of himself as King and Lord of all.

Instead of the word "judgment" in v. 31, I should prefer the Greek word itself which comes into our English—*crisis*. It signifies here the hour of destiny, the point where the great, long-pending issues of the conflict come to their final decision. The battle has been fought—with apparently varying fortunes and probabilities; but now the combat deepens; the struggle becomes desperate; Satan is doing his utmost and his worst. He has gained entrance into the heart of one of the twelve. "This is his hour and the power of darkness;" he has at length compassed the death of the Son of man, and the deep caverns of his pit reverberate with just one yell of fiendish exultation!—*but* one; no more! Alas for him; how soon the Crucified One rises a mighty conqueror!—rises, and lo! it appears that his very death on the cross has lifted, not *himself* alone for agony—but *all men* by its moral power of love. All men are lifted and drawn away from the grasp of the devil, and into sweet allegiance to him who hath "loved them and given himself to die for them."——Such is manifestly the course of thought in this wonderful passage.

As to the details of exposition: the "Prince of this world" contemplates Satan as having usurped a dominion never rightly his own; as having long held sway over the nations; but as being now prospectively vanquished and cast out from a world never his into "the place prepared for him and his angels."

The drawing of all to himself need not be pressed to the extreme of implying the actual salvation of all the race. The fact that Satan is thought of as having long maintained his usurped dominion as the Prince of this world should preclude this construction. Let it rather be held to mean that the morally attractive power of the cross is adequate to reach all varieties of the human heart; that it develops a power which legitimately impresses all; and that, in the ultimate result, it will reach the masses of the race with effective salvation.

The word "if" in the phrase—"if I be lifted up"—can not imply any contingency as to the future fact. Essentially the sense is, *when* I shall be; inasmuch as I am to be, therefore whenever it shall occur these will be the results.

34. The people answered him, We have heard out of the law that Christ abideth forever: and how sayest thou, The Son of man must be lifted up? who is this Son of man?

The people understood his being "lifted up" as implying his death—so far rightly. But they remembered that some of the prophecies respecting their nation's Messiah had spoken of the *perpetuity of his kingdom*. In fact there were many such prophecies. (See Ps. 72: 5, 7, 15, 17, Isa. 9: 7 and 60: 15, 19, 20 and Dan. 2: 44.)

It was however simply their mistaken inference that this perpetuity of his reign precluded his human death on the cross. They had yet to learn that their nation's Messiah was to die that he might conquer; that his death of agony was to be the very pivot on which should hinge everlasting victory and unutterable glory.

35. Then Jesus said unto them, Yet a little while is the light with you. Walk while ye have the light, lest dark-

ness come upon you: for he that walketh in darkness knoweth not whither he goeth.

36. While ye have light, believe in the light, that ye may be the children of light. These things spake Jesus, and departed, and did hide himself from them.

Noticeably Jesus makes not the least attempt to relieve their assumed perplexities. Did he see that these were only assumed and not really honest? Or did he pass them as trivial and unworthy of attention? Did he deem it better to hold them to things far more vital?——The latter view is at least in harmony with his reply;—Ye have light now—for a little while—light enough to walk by; therefore *use it while ye have it*. Soon darkness will settle down fearfully upon those who will not walk while their daylight shines. "While ye have light, walk in it:" believe in what truth ye really know: So shall ye be children of light, and the God of light will shed on your soul every ray ye may need in future.——With these monitory words, Jesus closes this discussion.

37. But though he had done so many miracles before them, yet they believed not on him:

38. That the saying of Esaias the prophet might be fulfilled, which he spake, Lord, who hath believed our report? and to whom hath the arm of the Lord been revealed?

39. Therefore they could not believe, because that Esaias said again,

40. He hath blinded their eyes, and hardened their heart; that they should not see with *their* eyes, nor understand with *their* heart, and be converted, and I should heal them.

41. These things said Esaias, when he saw his glory, and spake of him.

These are the words of John—his reflections upon the sad fact of the general and fatal unbelief of his countrymen. His narrative of the discourses, discussions, and moral efforts of his Master for the salvation of the Jews is now near its close. How often had both he and his Master "marveled at their unbelief"—marveled with great astonishment and most poignant grief, pressing often the question—*Why* is this? No wonder that long and thoughtful study of this fact brought to his mind the words of Isaiah here quoted—the first passage from 53: 1 which gives by prophetic anticipation the grief of their nation's Messiah over the almost universal unbelief of his covenant people; the second from 6: 9, 10—a part of the inauguration services at the induction of the prophet into his work, yet in the view of our author referring really to the same great fact of the nation's rejection of their Messiah through persistent unbelief and the moral blindness to which they were judicially abandoned in the righteous judgment of God

This is John's own comment:—"These things said Isaiah because he saw his glory and spake of him."——[" *Because,*" not " when," is the best sustained reading.]

In the closer examination of these quotations and their bearings upon the unbelief of the Jews, the most difficult and altogether the most important problem is to adjust their teachings to the moral relations and responsibilities of those hardened Jews so as to put in its true light the mutual action of human and divine agency in the case. Did the Jews reject Christ in unbelief *for the purpose* of fulfilling Isaiah's prophecies? Was it *impossible* for them to believe, and if so, in what sense impossible? Did the Lord blind their eyes *to the end* that they should not see and be converted?——These questions will suffice to indicate the points that seem to need our special consideration.——To meet, and in some measure at least to answer them, I suggest:

(1.) It is entirely legitimate grammatically to read v. 38, in its connection—not, "They did not believe *to the end* that, or *in order* that, the saying of Isaiah might be fulfilled;" but thus:— "They did not believe; *so that* the prophecy came to be fulfilled:"—the sense being this;—Inasmuch as they did not believe the prophecy was fulfilled. John does not assume or assert that those unbelieving Jews *intended, purposed,* to fulfill Isaiah, or even thought of fulfilling him. Nor does he mean to say that the Lord led them on into their unbelief *for the sake of* fulfilling prophecy. Nothing more is necessarily meant than that their unbelief did in fact fulfill Isaiah.*

(2.) The words—(v. 39) "They *could not* believe," are correctly translated. The Greek verb † here used can not be translated otherwise. The real question then is—*Why* could they not believe? What is the nature of this impossibility?——We have had the same problem already in John's gospel. Jesus used the same Greek verb (John 6:44)—"No man *can* come to me except the Father who hath sent me draw him." [The reader will revert to that passage and to the notes upon it.] The "drawing" in the case came through being "taught of God" by means of his truth and his Spirit. *Why* were not these Jews thus drawn by means of being taught of God's truth and enlightened by his Spirit? Their history gives the answer: They *would not be taught* in the way God had provided. They would not accept the Great Teacher whom he had sent. They would not believe that he came from God. They repelled the proof he gave them in his miracles.

---

* In the technical language of grammarians, the two very diverse senses of the word which stands before the subjunctive mood—expressed above in a popular way by the phrases—"to the end that"— and "so that"—are called—the former, the *telic;* the latter, the *ecbatic.* Writing for the masses I aim to use language with which they are familiar.——It seems scarcely necessary to give the arguments in support of the latter rather than the former of these senses.

† ηδυναντο.

They repelled the evidence that shone forth in his heavenly life, his loving spirit, his fidelity to truth and duty. They said he had a devil and was not fit to be heard. They even sought to murder the important witnesses to his great miracles. In every way they shut their eyes to the light of God and their heart against understanding and feeling the force of the truth of God. These and nothing less or other than these were the simple facts in their case. It was thus and only thus that it could be said—" He (the Lord) hath blinded their eyes—that they should not see." We must interpret the moral nature of the divine agency in this case by the known facts respecting the *mode* of that agency. So interpreting, we are forbidden to make this agency a direct one with intentional and purposed aim, producing its results by direct causation. We can not carry it beyond the line of a permissive agency—which means that God suffered moral causes to work out their legitimate results.

He suffered depraved human nature to run its self-persistent course, and to produce its natural, inevitable fruits. When those Jews *would not* believe; when they spurned all the light from heaven respecting Jesus their Messiah; when they repelled every influence that wisdom, love and tenderness could exert upon them; when they labored to quench all testimony for Christ even in the blood of the witnesses;—when they ascribed to the devil the miracles that Jesus wrought by the divine Spirit—what could this be less than the unpardonable sin? How could the result be less than a moral hardening of their own hearts which a righteous God for the safety and honor of his moral kingdom must visit with irretrievable damnation?——(3.) Our question legitimately involves not only the *kind* of agency which Jesus had in blinding the eyes and hardening the hearts of those Jews, but the *spirit* in which he worked this agency. The *heart of Jesus* in this whole case comes vitally into the main question. Fortunately on this point, we are left in no doubt whatever. Both Luke and Matthew have recorded his words at the moment when the sweep of his eye brought to his view, present and prophetic,—first, this moral hardness of unbelief, national, deep, damning; and secondly, the ruin that within a single generation was to whelm the holy city under the waves of a most terrific desolation.——As given by Luke (19: 41, 42)—" When he was come near, he beheld the city and wept over it, saying—*If* thou hadst known, even thou, at least in this thy day, the things that belong unto thy peace!—but now they are hidden from thine eyes."—In Matthew (23: 37, 38) on this wise;—" O Jerusalem, Jerusalem; thou that killest the prophets and stonest them that are sent unto thee; how often would I have gathered thy children together even as a hen gathers her chickens under her wings;— but ye would not! Behold, your house is left unto you desolate."——Now here but one thing need be said: If these were honest tears; if these were truthful words, uttering the real feelings of his soul, then it is simply an outrage to ascribe to Jesus the moral purpose to harden those Jewish hearts and bring upon them these rushing waves of desolation. We must dismiss—nay more—we must put utterly from our heart the possibility of any direct, purposed agency of God or of Jesus Christ to *make* those hearts hard and unbelieving, and so prepare them for this awful curse.——(4.) It is quite another thing that Jesus should deem it wise and perhaps unavoidable to let human depravity run its natural course and work out its legitimate fruits of moral obduracy unto terrible retribution. It is the law of our moral nature—indeed, of *all* moral natures in the universe, that light sinned against, conscience resisted, progresses onward into deeper hardness and yet more blind and mad infatuation,—until there is no remedy. The tendencies and fruits of such sinning go to set at nought all remedial agencies and to drift the soul into the vortex of perdition.——Now this being the natural and inevitable law of persistent sinning, working the more surely and rapidly according to the measure of light sinned against, and of mercy despised, why should not Jesus let this law take its course in the case of those who "set at nought all his counsel and would none of his reproofs"—who had the light of heaven as it came down in its glory, beaming forth from the very face of Jesus in his words, his miracles, his tears?

It is not wise or well to complain or to stumble because some of the sacred writers on occasion put the divine agencies in the permission of sin in the very bold and strong form which we meet with here. It was by no fault or mistake of theirs that they saw God's hand in *the permission of sin*, or in leaving the laws of a free moral nature to work on in their own way—to their own natural results. They had ground for believing and for saying of some sinners, that "because they received not the love of the truth that they might be saved, God would send them strong delusion that they should believe a lie, that they all might be damned who believed not the truth, but had pleasure in unrighteousness" (2 Thess. 2: 10–12). Such declarations should lift up their voice, loud as seven thunders along the pathway of self-hardening sinners. Let them never be ignored, never suppressed, never stumbled over as making God in the least responsible for any sinner's persistent unbelief.*

---

* The following comments of the Author in his Notes on Isa. 6: 9, 10 (pages 43, 44), may properly be introduced here:

Here the prophet receives his message. In v. 9 he is told what to *say;* in v. 10 what to *do,* or more strictly what should be the *effect* of his labor. The passage is peculiar in its form of statement, and therefore should be considered carefully. In v. 9 we can by no means take these imperatives in their direct sense as forbidding the people to understand and perceive what God is saying. They must therefore be taken as solemn irony, so put in the hope of arousing their dull hearts to serious thought. "Go on hearing, since so you choose and will: go on hearing and not understanding; go on to see and yet

42. Nevertheless among the chief rulers also many believed on him; but because of the Pharisees they did not confess *him*, lest they should be put out of the synagogue:

43. For they loved the praise of men more than the praise of God.

The conviction of many chief rulers was gained, but not their hearts. This could not have been true gospel faith, for it fell short of making them Christ's servants and disciples. There was not moral power enough in it to make them willing for Christ's sake to be put out of the synagogue—not enough to make them love and value the approval of God above the praise that comes of men. It was therefore clearly a case of intellectual conviction of truth which yet fell short of inducing hearty obedience to this truth. A state of fearful sin is this,—holding back and resisting the legitimate influence of truth which they know and are compelled to admit to be truth.

44. Jesus cried and said, He that believeth on me, believeth not on me, but on him that sent me.

45. And he that seeth me seeth him that sent me.

perceive nothing." Alas! you will find ere long to your bitter cost that such a course is fraught with ruin and death! Why will ye madly pursue it? Our Lord seems to speak in the same way in Matt. 23: 32, "Fill ye up then the measure of your fathers."——V. 10 is addressed to the prophet, and like v. 9, is to be taken, not in a direct but in a modified sense; not as enjoining him to aim and labor to harden the hearts of the people and make their hearing dull and their seeing dim or unavailing; but as indicating what must be the incidental *results* of his best and holiest endeavors. "Go and deliver my messages to this people." They have resisted my call hitherto: they will again. Thus far they have shut their ears and closed their eyes; you need expect no better hearing and seeing from them hereafter. Despite of your most tender and earnest appeals, they will cleave to their sins; they will repel your invitations; scorn your entreaties; mock at the threatenings you proclaim, and press on in the way of rebellion and moral ruin. It is their set purpose, and they will persist in it to their certain death. The Spirit of the Lord has pressed them long and kindly, but with no good result, and now they must be made a terrible example of the ruin that comes on those who will "always resist the Holy Ghost."——This strong case, strongly stated, of moral obduracy of heart and of judicial visitation from God, manifestly made a strong impression upon at least the good men of the nation in future ages. We have proof of this in the fact that these verses are referred to by quotations more or less full in at least six passages in the New Testament. See Matt, 13: 14; Mark 4: 12; Luke 8: 10; John 12: 40; Acts 28: 26; Rom. 11: 8.——
Our Lord's use of it in the discussion which grew out of his parable of the sower (as in Mathew, Mark and Luke) was entirely in

46. I am come a light into the world, that whosoever believeth on me should not abide in darkness.

This emphatic public declaration of truths essentially taught before is made just here to meet the case of those half-way believers of whom the history has just spoken. Whoever believes on me believes not on me alone, but on him that sent me. I come into the world, a light to men, so that none who really accept my light need abide in darkness. Let all half-hearted believers take notice and beware less they miss the light of God!

47. And if any man hear my words, and believe not, I judge him not: for I came not to judge the world, but to save the world.

48. He that rejecteth me, and receiveth not my words, hath one that judgeth him: the word that I have spoken, the same shall judge him in the last day.

"Hear my words and *keep*" [so the best authorities have the text]—"keep them not"—a very close fitting description of the class of believers spoken of vs. 42, 43. "I judge him not" *now*— the emphasis being on now. I am not here now to judge men but to save: I shall come in due time to judge. The word that I have spoken will appear in that great judgment day as a swift harmony with its drift and purpose as it stands here in Isaiah, *i. e.*, illustrative of that judicial blindness to which God leaves sinners who resist his Spirit and set at nought his merciful endeavors to enlighten and save them.——The phraseology of Matthew (13: 14) and of Paul (Acts 28: 26) is slightly modified from that of Isaiah. It is not, "Shut thou their eyes," but "their eyes *have they* closed." This change makes God's permissive and judicial agency less prominent, and the sinner's own voluntary agency more prominent. The latter agency Isaiah most fully and surely implies; and the former, neither Matthew nor Paul would exclude.——It should be noted that these Apostles, Matthew and Paul, quote from the Septuagint which reads, "The heart of this people has become gross; with their ears they hear heavily" (in dullness), "and their eyes have they shut lest they should see with their eyes," etc. This is entirely correct in sentiment, yet does not bring out in its full strength the divine agencies in withdrawing his Spirit and giving up self-hardened sinners in judgment to their own free and guilty choice of rebellion and death. It puts this guilty choice and this persistent refusal of the sinner in the foreground as facts never to be ignored. And rightly. The indorsement of this view by our Lord, as in Matthew (13: 14) and by Paul (Acts 28: 26) may be taken as a timely suggestion and caution against over-straining the divine agency in the judicial hardening of the persistent sinner. It would be ineffably revolting to give it such a construction as would ignore God's love and pity for even the guilty sinner, or his sincere and earnest desire that they would, any and all, turn from their sins and live."

witness for their condemnation, for it will show that they had abundant light for their salvation, but shut their eye and heart against it.

49. For I have not spoken of myself: but the Father which sent me, he gave me a commandment, what I should say, and what I should speak.

50. And I know that his commandment is life everlasting: whatsoever I speak therefore, even as the Father said unto me, so I speak.

These words recapitulate and re-affirm certain points of most vital testimony in the public debates of Jesus with the Jews, and come in appropriately here at the close of those debates and discussions. Of these points none could be more vital than— (*a*.) His mission from the Father—that his words were not his own but the Father's, sent through himself to dying men; and (*b*.) That obedience to God's great message through Jesus would insure everlasting life. These great truths will bear repetition, and the most earnest, emphatic announcement. The issues of life are in them. To accept them as true and obey them as duty will carry life into souls otherwise dying and sure of death.

CHAPTER XIII.

Jesus with his Disciples.

JOHN XIII–XVII.

There is method in this gospel history by John. It is throughout a history of Jesus who is always one party in all its various scenes and transactions. The second party, shown with him, is not throughout the same, but varies with the shifting of the scenes. We might arrange the book into sections on this principle—the *varying second party.*—

(1.) We see Jesus (chap. 1–4) in his *relations to individuals:*— *e. g.* John the Baptist; Nicodemus; the woman of Samaria: besides which in chap. 2 we see him in a group of family friends.

(2.) In chap. 5–12 we see him in his relations to the unbelieving, questioning, cavilling Jews (high priests and Pharisees)—the historic incidents being introduced mainly for the purpose of presenting the discussions, arguments and exhortations to which those incidents gave occasion.

(3.) In chap. 13–17 we see *Jesus with his disciples*—this section being made up almost exclusively of free conversations, farewell counsels, expressions of sympathy, love and confidence: closing appropriately with prayer.

(4.) In the next section we see *Jesus with his murderers*, and have the betrayal, the arrest, the mock-trial and the crucifixion.

(5.) Finally, in chapter 20 and 21 we see him the risen Jesus, *with his disciples again*, for parting words of sympathy, reproof and counsel.

With this chapter 13, we enter upon the section which presents Jesus in special communion with the twelve. He saw in the nearer future (what they did not)—the fearful strain of that trial to which their faith must needs be subjected when he should be seized by ruthless hands and hurried away to a death of shame and agony. In the more remote future he saw that his resurrection and ascension would leave them alone in the world—alone not only but almost utterly friendless; not friendless only, but encompassed on every side with hostile powers—the civil and religious authorities of the land in deadly antagonism, watching them with Argus-eyed jealously—in the intense bigotry of their fiery zeal, thinking that to kill these followers of the despised Nazarene would be to do God service. Into such a cold, hostile world Jesus knew that his disciples would be launched at his death;—and not only launched forth to live themselves as best they could, wherever they might; but to *do* a momentous work; to lay the foundations of the Christian church; to begin the evangelization of the wide world—yea, to "go forth into all the world and preach the gospel to every creature."——Did it not seem in the last degree preposterous to put a few Galilean fishermen and converted tax-gatherers to such a service?——Manifestly there were many things to be said to them and done for them by way of *preparation* for the life-work that lay before them when their Head should have been taken away.——How much and what preparation they did require can by no means be adequately appreciated without very careful attention to the leading elements in their religious thought and life at the time when this section of their history opens. To this, therefore, let us for a moment turn our attention.

When Jesus passed his eye over the twelve as they sat around this Passover* board and thought over their adaptation to meet the trials and do the work before them, what were the points that would most impress his mind and shape his farewell words?

1. With the exception of one traitor—soon withdrawn—the rest had some true Christian faith and love, yet faith and love that greatly needed culture and invigoration.

2. They had been in the school of Christ several years; had learned some precious truths, but had much more yet to learn. Many words of Jesus, more than once heard, were yet but half understood and needed to be recalled, reconsidered, and their deeper significance more thoroughly apprehended. Especially it

---

* The question whether this was *the* Paschal supper of the Jews has been hotly contested. We can not debate the point here, but will for the present assume that it was.

should be noticed that their early Jewish misconceptions of the Messiah's kingdom as being of earthly sort needed to be expelled, and the true spiritual conception of it rooted immovably in their place.

3. To face and bear those near impending persecutions which Jesus foresaw and they did not, it was vital that they should be not only forewarned but thoroughly forearmed. Every thing that farewell words could do to deepen their love to their Master and his cause; to lift their souls above fear, and pain and even death for his sake; would be eminently in place in this eventful night-interview.

4. Comprehensively let it be noted that every one of these great defects in their Christian character and great necessities for their future work combined to constitute a demand for the presence and work of the Holy Ghost. If Jesus could be with them as he had been, he might encourage, inspire and guide them. But he is going up to the Father, and therefore the Spirit of truth must needs come in his place to do all and more than all the work which Jesus had been doing. There is much therefore to be said concerning the Spirit's mission and work. Nowhere could this be more in place than here and now.

Bearing in mind these facts and features in their spiritual state, and in their approaching orphanage, persecutions, and immense labors, we shall the better appreciate the meaning, the fitness, and the force of the words and deeds of Jesus during this eventful night with his disciples.

In this chapter the central fact is the washing of the disciples' feet, including the scene itself (vs. 1–5); the objection made by Peter (vs. 6–11); the practical application of this example (vs. 12–20); the disclosure respecting Judas the traitor (vs. 21–30); Jesus forecasts the glory of the nearer future (vs. 31, 32); apprises the disciples that he must soon go away (v. 33); gives the new commandment of mutual love (vs. 34, 35); and forewarns his too self-confident disciple Peter of his sad fall (vs. 36–38).

1. Now before the feast of the passover, when Jesus knew that his hour was come that he should depart out of this world unto the Father, having loved his own which were in the world, he loved them unto the end.

2. And supper being ended, the devil having now put into the heart of Judas Iscariot, Simon's *son*, to betray him;

3. Jesus knowing that the Father had given all things into his hands, and that he was come from God, and went to God;

Here are the antecedents of the feet washing, presently to be described, including the external circumstances, and especially the internal thoughts and facts present to the mind of Jesus and to be taken into account by the reader that he may the better appreciate the transaction.

It was immediately before the feast of the passover. The preparations for this feast were made and the supper hour had come. The clause which stands in our version, "supper being ended," should rather be read: Supper being on hand; or, it being supper time. Literally it is, *supper being*—i. e., being in progress.

——Moreover, the purpose to betray his Master having been already instigated in the soul of Judas by the devil and accepted by the traitor, the agencies were at work for his speedy arrest and crucifixion. All this Jesus knew. He knew therefore that he was soon to depart out of this world unto the Father. The thought that he must so soon leave his chosen disciples quickened his love toward them. He had loved them tenderly before; this love threw into the background all thought of his own impending agonies, and blazed forth with fresh ardor at this point—so near the end of his personal communion with them upon earth.

——He is now about to perform for his disciples the most menial service known to the usages of Oriental life—that of washing their feet. The historian would remind us that Jesus did this with the full knowledge and under the present power of the thought that the Father had given all things into his hand, making him the Infinite King and Lord of the universe, and that he had come forth from God, having been from eternity "with God" and truly God; and was just about to return to "the glory he had with his Father before the world was." In a case of such apparent self-abasement, you might have thought (had you seen it) that he must have been oblivious to his infinite dignity; unaware and for the time at least unconscious of his Sonship to God and of his prospective exaltation to the throne of the universe—but no! That view of his consciousness is altogether wrong. John would forewarn you against it in the outset. This washing of the disciples' feet was done by the Master under the fullest sense and consciousness of his superlative glory before the Father. The act can not be properly appreciated by his people save as they hold fully in mind this present consciousness of Jesus in the transaction.

4. He riseth from supper, and laid aside his garments; and took a towel, and girded himself.

5. After that he poureth water into a basin, and began to wash the disciples' feet, and to wipe *them* with the towel wherewith he was girded.

He rose from the supper-table before the repast had fully commenced. The guests had taken their half recumbent positions around the table in the usual Oriental style, reclining upon the left side, resting on the elbow, leaving the right hand free for service in eating, and with feet extended outward. He then "laid aside his garments" (so the record has it)—the outer garment certainly, and possibly the inner one also; on this supposition, supplying its place in part with the large towel girded about the waist which he used also for wiping the feet after the washing. In Oriental experience, washing the feet was regarded as a luxury to the subject, but in Oriental idea, a most menial service for the operator. None but the lowest class of servants were expected to perform it. Its rigid restriction to this class was due not so much to its being laborious or offensive, as to the power of a caste feeling which, as is well known, is wont to go far beyond the intrinsic reason of things. We shall fail to appreciate this act of the Master unless we take into our estimate the current caste notions of the people among whom it was done. In this act Jesus became a servant of servants to his disciples. He showed that to serve was the business of his life, and in his view was not to his shame but to his glory. It was an example to illustrate a principle—the same principle which is stated to be the purpose of his mission to earth—"The Son of man came not to be ministered unto, but to minister, and to give his life a ransom for many" (Matt. 20: 28).——More is said below of its purposed moral application to his disciples in that age and, indeed, in every other.

6. Then cometh he to Simon Peter: and Peter saith unto him, Lord, dost thou wash my feet?

7. Jesus answered and said unto him, What I do thou knowest not now; but thou shalt know hereafter.

8. Peter saith unto him, Thou shalt never wash my feet. Jesus answered him, If I wash thee not, thou hast no part with me.

9. Simon Peter saith unto him, Lord, not my feet only, but also *my* hands and *my* head.

10. Jesus saith to him, He that is washed needeth not save to wash *his* feet, but is clean every whit: and ye are clean, but not all.

11. For he knew who should betray him; therefore said he, Ye are not all clean.

Verse six opens, not "then cometh he," but *consequently* (Greek, ουν), *i. e.*, in the course of this operation. Peter being one, his time would come; whether first in order, or not, does not appear.——As usual, Peter is impulsive and very out-spoken. Did he ever have a thought or impulse but it was a *live* one, and would burst out?——It seemed to him very repulsive—a very improper thing in his divine Lord—this getting down upon his knees (perhaps) and applying water to other people's dirty feet. "Lord" (said he) "dost *Thou* wash *my* feet?" He could not see the propriety at all.——The first reply of Jesus, throwing the reason of it upon the judgment of the Master, did not relieve Peter's mind. Jesus suggested that if he could not understand it now, he would at some future time. Peter, less considerate than he might have been, did not propose to take this strange operation upon trust, and therefore, under the impulses of his deep sense of its impropriety, exclaimed, "Thou shalt never wash my feet!" It might be very suitable, he probably thought, for me to wash *thy* feet; but never shalt thou wash mine!——As was his wont, Peter spoke very strongly; for he felt so. Perhaps we ought not to blame him severely; yet had he not seen enough of his Master to justify an unfaltering confidence that he never could do any thing improper, unreasonable; never a thing that had not a good meaning in it? These words of Peter have quite too much the air and tone of a *rebuke*—which as from him toward Jesus was entirely out of place. ——The reply of Jesus—" If I wash thee not, thou hast no part with me"—brought Peter round at once and most entirely. Lord, if that is the case, wash me never so much; " not my feet only, but also the hands and the head."——To understand the final reply of Jesus (v. 10) it should be noted that our version has the same word " wash " repeated—" He that is *washed* needeth not save to *wash* his feet," but the original, as spoken by Jesus, gives us two words—differing in their usage; the first used for a full bath; the second, for washing only particular portions of the body —as the hands or the feet. The primary sense of the words of Jesus must therefore be this: He who has taken the full bath—*i. e.*, of the whole person, has no occasion to wash more save his feet, for in coming from the bath his bare feet may have been soiled. So much for the primary meaning. It assumes the habit of frequent *full* ablutions, and the yet more frequent washing of the feet only. In preparation for this passover, the disciples (supposably) had taken their full bath, perhaps before they left Bethany. Now, after the walk into the city, only the feet needed washing.*

" Ye are clean, but not all of you "—looked toward the spiritual sense of " clean." Ye are washed from sin—all of you save the traitor Judas. The remark has importance as showing that washing here has some reference to its figurative or spiritual import.

The deep significance of this washing of the disciples' feet by their Lord remains still for inquiry. Shall we assume that it means nothing beyond moral cleansing, analogous to the physical cleansing by water? So some have supposed, and therefore have found here only another Christian ordinance, corresponding closely to baptism. Carrying out this analogy, they compare the full bath to regeneration; the partial washing, as of the feet, that may follow from time to time, to subsequent special cleanings from sins of later life as they may occur.

It seems to me this construction fails to reach the bottom significance of this feet washing. It overlooks the menial character of this service and consequently misses the illustration of blended

---

* Following the Sinaitic manuscript, Tischendorf omits the Greek words for " other than the feet;" but other authorities mainly retain them. If omitted, their significance must be implied.

humility and benevolence which shines forth in it. As has been already said, in washing his disciples' feet, Jesus filled the function of the humblest servant. He gave himself to *serve* his people. He put in act what he long before put in word—"The Son of man came not to be ministered unto, but to minister." In this symbol he bore our griefs and carried our sorrows; nay, more, he went calmly and lovingly into service deemed vulgar, servile, low —fit emblem therefore of the scorn and shame, the spitting and buffeting which culminated at length on the cross in a death at once of agony and dishonor.——Such service of shame and suffering Jesus came to render for his people. He foreshadowed it in the menial service of washing his disciples' feet. "If I wash thee not, thou hast no part with me," would therefore, in this view of its significance, mean, if thou canst not accept my menial and most humble service, as of one who is to bear thy griefs and carry thy sorrows, "despised and rejected of men," thou canst have no part with me.——In this view of the significance of the whole transaction we may better understand why there is no need save to wash the feet. If humiliating and painful self-sacrifice for other's good was the thing to be shown, washing the feet sufficed to show it, and no further or other washing could add to its value.

Thus far we have considered this act of feet-washing, without reference to any special circumstances at or near the time, which might intensify its significance. Let us now recall the incident stated both by Matthew (20: 17–28), and by Mark (10: 32–45)— that when Jesus was going up to Jerusalem to attend this very passover, the mother of Zebedee's children (James and John) came to him with a very special request;—"Grant that these my two sons may sit, the one on thy right hand and the other on thy left, in thy kingdom." As Mark has it the two sons themselves came, seeking to commit Jesus to the granting of their request before they had indicated what it was;—"We would that thou shouldest do for us whatsoever we shall desire." With more of mildness and less of sharp rebuke than we should expect, Jesus replied—"Ye know not what ye ask;"—there will be more of suffering and toil in reaching the honor ye seek than ye dream of. The honors of my kingdom come, not as ye are thinking, but only through the baptism of suffering and blood.——This adroit push of the two brethren to be in advance of all others in their application for the chief honors of the coming kingdom excited the indignation of the other ten. The resulting unpleasantness seems not to have altogether subsided when they came around this supper-table. For Luke (22: 24), speaking of "a strife among them which should be accounted the greatest," locates it in the midst of the scenes of this supper. This shows at least that the spirit of aspiration for pre-eminence had not subsided but was still rife even here. Some critics suggest that by Jewish usage, the feet of all the party were to be washed at this table; that as Jesus and his twelve employed no servant for their menial work, this service necessarily devolved upon some one of their number; that in the present case, no one offered himself for this service, but in far other spirit each was ambitious to get the first honors in the expected kingdom; and that, therefore, Jesus rose from the table and performed the service himself. It will be readily seen that under such circumstances the act must have been a pertinent and pungent rebuke, which could not be soon forgotten.

12. So after he had washed their feet, and had taken his garments, and was set down again, he said unto them, Know ye what I have done to you?

13. Ye call me Master and Lord: and ye say well; for *so* I am.

14. If I then, *your* Lord and Master, have washed your feet; ye also ought to wash one another's feet.

15. For I have given you an example, that ye should do as I have done to you.

16. Verily, verily, I say unto you, The servant is not greater than his lord; neither he that is sent greater than he that sent him.

17. If ye know these things, happy are ye if ye do them.

Is it not somewhat surprising that there could be the least occasion to suggest that this transaction was intended as an example? Why did not every disciple catch the spirit of it at once, and feel the power of its rebuke of his own selfishness? We must conclude that the temper of the disciples on the point here involved was far on toward the opposite pole—utterly unlike what Jesus desired and was laboring to inculcate.——Do ye understand what I have been doing? Ye call me your Lord and your Master [Teacher]; so far, well; for I am.——Ah, did they realize how high he stood above them in purity, in dignity, and in glory? Did their minds take in at all adequately the moral force of this transaction as done by the Infinite Son of God upon and for themselves—weak, vile; yet aspiring and proud mortals?—— " Verily, verily, (the usual emphatic words) I say unto you, the servant is not greater than his lord,"—and should never feel himself above any service which his lord is willing to do. It is one thing to know this principle of obligation and this rule of duty—quite another to obey it. Blessed is the man who shall *do*—who shall bring his very spirit and life into harmony with this law of self-sacrificing service for others' good! Manifestly the Master felt a painful fear lest even these most favored and best trained disciples would fail to take home to their heart and to work into their life this first law of Christian living. Alas! that there should be so much reason for this fear as to all his professed disciples, from that day onward.

On the question, What constitutes obedience to the example of Jesus in washing his disciples' feet? it seems hardly necessary to say—It lies in the spirit; not in the letter. As to the letter—the mere outside act, the washing of another's feet is an entirely different matter now from what it was then. Climate and modes of protecting the feet have made some of this difference; the usages and ideas of social life have made this difference yet much greater. It is simply preposterous to assume that obedience to Christ's example demands in our age and times the identical thing which he did.—Yet let not this fact weaken our sense of obligation to follow his example. All that his example meant then, it means now. The real service which the law of Christ demands of us is not abated by the least jot or tittle in consequence of the change in social customs which renders it improper now to wash one another's feet. It were more than a misfortune to lose the sweet power of this divine example; it were worse than a blunder to miss its precious influence toward the crucifying of human selfishness and the culture of Christian humility and of loving service toward all the Christian brotherhood.

18. I speak not of you all: I know whom I have chosen: but that the Scripture may be fulfilled, He that eateth bread with me hath lifted up his heel against me.

19. Now I tell you before it come, that, when it is come to pass, ye may believe that I am he.

20. Verily, verily, I say unto you, He that receiveth whomsoever I send receiveth me; and he that receiveth me receiveth him that sent me.

"I speak not of you all"—for there is one among you whose heart is not with me but against me. "I know whom I have chosen;" he is not one of them. In this apostasy the scripture is fulfilled which long since said; "He that eateth bread with me"—bound therefore to me in most sacred bonds of friendship—hath turned away from me, lifting his heel against me in ruthless violation of all duty and honor.——The scripture referred to here is Ps. 41: 9,—said probably of the treachery of Adonijah and his associates. (See my notes on the Psalm.) It was fulfilled in the case of Judas in the sense that this case *filled out fully* the very idea of David in the Psalm. The same thing which befell David befell David's greater Son also.——As is quite common, the connection between the event and the scripture is not that Judas turned against Jesus *for the sake* of fulfilling an ancient scripture considered as a prophecy, but simply that, in this treachery, there was a filling out again of the same crime of heartless and guilty treason.

The reader will scarcely need to be reminded that in all Oriental lands the rights of hospitality are deemed most sacred. Whoever has eaten bread or salt with another, is pledged to eternal friendship. The man who should lift his heel against a friend with whom he had eaten at the same table would doom himself to the deepest infamy.——Jesus forewarned his disciples of this treachery in Judas that it might not take them by surprise, nor suggest the inquiry—Did our Master fail to read the heart of Judas, and was he surprised in this outbreak of treachery? He would have their faith in him the rather confirmed by the developments which he had foreseen.——"Believe that I *am*"—am all I have ever claimed to be—the great "*I am*." (See John 8: 58, and 8: 24).

V. 20 is doubtless in place here, and must have some connection of thought with what precedes and follows. It behooves us to inquire for this connection. May it be this?——The treachery of Judas is before the mind of Jesus. The guilt of this treachery lay in the light sinned against, and in the position of high honor and dignity from which he had fallen. He was one of those whom Jesus had sent forth to preach the gospel. His functions were of such exalted honor that whoever should receive him would virtually receive Jesus himself. To receive Jesus was equivalent to receiving the Infinite Father who had sent him. ——From this high brotherhood of relationships with the Son of God and with the Father, Judas had utterly and basely fallen! He had shown himself to have no appreciation of this high honor; no sense of the obligations it imposed; no heart in sympathy with its exalted service. Thirty pieces of paltry silver weighed more with him than all this!

21. When Jesus had thus said, he was troubled in spirit, and testified, and said, Verily, verily, I say unto you, that one of you shall betray me.

"Troubled in spirit"—the same word we met in the scenes at the grave of Lazarus (John 11: 33)—indicating deep and painful emotion—it seemed so inexpressibly sad that one of his chosen twelve—one who had sat beside him at table; was sitting (perhaps) next him at this moment—who had been lifted so high in privilege and honor, and in the possibilities of a noble life, should turn against him in the foulness of the basest treason!——It should engage our thoughtful notice that the deep emotions of Jesus were not (apparently) indignation toward such meanness, nor resentment in view of such treachery; but unspeakable pity and sorrow over this fearful fall! "One of you" whom I have loved so tenderly, and ministered unto so long—one of you must go down to an unutterably hopeless perdition, and make a total wreck of his own well-being forever! As the story is recited by Matthew and Mark, Jesus had this fearful ruin vividly in mind: " Woe to that man by whom the Son of man is betrayed! Good were it for that man if he had never been born!"

The time had come for Jesus to announce this sad fact to his yet faithful disciples—but we notice he approaches it gradually, not calling out Judas at once by name, but saying with the usual solemn asseveration—" One of you shall betray me." It was no doubt morally wholesome to put the matter first in this indirect way. It wakened them to earnest thinking and to personal self-examination.

22. Then the disciples looked one on another, doubting of whom he spake.

23. Now there was leaning on Jesus' bosom one of his disciples, whom Jesus loved.

24. Simon Peter therefore beckoned to him, that he should ask who it should be of whom he spake.

25. He then lying on Jesus' breast saith unto him, Lord, who is it?

26. Jesus answered, He it is, to whom I shall give a sop, when I have dipped *it*. And when he had dipped the sop, he gave *it* to Judas Iscariot, *the son* of Simon.

The other evangelists present this scene with some variations and with more or less additional circumstances. Matthew (26: 21–25), and Mark (14: 18–21) make very prominent the agony of sorrow and solicitude which this announcement—"One of you shall betray me"—brought upon their souls. "They were exceedingly sorrowful and began every one of them to say unto him—"Lord, is it I?" As they relate the case, Jesus answered their inquiry and pointed out the traitor by saying (as in Matthew) "He that dippeth his hand with me in the dish, the same shall betray me;" and in Mark—"It is one of the twelve that dippeth with me in the dish." Luke treats these points in a less specific way, giving only the general statement.—"The hand of him that betrayeth me is with me on the table" (22: 21). These slight variations by no means impair the general accuracy of these independent narratives.——Only John brings out his own special agency in identifying Judas. How could John ever forget these facts? He sat next to Jesus on the right, almost leaning into his bosom, therefore in a condition to put his question in an undertone—to which Jesus seems to have given his reply so audibly as to be heard by all at the table. It is plausibly supposed that Judas sat next to Jesus on his left, so that Jesus could readily pass to him the morsel of bread ("sop") after dipping it in the common dish. This near position of the traitor at this table gives special emphasis to the words—"He that eateth bread with me;" "lifted up his heel against me;" "one of you"—among the nearest to my person, and one among the most honored. Alas, that *he* should betray me, and go away to a doom at once so guilty, so hopeless, so dreadful!

Throughout this book John is wont to designate himself as "the disciple whom Jesus loved." (See John 19: 26, and 20: 2, and 21: 7, 20, 24).——Assuming that this descriptive phrase came from John himself, what shall we say of the spirit it manifests? Is it assuming and consequential, as if John would suggest the high distinction which he enjoyed in the esteem and love of his

Master? Or is it really modest and humble, the author purposely implying that the marvel of his life had been that Jesus *could* love such a man as he? Or does the phrase make no special manifestation of John's spirit, resting upon the simple fact that being a relative, an early, and in the main a steadfast disciple, he had enjoyed a very special intimacy with Jesus?——Of these alternatives, the first is too revolting; the second is admissible and pleasant to admit; the third is not specially objectionable.

27. And after the sop Satan entered into him. Then said Jesus unto him, That thou doest, do quickly.

28. Now no man at the table knew for what intent he spake this unto him.

29. For some *of them* thought, because Judas had the bag, that Jesus had said unto him, Buy *those things* that we have need of against the feast; or, that he should give something to the poor.

30. He then, having received the sop, went immediately out; and it was night.

"Satan entered into Judas," taking advantage of the open door to his soul, for this exposure fired up his resentment and made him desperate. Now (said the devil to him) you may as well strike; you can never go back; all confidence in you is lost here; get the money while you can—and Judas thought so too.——The next steps were all downward. Jesus simply remarked—"That thou doest, do quickly." The eleven were not in the secret; and speculated to small purpose what the Master could mean. Judas went immediately out, to close the arrangement with the priests; night set in; the dread event came on apace.

Will it be a useful study of human nature to pause here a moment over this Judas Iscariot?——We naturally ask: What kind of a life had he lived since his call to be a disciple and his public enlistment into the service of Jesus? Nothing appears on the record of its earlier stages to mark him as the future apostate; nothing to show that the eleven suspected him rather than any other one of their number when Jesus astounded them by declaring, "One of you shall betray me." It is supposable that he had thought most of the earthly side of Messiah's kingdom; looked for a good time in Jerusalem when Jesus should take his throne there, and perhaps had felt discouraged of late by the opposition and by the slow progress in the line of his hopes. We may also consider that Satan helps such professors to keep up a fair appearance, to rein in their earthward propensities, or at least the manifestation of them.——Perhaps Judas enjoyed the society of good, kind brethren; had some relish for the social side of their Christian life, and having committed himself to Christ in hope of selfish good, did not see his way clear to withdraw without dishonor. So he may have managed to keep up appearances though heartless as to all real sympathy with the spirit of his Master.———Are there not such professed followers of Jesus in the churches of our age?———But why did not his better impulses recoil from betraying his Master?———Satan has his ways of keeping in the background the revolting aspects of sin. He may have whispered to the soul of Judas after this manner: The enterprise of your Master is not as hopeful as you expected; he manages badly for the best success; the money does not come in well and you are scarcely paid for your services; you need a little more money very much, and ought to have it. Besides, if Jesus goes into their hands, he can easily get out again by using his miraculous powers. You have not been quite well treated and may properly take some redress, etc.———The other side of the case was somehow strangely kept in the dark—the kindness he had experienced from his Master; the love that had been shown him; his positive conviction that Jesus was not only innocent but unselfish, benevolent, worthy of his deepest gratitude and his purest love and service; the unutterable wrong, sin, and shame of turning against so good and glorious a Friend—to all these thoughts he was strangely oblivious. But, oh, how did they come rushing upon his poor soul after the awful deed was done!——— Alas! is there any deception like that of sin? Is there any folly and madness possible to human souls like this which Satan fosters and works into force upon the human will till the sin is past and only its horrors remain!

31. Therefore, when he was gone out, Jesus said, Now is the Son of man glorified, and God is glorified in him.

32. If God be glorified in him, God shall also glorify him in himself, and shall straightway glorify him.

When Judas had gone out, the mind of the Master instantly grasped the coming result—the betrayal, the arrest, the death of agony, and what is specially to be noted, the ultimate fruit—glory to God and supreme exaltation for his Son. It is refreshing to note that these remotest results came to the front in his prospective view of his death, and that he saw them so near at hand—" shall *straightway* glorify him."

33. Little children, yet a little while I am with you. Ye shall seek me; and as I said unto the Jews, Whither I go, ye can not come; so now I say to you.

Not dazzled in the least for an instant by this prospective glory, his thoughts of love and tenderness return to the dear ones before him: "Little children," I must leave you soon. A sense of loneliness and desolation will come over you, I know; ye will seek me and long for the return of such precious hours of fellowship as we have enjoyed; but ye can not, for a time, come where I am to be. Nothing remains for you but to pass your remaining life on earth without my bodily presence. To prepare you better for this earthly life, I have many things to say.

34. A new commandment I give unto you, That ye love one another; as I have loved you, that ye also love one another.

35. By this shall all *men* know that ye are my disciples, if ye have love one to another.

These expressive words, so full of wisdom and of love, should be considered in the light of that recent disturbance of feeling, "the strife among them which should be accounted greatest," and the ambition of James and John to have first seats in his kingdom—which had stirred the indignation of the other ten disciples. It would be most dangerous, nay more, ruinous even to their cause, if such jealousies should supplant their mutual love, after their Master should have passed away. They absolutely *must* hold together in the spirit of real love for each other —such love as Jesus had felt and shown for them—or their work must utterly fail. Such love would show the world that they were disciples of Jesus, for the world never meets such love elsewhere than among his followers. The philosophies and wisdoms of earth have always failed to beget such fraternal love in human society—and always will. Reasonably, therefore, will sensible men for evermore infer that such mutual love proves discipleship in the school of Christ. It is therefore intrinsically one of the great vital powers of Christianity, working internally to augment the solid strength of Christian bodies; and working externally to enforce the conviction upon the world that such love of brethren is heaven-born, and witnesses with all the force of demonstration that these loving souls are Christ's disciples.

36. Simon Peter said unto him, Lord, whither goest thou? Jesus answered him, Whither I go, thou canst not follow me now; but thou shalt follow me afterwards.

37. Peter said unto him, Lord, why can not I follow thee now? I will lay down my life for thy sake.

38. Jesus answered him, Wilt thou lay down thy life for my sake? Verily, verily, I say unto thee, The cock shall not crow, till thou hast denied me thrice.

These words of Peter connect themselves logically with what Jesus had said (v. 33) of going away. Perhaps the intervening words about loving one another did not arrest his attention—at least they did not divert it from that previous remark by Jesus about going away from his disciples.——He is curious to learn *where* Jesus proposed to go. Jesus intimates that his going would be by death, and that Peter might come to him at some future time. The ardor of Peter's soul may be seen in the feeling—Why may I not follow thee *now?* How can I endure to live here without thee? I am ready to die for thy sake.——Ah! Peter, those noble impulses lack the solid base and the firmness of purpose which experience, culture, trial, and grace may yet give. There are deeds in thy nearer future that will astound thy friends and thyself!——How he felt when Jesus forewarned him of his fall we are not told. It should have made him watchful, self-distrustful, prayerful. We fear it failed of these results. Probably he was perplexed and scarcely believed it.——It is supposable that the words passed somehow out of his mind—until that "*look*" of Jesus which brought the cock-crowing to mind, and this admonition too, and made him weep—oh, most bitterly!

——oo:☙:oo——

CHAPTER XIV.

This chapter reports the conversations of Jesus with the eleven at the supper-table where they ate the Passover, until they adjourned to go over the Kidron to the garden of Gethsemane.—— The great central fact which shapes this entire discourse is that Jesus is soon to be parted from them, leaving them to do battle for his cause alone. Hence it became vital to minister moral strength to their faith; to open more fully before them the blessedness of the future life; to give them new light and new promises as to prayer, and not least, to reveal to them the mission and work of the Comforter; and in the same connection, to assure them of fresh manifestations of himself and of God the Father, conditioned upon their steadfast obedience to his commands. Such, therefore, is the general current of thought in this precious chapter.

1. Let not your heart be troubled: ye believe in God, believe also in me.

The death of Jesus would naturally fill their hearts with trouble—not grief only for the loss of one so honored and so dear, but anxiety, trouble in view of their own personal danger; in view also of the responsibilities of their work and of the sudden withdrawal of One upon whom they had been wont to lean so absolutely and with such sweet confidence. Therefore Jesus admonishes them "not to let their hearts be troubled." It is their privilege to trust in God and in himself, as truly and as fully as ever, and indeed far more fully than ever yet.——In the last clause of the verse the Greek verb for "believe," being repeated in precisely the same form with reference to "God" as to "me" [Jesus] may grammatically be either indicative or imperative; so that we may translate it in either of the three following ways: (1) Both indicative;—Ye do believe in God; ye do believe in me:—(2)

Both imperative;—Believe ye in God; believe ye also in me:—or (3) Either of the two indicative and the other imperative; *i. e.* Either—Ye do believe in God; believe ye also in me; or Believe ye in God; ye do believe in me.——The best is the second of these alternatives, making both clauses imperative;—Believe ye in God; believe ye also in me. They needed this exhortation to more faith in both God the Father and God the Son. So far as appears there is no reason to assume that their faith in God was already perfect, so that they only needed to bring up their faith in Jesus to the same perfection. To interpret thus—As ye already believe in God as fully as need be, so give your confidence in like fullness to me—rests on nothing in their previous history or experience, and is therefore gratuitous. It is better to interpret the exhortation as urging equally and alike more faith in God and more faith in Jesus.

2. In my Father's house are many mansions: if *it were* not so, I would have told you. I go to prepare a place for you.

3. And if I go and prepare a place for you, I will come again, and receive you unto myself; that where I am, *there* ye may be also.

The course of thought is—I must leave you; but it is only for a short time. Indeed one object in my going is to prepare a place where we may dwell together forever.——"In my Father's" [great] "house are many *mansions*"—places of abode—not precisely equivalent to *palaces* as if the leading idea were magnificence, splendor; but places for permanent abode where we may dwell together.——There was none of the coldness of formality, none of the reserve of a half distrustful friendship, manifested in saying—"If it were not so, I would have told you." I withhold nothing from friends so dear which it is important for them to know.——The best textual authorities read—"I would have told you, *for* I go to prepare," etc.——"*If* I go"—the word "*if*" not implying the least doubt as to his going. It is equivalent to saying, "When I shall have gone and prepared a place for you, I will come again and receive you to myself."——This must refer to Christ's coming *in the death* of his saints. At and in their death he comes to receive their souls to himself, to bear them up to his Father's mansions where he has prepared a place for them that they may be where he is. This passage has great importance because of its bearing upon the true sense in which Jesus speaks of coming to his people—or rather I would say—upon *one* of the senses in which he was to come again, for there are other comings besides this.*

"Many mansions"—but for whom? Observe, Jesus does not say many mansions *for you*—does not imply that the mansions

---

* See this subject treated more fully in the Appendix.

previously there were prepared and intended for his redeemed people. It should be considered that these disciples had heard of angels in heaven, "beholding always the face of the Father," and they might also have heard of various orders of unfallen beings—"principalities and powers in the heavenly places." It was pertinent therefore for Jesus to suggest that his Father's house had mansions for all these, and that still there was a place also for his disciples which he would put in order for their reception.

This brief but rich allusion to the future reunion of Christ's people with himself should not be passed without a few moments' attention to its salient points—as *e. g.*

(1.) It has *definite locality*—in opposition to the notion that heaven has no locality; means nothing but happy existence, with not the least regard to *place*.

(2.) As to *place where*, we learn nothing here save what is incidentally implied, viz, that this place prepared for Christ's people is in the same great house of our Father in which are the mansions for we know not how many orders and families of his unfallen children. Jesus testifies that there are many such mansions, and more than intimates that he will fit up yet other places of abode, of the same sort, for the new accessions gathered by his grace from the fallen sons of earth. So much then as to the future home of his people we may regard as made certain.

(3.) The notion that the future abode of Jesus with his people is to be *on this earth* after it shall have been purified by the final conflagration, is not only unsupported by revelation, but is in direct conflict with this testimony from Christ. We can afford therefore to dismiss it to its place among the fancies, thankful that something at once better and surer is provided.

(4.) It should be spoken of gratefully that this very brief allusion to the heavenly place carries in it the best possible elements of blessedness; viz. *being with Jesus where he is*. Let this be enough for us to know. Nothing could be better. May we not almost say—Nothing can add to the blessedness of this companionship and ever-abiding presence. It matters little to us *where* among the celestial bodies of the boundless universe the locality may be; what its relations in space may be to other worlds; what its surroundings; what its possibilities of acquaintance with the vast universe of matter or of created mind. The one all-comprehensive fact, itself sufficient though it were alone, will be that this everlasting home is to be *with Him* we love, with him who hath loved us; who wears our nature and takes us to himself as his redeemed brethren.

4. And whither I go ye know, and the way ye know.

5. Thomas saith unto him, Lord, we know not whither thou goest; and how can we know the way?

6. Jesus saith unto him, I am the way, the truth, and the life: no man cometh unto the Father but by me.

Ye must surely understand ere this that I refer to my own death as the going, and to heaven as the place whither. Ye must therefore know the *way* by which human beings reach that other world.——Noticeably the thought of Jesus is not at all upon the direction in space, or the convoy of agencies for transportation, or attendants upon this transit from earth to heaven:—nothing of this sort. He thinks only of the "*way*," taken in its spiritual sense, *i. e.* of himself as the only way to that blessed life above. He had already illustrated the same truth under the figure of "the door" into the sheep-fold, and had taught it in plainest terms by the promise of everlasting life to those who believe in himself.——"Way;" "truth;" "life"—abstract terms of most comprehensive import. I am myself the "*way*," for only by and through me can men reach that blessed state. I reveal all *truth;* I give all real *life*. No man cometh to the Father save by me. ——In v. 4 the Sinaitic and Vatican manuscripts (whom Tischendorf follows) give the text; "Whither I go, ye know the way." ——Thomas in reply made two points; the place whither and the way by which, and said that not knowing the first they could not understand the second. Jesus adds nothing more respecting the place whither, but answers to the more important point—the way to gain it.

7. If ye had known me, ye should have known my Father also: and from henceforth ye know him and have seen him.
8. Philip saith unto him, Lord, shew us the Father, and it sufficeth us.
9. Jesus saith unto him, Have I been so long time with you, and yet hast thou not known me, Philip? he that hath seen me hath seen the Father; and how sayest thou *then*, Shew us the Father?

Twice in this connection Jesus had spoken of the Father; in v. 2, of his Father's house as their own future abode with their Lord Jesus; in v. 6, as one to whom they must needs come through himself;—but did they really know this Father? Jesus tacitly assumes that they do not—at least that they needed a yet deeper and more full knowledge of him. Therefore he says— "If ye had known me thoroughly, ye would have known my Father also." From henceforth, since I have revealed myself to you so fully—since I have shown and am about to show you the depths of my heart of love, ye will know the Father and may consider that ye have seen not me only but him.——Philip does not quite understand these allusions to the Father. In saying— "Lord, show us the Father and it sufficeth us," he may perhaps have had his mind upon the case of Moses—"I beseech thee, show me thy glory;" when the Lord replied—"I will make all my goodness pass before thee," etc. (Ex. 33: 18-23).——"It sufficeth us"—breathes a precious spirit. If only we may have such revelations of the Father as thou, our heavenly Teacher, canst surely give, it shall be enough for us; it will meet the greatest and most deeply felt want of our souls.——The answer of Jesus is perfectly definite and lucid, and also entirely in point. I have been with you a long time, and hast thou not known me, Philip? If thou hast really seen me, thou hast seen the Father. I am the very manifestation of the Father to men. My words, my character, my life, reveal to men nothing save what is in the Father also—omit nothing that is in him. The revelation I make of the Father is therefore perfect.——The truth taught here has immense significance. Jesus, the revealer of God the Father to men; the perfect representation of the Father's character; of the Father's love, of the Father's compassion for sinners, of his interest in their salvation, of his love for the penitent and believing; of his patience, sympathy, tenderness, and eternal faithfulness to all his promises in their behalf.——It is one of the infirmities of the human intelligence that its conception of a God never seen by human eyes—never brought near in his distinct personality, but revealed only in his works of nature, his agencies of providence, his written word, and such testimonies as he may give to man's inner consciousness, should seem indefinite, dim, cold, distant. How wonderfully do all our conceptions of God become distinct, clear, vivid and intensely impressive when we have him brought before our very eyes and home to our souls in the person of the incarnate Jesus! As seen in Jesus Christ, God meets us in all the varied moods of our inner and outer life; in every variety of circumstances; in sorrows and in joys; in darkness and in light; in depressions and doubts, and no less in our days of trust and peace:—for with the life of Jesus before us and taught to see God in this life, we have the very Father himself brought home to our mind's conception and to our heart's sensibility in every possible phase in which we can need to see or feel a present God. O how near we come to the Great Father when we are introduced to him by his incarnate Son, our human brother! How definite and precious may our thoughts of him become when we understand that we may shape them upon the model of Jesus, made manifest in human flesh!

10. Believest thou not that I am in the Father, and the Father in me? the words that I speak unto you I speak not of myself: but the Father that dwelleth in me, he doeth the works.

11. Believe me that I *am* in the Father, and the Father in me: or else believe me for the very works' sake.

The form of question seems to imply that Jesus had said this before, and that Philip ought to have believed it. Art thou still slow of heart to believe what thou hast heard from my lips already—"that I am in the Father and the Father in me"? (chap. 10: 38). The same expression occurs subsequently (14: 21, and

17: 21, 23).——No human language can be framed to express a closer relation than these words express—"I in the Father, and the Father in me." It has been well said that the most intimate relationships known to human society fall below this; for we never say—The patient is *in* his physician; or the client *in* his advocate; never that the soldier is *in* his commander; the pupil *in* his teacher;—never that the parent is *in* his child nor the child *in* his parent. These human relationships give us precious illustrations of trust, confidence, sympathy, affection;—but the great depth of oneness, reaching almost to the point of complete identity—such as this language gives us—finds no adequate illustration in human relationships. How much it does in fact mean, who can tell? Where all human analogies fail us, our conceptions are (may we not say?) necessarily feeble and imperfect.

The definite points that follow are tangible. "The words that I speak unto you, I speak not of myself." Jesus had often insisted upon this point—that he came among men to speak, not on his own authority, but on that of his Father—words not only concerning God, but *from* God—the very words the Father had given him to speak.——So also of his "*works*"—The Father who dwelleth in me, doeth these miraculous works which are wrought through my voice and hand.*

Again Jesus adduces his miracles to confirm the testimony of his personal word: "Believe me"—my own declaration—"that I am in the Father and the Father in me;" or if you ask more and higher testimony, believe me on the ground of these miracles—("for the very works' sake").

12. Verily, verily, I say unto you, He that believeth on me, the works that I do shall he do also; and greater *works* than these shall he do; because I go unto my Father.

The double asseveration, "Verily, verily," implies as usual that Jesus here advances to a new announcement of special solemnity and importance. What is it? Especially, what are those "works" which believers shall do, the same essentially as his own, and even greater? And what are the force and bearing of the reason assigned—"Because I go to the Father"?

In the antecedent context the "works" spoken of include miracles unquestionably. We need not say—denote miracles to the exclusion of all other works, but they obviously include miracles and make them prominent as testimony from the Father. Does Jesus mean to say that his believing people will work miracles equal to his own, and even greater?

In the decision of this question the points to be considered are these:

*The better sustained text has it—not "*the* works," but "*his* works"—in the sense—his own works are wrought by and through me.

(1.) That in the passage where Jesus first speaks of his "works" in relation to the Father's (John 5: 17-25), these "works" include the raising of dead souls to new spiritual life as well as the working of miracles in the natural world. Therefore the idea of spiritual works, wrought in the realm of the spiritual life, is not foreign from the thought of Jesus in the usage of this term "*works.*"

(2.) That subsequent to his resurrection and ascension his believing disciples *did* perform miracles in the natural world as well as works of converting power in the spiritual world. The power to work miracles was definitely promised them (Mark 16: 17, 18). Yet it must be said, there is no intimation that these miracles were to be, or actually were, "greater" than those wrought by Jesus in person.

(3.) The reason given—"Because I go to the Father"—must look to the promised gift of the Spirit. This gift was made directly contingent upon his going: "It is expedient for you that I go away; for if I go not away, the Comforter will not come unto you; but if I go away, I will send him unto you" (16: 7).—— In the decision of our main question, very great force must be accorded to this last consideration because, standing as the reason for the greater works, it shows what was specially present to the thought of Jesus in these words.——It is therefore with special regard for this last consideration that I would interpret these "greater works" to mean the spiritual fruits of their labors, particularly as wrought by the fresh and copious effusions of the Divine Spirit. Jesus had in his eye the scenes of the great Pentecost and those continuous manifestations of the Spirit's power of which Pentecost was the beginning and the type.——Of his personal feelings in the view of that sublime manifestation of spiritual power, we are reminded that as John the Baptist said of Jesus—"He must increase but I must decrease," and said it with no pain of heart from the thought of being eclipsed by the brighter glory that came after, somewhat so, Jesus saw that the Holy Ghost, the Spirit of Truth, coming to take his place as a helpful presence and power with his people, would do greater things through those human instrumentalities than himself had wrought. He too foresaw this with no thought of sadness in being eclipsed by the greater brightness of the new manifestations. It was in his heart to honor the work of the Spirit. It is always in his heart that we *should do the Spirit honor.* No sentiment in our heart can be more grateful to him—none more vital to our spiritual life—none more conducive to the triumph of truth and to its effective force on the earth.——Let it then be carefully considered that these "greater works" to be done by those who believe in Jesus are not supposed to be due to improved methods of Christian work, nor in any large measure to progress made in Christian doctrine, nor to greater zeal in the laborers—to nothing in short that is merely or even mainly human and of man. No; the reason—"Because I go to the Father"—looks toward the mission of the Spirit as constituting this new accession of power. This fundamentally is its source and fountain. He comes to work through human instruments. So working he may bring into service better methods of Christian labor; a purer Christian doctrine; a truer zeal and a more thorough self-denial and consecration;—yet in all this, "the excellency of the power shall be evermore of God and not of man."

13. And whatsoever ye shall ask in my name, that will I do, that the Father may be glorified in the Son.

14. If ye shall ask any thing in my name, I will do *it*.

It should not surprise us that this line of thought brings up *prayer* as the next subject. Indeed it seems to me that the better punctuation connects v. 13 closely with v. 12 in this sense; Greater works than these shall he do (1.) Because I go to my Father; and (2.) Because, "whatsoever ye shall ask in my name that will I do"—a second reason why believers in Jesus after he shall have gone to the Father will do the "greater works"—viz. he appears before the throne as their Great Advocate and Intercessor, and so will secure the utmost efficiency to believing prayer.

These words—supremely rich in meaning—demand careful attention. The points to be considered are——

1. That here is "progress of doctrine" in regard to prayer—an advance in the agencies provided for prevailing prayer and in the light which reveals them. It is a new thing that Jesus the incarnate Son is now in heaven, "exalted as a Prince and Savior to give repentance and remission of sins" (Acts 5: 31); an Advocate with the Father; "a great High Priest passed into the heavens." His presence and agencies there are so revealed to us that we can see intelligently an enlarged foundation for richer spiritual blessings in answer to prayer and for greater assurance that they shall be given.

2. What is implied in asking in Jesus' name?——That we are in sympathy with his work; that we ask blessings upon his kingdom and its interests, and not upon ourselves apart from that kingdom and those interests; that we plead on the ground of his worth and not our own—because *he* is worthy, and not because we are; also that he and not we may be honored thereby. We put his name forward and not our own—appearing at the throne of the Father (so to speak) *behind* that name of Jesus and not otherwise.

3. Bearing upon the mutual relations of the Father and of the Son, we may properly compare the passage before us with John 16: 23; *here*, "Whatsoever ye shall ask in my name, that will I do;" *there*, "Whatsoever ye shall ask the Father in my name, He will give it you." The Father and the Son are *at one*—in perfect harmony in this matter of answering prayer offered in Jesus' name. It would seem that each has a common interest and a common agency; indeed, that the case is such that these forms

of statement are essentially interchangeable—"what things the Father doeth, those doeth the Son likewise."

4. The reason assigned—"That the Father may be glorified in the Son"—implies that the Father accounts it his honor to hear the intercessions of the Son; to show before the universe that he loves and honors the Son, and approves his benevolent self-sacrifice for man. The whole scheme of human salvation is no less truly an outgrowth of the Father's love than of the Son's. While it is said on the one hand that "God so loved the world that he gave his only-begotten Son," it is also said that the Son came to seek and to save the lost—came under the impulses of his own infinite love. Of this self-sacrificing love the Father delights to show his approbation.——The appropriate inference from this is—that all prayer, honestly made in the name of the Son, will be surely and joyfully answered by the Father because he loves to honor his Son, and to glorify himself before the universe thereby.

5. But there will arise the question of *limitation* as to things that may be asked in Jesus' name. What shall we say of the apparently unlimited "*any thing*"? Does this promise authorize Christians to ask *any thing they will*, with the certainty that it will be granted?

In my view this promise carries with it its own limitations—all there are—all there need be. The blessings sought must be *blessings*—not *curses;* must be such as can be asked in Jesus' name—for the glory of God in the scheme of human salvation. No provision whatever is made under this promise for men to ask for what are blessings only in the seeming, and to "consume upon their lusts." The condition of asking in Jesus' name utterly precludes all those things from the class of subjects appropriate for this prayer. Countless things of an earthly nature—health, prolonged life, food, raiment, comforts of varied sort—these may be prayed for in sympathy with Christ, for the ends of his kingdom according to our honest judgment; and if God should judge as we do, he will grant them; otherwise, we ought not to wish him to do so. If our heart is in sympathy with his kingdom, we shall of course defer sweetly to his wisdom in all such subjects of prayer. Those things—a large class—which on the great whole *may* be or may *not* be blessings, must find their necessary limitation in God's wisdom. But those things which, in their very nature, must be blessings, and never can be evils, fall entirely within the range of this promise. If we ask them in true sympathy with Jesus, asking really in his name, so that in giving them the Father may be glorified in the Son, they are sure. This promise, therefore, is as free from limitation as we ought to wish; is as broad, as rich, as sure, as it can be reasonable for us to desire.

15. If ye love me, keep my commandments.

16. And I will pray the Father, and he shall give you another Comforter, that he may abide with you for ever;

17. *Even* the Spirit of truth; whom the world can not receive, because it seeth him not, neither knoweth him: but ye know him; for he dwelleth with you, and shall be in you.

Toward a superior, obedience is the natural outgrowth and expression of love. The profession of love avails nothing without it. In this case, as between Jesus and his disciples in every age of time, he is the superior, with infinite right to command. Consequently there is always infinite reason why his people should render to him the love of their heart, and the natural expression of this love in the fullest obedience.——There is yet another view of the case. Jesus has work to be done by his people. The same salvation which has blessed their souls so abundantly, he would have them carry (instrumentally) to other souls, that they also may in like manner be blessed. As Jesus rejoiced with great joy in giving to them these blessings of his dying love, so does he long with great longing to see like blessings borne to other souls. This is the work to which he calls his people. By all the love they bear to their own Savior; by all the gratitude they feel toward him for their own salvation; by all the sympathy they have in his enterprise of saving a world from its sins—they are bound most sacredly to "keep his commandments."
——In view of the circumstances of his disciples then present, Jesus would say, I am to leave you and go away. If in my absence ye would express your love to me, this is the way to do it—"Keep my commandments;" conform your heart and life to my expressed will; perform with all diligence the work I give you to do; spare no pains to understand what my will concerning you is that ye may do it. This is the requital I ask for all the great blessings I have given you; this the testimony I look for of your love to me.

Note further: This injunction of obedience stands here as the condition of a special promise. "Keep my commandments;" so, or then, on this condition, "I will pray the Father in your behalf, and he will give you another Comforter."

We have reason for the deepest interest in learning all we can respecting this promised Comforter. Our sources of knowledge as to his mission and work are—(1) The names given him: "Comforter," "Spirit of truth," "Holy Spirit," etc.—(2) The functions assigned him—things he is said to do:—*e. g.* To "dwell with you and be in you;" to "abide with you forever;" to "teach you all things and bring all things to your remembrance whatsoever I have said unto you" (14: 26); to "guide you into all truth and show you things to come" (16: 13); in the words of Jesus, "He shall testify of me" (15: 26); "he shall glorify me, for he shall receive of mine and shall show it unto you" (16: 13, 14).—(3) That he shall be "*another* Comforter" as compared with Jesus himself, in this respect filling the place left vacant by Jesus when he withdrew his personal presence. As Jesus was to them a perpetual comforter, so shall the Spirit of truth become their comforter, being to them a second Jesus—a successor to Jesus, filling his place permanently to the end of the world.——So much Jesus taught respecting the Comforter during the conversations of this eventful night.

The word chosen here as the leading name for the divine Spirit —" Comforter "—is specially adapted to the circumstances of the disciples, then to be left in a sort of orphanage. They would need *consolation*. They had been blessed with a Friend whose words were always sustaining, consoling, cheering, morally bracing to the soul. By his words of sympathy, counsel, caution, sometimes of reproof, they had been sustained and kept during the years of their pupilage under him. When he should leave them, they would need another such Comforter. Hence it was fitting not only that Jesus should provide one, but that he should present him under this name, that they might look to the Spirit for the same sympathy, counsel, consolation, which they had been wont to obtain from Jesus himself.

The Greek word, translated "Comforter," is sometimes transferred into our language—Paraclete. The primary sense of the root is to *call;* the sense of this compound with *para*, is to speak on terms of intimacy [*with*], and hence to speak kindly, to one's comfort and consolation in trouble: also to instruct and to admonish or reprove, in cases where the truest friendship would require it.——Furthermore, the word is used of one who speaks not only *to us* in intimate friendship, but *for us to another* as an advocate, intercessor.——Such are fundamentally the functions of the Spirit as indicated by the name "Comforter."——It should be noted that these are his functions toward Christians, the followers of Jesus. Toward the world—toward men in their sins, his work is not that of comfort, consolation; but of reproof, rebuke, conviction, as we shall see (John 16: 8-11).——It will be readily seen that the descriptive points which define his service for true disciples coincide entirely with the significance of this descriptive name—Paraclete, Comforter.

Let it be noted, moreover, that, as said here, Jesus prays to the Father, and the Father, in answer to his prayer, gives the Comforter. In another passage (14: 26) Jesus says—" Whom the Father will send in my name;" and in yet another (15: 26), " Whom I will send unto you from the Father;" and also (16: 7), "If I depart, I will send him unto you." These various modes of expression are seen to be in harmony when we consider that the Father and the Son act jointly and co-ordinately in the sending of the Spirit. In certain aspects the sending may be ascribed to the Father; in certain other aspects to the Son. Apparently the most precise statement is this in the passage before us—Jesus praying, and the Father, in answer to his prayer, sending.——The great discussion of the Middle Ages—whether the Spirit proceeds from the Father *and* from the Son, or only from the Father, has been mostly logomachy—a mere war of words.

This Comforter is to "abide with you forever"—a ministration which shall continue to the end of the world—not to be closed as my personal ministrations in the flesh are to be by my death.

This presence of the Spirit, men of the world "can not receive," because they neither see nor know him. So long as the spirit of the world rules in their souls, they have no heart—*i. e.* they care not either to see or to know him. This does not say that they might not have his presence if they sought it: might not hear his voice if they would listen to it reverently and obey it honestly. It simply means that in the spirit of the world— *i. e.* of selfishness and sin—of pleasure-loving and seeking—they give no ear to the Spirit; never put themselves in communion with his presence; have no heart for his teaching and counsel; know him not.——But ye, my disciples, know him, for he is infinitely near to you, dwelling within you, abiding in you.

This blessed truth of Christian experience found its early illustration from the case—very familiar to all Jewish Christians—of the Shechinah—the visible glory of God in their ancient temple. Under this figure, the Christian body became a temple of the Holy Ghost. He dwelt in this temple, as of old the glory of God reposed above the mercy-seat beneath the cherubim, in the deep recesses of the most holy place.

18. I will not leave you comfortless: I will come to you.

Where the Greek has the word "orphanous," equal to *orphans*, our translators put it "comfortless," to keep up the harmony with the word "Comforter." Orphans gives the more exact sense. They would be as children left alone in the world—father dead, mother dead. But Jesus would not leave them so. "I will come to you," he said—said it manifestly with reference to sending the Spirit to dwell with them as a near and dear and perfect Friend. The Spirit would fill the place of his own presence. They would have no occasion to regret the change by which Jesus should go (bodily) and the Spirit come (spiritually).

19. Yet a little while, and the world seeth me no more; but ye see me: because I live, ye shall live also.

It was but a little while and death would remove his bodily presence. Then the world with their eye would see him no more. Ye (said he to his disciples) will see me still—not with the eye of flesh, but with the eye of the inner soul. Yet strictly speaking, this vision of Jesus is by means of the Spirit, of which Jesus said in this very discourse—"He shall receive of mine and shall show it unto you. He shall testify of me; he shall bring all things to your remembrance whatsoever I have said unto you." No work of the Spirit in the souls of God's people is made more prominent in these discourses—none can be in itself more vital and precious—than to *reveal Jesus*. His perfect ability to set all truth respecting Jesus in beams of sun-light before the Christian's thought and apprehension qualifies him for this service. Jesus might fitly say of those who had these clear and impressive revelations, "Ye see me."——Such seeing bears home to the soul a vivifying spiritual power. "Because I live, ye shall live also." Because, though I go away in death, this dying is not ceasing to be—is not ceasing to act and to fill all the functions of real life, but is rather, to rise to a mightier life-power and to a more blessed existence. Because I receive this great accession of life-forces in my ascension to the Father, so shall ye live also, with life renewed and mightily invigorated and intensified. The gift of the Spirit shall breathe new life into your souls. Ye need not fear that my death on the cross is destined to lessen my power to sustain and to comfort you in your Christian life, for it will rather bring to you a quickened life, of intenser energy and richer blessedness.

20. At that day ye shall know that I *am* in my Father, and ye in me, and I in you.

This passage has special interest on two grounds: (*a*.) That it places side by side the relation of Jesus to the Father on the one hand and to his people on the other, implying some degree of analogy between these respective relationships.——If we inquire more deeply into the points contemplated in this analogy, we need be in no doubt that it looks, at least in part, towards the *spiritual life*—a precious union of heart, a relationship of sympathy and love.——Does it look also, more fundamentally, toward some analogy in the relationship of *being*, comparing Jesus related to God as a son on the one side, with Jesus, related to his people as a brother on the other side? Who can tell?

(*b*.) The other point of interest in the passage lies in the word "*know*." "At that day ye shall *know*." It will be a new knowledge, known before but poorly and imperfectly if at all. Exegetically we must find the significance of this knowledge in the line of the speaker's thought as brought out particularly in vs. 21, 23:—"I will love him, and will manifest myself to him." "My Father will love him, and *we* will come unto him and make our abode with him." Under the light and inner glory of such manifestations—Jesus to the believing and obedient soul; Jesus and the Father also, to every such loving and obedient one, even to the extent of coming to him and abiding with him—the soul thus visited, not with manifestations only but with the very presence of the Son and of the Father—can not but *know*, as said here, both that Jesus is *in* the Father and also *in* his people. It is the knowledge of experience, using this word in its broadest sense—a knowing that comes of the witnessing presence of God in Christ to the human soul.

21. He that hath my commandments, and keepeth them,

he it is that loveth me: and he that loveth me shall be loved of my Father, and I will love him, and will manifest myself to him.

To "*have* the commandments" of Jesus implies careful study, diligent inquiry and docility. To "keep them" involves the true spirit of obedience—the one deep, changeless purpose to do *all* his known will. This is the legitimate evidence of true love to Christ. He can accept no lower evidence than this; but he will most joyfully accept this evidence, and give every obedient, loving soul the testimony that he accepts it. This is what he declares here. "He that loveth me shall be loved of my Father," or as said most directly in v. 23—"My Father will love him," for the Father rejoices greatly to see his Son honored truly and loved with the love of honest obedience. "I also will love him, and will manifest myself to him"—causing him to *know* that I love him; revealing to him my face and favor; answering his prayer; renewing his spiritual strength; witnessing by my Spirit to the love I bear him.——Of course the fulfillment of this promise lies in the field of human consciousness and personal experience. Each Christian must learn its inner meaning for himself alone. Inasmuch as to *manifest* is to *show*—to cause one to *see*—therefore for Jesus to manifest himself is to make himself seen and known. Consequently, this revelation must be made to each individual soul, for himself to see and not for another; also to see for himself and not for any other.——A statement essentially the same yet somewhat more full, we have in v. 23.

22. Judas said unto him, not Iscariot, Lord, how is it that thou wilt manifest thyself unto us, and not unto the world?

This other disciple bearing the name Judas—(the "Jude" of the Epistles)—to be broadly distinguished from Iscariot who was not there and was never to be among the chosen again—could not understand how Jesus would show himself to his disciples and not to the world. He was grasping some new idea about an inward manifestation, not visible to the godless eye, and yet the mystery puzzled him. How could it be? Fortunately this question brought to them from the Lord a renewed statement of essentially the same truth, yet with clearer light upon some of its aspects.

23. Jesus answered and said unto him, If a man love me, he will keep my words, and my Father will love him, and we will come unto him, and make our abode with him.

Observe (*a*.) The natural connection between love and obedience is put here, as compared with v. 21, in new form:—*there;*—"He that hath my commandments and keepeth them, he it is that loveth me:" *here*—"If a man love me, he will keep my words.' The fact is the same—but in other form of statement. ——(*b.*) Jesus had said before—"I will love him:" here, only—"The Father will love him."——(*c.*) Instead of the word used before—"manifest"—he says here; "will come unto him and make our abode with him." This new form of statement was obviously designed to answer the question put by Jude—"*How* wilt thou manifest thyself to us and not to the world?" We will come to him and dwell with him. You can surely understand that a man will easily learn to know those who come to him and live with him; "abide with him;" give him their every day presence; their constant communion. If a man can not know thoroughly and intimately those who come and abide with him in all the intimacies of every-day life, what can he know?——The mystery of the point *How?* as it lay in the mind of Jude, here is no attempt to explain to men of the world that they might understand it. It was enough to explain it to Jude and to the disciples—an explanation equally good for all disciples in every age. Every disciple—loving and obedient—will know what these manifestations mean when Jesus and his Father shall come to him and make their abode with him; when they shall become inexpressibly near to his conscious spirit; when he shall *know* the presence of Jesus and the presence of the Father; when the spirit of adoption is living and strong in his heart whereby he says spontaneously—Father; Father.

It will be readily seen that this promise is put on one definite condition, viz. love and obedience—that love which begets obedience. Every believer who has such love as begets and insures honest obedience to Christ's commandments—including both knowing and keeping—has this promise to claim as his own. It is made sure to him. No promise in the sacred word is stated more definitely; none is connected with its one condition more simply and closely; none is therefore more easily understood and more readily made available.

We should greatly wrong ourselves if we were to pass these words of Jesus without taking special note of what he says of himself and of the Father as bearing upon his *true divinity*, and yet *distinct personality*. Perhaps we shall see this better if we make the supposition that Jesus is only a distinguished human teacher, of the same sort as Peter and John. Then on this supposition, we should be forced to ask—What can he mean by claiming for himself the love and obedience of his people in the same sense and degree in which love and obedience are claimed for God the Father? What can he mean by promising to manifest himself to his loving and obedient friends in such ways as the world can not see and can not know?——By what authority can he promise that such friends of his shall be loved of his Father, God? By what right does he pledge to them the Father's love? More still: Is it not impudent presumption in him to put himself on the same level with the Father and say—"*We* will come to him and make our abode with him"? Was Jesus com-potent to make such pledges in honesty and truth? If so, then he is far more than a merely human teacher. If so, he can be nothing less than the Infinite Son of God.

Observe also that he does not by any means identify himself with the Father. Every word of our passage rests upon the assumption of distinct personality. "I will love him;" "my Father will love him;" "*we* will come unto him and make our abode with him." If this does not imply and involve distinct personality, what human language can?——If there is mystery in the mutual relation of the Son to the Father, be it so. Here is no attempt to explain the mystery; but the fact of distinct personality is put in words than which none in our language—none in any human language—can be plainer.

24. He that loveth me not keepeth not my sayings: and the word which ye hear is not mine but the Father's which sent me.

Statements of special importance in the Scriptures are often strengthened by being put in both the positive and the negative form. In vs. 21, 23, we found the positive form; here, the negative: "He that loveth me not keepeth not my sayings." The non-loving are of course non-obedient. I say all this, not on my own authority alone, but on that of my Father who has sent me—a statement often repeated by Jesus, as a thing never to be forgotten or left out of account.

25. These things have I spoken unto you, being *yet* present with you.

26. But the Comforter, *which is* the Holy Ghost, whom the Father will send in my name, he shall teach you all things, and bring all things to your remembrance, whatsoever I have said unto you.

So much I have said to you while present; the rest—the many things more which you will need to know—will be taught you by the Holy Ghost. This was the very place and time to put in strong light the work of the Spirit *as a Teacher*. He was to supplement the teaching of Jesus—to teach the many more things—the "all things"—they might need to know. Moreover, he would not only reveal new truth as they might be prepared for its revelation, but he would bring to their remembrance what Jesus had said, recalling it for a more full illustration, and a deeper spiritual impression. For it can not be denied that the disciples had been dull and slow of understanding as to many things Jesus had said. Their previous misconceptions of the nature and genius of his kingdom had often misled them, had often darkened their minds, and retarded their reception of the simple truths of the gospel. The death and resurrection of Jesus struck down many of their cherished notions, and consequently had brushed away the mists and clouds so as to let in heaven's clearer light.

If Jesus had continued among them after his resurrection not forty days only, but forty years, talking with them as with the two brethren on the way to Emmaus he would have done much of this work himself;—but this was not the better plan. Ascending to heaven, he sent down the Spirit of truth on this mission of spiritual instruction—not by taking two or three only at once—but myriads if need be at the same moment;—not for forty years only, but for all the years thenceforward even to the end of the world.

27. Peace I leave with you, my peace I give unto you: not as the world giveth, give I unto you. Let not your heart be troubled, neither let it be afraid.

The only right interpretation of this verse is the Oriental—that which is based upon all Oriental usage. According to this usage "peace" is the heart's benediction—the utterance of loving farewell words; expressions of earnest good will; prayer for all peace and prosperity. The usage runs through all Old Testament times; the salutation, "Peace" (shalom) we hear often in its history of common life, *e. g.* Gen. 43: 23, and Judges 19: 20, and 1 Sam. 25: 6, etc. Also in the New Testament, compare Matt. 10: 13, and Luke 10: 5, 6; Gal. 6: 16, and Eph. 6: 23. To this day the Arab gives his friends his "salam," repeated and still repeated according to the fullness of his heart or the homage he pays to the conventional forms of social life.

Jesus says—I am about to leave you; I give you my blessing; I leave it with you; and mark this—not as the world give; not at all in their spirit of form and ceremony; not in words void of heart, empty of love; but with overflowing soul and with abiding friendship, enduring sympathy, the most tender concern for your welfare. Let this suffice to sustain your souls under the pressure of the sternest trial. Let not your heart be troubled or afraid. Ye know my love for you; ye shall have occasion to know my power to save and the fullness of my promised consolations.

28. Ye have heard how I said unto you, I go away, and come *again* unto you. If ye loved me, ye would rejoice, because I said, I go unto the Father: for my Father is greater than I.

The point of critical interest here lies in the words—"My Father" (or as in the improved text "the Father") "is greater than I." "Greater," in what sense? Must it necessarily mean "greater" in the essential elements of his being—*i. e.* of a higher nature; of attributes really divine—with the implication that those of Jesus are less than divine?——Or may these words of Jesus mean in this connection, only greater in *position*—greater as being exalted above all the incidents of such a world as this—so that for Jesus to go there will be to exchange a life of sorrow, humiliation, trials manifold, for one of infinitely higher dignity and blessedness?——In making our choice between these two possible alternatives, two things may safely be said, and perhaps these include all that can be affirmed safely.

(1) That the latter construction meets the exigencies of the passage; *i. e.* it gives a good reason, and doubtless the true reason, why they should rejoice in his going to the Father. In his going they could not rejoice on their own account, so far forth as their own interest, pleasure, comfort, were concerned; but *for his sake* they would rejoice, because to him this going to the Father would be exaltation in place of humiliation; glory instead of shame; bliss forever, and no more sorrow.——Thus the logic of the passage demands that the word "greater" should refer to position, and not necessarily to the essential elements of being. Around the Father's throne would be supreme dignity and glory, to which the Son would be at once exalted upon his ascension to the Father. This view is sustained fully by the current of apostolic teaching in regard to the ascension of Christ and the glory that should follow.

(2) On the other hand, it is by no means apparent that the other proposed construction—The Father greater than I in his essential nature—can meet the logical demands of the context. Admit for argument's sake that the sense is—The Father a greater being than I in his essential nature, would this be any more a fact after the ascension of Jesus than before? Would it bring any new accession of happiness to the Son after his ascension?—*i. e.* would it be any apparent reason why the disciples should rejoice because Jesus was going to the Father?

29. And now I have told you before it come to pass, that, when it is come to pass, ye might believe.

I have spoken thus freely of my death and of my subsequent ascension to the Father that when ye shall see these things, ye may have the more assured confidence in all I have said and in all that I am. Thus when your straining eyes shall follow me rising toward heaven till the opening cloud shall encompass me and take me from your sight, ye may return to your work, not with waning but with growing confidence; not with deeper sadness, but with sublimer joy.

30. Hereafter I will not talk much with you: for the prince of this world cometh, and hath nothing in me.

What I can say to you now must be limited; our time is short. The Prince of this world—Satan—is coming shortly: he will find no foothold in me; no avenue of approach; no point open to his assault; nothing upon which his tempting arts can take hold. The conflict will be on his part desperate; but as to the issue, we have nothing to fear.

31. But that the world may know that I love the Father;

and as the Father gave me commandment, even so I do. Arise, let us go hence.

All these things I have said and done that the world may know that I love the Father, and have done all in obedience to his commandment. The sweet consciousness of this was the joy of his soul. The testimony of it he had sought in all honesty to bring before men that they might see reason to accept his mission and believe in him to their salvation.

At this point, the conversation around the passover table seems to have closed. Preparations were soon made to leave the city and go as usual across the Kidron to the Mount of Olives. The next allusion to place locates them in the garden of Gethsemane. Yet we infer from John 18: 1 that the discourses recorded in chap. 15 and 16 and the prayer of chap. 17, occurred in the city before they left; but more definitely *where;* whether in the house in which the Passover was eaten or elsewhere, does not appear.

CHAPTER XV.

The aim of Jesus in this precious discourse is to impress upon his disciples a sense of spiritual dependence upon himself; to reveal the conditions of obtaining from himself perpetual strength; to testify to his love for them and to intensify their love to himself; to forewarn them of hatred from the world—from which he passes to speak of the great sin of those who rejected him, closing with a renewed allusion to the promised Comforter and to his work, with which their own personal agency should co-operate.

1. I am the true vine, and my Father is the husbandman.

2. Every branch in me that beareth not fruit he taketh away: and every *branch* that beareth fruit, he purgeth it, that it may bring forth more fruit.

3. Now ye are clean through the word which I have spoken unto you.

In Isa. 5: 1–7 the Lord's people are put as his vineyard upon which he expends his care in culture, and from which he looks for fruit often in vain. This figure is here expanded with some modifications, especially that which makes Jesus the vine and his people the branches, bearing or not bearing fruit according as they meet their moral responsibilities.——I understand Jesus to call himself the "*true* vine," in the sense of real, genuine—one that honestly fulfills its legitimate function of nutrition to its branches. Perhaps he meant to intimate that in himself the figure of vine and branch became thoroughly appropriate to express the relation between himself and his people.

In speaking of the treatment of the non-bearing and of the bearing branches, the original Greek makes its contrast more clearly and yet tersely than our English version: thus: Every non-bearing branch he *taketh away;* * every branch that beareth, *he taketh away from it;* † *i. e.* taketh away the superfluous shoots that rob the young fruit-clusters, abstracting nutriment to give it to useless foliage and tree-growth. The antithesis between taking away the whole branch that promises no fruit, and taking away *from that branch* its superfluous growths, is put at once clearly, tersely, and forcibly.

Our English has yet another infelicity in the use of the words "purge" (v. 2) and "clean" (v. 3). The old English word "purge" has become obsolete except as it has saved itself from utter oblivion by linking itself with professional phrases, *e. g.* in the usage of courts of law—to purge one's self is to clear himself of alleged offense; while in the physician's dialect, "purge" retains yet another and a very definite significance. With these exceptions the word has deceased.——Few English readers would suspect that "clean" (v. 3) means the same as "purged" (in v. 2), yet the original gives us a word of the same significance, from the same root. The connection of thought demands the same sense—which in both cases might better have been put—"pruneth"—"pruned"—in the sense of cutting away superfluous and damaging growths.

As bearing upon the use of figures like this of the vine, let us note that it is only to carry out the figure that a branch (one of Christ's disciples) is said to be *"in me"* (Christ) and yet not bear fruit. He might be in Christ *by profession*—numbered and named among the disciples; but really *in Christ*, in the strict sense, he could not be, without bearing some fruit. Indeed, Jesus himself affirms below (v. 5)—"He that abideth in me and I in him, the same bringeth forth much fruit."——In the literal vine there are often branches which are not fruit-bearing. Correspondingly, in the spiritual life, one might be,—as it should appear to others' eyes—*in Christ*, and yet, if he bore no fruit, this fact would show that for the time at least, the vital, life-imparting connection with Christ is suspended. *That* professed Christian should take the warning—not to say the alarm—lest death supervene.

The blending of literal terms with figurative is seen (v. 3); "Ye are *pruned* through the *word* which I have spoken unto you." "Pruning" is in and of the figure; the "word" is of that which the figure represents—the literal Christian heart or character. Jesus had been pruning away the non-bearing branches by his words of instruction, reproof, correction. The spoken words were

* αιρει. † καθαιρει.

the pruning knife; but in strictness, the "pruning" is figure; the "word" is literal.—Moreover, let it not be thought to mar the beauty or force of this figure that Jesus himself does this pruning, although in the outset the Father is the husbandman and Jesus the vine. In some aspects Jesus *is* the vine; in other aspects he has the care of the pruning. The figures of scripture are plain and instructive, even although they sometimes fall short of meeting all the demands of our rules of rhetoric.

4. Abide in me, and I in you. As the branch can not bear fruit of itself, except it abide in the vine; no more can ye, except ye abide in me.

5. I am the vine, ye *are* the branches. He that abideth in me, and I in him, the same bringeth forth much fruit; for without me ye can do nothing.

6. If a man abide not in me, he is cast forth as a branch, and is withered; and men gather them, and cast *them* into the fire, and they are burned.

Here the branches are thought of, mostly, as intelligent and morally responsible—as personally active in forming and maintaining in due force the living connection with Christ the vine; *i. e.* the discourse shades off gradually from the figure—the vine-branches in husbandry—to the thing illustrated by the figure, viz. the human soul as being in Christ. The figure, however, still helps us to apprehend the spiritual fact.——The central idea in these verses is the *abiding;* the sustained life-connection of the soul with Christ. As the branch, severed from the parent vine, is cut off from nutrition, can bear no fruit and dies; so the soul that abides not in Christ can bear no fruit—can not even *live*—but withers, dies, is cut away, fit only for burning. Human souls, abiding in Christ, bear much fruit; severed from him, as a branch may be severed from its parent stock, they can do nothing. The sense of the original in the phrase (v. 5) "*without me* ye can do nothing," is precisely this;—*apart* from me—severed from me like a branch cut off—ye are powerless as to spiritual fruitage. ——The reader will note that this abiding in Christ is presented as a moral duty, a thing of obligation—proper to be enjoined by command. Some of the care and culture therefore devolve upon what in the figure are branches, but in reality are morally responsible human souls.

Let no one pass these words—so richly freighted with precious thought—truths most vital to all Christian living—without solemn personal endeavor, first, to comprehend their significance; and then, to appropriate all their wealth of instruction to his own new and divine life.

7. If ye abide in me, and my words abide in you, ye shall ask what ye will, and it shall be done unto you.

By the most natural relations of thought, Jesus passes from "*abiding in him*" to *prayer*. Verily it is chiefly by prayer that this abiding is to be maintained and kept in vigor. Prayer holds on to the arm of Jesus; or more in keeping with the figure, it is the channel of life-sympathy and life-power, corresponding to the tubes and ducts through which the vital juices flow and reflow between vine-stock and fruit-branch. Prayer! it lives on Christ, and draws invigorating force evermore from that life-fountain.

The promise, standing here with its condition, is complete in both its main parts—the conditions so clear that none need mistake them; the blessings promised so rich that none need wish them more so.——As to conditions, we note the slight change which is essentially explanatory—from "abide in me and I in you"—to "abide in me and *my words* in you." While it stood "I in you," the human duty and agency were less clear, for even an honest, truth-seeking heart might say—What can I do to keep Christ abiding in me? But when Jesus substitutes "my words" for "I," we see at once how the thing is to be done. We are to hold his words close to our own living, loving heart; study their significance; absorb their living force; breathe their spirit; conform our voluntary activities evermore to their demands. He who loves Christ's words and keeps them in abiding force upon his own moral nature certainly has Jesus himself abiding in the heart.

Fulfilling these conditions "ye shall ask what ye will, and it shall be done unto you." What richer promise could the very soul of want frame for itself? What more should the children of poverty and need desire than the privilege of asking what one will, to be granted him?

But is not this promise too broad and too rich for God to make and to fulfill? Does it not transfer too much power to mortals? Who will remain Ruler of the universe and Manager of all mundane things when the whole sacramental host shall come up to the measure of this great promise and every one ask what he will—God being pledged to grant it?——We may dismiss all fear lest the Lord should make promises, blind to their possibilities of danger. In this case the safeguard lies essentially in the conditions. "If ye abide in me and my words abide in you," ye will be most entirely in harmony and sympathy with the will of God, desiring what he desires; valuing above all else what he most desires for you, and desiring nothing save what will (as ye judge) meet his approval and subserve his glory. If in any point ye should misjudge, God will see it (as you should wish him to do), and withhold it (as ye would pray that he might). Would not this work well and safely for God's kingdom?

8. *Herein is my Father glorified, that ye bear much fruit; so shall ye be my disciples.*

Standing in this connection, these words seem to have two main objects:—(1) To afford additional ground for confidence that God will answer prayer, doing for us whatever we ask because to do so is vital to our bearing much fruit:—(2) To show that Christian fruitfulness honors God and consequently must be most grateful and pleasing to him. Such fruit-bearing is altogether in harmony with his own nature—always "doing good to all"—"his tender mercies evermore over all his works." In one important view this is what men are converted for, viz. that they may be laborers together with God to put forward God's own work of salvation in a world of lost men.

"So shall ye be my disciples"—for this and only this is learning truly of me; imbibing my spirit; walking in my footsteps. For this I have called, taught, trained you all; this work, therefore, I expect at your hands.

9. *As the Father hath loved me, so have I loved you: continue ye in my love.*

They could not doubt that the Father loved his Son Jesus; there might be ground for doubt or fear whether Jesus could love them. This statement was therefore well adapted to confirm their conviction and sense of the love of their Master.——The exhortation—"Continue ye in my love," assumed that they might forfeit and alienate his love. Let them take care to avoid every thing that could tend to this result; let them also cultivate and cherish whatever would serve not only to perpetuate but to intensify his love for them.

We must not omit to notice how very timely these words were, considering how soon these disciples were to be left alone, under circumstances in which the sense of Jesus' love would seem to be their only remaining consolation, and their only source of courage to heart or hope.

10. *If ye keep my commandments, ye shall abide in my love; even as I have kept my Father's commandments, and abide in his love.*

It was kind as well as considerate in Jesus to tell them how they might retain his love, "*abide*" in it, according to the figure of branches abiding in their vine. They must "keep his commandments." This keeping would be the proof of their love (as he had often said); and it would ensure his continued love to them. To enforce this, he appeals to his own case as toward his Father. Their relation to him was the same as his to his Father.

11. *These things have I spoken unto you, that my joy might remain in you, and that your joy might be full.*

In these exhortations Jesus had two objects, viz. his own continued joy in them, and their augmented, completed joy in him. In the opposite course, they would bring bitter grief to him; and not woe only, but ruin upon themselves. Would they not think of this contrast and strive to appreciate its moral force?

12. This is my commandment, That ye love one another, as I have loved you.

13. Greater love hath no man than this, that a man lay down his life for his friends.

14. Ye are my friends, if ye do whatsoever I command you.

This command—"Love one another"—is repeated here (see 13: 34), even with the same words annexed—"As I have loved you"—which we may take as at once the *standard* or *measure*, and also the *motive*, of this new command. We may suppose it repeated here for the twofold reason—that it lay so near his heart; and that he wished to enlarge upon the appended clause considered as a motive. "*As* I have loved you;" but consider how great this love of mine toward you has been, and how you will properly look upon it when you see me die for you. No manifestation of love can be stronger than to lay down one's life for his friend. What more, what beyond this can man possibly do? He has no costlier gift to bestow—no greater sacrifice to make. But precisely this is what Jesus does for his friends. Now he asks them to show themselves his friends by doing what he commands. Does he not imply—I ask of you nothing more? So much—for my life laid down for you—I have the right to ask; so much you will surely do for your dying Friend!

15. Henceforth I call you not servants; for the servant knoweth not what his lord doeth: but I have called you friends; for all things that I have heard of my Father I have made known unto you.

The word *confidential* gives the pith of this verse. Jesus treated his disciples as his *confidential* friends. They were not "henceforth"—for the statement looks somewhat more to the future than to the past—to be mere servants for toil and drudgery —to do service not knowing why this rather than any thing else; but as friends, taken by the Master into the fellowship and confidence of co-workers, intelligent helpers, who should understand the nature and object of their work, and feel consequently a personal interest in its results.——We can not withhold the remark that he who spake these words *understood human nature*—knew full well how powerfully such expressions of confidence impress responsibility, draw out the heart, inspire endeavor.

If it be said that this verse runs in a very different strain from 13: 13, 16, "Ye call me Master and Lord, and ye say well, for so I am," etc., the reply is—even so; the strain *is* different; the object is different and each good and noble in its place. Yet there is no conflict whatever between the two. The earlier statement contemplated his real superiority, his higher dignity; but was utterly far from thrusting the disciples into the position of servility. This latter by no means denies Christ's infinite superiority; yet it does imply great condescension—a sympathy and fellowship which rest—may we not say?—upon a common humanity, and upon the confidence which real love begets where it safely may.——"All things which I have heard of my Father," pertaining to the scheme of salvation—to the methods, encouragements, inspirations for Christian work; all the things needful for your guidance and efficiency—I have made known unto you. As ye contemplate this great wealth of truth, pause and think of it as the outflowing of my confiding heart toward you as laborers together with God; regard it as said to you because ye are my friends, as to whom I have no concealments—nothing other than fraternal confidence.

16. Ye have not chosen me, but I have chosen you, and ordained you, that ye should go and bring forth fruit, and *that* your fruit should remain; that whatsoever ye shall ask of the Father in my name, he may give it you.

The choice which brought these men rather than others into the family of Jesus and into the first group of apostles was made by Jesus, not by them—was his choosing of them, not their choosing of him. He set them apart by ordination to their work, with these two great objects—both of a sort to be brought out pertinently here, viz, that they should bring forth much and abiding fruit: and that they might be models of prevailing prayer—evincing its principles, its methods, and glorious possibilities. Let them take courage even to the point of full assurance of success in their work.——What could be more inspiring? Called of Jesus into his service with such a calling, for such ends, with such sustaining forces—how "strong in the Lord" it was their privilege to become!

Need we say less of all their successors in every age, and not least, our own?

17. These things I command you, that ye love one another.

I have enjoined upon you several precepts; let them all bear upon this one great, freshly announced duty—that of love to one another. My heart feels this most deeply: how can I forbear to repeat it and to make every thing converge to enforce it?

18. If the world hate you, ye know that it hated me before *it hated* you.

19. If ye were of the world, the world would love his own; but because ye are not of the world, but I have chosen you out of the world, therefore the world hateth you.

20. Remember the word that I said unto you, The servant is not greater than his lord. If they have persecuted

me, they will also persecute you; if they have kept my saying, they will keep yours also.

21. But all these things will they do unto you for my name's sake, because they know not him that sent me.

"If" (v. 18) supposes no doubtful contingency. The world will hate you. When you feel its hatred malign and scornful, then consider for your comfort that your Master bore the same before it fell on you. Let there come, with the world's scorn, this consolation, that it proves you not of them—not of their party, but of mine. Ye can afford to bear their hatred for the sake of my love. Moreover, remember what I said to you about servant and Lord. If they abuse the Lord, ye should expect them to abuse the servant no less. Consider; they have persecuted me; they will you. If they had kept my saying, ye might hope they would keep yours; but since they have rejected mine, ye must expect nothing better.——"Do unto you for my name's sake," means because ye bear my name. Because they hate me, they will also hate mine.——They hate me and mine also because they refuse to know that my Father hath sent me. They have set at nought the testimony I have given them of my mission from the Father. In this ignorance and blindness which themselves have chosen, they must remain my enemies and die in their sins.

22. If I had not come and spoken unto them, they had not had sin; but now they have no cloak for their sin.

23. He that hateth me hateth my Father also.

24. If I had not done among them the works which none other man did, they had not had sin: but now have they both seen and hated both me and my Father.

25. But *this cometh to pass*, that the word might be fulfilled that is written in their law, They hated me without a cause.

The underlying doctrine here is that light sinned against both heightens and measures the guilt of sin. So far indeed does Jesus carry this point that he speaks as if those Jews would have been without sin—sinless—if he had not come among them and spoken to them, doing before their eyes miraculous works never done by mortals. But we must construe these words as referring to the sin of rejecting his mission, and not to every other form of sin. That sin of unbelief toward himself was specially in his mind: it is therefore legitimate to interpret his words as referring to that sin only. So construed, they would doubtless have been without sin if they had had no light at all as to his claims to be the Son of God and their promised Messiah.——This hatred of Jesus involved also hatred of his Father. Through the preaching of Jesus they had come to know more of God the Father, and hence their hatred of him became more intelligent and more damning.

In these facts those ancient scriptures (Ps. 35: 19, and 69: 4) had their significance filled out. Holy men of old had this plaint to make; why should not Jesus also? and his faithful followers no less?

26. *But when the Comforter is come, whom I will send unto you from the Father, even the Spirit of truth, which proceedeth from the Father, he shall testify of me:*

27. *And ye also shall bear witness, because ye have been with me from the beginning.*

Jesus repeats here many things said before (14: 16, 17, 26) of the Comforter, and obviously for the purpose of bringing out more fully his witnessing agency for Christ. In the context Jesus had spoken of himself as maligned, hated, rejected by the men of his generation—the "world" of those times—before whom he had testified as to his mission from God. When they shall have put him to death, will this testimony of his be quashed—its force be exhausted, and its light extinguished forever? No, indeed. The glorious Spirit of truth, proceeding from the Father, will take up the theme and testify for Jesus through tongues of flame, and with transcendent, convincing power.——Ye too shall bear witness for me because ye have been with me from the first, personally familiar with my teachings, my miracles, my life.——The hour would come—was not far hence even then—when such words from Jesus would be supremely inspiring. How they must have come up to their minds afresh amid the glories of the Great Pentecost! How the witnessing testimonies of that scene must have quenched the fear of the disciples lest their Master's claims and cause were doomed to go down in dishonor and oblivion!

CHAPTER XVI.

This chapter closes the conversations of Jesus held with his disciples prior to the scenes of Gethsemane. The central thought is—the approaching separation—Jesus soon to leave them and return to the Father. In view of this near event, he apprises them of the persecutions they must meet (vs. 1-4); assures them there is occasion rather for joy than for sorrow in his departure, for his going is to be followed by the Spirit's coming (vs. 5-7); shown in what the Spirit will do; (*a.*) as toward the ungodly (vs. 8-11);—(*b.*) for themselves, especially in revealing Jesus to their souls (vs. 12-15). The transient pain but ensuing joy consequent upon his leaving them, and their subsequent coming to him, are put (in vs. 16-22). The subject of prayer recurs again (vs. 23-27), and also the leading theme—his return to the Father and its results to themselves, with closing words of consolation (vs. 28-33).

1. These things have I spoken unto you, that ye should not be offended.

2. They shall put you out of the synagogues: yea, the time cometh, that whosoever killeth you will think that he doeth God service.

3. And these things will they do unto you, because they have not known the Father, nor me.

The merely English reader may need the caution not to take the word "offended" in the sense of being displeased. It means only being stumbled—*i. e.* perplexed, puzzled, and perhaps conseqently discouraged. Jesus forewarns them of impending persecution, to the end that it should not take them by surprise, but should rather confirm their faith in himself. The religious authorities of the Jews would excommunicate them from their church [synagogue], and with a perverted and terribly bigoted conscience, would shed their life-blood, and think it a religious offering acceptable to God. All this because they had not known God the Father nor his Son. They assumed that they knew God; no mistake could be greater. They *would not* know him; they were in no.mood of mind to receive the real truth respecting either the Father or the Son.

4. But these things have I told you, that when the time shall come, ye may remember that I told you of them. And these things I said not unto you at the beginning, because I was with you.

5. But now I go my way to him that sent me; and none of you asketh me, Whither goest thou?

6. But because I have said these things unto you, sorrow hath filled your heart.

These forwarnings of persecution might pass from their minds for a season, but would be recalled when the bloody scenes should open, and might then serve to confirm their faith in Jesus as both foreknowing all, and in his compassion and wisdom, laboring to prepare them to meet even the worst with courage and joy.——On v. 5—"None of you asketh me," etc., the reader will naturally say—Did not Peter (13: 36) ask this very question, "Whither goest thou?" and did not Thomas (14: 5) remark, "Lord, we know not whither thou goest?"—The explanation probably is that the question *Whither* had excited much less attention than he had a right to expect. The disciples were engrossed with other things—brooding sadly over their own prospective bereavement, rather than turning with inquiring thought toward the future of their Lord. Was there not a shade of selfishness in this?

7. *Nevertheless I tell you the truth; It is expedient for you that I go away; for if I go not away, the Comforter will not come unto you; but if I depart, I will send him unto you.*

It was in part to meet this extreme solicitude as to their own case when Jesus should have gone that he here declares emphatically that even *for them* (no less than for himself) it was well that he should go.——"Expedient"—in the sense of profitable, conducive to ends that were of the very highest value to his kingdom. It would be expedient because the coming of the Comforter hinged upon his own going. If I go not, he does not come. When I go, I shall send him to fill and more than fill my place.

The truth here taught most explicitly is too vital to be passed without attention. Comparing the spiritual work respectively of himself here in the flesh with that of the Comforter, he represents the latter as being most effective, most fruitful, and therefore most to be desired by his people. To show how and why this is the case, he adduces—(1) His agency upon unbelievers—men in their sins; and (2) His functions as to believers—guiding them into all truth; imparting such truth as God might send through him; revealing things to come; but especially, setting forth in new light all they needed to know of Christ—"receiving of mine and showing it unto you."——(3) By no means least in importance is the fact that the agency of the Spirit has no limitations of *place* or *time*. The presence of Jesus in the flesh was of necessity restricted to few—sometimes to the most favored three; usually to the chosen twelve; more rarely to a somewhat enlarged circle of friends, or to a listening group of hearers, yet always under the limitations of one human voice, and of the physical endurance of one living man. But the Spirit is simply Omnipresent, and of never waning, never wearied energy—bounded by no limitations of space or time or power. In every land, at every hour, among the countless peoples of the wide earth simultaneously, his work may go forward, only the more effectively as the numbers brought under his influence shall be multiplied. What an accession of power—what an augmentation of forces—is to come from this substitution of the presence of the Divine Spirit for the personal presence of Jesus in the flesh!——Those who express such impassioned longing for Jesus to come again to earth in his visible person, to reverse the whole scheme of spiritual agencies, and to set us back to the state of things in Judea and Galilee, would do well to consider the significance of these declarations. If believers were to have the presence of Jesus only through their bodily eye, how would the uncounted millions in all the continents of the earth deplore their loss! Of how little avail would be all the pilgrimages possible to human flesh to get a moment's vision of his bodily form, and to hear one word, if they might, from his living voice! In what terms, then, shall we express the folly of longing and praying that Jesus would come again to earth to show his people his human body under the same laws of limitation as when he taught in the temple or sat around the passover board in the holy city! As if it were expedient now—not for him to be in heaven and the Spirit on the earth—but, reversing this present order, and falling back upon the former system—to let the Spirit return to the heavenly spheres, and Jesus come to manifest his human body before human eyes as of old!

The theory underlying these notions as to Christ's visible coming seems to be that the plan of the gospel dispensation as set forth by Jesus in these chapters might be very much improved by returning to the methods in force during his public ministry, before his ascension, and before the Great Pentecost;—in other words—that it was a mistake to suppose it "expedient for you (Christians) that I should go away and the Comforter come."

If any should reply to this that the limitations of human flesh are to be ruled out by the resurrection body and by new modes of spiritual existence—*i. e.* by bringing down to earth not Jesus only but heaven itself; then I answer—This theory or scheme, instead of improving gospel work, rules it out entirely; instead of introducing mightier spiritual forces to sustain the Christian life and to convert sinners to God—puts an end to probation; shuts down on the age of mercy for lost men; abandons the conversion of the world to Christ, and puts the Christian heart in the attitude of saying—O for an end of this working for Christ toward human salvation! O for the heavenly rest, in place of this weariness of toil!——To all which the fit reply is—By what right are we praying God to desist from his scheme of converting the world to Christ? With what reason are we putting our opinion against the expressed opinion of Jesus as to the expediency of his going away that the Spirit may come? With what face do we ask to be excused from labor and to have our pay before our day's work is done?

As bearing with great weight upon the expediency of Christ's going away that the Spirit might come, let the reader consider carefully that as the case is put here, his going is made the definite condition of the Spirit's coming. If Christ does not go, the Spirit does not come. Now does not this imply that if Christ returns to earth again, the Spirit also returns to his own heaven? Why not? Especially must this question—*Why not?* carry great force if we take into account that Jesus makes the sending of the Spirit hinge upon his own prayer before the Father's throne: "If I go I will send him unto you;" "I will pray the Father and he shall send," etc. For reasons that lie in the economy of the heavenly world, Jesus must appear there in person before the Father, interceding for the Spirit as the condition of his being sent. It does not devolve upon us to set forth and explain the reasons underlying this divine arrangement; yet nothing could be more presuming—perhaps nothing more offensive to God—than to assume that he has no good reasons for requiring Jesus to be there in order that the Spirit may be here; or to assume that the Father would readily modify this arrangement to meet human schemes.

Perhaps it would startle some admirers of the pre-millennial advent scheme to find that according to these scriptures, if Jesus returns to be here in the flesh as he was in Judea of old, the Spirit also returns to his former place and his special agency among men is superseded by the visible presence of Jesus, reigning here, not praying there. It ought to startle us if we find that our speculations are reversing the order of the divine plans.

8. And when he is come, he will reprove the world of sin, and of righteousness, and of judgment:

9. Of sin, because they believe not on me;

10. Of righteousness, because I go to my Father, and ye see me no more;

11. Of judgment, because the prince of this world is judged.

To prove that it *is* expedient for himself to go and the Spirit to come, Jesus proceeds to state what the Spirit will do;—first, as to the ungodly—the "world" in their sins. In general his work as to sinners is to *reprove* them; *i. e.* to enforce conviction as to their sin; to bring the truth that shall convict before their intelligence and to make it effective upon the conscience. Then, with remarkable method and consequent clearness, he makes three distinct points as to which he will reprove or convict them; viz: *sin; righteousness;* and *judgment.* Then resuming each point separately, to show more particularly what the Spirit will do, he says;—"Of sin because they believe not on me." The sin of not believing on Jesus is the capital sin—the one great, comprehensive, all-inclusive sin of ungodly men. All other sins could be forgiven and their power on the heart broken—if the sinner would believe on Jesus. No sin other than this so deeply insults the Lord of glory; no other so cruelly wounds his heart; none other so fatally baffles his efforts for that sinner's salvation, or so surely dooms him to remediless woe. Appropriately, therefore, will the Spirit concentrate his efforts to set before every sinner's eye the guilt of not believing on Jesus.——This accords with the experience of all truly convicted souls, and is in harmony with the soundest philosophy.

The Spirit when he comes will plead for Christ; will testify to the sin of setting him at nought and despising his salvation; will make this cruel, damning sin stand forth in the sunlight of infinite truth before the sinner's soul.——From which we pause here only to suggest these two deductions:—(*a.*) That the Christian laborer who would be a worker together with God in saving sinners should press this point above any and all others:—(*b.*) That the sinner who has any wish to be converted and saved should fix his eye on this great sin; should consent to see its enormity and to feel its guilt; and should of course turn from it by coming to Jesus in penitence, in love, in simple trust for salvation.

Next; the Spirit "will reprove the world *of righteousness*"— "because (said Jesus) I go to the Father and ye see me no more." Of *whose* "righteousness"? Of his who goes to the Father. Moreover, the nature of the case forbids us to think of the sinner's righteousness, for he has none; or of the word as applying to any other than Jesus.

"Righteousness" must here have essentially the sense of rightness—the truth and justness of his claim to be the Son of God, sent of God to men with revelations of truth and messages of mercy. The Spirit will vindicate the rightness of this claim of Jesus by appealing to his resurrection and ascension to the Father. This is every-where the doctrine of the New Testament; the resurrection of Jesus was the supreme testimony to his Messiahship. If he had failed to rise again, there would have been no Savior; all the preaching of the apostles would have been in vain (1 Cor. 15: 13–15); all faith in him vain; all men would be hopelessly in their sins.——In harmony with this construction of these words was the whole history of apostolic practice and preaching. They chose their twelfth man to fill the place of Judas that he might (as they said) "be a witness with us of his resurrection" (Acts 1: 21, 22). They began with preaching— "This Jesus hath God raised up, whereof we all are witnesses" (Acts 2: 32). The voice of that history is—"With great power gave the apostles witness of his resurrection" (Acts 4: 33). The text and theme of Paul's preaching at Athens was "Jesus and the resurrection" (Acts 17: 18).——Thus was the righteousness of Jesus set forth before the men of that generation. He was proved to have been sent of God because God raised him from the dead, and set him at his own right hand in the heavenly places far above all principalities and powers (Eph. 1: 20, 21).

"And ye see me no more"—no more till the Spirit's work of convicting and saving sinners is finished; no more till I come again to close this scene of earthly probation and inaugurate the era of eternal retribution.

"Of judgment because the prince of this world is judged." In the usage of Jesus "the prince of this world" is no other than Satan (John 12: 31, and 14: 30). He is "judged" when the hand of the Almighty falls heavily upon him, blasts his schemes; confounds his wisdom; overwhelms his power; makes his utmost wrath work out God's praise. Satan plotted the murder of Jesus; made Judas and the Jewish Sanhedrim his tools; and compassed his crucifixion. Then, did he not exult over his fallen enemy?—Ah! but when that death of Jesus proved the salvation of the world and his own utter fall; when his supposed victory brought only disaster to his kingdom and ruin to his cause; when he whose eye swept the realms of the spiritual world reported—"I beheld Satan fall as lightning from heaven"—then how suddenly did his fiendish exultation give place to chagrin and shame! In this sense Satan was "*judged.*" This defeat was a visitation of righteous justice from the Almighty—a foretoken of his final doom;—and, what is not less in point here—a beginning and foreshadowing of the righteous judgment of God upon all the armies of Satan, all his followers, servants and sympathizers, of earth or hell. Persistent sinners of whatever race or world might mark the fall of their captain and read in it their own approaching doom.——Of this great fact, the Spirit of God when he came would convict [convince] the world. We may suppose this to have been one of the elements of that convicting power which fell on the gathered thousands at the first great Pentecost. They not only saw their sin in rejecting and murdering Jesus, and the righteousness of Jesus vindicated by his resurrection and ascension to the Father; but they saw Satan hurled down from the high place of his power at the very point where he thought himself the conqueror. The doom of Judas the traitor lay in their eye, suggesting terrible premonitions of like doom for all the enemies of Jesus.

12. I have yet many things to say unto you, but ye can not bear them now.

13. Howbeit when he, the Spirit of truth, is come, he will guide you into all truth: for he shall not speak of himself; but whatsoever he shall hear, *that* shall he speak: and he will shew you things to come.

14. He shall glorify me: for he shall receive of mine, and shall shew *it* unto you.

15. All things that the Father hath are mine: therefore said I, that he shall take of mine, and shall shew *it* unto you.

Protracted as this last series of conversations was, many things remained unsaid. Precisely what these many things were we can know only so far as we infer them from the future revelations made through the Spirit. Whether the disciples could not bear them then because of physical weariness, or because so many new things had been crowded upon their minds during this eventful evening, or because their Jewish misconceptions of the Messiah were still too stubborn and misleading—does not clearly appear. It was an eventful moment. A thousand things crowded upon the mind of the Master as he looked down into the great crisis of his own agony, over into the fearful trials that awaited his scattered sheep when their Shepherd should be smitten, and beyond into the new fields of Christian life and Christian work to open when the Comforter should have come: how could he say all that pressed upon his laboring mind?

It was a relief that the Spirit of truth was so soon to come and be their Great Teacher in things divine. We note that here the Spirit is not called (as before) "the Comforter," but "the Spirit of truth"—the Teacher divine—to guide them into all truth, to speak what he should hear as his message from the Father and of the Son, including also "things to come"—such future events revealed in prophecy as the exigencies of the times might require.——Jesus gives special prominence to one momentous fact, in the words—"He shall glorify me; for he shall receive of mine and shall show it unto you." "Receive of mine," in the sense of receiving what concerns me—the truth that reveals my person, character and works; the messages I send through him; all that pertains to me which my people may need to know for their consolation, quickening, joy, and efficiency in my work. *The Spirit is to be the Great Revealer of Jesus to his people.*

The things of Jesus are the staple of his messages to men—the matter which he is pre-eminently to teach.——But let it be noted—this must not exclude whatever truth relates to the Father. "All things that the Father hath" (said Jesus) "are mine." It was in view of this fact in our mutual relations to each other that I said—"He shall take of mine and shall show it unto you." Ye will understand that I by no means exclude the truth ye need to know respecting the Father. All that truth is in a sense mine, for while I have been among you I have always said that I came to reveal the Father and have made this my chief concern. The Spirit of truth takes up the same work, revealing both the Father and the Son.

In four several and successive passages from the lips of Jesus (viz. 14: 16, 17, 28 and 15: 26, and 16: 7-15) we have had a very full and an incomparably precious exposition of *the work of the Holy Spirit* upon human souls. It is so full as to include his action upon believers and also upon the unbelieving world. These passages above any others in the Scriptures, are to be studied if we would gain the full light of revelation on this subject and would eliminate whatever errors may be current in regard to it.

In the light of these passages let me call attention to two misapprehensions as to the work of the Spirit which are (as I suppose) more or less prevalent in our age, viz:

·1. That his work is to create capabilities for right moral action—*i. e.* to implant the necessary faculties, or at least to *impart the power to use* the faculties of the soul which are requisite for right action.

2. That his work is to produce emotion, feeling, sensibility; and that he acts upon the emotional nature rather than primarily upon the intelligence and conscience.

To place these views under the light of our passages, I remark as to the first—

1. It is one thing to *create capacities* for right moral action, and quite another to *induce men to use* capacities already in existence. The former is the error now in question; the latter, its correlated truth.

The attentive reader will readily notice that these passages say nothing which implies that the Spirit creates new moral faculties, or even imparts a new and previously unknown power to use such faculties aright. On the contrary every thing said here contemplates an entirely different agency from that of an original creation of faculties.——For observe:—The Spirit is "another Comforter" as compared to Jesus—a second Jesus—taking up and doing for his people the same work which Jesus did for them during his earthly life. But this work of Jesus was not to make new faculties, but was to teach men how to use them—to *instruct* as to duty and to *persuade* men to do it. Such therefore was to be the work of the Spirit.——Note also that the Comforter is definitely described as "*the Spirit of truth*"—the Spirit who uses truth to produce the moral effects which he labors to secure. With most entire definiteness it is said—"He shall *teach* you all things and bring all things to your remembrance whatsoever I have said unto you"—all which is action upon mind by means of truth.——Note also that what is said of his agency upon "the *world*," *i. e.* the unbelieving, is all put in one word, "*reprove*," in the sense of convict, enforce conviction as to sin, righteousness, and judgment. This is action upon a mind supposed to be already in possession of intelligence and conscience—the faculties requisite for moral action. It assumes the existence of such powers, and brings the truth to bear upon minds so constituted, to produce this conviction of sin.——Thus these passages in which Jesus unfolds the work of the Spirit lend their entire force to the doctrine that the Spirit acts *by means of truth* upon minds already endowed with the requisite powers for right moral action, and *against* the notion that his work consists in creating such powers, or in imparting the ability to use them.

If to break the force of these considerations, appeal be made to other scriptures which speak of being "*born* of the Spirit," and of being "*created* anew in Christ Jesus," let regard be had to two points of reply:—(*a*) Whether these be not figurative rather than literal expressions: *i. e.* figures taken from changes wrought in the natural, material world, and applied by figurative license to analogous moral changes in the free moral attitudes and activities of the mind:—and (*b*) whether in our endeavor to reach the precise nature of the Spirit's agency, we ought not to depend on these words of Jesus which are as explicit, definite, and exact as language can ever be, rather than upon expressions which are so obviously figurative.

2. A second misconception assumes that the Spirit acts directly

upon the emotional nature and that his object is to produce emotion rather than conviction and a moral change in the will. On this point we need to discriminate between direct purpose and incidental result. Instruction in truth aims directly at conviction of duty and obedience to this conviction. Yet indirectly, incidentally, such conviction will naturally result in more or less emotion. But to make emotion the *aim* and *purpose* is a totally different thing. Some preaching is purposely sensational, exciting, shaped to intensify the emotions. Another style of preaching aims to impart and impress truth and so to convict men of sin and bring them to duty. As shown in these passages, the agency of the Spirit moves altogether in the latter line—instruction, moral conviction, obedience to the truth. To suppose therefore that the Spirit *aims* to produce emotion is by no means warranted by these representations of his work.——It will follow from this view of his work that we are not to judge of its depth and amount by the emotional excitement which may appear, but from the deep moral conviction and the radical change as to obedience to God which may result.

Finally, these views of the work of the Spirit are in the best sense practical, particularly because they show how we may promote and facilitate his work; and also how, through misapprehension of what his work is, we may retard it—not to say, frustrate it altogether.

Obviously it is expected of us that we profoundly honor the work of the Spirit; invite and welcome his presence; of set purpose, do the utmost in our power to promote the work he would do and the results he would secure.——For this purpose it is vital that we close our mind against diverting thought, and open it most fully to the truth of God. We are made capable of self-control in this matter, and can, if so we will, give our attention seriously to those subjects which we know the Spirit would fain teach and impress. Serious meditation on such themes naturally promotes the work which the Spirit seeks to do in our souls. As in the case of the disciples the Spirit would recall the words of Jesus to their remembrance, so we may read those same words and invite the Spirit to teach us their deep significance and make them words of power and life to our hearts.——In this line of purposed labor and moral effort, we may become "workers together with God" for our own spiritual profit and for the profit also of others.

16. A little while, and ye shall not see me: and again, a little while, and ye shall see me, because I go to the Father.

17. Then said *some* of his disciples among themselves, What is this that he saith unto us, A little while, and ye shall not see me: and again, a little while, and ye shall see me: and, Because I go to the Father?

18. They said therefore, What is this that he saith, A little while? we can not tell what he saith.

19. Now Jesus knew that they were desirous to ask him, and said unto them, Do ye inquire among yourselves of that I said, A little while, and ye shall not see me: and again, a little while, and ye shall see me?

20. Verily, verily, I say unto you, That ye shall weep and lament, but the world shall rejoice; and ye shall be sorrowful, but your sorrow shall be turned into joy.

21. A woman when she is in travail hath sorrow, because her hour is come: but as soon as she is delivered of the child, she remembereth no more the anguish, for joy that a man is born into the world.

22. And ye now therefore have sorrow: but I will see you again, and your heart shall rejoice, and your joy no man taketh from you.

The great fact that he must leave his beloved disciples so soon can not be out of mind long.—"A little while"—here only a few hours—and he must go from their presence by death. Again, it would be but another "little while"—three days only—and they would see him again, risen from the dead. We must interpret the second "little while" on the same scale of measurement as the first. So doing, we must refer it to his resurrection, and not to any event more remote; e. g.—not to any supposed second coming; not to his meeting them after their individual death.—— The reason why, after a little, they should not see him, was— "Because I go to the Father." They must have learned ere this that these words from his lips meant his own death. For in the very opening of these discourses on this evening, Jesus had said (John 14: 2): "In my Father's house are many mansions;" "I go to prepare a place for you." This certainly was going to his Father's house and home by means of dying.—But the words now spoken embraced somewhat more, viz: a second "little while," after which they would see him. This was a new fact; what could it mean? They talked about it among themselves (in an under-tone perhaps), possibly ashamed of their dullness of apprehension, or fearing lest their inquisitiveness might be out of harmony with the deep solemnity of these moments. But Jesus either heard their whispers or knew their hearts otherwise than through their words, and therefore proceeds to meet the point of chief importance by an illustration;—that of a woman in childbirth whose transient pangs are followed with the luxury of joy over "a man born into the world." So they would have a few most desolate days, bereaved, bewildered, trembling with fear for their own lives, borne down with sadness in the loss of such a Friend, shocked with the sudden sinking of such hopes as they had still cherished in the promised King of Israel, coming in the name of the Lord to set up something they thought of as a "kingdom." It is hard for us to take in all the elements of that fierce conflict of thoughts and emotions, which raged in their smitten bosoms when they really saw their Master hung upon the cross till he was certainly dead!——This rush of the waves of sorrow Jesus foresaw, and therefore kindly gave them these words among the very last—good to be recalled to mind in the bitterness of that anguish. He did not care to go into a very minute explanation of the shortness of these two periods—the first and the second "little while"—but he did say—"I will see you again, and your heart shall rejoice." The historian verifies the fulfillment of this prediction, remarking upon their feelings when Jesus showed them his hands and his feet with the nail-prints still fresh;—"Then were the disciples *glad* when they saw the Lord" (20: 20).——It was no insignificant thing to add—"And your joy no man taketh from you." For, the ground of this joy could never pass away. Jesus lived again—to die no more. He had said (and they would know the truth of it more and more forever)—"Because I live, ye shall live also." Their joy in such a Savior no man could take away. Fire and fagot could not burn it; prison or exile could not cramp or crush it; never so many waves of bloody persecution could not quench it. Ah! no indeed; it would live and glow with purer bliss by reason of whatever efforts the wrath of men or devils might seek to take it away.

23. And in that day ye shall ask me nothing. Verily, verily, I say unto you, Whatsoever ye shall ask the Father in my name, he will give *it* you.

24. Hitherto have ye asked nothing in my name: ask, and ye shall receive, that your joy may be full.

It is a point of some practical importance to determine whether in the words—"In that day ye shall ask me nothing," Jesus meant to forbid (or even advise against) the address of prayer to himself. Does the antithesis involved in this verse lie between addressing prayer to Jesus on the one hand and to the Father in the name of Jesus on the other? If so, and if the words—"In that day"—mean not only "*in*" but evermore *after* that day, then prayer should not be addressed directly to Christ, but always to the Father in the name of Christ. Is this the Scripture doctrine, and is it also the Apostolic practice?

This question stated thus broadly we may wisely defer till we have examined this passage in its connection. Examining it thus, we shall see that "asking Jesus" had been an every-day business for fully three years. But this free, face-to-face questioning was about to close. That this gives the sense of "asking me," in v. 23, is made more than probable by the occurrence of the same verb in this sense, v. 19—only four verses back; "Jesus knew that they were desirous to *ask* him." This unrestrained freedom of question had been the law of their life under their Great Teacher. Their words fell on his earthly ear; his replying words fell on theirs. But after his ascension this form of asking Jesus must cease, and instead of it must come praying to the invisible Father in the name of that Jesus whom they had been wont to ask as they would while visibly present with him, but whom henceforward they must think of as having passed into the heavens, and evermore making intercession for his people there. The latter method of obtaining blessings would not fall in anywise below the former. They might ask the Father in heaven as freely as they ever had the Son on earth. They might use the name of Jesus in coming to the Father as really as they had ever used it in addressing him face to face. The methods of prayer [asking] were then to change: "Hitherto ye have not asked the Father in my name;" henceforward, this new way is open; "Ask and receive, that your joy may be full."

In this view the antithesis lies between asking Jesus in the freedom of personal conversation in the flesh on the one hand; and asking the invisible Father by prayer in the name of the risen Jesus on the other. The transition from the former method to the latter was then just at hand, and nothing could be more natural or appropriate than for Jesus to connect the former method with the latter by words like these. It would help them to realize how freely and fully they might still and evermore present their prayers to the Father in the name of Jesus.

Under this construction of his words Jesus did not intend to forbid them to address their prayer to him in heaven after his ascension. They certainly did not understand him to forbid this, for Stephen, full of the Holy Ghost, died with prayer to Jesus on his lips (Acts 7: 59, 60), and so current was this practice in apostolic times that Paul describes Christians thus;—"All that in every place call upon the name of Jesus Christ our Lord" (1 Cor. 1: 2).

25. *These things have I spoken unto you in proverbs: but the time cometh, when I shall no more speak unto you in proverbs, but I shall show you plainly of the Father.*

Speaking "in proverbs" as contrasted with speaking "plainly" (both in v. 25 and in v. 29) is the difference between using figures of speech, illustrations; *e. g.* of the "*door*" to the sheep-fold; of the shepherd and his sheep (John 10); or of the vine and branches (John 15);—and using the plainest and most direct words for the very thing intended.——The "showing plainly of the Father" must be referred to his teaching them by means of the Comforter, the Spirit of truth, who, as said above (vs. 13–15), would reveal Jesus to them; "He shall receive of mine and shall show it unto you"—more plainly than his own lips had ever done.

26. *At that day ye shall ask in my name, and I say not unto you, that I will pray the Father for you:*

27. For the Father himself loveth you, because ye have loved me, and have believed that I came out from God.

Here we must notice the special turn of thought: "I say not unto you that I will pray the Father for you." Observe; Jesus does not say—I shall never offer such prayer in your behalf; but he says a very different thing from that. He means—I would not have you think that the Father has no love for you, or that you will get his ear only because he loves me. While it is every way proper that you should ask in my name, I wish you to know that the reason for your praying in my name is not by any means because the Father has personally no sympathy—no love for you. He certainly has. He loves you as truly as I do. He loves you because ye have loved me, and because ye have believed that I came forth from God. It is a matter of profound interest to him that some from this fallen race have had faith in his mission of his Son and have received him as their own Savior; have learned of the Father through his lips; have believed on the Father by reason of what they have learned through his Son.

28. I came forth from the Father, and am come into the world: again, I leave the world, and go to the Father.
29. His disciples said unto him, Lo, now speakest thou plainly, and speakest no proverb.
30. Now are we sure that thou knowest all things, and needest not that any man should ask thee: by this we believe that thou camest forth from God.

The point made in v. 28—often repeated in various form—seems now at length to be understood and fixed in their minds. Consequently they now have a broader view of Christ's foreknowledge and a deeper sense of it; which serves to confirm their faith that he came really from God.

31. Jesus answered them, Do ye now believe?
32. Behold, the hour cometh, yea, is now come, that ye shall be scattered, every man to his own, and shall leave me alone: and yet I am not alone, because the Father is with me.
33. These things I have spoken unto you, that in me ye might have peace. In the world ye shall have tribulation: but be of good cheer; I have overcome the world.

No doubt Jesus was glad of this apparent quickening of their faith in himself;—but were they aware how soon and how sorely it would be shaken? It may be well to remind them that they are on the eve of fearful peril. A terrible strain upon their fidelity, courage, and practical faith in him would presently come upon them. They would be scattered every man to his old home associates. All the disciples would forsake him and flee; and

Peter—alas!—but he had already told them of his coming fall. ——But observe; Jesus does not stop here to rebuke or reproach them, or even to tell them how deeply he should be grieved; but turns the course of thought. "Yet I am not alone:" I shall not be alone when ye all forsake me; for the Father is and will still be "with me." I have said these things not to make you sad— not to rebuke you beforehand; but with far other purpose; viz. that in me ye might have peace. I did long to assure you of my love and sympathy, though I have in my eye even now the fact that ye all are soon to forsake me in my hour of bitterest woe.

And thus this series of conversations, of unparalleled significance, of inexpressible sweetness—precious above all other words that ever fell from those sacred lips—came to its close. It only remained to Jesus to pour out his full soul in prayer—prayer for the men he loved most tenderly; for men whose pending perils he foresaw clearly; whose moral frailties lay vividly before him, and whose need of help from above he therefore saw to be exceedingly great and demanding.

CHAPTER XVII.

This entire chapter is prayer—the longest prayer of Jesus on record; offered in circumstances of the deepest interest both to himself and to his disciples. Noticeably, it is not mainly prayer for himself—that he might endure to the end and drink submissively the cup of sorrows soon to be pressed to his lips; but, almost exclusively, it is prayer for his beloved disciples whose foreseen perils and whose moral weaknesses were a sore burden upon his heart. In words most simple; in thoughts most weighty; in choice of points for petition embracing with wonderful grasp the grand elements of the Christian life—this prayer for every reason commends itself to our profoundest study and contemplation.

1. These words spake Jesus, and lifted up his eyes to heaven, and said, Father, the hour is come: glorify thy Son, that thy Son also may glorify thee.

"These words" are those recorded in chap. 13–16. Having uttered these, he passed naturally to prayer. His full heart demanded this expression of its yearning, longing desires for his people. "Father"—no form of address could be more appropriate—Oh thou universal Father—in the highest sense *my* Father;—as such I now come to Thee. It should be noted that the first five verses are specially personal to Jesus himself, expressing his own individual relations to the Father.——"The hour has come;"—the hour long anticipated, most eventful, toward which my whole earthly life has looked and all its labors have been shaped—this great hour of crisis, of issues, of consummation—of trial, pain, arrest, torture, conflict with Satan, death, resurrection, ascension, triumph, eternal glory—how do the grand issues of my earthly mission culminate upon this momentous hour! and yet though these issues, specially personal to Jesus were so absorbing, another class of interests are here perhaps even more pressing—those of his little flock, for they are to be left among devouring wolves—their shepherd smitten and the sheep scattered; their faith fearfully tried; their souls perplexed, bewildered, staggered;—Oh, how could their compassionate Master leave them without pouring out the prayer of his burdened heart in their behalf!

"Glorify thy Son." We pause in the presence of this petition. No other spirit save one of profoundest reverence befits us when we assume to interpret such words uttered by the glorious Son of God. Yet they are here to be studied and to be understood as best we may. It seems to me supremely important that our apprehension of their meaning should be at once *clear* and *just.*

We recognize Jesus who offers this prayer as "God manifest in human flesh," meaning by this that the divine person, named in this gospel by John "the Word" [Logos] became mysteriously united with the human person, born of Mary.——These points are brought to view here only as bearing upon the prayer of Jesus. Do we not make some advance in our conception of his prayer when we consider that in its very nature and relations prayer is *of man*—is human; and that, consequently, as offered by Jesus it assumes that his human consciousness is in the foreground and is made specially prominent?——With this view, I suggest whether we should not interpret the prayer—"Glorify thy Son"—to mean not merely—Lift him at once from his earthly humiliation to his heavenly glory; but rather—Bear him through these scenes of his earthly trial, now instantly pending: help him to be true to his mission of suffering, shame, and death; to drink the cup of woe which Thou, Father, hast given him to drink: strengthen him that through thy help he may manifest before the universe thy love for lost men, and may glorify Thee amid this fearful ordeal of torture and temptation. Glorify thy Son by making him more than conqueror through these last and sorest conflicts, so that he may glorify Thee—fitly representing thy love for those in whose behalf he dies.

2. As thou hast given him power over all flesh, that he should give eternal life to as many as thou hast given him.

The first word in this verse "as" [better read *according as*] is specially significant because it logically connects the words that follow with those that precede. Be pleased to answer my prayer,

"Glorify thy Son," *in accordance with* that grant of power over all the race conferred on him to the end that he might give eternal life, etc. As the Father had endowed the Son with this power over human souls, in the realms of providence and grace, for the grand purposes of salvation—the salvation of the "given" ones—all who are really saved at last—so now in this hour of crisis he prays to be girded with strength to bear and to go triumphantly through these scenes of fiercest conflict and of most perilous responsibility. Now if ever [he would say], O my Father, I need thy sustaining hand that I may truly honor thee. Only with thy present help can I meet this fearful crisis with honor to thee and to myself. Thou knowest well the work I have undertaken—this giving eternal life to all whom Thou hast given to me.——In support of his plea it was in place as an indirect argument to suggest this final purpose—the eternal life of the "given" ones—and to refer thus to the fact that they had been *given* by the Father. He was thus an interested party. His hand and counsel were in the scheme. Jesus asked only that he might be sustained to carry through a scheme which had its origin in the Father's love—for the accomplishment of which the Father had already given him "power over all flesh." He now needs and asks more blessings in the same line, on the same principle, for the same ultimate purpose.——The Greek reader would notice that for the words translated—"as many as"—he finds the Greek word for *all* in its neuter form—the precise sense being therefore—to the mass, thought of as a body—a *whole*.

3. And this is life eternal, that they might know thee, the only true God, and Jesus Christ, whom thou hast sent.

That "life eternal" which he is to give to believers, in its simplest conception, is the practical knowledge of God the Father and of his Son. It is not merely to know that Jehovah *is* the one true God and that Jesus is his Son; but to *know them as such*. Of course such knowing involves the adjusting of the heart and of the life to this knowledge. It signifies that what is thus known of God and of his Son is received in love; is wrought into the very life of the soul; develops the spirit of loving obedience, and the simple trust of faith—so that thus knowing God intelligently, they become in spirit and life his children through the salvation provided in Jesus his Son. The word "know" thus used becomes signally emphatic, or shall we say, all-comprehensive; inclusive of the moral acts and states to which such knowledge legitimately tends. It is the knowledge of truth, made effective by the Spirit of truth, according to the legitimate potency of such truth, so that the human heart yields itself to its molding power.

4. I have glorified thee on the earth: I have finished the work which thou gavest me to do.

So far I have done the work undertaken, to the honor of the Father. This was his sustaining consciousness, and seems here to be made the basis for the plea that follows:—"Glorify thou me," etc. (v. 5).——At this point the great work was mostly finished, yet not entirely. The last words of Jesus on the cross as reported by John were—"It is finished" (19: 30). Then the suffering was indeed endured; all that belonged to the stage of humiliation was past, and only the glory remained.*

5. And now, O Father, glorify thou me with thine own self with the glory which I had with thee before the world was.

In the interpretation of the words (v. 1)—"Glorify thy Son," there seems good reason to refer them in part (yet perhaps only in part) to blessings needed in the immediate future, for whatever of endurance and trial lay directly before the Great Sufferer. The allusion to the "power over all flesh" as given him, seemed to contemplate more blessings of similar sort, needful to perfect the entire work undertaken for the salvation of men. But in this verse (as in v. 4) Jesus seems to stand in thought at the point of consummation, where he looks upon the period of his humiliation as closing, and lifts up his prayer for the glory that lay beyond. Bring me home to that glory in which I dwelt with thee in the eternal ages before this world's creation.——"With thine own self" is not equivalent to—*by thine own power*—but means, *along with* thyself. Raise me to that former position of coequal dignity and glory in which I dwelt from eternity "with God." Closely construed it would seem that in this prayer the divine—not the human—consciousness is in the foreground—the word "I" in the phrase—"which I had with Thee"—representing the Logos especially; the eternal Word, who was from the beginning "with God." †

6. I have manifested thy name unto the men which thou gavest me out of the world: thine they were, and thou gavest them me: and they have kept thy word.

7. Now they have known that all things whatsoever thou hast given me are of thee.

8. For I have given unto them the words which thou gavest me; and they have received *them*, and have known surely that I came out from thee, and they have believed that thou didst send me.

---

* The improved text puts the verb "finished" in the form of its participle—"Having finished the work," etc.

† This view of the *divine* personality as prominent in this prayer, must be taken unless we adopt the opinion held by some that the human nature of Jesus also, as well as the divine, was pre-existent —"before the world was."

From this point onward Jesus prays especially for his people.——"Manifested thy *name*"—in the sense of thyself, thy character, and particularly thy great love and thoughts of mercy for lost men. To those whom the Father had given him had these revelations of God been made. All others had repelled his teachings. This mode of putting the case kept prominent the antecedent agency of the Father in regard to the salvation of Christ's people and made that agency an argument in his plea.——"They have kept thy word"—revealed to them through my ministry. Now therefore thou wilt surely remember them with mercy in their present and pending emergencies.——"All things which Thou hast given me"—both words to be spoken and deeds to be done (miracles included) are of Thee. They have joyfully recognized this. The words which Jesus had received from the Father for men, they had accepted in faith and in love.——"Have known surely"—were better read—not "surely," but truthfully—the point being not so much the certainty as the correctness—the exact conformity to the truth. The points stated here as truthfully known are put in two forms, essentially equivalent; viz. that I came out from God; and that Thou (God) didst send me.

9. I pray for them: I pray not for the world, but for them which thou hast given me; for they are thine.

10. And all mine are thine, and thine are mine; and I am glorified in them.

Should this negative statement—"not for the world"—be construed in its fullest and most absolute sense—never, at all; or, only in a qualified sense—*e. g.* I am not praying for the world *now*, or not for them specially: but I do pray specially for these my disciples.——The latter view seems to me the true one, inasmuch as below (vs. 21, 23) Jesus expresses a real interest for the world—"that the world may believe that thou hast sent me;" "that the world may know." Moreover, elsewhere the broadest benevolence is affirmed;—"God so loved the world," etc. (John 3: 16). "God sent not his Son into the world to condemn the world, but that the world through him might be saved," etc. (John 3: 17). It seems legitimate therefore to construe this prayer thus: I pray now especially for them.——A prominent point in this plea is that these men had been given to him by the Father—really belonged to the Father ("they are thine"), and indeed belonged by the same tenure to both the Father and the Son—each having in them a common right of property. Of course this conception of property is borrowed from human relationships; but is at once clear in its significance and precious in its bearings.

11. And now I am no more in the world, but these are in the world, and I come to thee. Holy Father, keep

through thine own name those whom thou hast given me, that they may be one, as we *are*.

12. While I was with them in the world, I kept them in thy name: those that thou gavest me I have kept, and none of them is lost, but the son of perdition; that the Scripture might be fulfilled.

Here then is property jointly owned by the Father and the Son, to be taken care of. Jesus has had them in special charge while with them in the flesh: but he is now to go from them to the Father. Hence he prays the Father to keep them.——It is not quite clear what our English translators meant by the word "*through*"—"through thine own name." Usually this preposition signifies—*by means of;* but in this case it translates the Greek word for *in*—the very same which in the next verse they have translated "in"—"I kept them *in* thy name." There can be no good reason for translating the same word "through" in v. 11 and "in" in v. 12.——Moreover, not only is the Greek original the same, but the connection and relations are the same. Jesus prays to the Father to do precisely what he himself has been doing. "While I was with them I kept *in* thy name;" now that I leave them, I pray thee to keep them *in* thy name. The sense therefore must be—keep them in the knowledge and love of thy name—"name" being synonymous with revealed character.

We must note also that in both v. 11 and v. 12 the improved text gives us—not "those whom" (masculine plural), but *which* (neuter singular), referring to *name*, the sense being—thine own name which thou hast given me. Then v. 12, closely translated, would be—"While I was with them I was keeping them in thy name which [name] thou gavest me, and I guarded [them] and none of them is lost," etc. He had kept all of them safely in the knowledge of his Father's name, except the traitor, in the loss of whom the Scripture was fulfilled.

13. And now come I to thee; and these things I speak in the world, that they might have my joy fulfilled in themselves.

I say these things in the world, while yet with them in the flesh, in order that they may have in full measure the same joy in thee which I have. This must be the sense of "*my* joy"—the very joy which I have in my Father. I wish to show them that they may love and trust the Father even as I have done and may have the same joy which I ever have in this love and trust.—— Would not this be a blessed experience?

14. I have given them thy word; and the world hath hated them, because they are not of the world, even as I am not of the world.

I have given them thy word and so have kept them. But now that I leave them, new dangers will beset them from external sources—*i. e.* from a hostile world, hating them because they are not *of it* as I am not. Both they and I are of another class, having no sympathies in common with a selfish, wicked world.

15. I pray not that thou shouldest take them out of the world, but that thou shouldest keep them from the evil.

16. They are not of the world, even as I am not of the world.

It might seem a very simple and perfect protection for them to take them out of the world, but we are not ready for that. I do not pray for that; but that thou shouldest keep them from the *Evil One*—not from evil in the abstract, but from the Master Spirit of evil—Satan—who has always fought me and will fight them.——In 1 John 2: 13, our translators have rendered the same Greek words as these (both the noun and the article)—"Ye have overcome *the Wicked One.*" Both consistency and philology required that they should translate this passage in the same way.

17. Sanctify them through thy truth: thy word is truth.

Make and keep them holy through thy truth—that of thy revealed word. We need not construe this prayer to exclude the agency of the Spirit. Let it rather include this agency, since the Comforter is evermore the Spirit of truth, teaching, suggesting, impressing, fulfilling his functions as a Sanctifier by means of God's revealed word of truth.——Sanctifying human souls should not be considered a mystical process, in such a sense mysterious that we can get no clearly defined conceptions of it. Far otherwise. The fact that it is effected "*through the truth,*" brings it within the pale of our own consciousness—a subject of study and of distinct intellectual apprehension. To assume it to be a mystical operation can never be otherwise than misleading and pernicious.

18. As thou hast sent me into the world, even so have I also sent them into the world.

On essentially the same mission, viz: to testify for God; to reveal God to men; and at this point, especially to preach the gospel. Jesus could not have meant that they had the same work as himself in dying to make propitiation for the sins of the world; but—as to the point then present in thought—viz: the agency of revealed truth to sanctify and save men—their work was substantially a continuation of his. As the Father had sent him with great and glorious messages of truth to men, so did he send them.

19. And for their sakes I sanctify myself, that they also might be sanctified through the truth.

As applied to Jesus, the word "sanctify" must have its primary, not its secondary sense—the primary being—to *set apart* for holy purposes; the secondary—to purify from sin. Only in the former sense could it be used of Jesus. But it might be used as to his disciples in both senses or in either. Jesus meant to say that he set himself apart with supreme devotion to the sanctification of his people—the purifying of their hearts by *faith*—which is equivalent to saying "*through the truth.*" Faith stands related to truth. Faith receives the word of God as true, and thus secures to the believer the legitimate moral forces of truth.

20. Neither pray I for these alone, but for them also which shall believe on me through their word;

21. That they all may be one; as thou, Father, *art* in me, and I in thee, that they also may be one in us: that the world may believe that thou hast sent me.

22. And the glory which thou gavest me I have given them; that they may be one, even as we are one:

23. I in them, and thou in me, that they may be made perfect in one; and that the world may know that thou hast sent me, and hast loved them, as thou hast loved me.

Not for these eleven disciples alone do I pray, but for all who shall come into faith through their preaching, onward down through all the ages.——For *what* does he pray, in their behalf? "That they all may be one;" this is the burden of the prayer—illustrated, reiterated, and its anticipated results stated—viz: "that the world may believe," etc.—— *What then is this oneness?*

Something more and better than a denominational, organic unity of the church, as opposed to diverse organizations. It might involve this by involving and including the spirit which would insure it; but this precisely and this only it can not be. There is nothing in the passage that suggests this as the main idea. There was nothing in the circumstances of Jesus at that moment which would naturally bring this sort of oneness before his mind. The entire description with its illustration leads to a different and vastly higher view; "As thou, Father, art in me and I in thee; that they also may be one in us." There can be no simpler way to indicate entire unity—perfect oneness—than this—one person *in* another. We need not push the sense of the word "*in*" so far as to constitute identity and to absorb and rule out individual personality. Stopping short of this, it gives us the completest conception of moral oneness which human language can express. Morally, Jesus and the Father were *at one:* the same love, the same purity, the same glorious spiritual life, lived and reigned in each and in both. The prayer of Jesus is that his people may all be one in us (the Father and the Son) in the same sense of moral, spiritual union.——"The glory" (v. 22) must refer to that honor, dignity, exaltation, which the Father had prospectively given to the Son; to which the Son was soon to be raised.—"This" Jesus says, "I have given to them as thou hast given it to me." The bestowment of this glory would still conduce to the same great end—moral, spiritual oneness; would be given for the sake of this result—"that they may be one, even as we are one."——Still the precious idea is expanded and reiterated; "I in them and thou in me, that they may be made perfect in one." Is it not worthy of special thought that here this *oneness* (if we may coin a word) is not put as reciprocal—(I in them and they in me; I in thee, Father, and thou in me)—but in each case the greater is *in* the less—the superior is *in* the inferior; for the Father is said to be *in* the Son and the Son also is *in* his people. The higher condescends to come down and manifest his presence and power in the lower, obviously to *uplift*—to raise up into a higher plane of spiritual communion and fellowship. As the Father brings himself into spiritual communion with the Son (considered as incarnate), so does the Son bring himself into spiritual communion with his people. This constitutes Jesus the connecting link—the uniting agent—between the Father and each true believer.——When the lower is spoken of as in the higher; as for example, believers are said to be in Christ as branches are *in* the vine, the connection is specially one of faith, dependence, trust on their part, bringing them into such relations to Jesus that currents of sustaining life-power flow from him to them, as from the parent vine to the inhering branches; or as the vital nervous force flows from the brain [the head] through the entire human organism [all the members]. But in our passage the mode of stating the law of spiritual union—*i. e.* the higher party *in* the lower—makes prominent the idea of condescension—of coming down to lift up the relatively lower party into the relationship of sublime communion and fellowship—a communion born of divine love and made effective through the sanctifying agency of God's truth and Spirit. Human souls made in God's image are *inspirable*—capable by virtue of their created constitution, of being pervaded and permeated thus with God. No higher quality—capability—than this in man's nature can possibly be conceived of. ——A noticeable addition is made (v. 23) to the clause—"that the world may know that thou hast sent me;" viz: "And hast loved them as thou hast loved me." Exalting them to the same heavenly glory with Jesus would serve to show this. But going deeper than this external glorifying, and contemplating the moral, spiritual renovation of their natures, and consequently the bringing them into moral oneness with Jesus and with the Father, we shall see that this must testify to the same love of the Father toward them as toward his Son.——Is not all this surpassingly wonderful?

24. Father, I will that they also, whom thou hast given

me, be with me where I am; that they may behold my glory, which thou hast given me: for thou lovedst me before the foundation of the world.

The genuine tenderness, sincerity and condescension of Christ's love for his people could not easily be put in more touching form than this: I would have them very near me—with me—so that they may behold my glory which thou hast given me. I know they will enjoy it. I too shall rejoice to see them enjoy it. Human friendships are full of such manifestations. Who does not love to have his personal friends see and sympathize with his own honors—his real and worthy success in his labors? How then could Jesus show his disciples more clearly that he holds them as his beloved, confidential friends, than by this prayer that they may rise to behold his own eternal glory and rejoice with him in his immortal honors and triumphs?

25. O righteous Father, the world hath not known thee: but I have known thee, and these have known that thou hast sent me.

Why does Jesus choose the word "righteous" to apply to the Father in this connection?——I suggest this: that "righteous" involves moral discrimination between good and evil; good-doers and evil-doers. The thought—underlying and implied—may be this: I have prayed that these whom thou hast given me—sanctified through thy truth—may be with me in my heavenly glory. Why do I not ask the same for all the world?——A righteous God could not grant it. "O righteous Father, the world have not known thee." They would not receive my testimony of thee; they have loved darkness rather than light because their deeds are evil. There can be no home for them in the pure and glorious heaven. "But I have known thee, and these have known that thou hast sent me," and therefore are preparing to know thee with the perfect knowledge of heaven.

26. And I have declared unto them thy name, and will declare *it*; that the love wherewith thou hast loved me may be in them, and I in them.

I have begun already to reveal the Father to them: I have more yet to reveal and to manifest to their obedient and loving hearts. I shall pursue this work to the end that the love thou hast for me may go forth also toward them—that thou mayest love them as thou hast loved me; also that I myself may be in them in yet greater perfection.

Thus closes this wonderful, glorious prayer. Were truths more sublime ever uttered, or thoughts more inspiring to Christian souls, or more consoling to men looking forward to perils and conflicts which might be unto death? Studying it as heard by the chosen few in that eventful moment, we can scarcely restrain the inquiry—Did they comprehend the grandeur of these sentiments and feel the mighty inspiration of such sympathy, and were their souls lifted up by the anticipation of such communion and fellowship with the risen Jesus and with the Infinite Father? Did they say within themselves—Now we can endure any thing bravely for such a Friend; now we can surely count it all joy to go with him to prison and to death for the love we bear him and for the glory that is so soon to follow?

We can not know precisely what the then present impression of this prayer was upon the disciples; but we may doubtless believe that after Jesus had gone up into heaven before their eyes and the Spirit began to bring these things to their remembrance, then they began indeed to drink in their grand inspirations, and to feel their sustaining power. It is sweet to think how the people of God all down the ages have delighted to read the words of this prayer and to feel the spiritual power thereof.

CHAPTER XVIII.

This chapter and the next comprise the selection made by John, from the historic incidents of the Savior's passion, including his arrest, trial, crucifixion and burial. Each of the four gospel historians has made his own several selection from among this group of incidents, Matthew and Mark following with slight variations the same general principle of selection, so that in the main their accounts are parallel with each other; while Luke and John each contain a considerable amount of new matter, peculiar to themselves. Hence it is only by bringing these several histories together and allowing them to supplement each other that we get the full view of what is revealed in respect to the final passion of the world's Great Sufferer.

Much the same might be said of any other considerable chapter of our gospel history, and being said, might become an argument for treating it in this complementary method. Thus far in this volume I have confined myself mainly to the record given us by John. In treating the two chapters next ensuing, I propose to notice briefly those main points of the history which, being omitted or less fully stated by John, are brought out more fully by the other historians. I am induced to adopt this method by the exceeding great interest and importance of the subject.—— Moreover what John has said will be better understood when supplemented from the parallel records. There is the more reason for this course in a commentary upon these chapters of John because it is more apparent here than elsewhere in this book that he regarded it as only supplementary—*i. e.* wrote it, aware of what others had written before him, and therefore (probably) omitted certain things because they had been fully recorded already by his brethren.

This chap. 18 gives the scenes of the arrest (vs. 1-14); the course of Peter, resulting in his sad denial of his Master (vs. 15-18, and 25-27); and in part, the incidents of the trial before the high priest and before Pilate (vs. 19-24, and 28-40).

1. When Jesus had spoken these words, he went forth with his disciples over the brook Cedron, where was a garden, into the which he entered, and his disciples.

This passing over the brook Cedron (otherwise Kidron) which skirted the city on the east, brought them to the foot of the Mount of Olives, and to that ever memorable garden known in the other evangelists as Gethsemane. The word "garden" should not suggest here a spot under cultivation for vegetables, flowers, and perhaps summer fruits; but rather, an orchard—in this case devoted, as we may infer from the significant name, to the olive. It was a sweet and calm retreat from the turmoil of the great city, perhaps under the care of some well-known friend, but at least a place often frequented by Jesus and his disciples, and as we may well suppose, sacred to the double purpose of rest and of prayer. This was Gethsemane. Here, there fell upon the human soul of Jesus that mighty agony which human language seems to falter in every attempt to describe. Mark says, "He began to be sore amazed, and to be very heavy, and saith unto them—My soul is exceeding sorrowful unto death; tarry ye here and watch." Matthew records most fully the words of his prayer:—"He fell on his face and prayed, saying, O my Father, if it be possible, let this cup pass from me; nevertheless, not as I will but as thou wilt."——Returning to the disciples and finding them asleep (alas, for human infirmity—not to say also for deficient sympathy!)—he saith to Peter, as if to remind him of professions of love, scarcely yet cold upon his lips:—"What! could ye not watch with me one hour?"——But mark the tenderness of his own apology: "The spirit indeed is willing, but the flesh is weak."——Still there comes no relief from the dreadful burden, and again he withdraws from them (Luke says "about a stone's cast"), and pours out his soul in prayer: "O my Father, if this cup may not pass from me except I drink it, thy will be done." Returning to the chosen three once more, he finds them asleep again.—Ah, the pain of such neglect!—the fearfully suggestive power of its intimation that even his redeemed people will not (always) stand by him in his most bitter need.

In the general outline of this scene, Matthew and Mark are altogether at one—the points made by each being substantially the same; the differences being little else than verbal. Luke adds two or three incidents; *e. g.* that "there appeared unto him an angel from heaven, strengthening him:" and that "being in an agony, he prayed more earnestly, and his sweat was, as it were, great drops of blood falling down to the ground." What messages of love and sympathy this ministering angel brought from heaven, are not on record (we may wish they were)—but it is a comfort to think that when all human sympathy failed him so deplorably, angelic sympathy came to his relief.——As to the sweat, said to have been "as great drops of blood," the prevalent opinions of critics concur in this sense: great drops of sweat colored with blood—not in appearance only, but in fact a bloody sweat. It is highly improbable that a profuse sweat would be compared with great clots of blood, if the only point of comparison was the size of the drops and the sweat were really bloodless. That such bloody sweat is physiologically possible under intense agony, seems to be a well authenticated fact, though the cases are exceedingly rare.

In speaking of the sleep of the disciples, Luke puts it—"sleeping for sorrow." This result of sorrow is scarcely supposable save in the case where great sorrow has served to exhaust human endurance—which would bring the fact as an apology under the other statement—"The flesh is weak." Really this is the only apologetic plea which this case admits. The preceding day and evening had been one of intense excitement—of exhausting interest and thought.

The inspired accounts of the scenes in Gethsemane are rounded out by the writer to the Hebrews (5 : 7, 8); who says of Jesus— "In the days of his flesh when he had offered up prayers and supplications with strong crying and tears to him that was able to save him from death, and was heard in that he feared:— Though he were a Son, yet learned he obedience by the things which he suffered."——This passage, being a sort of comment by an inspired apostle upon the scenes of Gethsemane, should have weight in the interpretation of those scenes. It recognizes the fact of most earnest prayer; that this prayer was offered as to "one who was able to save him from death;" and that in some important sense the prayer was heard and answered. In *what sense* is one of the chief questions in interpreting the words and scenes of Gethsemane.——The clause translated—"was heard in that he feared"—is not only obscure in the English but somewhat doubtful in the Greek.*——The choice lies between these two constructions: (*a.*) "Being heard [and delivered] from the thing he feared;" and (*b.*) Being heard from † [because of] the piety, *i. e.* of his prayer—because of his profound submission to the Father's will. The former construction assumes it a case of "constructio pregnans"—*i. e.* one which involves the idea of another verb. It also takes the noun translated "fear" ‡ in a

---

* εισακουσθεις απο της ευλαβειας.   † απο.   ‡ ευλαβειας.

sense unknown to the New Testament—its only N. T. sense being *godly fear*—true piety; and never the dread of some danger.
——The latter construction takes the preposition * in an unusual yet not inadmissible sense, and seems to require the word for *his* instead of the article—because of *his* piety. Hence there are somewhat grave difficulties in either construction;—less, however, (grammatically and lexicographically) in the latter than in the former.——But without deciding absolutely between these constructions, let it suffice to say that both concur in this point—that the prayer of Jesus in Gethsemane was in some important sense answered.

Is it permitted us to approach this scene of agony and inquire reverently—*What were the elements of its great sorrow?*

In the first place it must be carefully considered that the human rather than the divine in the person of Christ is prominent here. It is not given us to know perfectly how it could be that the human should bear such relations to the divine as to suffer not only pains of body but pains of soul according to the normal laws of human suffering, *as if* the divine nature and powers were for the time, to a greater or less extent, in abeyance; but such seems to be the fact. As we have more than once had occasion to suggest in reference to the prayers offered by Jesus—*prayer is human;* and hence the prayers of Jesus must assume that the human in his compound nature is in the foreground. He prays *as man*—not as God. These scenes in Gethsemane were full of prayer—were certainly as human as prayer is human. So far as we can comprehend them, the sufferings that evoked those prayers were those of his human soul.

Reasoning therefore upon these assumptions, we take into consideration all the known circumstances of the case, and thereupon suggest—

(*a.*) This was the hour of supreme, intense, undiverted *anticipation*. Other interests than his own personal suffering had received their due attention. Earnest thought had been devoted long to the case of his disciples. He had given large scope to his solicitudes, sympathies, counsels, and prayers for them—as we have seen all through the previous hours of this memorable evening. Now his own great "hour" draws nigh, and all the momentous scenes of his final sufferings rush upon his soul. We know how terribly the anticipation of suffering bears upon human nerves. Upon some temperaments and in certain respects it has less alleviations and seems more unendurable than the very suffering which is foreseen.

(*b.*) We must allow some place to the suggestive power of the circumstances immediately present;—*e. g.* that one of the chosen twelve is the traitor, reminding him how often he must be wounded in the house of his friends; that the three of his remaining eleven—most loved and most relied on, are sleeping instead of

---

* $\alpha\pi o$.

sympathizing, praying, watching; can not be induced either to pray or to watch with him, nor even to watch and pray for themselves in this hour of so much peril.—Moreover, he knew they would all within a few moments forsake him and flee; that the most earnest, enthusiastic, and outspoken of them all would deny him with oaths and curses. Alas! how bitter must these facts have been, considered not merely in themselves alone but in their suggestive power as indicating how unspeakably his soul must be tried all along the ages of the future by the infirmities and the sins of his professed disciples!

(c.) More yet must be ascribed to the assaults of Satan and his legions. To such assaults Jesus seems to allude in the words (Luke 22: 53): "But this is your hour *and the power of darkness.*" Also in these (John 14: 30): "For the Prince of this world cometh," etc. We may therefore assume that these were moments of fierce and fearful conflicts with Satan. It is but little that we can know, from the testimony of other human experience, of the foul suggestions, the hot temptations, of Satan; of the rapid succession of his thrusts, and the fierceness of his assaults; but we may safely say—he did his worst. He shrunk from nothing as too mean, too dastardly, too blasphemous, too horribly malign—which might (in his hope) break down the sublime purpose of the Holy Sufferer; or, failing of this, might inflict torture, harass with doubt, or enshroud with darkness and gloom. All and more than all (probably) that his children have ever suffered from Satan, or ever will, went into his cup in that dreadful hour—to the end that "having suffered, being tempted, he might the better succor those who are tempted."

(d.) To all this may we not add a certain fearful apprehension that he might fail under the dreadful burdens to be borne. Would his fortitude and patience be equal to the strain; would his soul abide true to its purpose through the entire long period of this anticipated horror and agony? It is at least supposable that Satan's temptations were plied on this point especially, and that a sense of human weakness heightened the agonizing apprehensions of this fearful hour. May not this have been a large element in the pains grouped under the word "*cup*" which he prayed so fervently might pass from him—the fear of some moral failure under his awful sufferings of body and soul upon the cross?—It should be considered that "cup" does not define the nature of the sufferings which fill it. We need not suppose it to denote mainly his death itself by crucifixion. There are grave objections to the supposition that he prayed to be excused from this death. Far more probable is it that he prayed against possible failure—that this was the fear which so agonized him in the garden, and that in this definite respect—from this dread apprehension—he was delivered in answer to his prayer. It is entirely clear that the agitation and horror which were so prominent in the garden passed away and left his soul calm and self-possessed. Never was moral heroism more calm than his when

Judas and his posse broke upon the stillness of Gethsemane and they led him away to the insults and injustice of their tribunals.

(*e.*) Coupled with all the rest, we must assume a very extreme physical nervous prostration—a state of exhaustion which may have almost robbed him of the power of endurance. He may have spoken from experience—even *present* experience—when he said for his disciples—"The flesh is weak." When we review the scenes of the previous day and evening; think of the mental tension, the draft upon his sympathies, the burden of such and so much responsibility; of the words he spake and the prayer he offered, coupled also with the wear of that flood of anticipations then rushing upon his soul, we shall have some data from which to estimate the nervous exhaustion of the Man of sorrows at this hour. That he became physically unable to carry the wood of his cross alone, and that under the agonies of crucifixion life became extinct long before Pilate supposed it possible he could have died, are collateral circumstances confirming this view of his physical exhaustion.

(*f.*) The point last to be named—of which we know least—can be only suggested—viz. that there may have been in some degree a hiding of the Father's face—a measure of the same experience which at the sixth hour of his passion extorted that most bitter wail which ever fell from human lips:—"My God, my God, why hast thou forsaken me?"—We could scarcely make a greater mistake than to estimate on the scale of our own experience the darkness and horror of his holy soul under such conscious suspension of the Father's manifested favor. For, be it considered, none of us have ever stood—none will ever stand—in the place of lost sinners before God, to "bear their sins" in the way of an atoning sacrifice. God has never hidden his face from us—has never "forsaken" us—while we were faithfully true to our love and service for him—and never will.——And not least—let it be considered that—to Jesus, who had never known such darkness *Godward* before—who had enjoyed the perfect bliss of the Father's light and love with never an intermission till then—this experience must have been inexpressibly agonizing, appalling. This may be the very thing suggested if not expressed in the word used by Mark (14 : 33)—"began to be sore *amazed*" *—a word which expresses both surprise and horror—as if some new experience was upon him—appalling and even astounding.

These are suggested as being (supposably) the elements of the great agony of Jesus in Gethsemane.

The reader will not make the mistake of supposing that these points are put here as actual knowledge. No such claim is made. It is not given us yet to know with absolute certainty what were the elements of that cup of woe. Of the surrounding circumstances we do know something; with the laws of our own human nature we may become in a measure familiar; of the words that

---

* εκθαμβεομαι.

fell from the lips of the Sufferer we have probably a somewhat full and certainly an authentic record. It has been my aim to form opinions and make suggestions based upon these data, confident that it must be morally wholesome to study the entire scene reverently, solemnly, tenderly—with our souls keenly alive to sympathy with him we love, and open to the full impression of what it was for him to "bear our griefs and carry our sorrows, that by his stripes we might be healed."

If the question be asked, Why did not John give some account of these scenes in Gethsemane? we can answer only by conjecture. We may be quite sure this omission was not due to any want of sympathy and interest in those scenes. We may remember that he (and he only) records that other very similar though briefer and less agonizing scene (viz. in 12: 27–30). His own personal recollections of the real Gethsemane could not have faded out, for he was one of the three, chosen by Jesus to be nearest him in that dark hour. No apparent reason for his omitting all record of this scene is more probable than this—that he knew it had been very fully described in three other gospel histories. He may therefore have felt that he had nothing to add to what had been fully and well said by others.——To this we may perhaps subjoin suggestively that those scenes did not seem to bear very directly upon the special object for which he compiled his history—"That ye may believe that Jesus is the Christ, the Son of God." Gethsemane revealed the *human* in Jesus rather than the divine.

2. **And Judas also, which betrayed him, knew the place: for Jesus ofttimes resorted thither with his disciples.**

Judas knew the place; he had been there often with his Master and the chosen disciples. He had reason to expect that after the labors and responsibilities of such a day in the temple among the gathered thousands, and after the scenes at the supper, Jesus would retire to this place of prayer for his accustomed communion with his Father.——But what a revelation is made here of the character of Judas! His definite plan is to break in upon Jesus while engaged in his private devotions and in the very place sacred to communion with God! Judas had been there scores of times, a witness to the devotions of his Master, but never in devout sympathy; never to pray himself. No hallowed associations with that sacred spot deterred his treason for one moment. It was a good time to find his victim apart from the multitude, alone with his God;—what more should he care for? Why should any qualms of conscience, or any notions as to the sacredness of communion with God hold him back from—the chance of making money by selling his knowledge of this secret place of prayer?

3. **Judas then, having received a band** *of men* **and officers from the chief priests and Pharisees, cometh thither with lanterns and torches and weapons.**

4. Jesus therefore, knowing all things that should come upon him, went forth, and said unto them, Whom seek ye?

5. They answered him, Jesus of Nazareth. Jesus saith unto them, I am *he*. And Judas also, which betrayed him, stood with them.

6. As soon then as he had said unto them, I am *he*, they went backward, and fell to the ground.

This "band" may possibly have been Roman soldiers, but probably were a detachment from the Levite guards of the temple. The word* is used of either. In the present case it was a rudely armed troop—"swords and staves," or bludgeons—not the weapons of the Roman soldier; besides that a Roman band would naturally take their prisoner at once before a Roman tribunal. The officers of the chief priests and Pharisees were of course Jews.——"Armed with lanterns and torches," as well as death weapons, because it was night and vital to their success that they should recognize their man.——Jesus, fully aware of their purpose, with no thought of either resistance or escape, "went forth," *i. e.* from the secluded retreat where his great agony of prayer had transpired, and surrendered himself to their hands. The other three evangelists concur in saying that Judas was to designate the man by the concerted signal of a kiss—and did so—professing the truest friendship to carry out the foulest treason! What could be more mean and vile?——John only of the four evangelists records that at the words of Jesus—"I am he," this armed posse "went backward and fell to the ground." Strange that this did not open the eyes of Judas and appall his soul with terror! Strange that his heart was not smitten with a sense of the dignity and majesty of the innocent man he was betraying! Strange that the priests and Pharisees present in that "band" did not think of fifty men sent twice to bring Elijah down from his mountain retreat, and ask themselves, What are we doing? Who is this man of Galilee that we can not stand before him?——Whether this "band" were made up of volunteers, or of picked men, we must suppose them men of average firmness —not of the sort whose manhood is sapped by a weak superstition —that they should be smitten with causeless panic. But they were sent on a cruel, unrighteous mission, and it may have been divinely ordered to give them one admonition (perhaps but this one) that their bloody purpose brought them into collision with the Infinite and righteous God.

7. Then asked he them again, Whom seek ye? And they said, Jesus of Nazareth.

8. Jesus answered, I have told you that I am *he:* if therefore ye seek me, let these go their way:

* σπειρα.

9. That the saying might be fulfilled, which he spake, Of them which thou gavest me have I lost none.

When they rose to their feet Jesus mildly repeated his question, "Whom seek ye?" and renewed his surrender of himself, asking only the favor that his disciples might go unmolested.—— The "saying which he spake" is supposed to be that in John 17: 12. The divine plan called for his life to be sacrificed, but equally, that the lives of his disciples should be spared, for the work yet before them.

10. Then Simon Peter having a sword drew it, and smote the high priest's servant, and cut off his right ear. The servant's name was Malchus.

11. Then said Jesus unto Peter, Put up thy sword into the sheath: the cup which my Father hath given me, shall I not drink it?

True to his own instincts and characteristics, Peter is for fight, with deadly weapons, and to the death—for, judging from the aim of this blow, he intended it to be more serious than it was.—— Did this quick resort to his sword come of his still cherished notions of a temporal kingdom, to be founded in force and sustained by arms? Whether so or not, it is plain that his Master's rebuke staggered, not to say stunned him, and that his soul gravitated suddenly from the extreme of rash boldness to pusillanimous timidity; that non-resistance did not come easy to him; and furthermore, that he became fearful that he had exposed himself to vengeance and had every thing to fear from being known as one of the disciples of Jesus. So one mis-step begat more.——This servant's name, omitted by each of the other evangelists, appears in John. The omission at the early date of the first three may have been prudent; the insertion at the late date of John's gospel was doubtless safe enough, and served to give an air of life-likeness to his history.——All the gospel historians speak of this sword-blow of Peter, as falling upon a servant of the high priest and cutting off his right ear. Luke only has told us that Jesus said—"Suffer ye thus far;" then touched his ear and healed him.——How Jesus expostulated with Peter is given most fully by Matthew (26: 52–54): "Put up again thy sword into his place; for all they that take the sword shall perish with the sword. Thinkest thou that I can not now pray to my Father and he shall presently give me more than twelve legions of angels? But how then shall the Scriptures be fulfilled, that thus it must be?"

12. Then the band and the captain and officers of the Jews took Jesus, and bound him,

13. And led him away to Annas first; for he was father

in-law to Caiaphas, which was the high priest that same year.

14. Now Caiaphas was he, which gave counsel to the Jews, that it was expedient that one man should die for the people.

In giving the details of this trial, John only has spoken of the preliminary examination as being before Annas. The point of transition from Annas to Caiaphas as presiding officer, if indeed it was made distinctly in fact, is not clearly put in the inspired histories. Matthew seems to say that Jesus was taken at once and at first before Caiaphas; next and last, before Pilate. Mark omits the name of the Jewish presiding officer, simply calling him "the High Priest." Luke also omits names; passes over the night session with no details of the examination; but notices distinctly the early morning session of the whole Sanhedrim. Whether the scenes recorded by John (vs. 19–24) were before Annas or before Caiaphas, or before both sitting on the same bench, seems to be left in doubt. If before Annas only, then John omits what transpired before Caiaphas during the night session.——This partition of responsibility between Annas and Caiaphas is of no special importance.——John is careful to identify Annas as the same who had previously advised the murder of Jesus (11: 49, 50).

Judas has done his part and got his money. Shall we follow him a moment to his end?——John drops his story here. From others we learn that when he saw Jesus condemned "he repented himself" (not the word used for gospel repentance); brought again the thirty pieces of silver to the priests and elders (which after the manner of ill-gotten gain was "eating his flesh as it had been fire," James 5: 3) saying—"I have sinned in that I have betrayed the innocent blood." To which, with the coldest sort of comfort, they replied—"What is that to us? See thou to that." All they cared for was their victim. What if he were innocent? They knew that before.——If you have done a wicked thing, that is your concern, not ours! Alas! Judas scarcely needed any one to tell him it was his concern. He not only knew this but felt it.——This accursed money;—his hand could hold it no longer; he thrust it down upon the pavement of the temple; rushed away; sought some elevated point and hung himself;—to which Luke adds (Acts 1: 18) that, "falling headlong, he burst asunder in the midst, and all his bowels gushed out."—A yet briefer record testifies what became of his immortal part:—"Judas by transgression fell that he might *go to his own place.*"—— The record in whole supplies two great moral lessons: one upon the innocence of Jesus; the other upon the wages of sin.

15. And Simon Peter followed Jesus, and *so did* another disciple: that disciple was known unto the high priest, and went in with Jesus into the palace of the high priest.

16. But Peter stood at the door without. Then went out

that other disciple, which was known unto the high priest, and spake unto her that kept the door, and brought in Peter.

17. Then saith the damsel that kept the door unto Peter, Art not thou also *one* of this man's disciples? He saith, I am not.

18. And the servants and officers stood there, who had made a fire of coals, for it was cold; and they warmed themselves: and Peter stood with them, and warmed himself.

These are the first erring steps of Peter. He followed Jesus—but "afar off"—to see what might befall him. So did another disciple whom the writer forbears to name. We may call him—the writer himself—this being his way of speaking of himself. It happened that John was known to the high priest, and so was permitted to enter the court-room. Peter not being recognized and fearing what might happen to himself, stopped outside the door till John brought him in. It seems to have been a casual remark of the door-maid, having no purposed bearing upon Peter's safety—"Art thou not also" (as well as John) "one of this man's disciples?" To which he replied—"I am not." Our author locates this as his first denial of his Lord.——Peter did not think it prudent to leave abruptly: it might excite more suspicion; and moreover he had not yet seen the end; so he throws himself among the servants around the fire—apparently as if one of them, while the trial of his Lord went on.

19. The high priest then asked Jesus of his disciples, and of his doctrine.

20. Jesus answered him, I spake openly to the world; I ever taught in the synagogue, and in the temple, whither the Jews always resort; and in secret have I said nothing.

21. Why askest thou me? ask them which heard me, what I have said unto them: behold, they know what I said.

22. And when he had thus spoken, one of the officers which stood by struck Jesus with the palm of his hand, saying, Answerest thou the high priest so?

23. Jesus answered him, If I have spoken evil, bear witness of the evil: but if well, why smitest thou me?

24. Now Annas had sent him bound unto Caiaphas the high priest.

From this account of the proceedings before the high priest, it is clear that the court was itself the accusing party; that the judge had no definite charge to make, but was laboring to find one. The question *what it should be* was an after consideration; the question whether it were just or not—was no consideration at all.——So they began with leading questions:—*Why* have you

been gathering disciples? And *what* have you taught them?—— With profoundest sagacity Jesus replied:—I have taught in public only—in your own synagogues and in your temple. Ask the people what I have taught; they know: "In secret have I said nothing." My gospel is for all the world; I teach nothing which I fear to have all the world and this court itself know perfectly.
——Matthew and Mark relate more fully the history of this examination, showing how earnestly and long they sought false witness against Jesus, but found none; how they labored to convict him of threatening to destroy their temple, but no two witnesses concurred to the same point. At length the high priest adjured him—put him under the sacred oath—to answer whether he were "the Christ, the Son of God." He could not remain reticent; this solemn adjuration before the high court of Israel made it his duty to answer, and the point itself, it had been the great aim and labor of his public ministry to affirm and set forth. He therefore solemnly reaffirmed it here—"*I am.*" To admonish them once more of their infinite peril, he subjoins—"Hereafter ye shall see the Son of man sitting on the right hand of power and coming in the clouds of heaven."——The High Priest expressed his horror; declared it blasphemy; and called for the decision of the council. They all said, "He is guilty of death."—— Thus before the highest Jewish tribunal, Jesus stands convicted of blasphemy and is therefore adjudged worthy to die. But the power to take life judicially had passed from their hands to the Romans. Hence they must needs take the case before Pilate.

25. And Simon Peter stood and warmed himself. They said therefore unto him, Art not thou also *one* of his disciples? He denied *it*, and said, I am not.

26. One of the servants of the high priest, being *his* kinsman whose ear Peter cut off, saith, Did not I see thee in the garden with him?

27. Peter then denied again; and immediately the cock crew.

These verses conclude John's record of Peter's fall. The second denial was in reply to a question put to him by those who stood with him around the fire; the third, to a question by a kinsman of that servant of the high priest whose ear Peter had cut off. This latter question would naturally suggest to Peter the thought of personal danger, and so become a special temptation to deny his Lord.——Close upon this third denial the cock crew.
Supplementing this record from the other evangelists, we learn that the more definite form of Christ's prediction was—"Before the cock crow twice, thou wilt deny me thrice;" that there was a first and second crowing of the cock—the first apparently unnoticed by Peter; but that the second suggested to him this solemn forewarning from his Master; that Peter "denied with an oath," or as reported by Matthew and by Mark—"began to curse

and to swear, saying, I know not this man of whom ye speak;" that Peter's provincial tongue betrayed his Galilean origin; that immediately upon the second cock-crowing, "the Lord turned and looked upon Peter," and that then Peter remembered those words of warning; suddenly "went out and wept bitterly," or according to Mark—"When he thought thereon, he wept."——It seems remarkable that John should omit this weeping and give no hint of Peter's repentance. Must we not suppose that he made up this record as supplementary, so that he might omit very important facts because they were fully recorded already?——It deserves notice that Mark, who is supposed to have written under the supervision of Peter himself, details the case more fully than any other gospel historian, and gives its darkest features. He gives in its full strength the cursing and swearing, but on the side of penitence says only "he wept;" while Matthew and Luke have it—"wept bitterly." Staunch honesty, real contrition and humility, make his statement of the offense very strong, but put no special emphasis upon the tokens of penitent grief.

28. Then led they Jesus from Caiaphas unto the hall of judgment: and it was early; and they themselves went not into the judgment hall, lest they should be defiled; but that they might eat the passover.

This "hall of judgment" was the Roman tribunal, Pilate being at this time the Roman Procurator, and consequently the judge. The High Priest and his Council carry the case before Pilate, not of choice but of necessity—as their only means to take his life judicially.——Notice how sanctimoniousness and crime consort together in the same bosoms—the spirit of murder firing their hearts, yet afraid to defile their hallowed garments or soil their holy feet by going into Pilate's judgment hall, inasmuch as they were soon to eat the holy Passover! * A ceremonial religion naturally divorces itself from sound morality—ceremonies superseding both love to God and love to man. Hence in the case of men under the influence of such religious notions, no amount of depravity or crime ought to surprise us.

The words, "That they might eat the Passover," open a question in regard to the time when our Lord and his disciples on the one hand, and the scribes and Pharisees on the other, ate the Passover. It seems clear that Jesus and his eleven had already eaten their Paschal lamb †—*i. e.* on the evening preceding this

---

* Jewish authorities on defilement inform us that going into the house of a Gentile made a Jew unclean for one day.

† The testimony of Matthew (26: 17-20); of Mark (14: 12-18); and of Luke (22: 7-15), that Jesus and his disciples did eat the real Passover seems to be as clear and strong as can be framed in human language. Thus Matthew:—"Now the first day of the feast of unleavened bread, the disciples came to Jesus, saying, Where wilt thou

hearing before Pilate. How then are we to explain it that these priests anticipate their Passover as yet future—being afraid of such defilement as might preclude them?

It does not fall within the plan of this work to give the history of the various controversies which have arisen over points of this nature. Let it suffice here to say that the solution most satisfactory to me rests upon a distinction between the eating of the Paschal lamb on the first evening of the Passover week, and the festival of the week which opened fully on the day following and continued through the seven days. This distinction being recognized and applied in this case, we may hold, in harmony with all the statements, that our Lord and his disciples ate the Paschal lamb on the evening preceding his arrest; that these priests and men of the Great Council, for aught we know, may have had their Paschal lamb at the same time (unless they neglected it to carry out this scheme of arrest); but that they had the great festival yet in prospect. Possibly they cared more for the festival than for the Paschal lamb itself with its bitter herbs.

29. Pilate then went out unto them, and said, What accusation bring ye against this man?

30. They answered and said unto him, If he were not a malefactor, we would not have delivered him up unto thee.

As they must not go in, Pilate comes out to them to inquire of what crime they accuse the prisoner. It was a hard question for them to answer the Roman Procurator. Their council had condemned him for blasphemy; but such blasphemy was no crime before Roman law. What should they do? First, they respectfully suggest that Pilate might take their judicial action upon trust—with so much respect for their justice and good sense as to believe that they would not deliver a man up to him for the sentence of death unless he were a bad man—a real bad-doer. If Pilate would only be so very kind as to make himself their tool and order a man to be crucified upon their sentence against

that we prepare for thee to eat the Passover?" . . . "I will keep the Passover at thy house." "They made ready the Passover, and when even was come, Jesus sat down with the twelve."——Mark gives his testimony with no less strength: "The disciples made ready the Passover;"—"In the evening he cometh with the twelve, and as they sat and did eat"—the exposure of Judas occurred, etc. ——Luke is no less positive: "Then came the day of unleavened bread when the Passover must be killed;" "They made ready the Passover;" "When the hour was come he sat down and the twelve apostles with him; and he said—With desire have I desired to eat this Passover with you before I suffer."——Such testimonies can not be overruled without impugning the historic veracity of these three evangelists. This is one of the vital points in the discussion. If the witnesses are reliable the testimony is decisive.

him as a malefactor, the case might be disposed of without trouble or delay.

31. Then said Pilate unto them, Take ye him, and judge him according to your law. The Jews therefore said unto him, It is not lawful for us to put any man to death:

32. That the saying of Jesus might be fulfilled, which he spake, signifying what death he should die.

Pilate does not fall into this trap so readily as they had hoped. But he says—Take him; judge him by your own law; and then execute your sentence by inflicting such penalties as lie within your powers.——Pilate seems to assume that the crime could not be one that deserved death, and therefore that some penalty falling within their authority would be amply sufficient for the ends of justice.

They reply—That will by no means answer our purpose. We must have his life; and it is not lawful for us to put any man to death.——Jesus had spoken of his death as a being "lifted up "— *i. e.* on the cross (John 12: 32, and 8: 28, and 3: 14); and death by crucifixion implied an execution by Roman hands—this being their method of capital punishment. The Jewish method (while they had the power) was stoning. Jesus foreknew that his death must be by Roman hands. The historian apprises us how the course of events was shaped to this result.

33. Then Pilate entered into the judgment hall again, and called Jesus, and said unto him, Art thou the King of the Jews?

34. Jesus answered him, Sayest thou this thing of thyself, or did others tell it thee of me?

John does not show how Pilate was led to put this question to Jesus. Luke remarks—"They began to accuse him, saying—We found this fellow perverting the nation and forbidding to give tribute to Cæsar, saying that he himself is Christ a king " (23: 2). John, perhaps, opens the case at an earlier stage, while it yet remained doubtful to Jesus how Pilate was induced to put his main question. Jesus therefore calls for Pilate's information:—" Did this question spring up in thy mind spontaneously; or did others tell thee?"——Before Jesus should answer that question, it was at least prudent to ascertain what Pilate meant by it; what he had heard, if any thing; and what his views of the nature of the charge might be.

It was to the credit of Pilate's sagacity and good sense that the clamors of the accusing Jews as given by Luke made but little impression on his mind. Very probably he saw that those charges must be false—as they were. The central point—that Jesus forbade tribute-paying to Cæsar—was totally false—the very reverse of the truth; and sufficed to discolor whatever else

in their words as reported to us had any semblance of truth—
e. g. that Jesus claimed to be a king. The main charge—that of
setting up a worldly kingdom in rebellion against the Roman
power—was worse than groundless, for it imputed to Jesus those
worldly notions of empire—so rife among the whole Jewish people, including these very accusers—which notions it had been the
labor of his life to oppose, and the great sorrow of his life that
he was able to oppose to so little purpose. Probably Pilate saw
the animus of this accusation, and knew very well that no such
sedition as they charged could have existed without his knowledge, or would have disturbed these restless, seditious Jews, if it
had been never so serious. He knew they were ready enough to
throw off the Roman yoke if only some leader powerful enough
might appear, to be their head. Hence he saw that they were
pushing this prosecution "for envy."

35. Pilate answered, Am I a Jew? Thine own nation
and the chief priests have delivered thee unto me: what
hast thou done?

36. Jesus answered, My kingdom is not of this world: if
my kingdom were of this world, then would my servants
fight, that I should not be delivered to the Jews: but now
is my kingdom not from hence.

"Am I a Jew?" seems a little sharp—as if his equanimity or
his notions of personal dignity were slightly disturbed by this
plain question from the prisoner.——The crime charged (he seems
to imply) must pertain to the Jewish religion. Thou shouldest
not expect *me* to be versed in those matters. Please not take me
for a Jew: I am a *Roman*. Thine own nation have brought thee
before me under the charge of sedition: it is my business to put
the question—What hast thou done?——To this Jesus answers
squarely: "My kingdom is not of this world." It differs totally
from the kingdoms of earth. It claims no civil jurisdiction;
exacts no tribute; forbids no proper allegiance to kingdoms
which are of this world; resorts never to force of arms. My
servants, you must have known, were not allowed to fight to
shield me from arrest. My kingdom comes not of human power;
was never won by the sword; has no earthly origin.——So far
the reply of Jesus is substantially *negative*—saying what his
kingdom *is not*. This sufficed to rebut the charge of treason.

37. Pilate therefore said unto him, Art thou a king then?
Jesus answered, Thou sayest that I am a king. To this end
was I born, and for this cause came I into the world, that I
should bear witness unto the truth. Every one that is of
the truth heareth my voice.

Thy words (Pilate seems to say) imply, however, that thou art
a king: how is this? Art thou really a king? If so, what sort

of a king?——Jesus meets this question also with most entire frankness. It is as thou sayest; I am a king. For it should be noticed that the words—"Thou sayest that I am"—are equivalent to—I am as thou sayest: it is as thou hast said.——I was born a king; I came into the world to reign as king, or what amounts to the same thing—"that I should bear witness unto the truth." For my kingdom is an *empire of truth.* "Every one that is of the truth"—whose heart receives and loves the truth—hears my voice and is one of my subjects—is a member of my kingdom. Thus it will be seen, Jesus does not object to the words used in the charge brought against him, but rests his defense upon his definition of their true meaning. In the sense in which he is a king, his claim to be one is no crime.——He came from heaven to earth to bring to men messages of truth; to reveal great truths respecting God and man; God's rightful claims; man's rebellion against those claims; the law God has enjoined; the guilt and condemnation of the race as sinners; the redemption provided through his Son, and the offer of free pardon to the penitent and believing;—such were the vital points in this great realm of truth of which Jesus is king. To receive and obey this truth is to render the homage and service due under this kingdom. Over all such obedient, loving hearts, Jesus reigns. This and such is his kingdom.

38. *Pilate saith unto him, What is truth? And when he had said this, he went out again unto the Jews, and saith unto them, I find in him no fault at all.*

39. *But ye have a custom, that I should release unto you one at the passover: will ye therefore that I release unto you the King of the Jews?*

40. *Then cried they all again, saying, Not this man, but Barabbas. Now Barabbas was a robber.*

Pilate said, "What *is* truth?" with a slight emphasis on "*is*," signifying, not that he never heard that word before; not that he had no idea of truth as contrasted with falsehood; but intending to ask—What precisely dost *thou* mean by "truth"? What is truth as the word cometh from thy lips? What kind of truth is that to which thou bearest witness, and which maketh thee a king?——Then suddenly checking himself as if this rising inquiry might lead where he chose not to go—perhaps recoiling from the subject as one likely to come too closely home to his own ungodly soul—or arresting the inquiry as being aside from his official business, he gave no opportunity for the Great Teacher to answer his question, but went out again to the waiting Jews to say—"I find in this man no fault at all." The charge of sedition which ye bring against him must be entirely groundless. He may have some peculiar religious notions; and perhaps he may have come down from heaven as he says:—I dare not—can not—condemn him to death. But (he adds) let me suggest a plan which will relieve both you and myself, viz. that according to your custom of having one prisoner released at this festival, ye consent that I release this Jesus—the king of the Jews.——Nothing could be more distasteful to the Jews; any thing else would please them better; all with one voice cry aloud—"Not this man, but Barabbas."——John remarks that this "Barabbas was a robber;" Mark, more fully, that he "lay bound with others who had made insurrection with him, and had committed murder in the insurrection" (15: 7)—in which points Luke concurs. Matthew and Mark inform us that "the chief priests and elders persuaded the multitudes to ask Barabbas and to destroy Jesus." So Pilate is again frustrated in his endeavor to satisfy at once his own convictions of right, and the demands of those infuriated, prejudiced, persistent Jews.

CHAPTER XIX.

The author concludes his narrative of the trial of Jesus before Pilate (vs. 1–16); speaks of the crucifixion (vs. 17, 18); of the title put by Pilate upon the cross (vs. 19–22); of the disposal of his raiment (vs. 23, 24); relates how Jesus committed his mother to John (vs. 25–27); the final death-scene (28–30); the body taken from the cross and pierced (31–37); then finally embalmed and placed in its sepulcher (38–42).

1. Then Pilate therefore took Jesus, and scourged *him*.
2. And the soldiers platted a crown of thorns, and put *it* on his head, and they put on him a purple robe,
3. And said, Hail, King of the Jews! and they smote him with their hands.

This scourging and these insults were concessions by Pilate to the malice of the Jews, made probably in the hope that they would be satisfied with these inflictions and would cease to demand his life. The effect on them was the very opposite; they were the more sure of their power and of Pilate's weakness. It was Pilate's capital mistake; he lacked the courage to stand up to his moral convictions. Perhaps he had not fully learned before that bad men, infuriatd with passion, are not to be managed by concession.——Note that the whole course of the trial before Pilate puts the charge of sedition in the foreground. We hear little of the charge of blasphemy, but Jesus is treated as one who pretended, claimed, to be the King of the Jews. Hence the form of these insults.——The better textual authorities begin v. 3— "And they came to him and said," etc.—making more emphatic the formal, perhaps insulting, approach, in the way of mock homage.

4. Pilate therefore went forth again, and saith unto them, Behold, I bring him forth to you, that ye may know that I find no fault in him.

5. Then came Jesus forth, wearing the crown of thorns, and the purple robe. And *Pilate* saith unto them, Behold the man!

Again Pilate comes out from his court-room to report to the Jews—No proof against the accused; I find no fault in him.—How much and what Pilate meant in his words—"Behold the man!" is not entirely clear. Perhaps this: You see him humiliated and insulted:—Will not this suffice you? You see also that he is powerless for any harm in the line of sedition—nothing but the pageant of a king. Why should ye fear mischief from such a man? Can ye not therefore on the ground of his harmlessness consent that I release him and let him go?

6. When the chief priests therefore and officers saw him, they cried out, saying, Crucify *him*, crucify *him*. Pilate saith unto them, Take ye him, and crucify *him*: for I find no fault in him.

7. The Jews answered him, We have a law, and by our law he ought to die, because he made himself the Son of God.

"When they saw him"—he having been for a season withdrawn from their view in the Roman court-room, into which it would defile them to enter. As he came again before their eyes, they raise yet more fiercely the cry—Crucify him! To this, Pilate replies—Take him and crucify him yourselves, if so ye will—on your own responsibility—not on mine. I find no fault in him, and I can not crucify a man whom I believe to be innocent of crime.—The Jews seem here to concede at least tacitly, that the charge of sedition is of no particular account, for they fall back upon their original charge—blasphemy. "We have a law, and by the law" (so the best authorities, instead of *our* law) "he ought to die."—The reading, "By the law," being accepted, is stronger, as the reading, "our law," is weaker—since this latter makes the law only a Jewish thing. They would fain claim for this statute the dignity and authority of universal law.

8. When Pilate therefore heard that saying, he was the more afraid;

9. And went again into the judgment hall, and saith unto Jesus, Whence art thou? But Jesus gave him no answer.

. 10. Then saith Pilate unto him, Speakest thou not unto me? knowest thou not that I have power to crucify thee, and have power to release thee?

That Jesus claimed to be the Son of God springs new thoughts in the mind of Pilate. What—he says to himself—can this mean? There is a strange dignity in his bearing; a tone and air of innocence as well as integrity that I can not understand. I wish I might be rid of this responsibility; how can I give command for his causeless murder by these maddened Jews?

Again he resumes his place on his tribunal to push his inquiries as to the origin, the birth, and sonship of his prisoner. To his surprise and somewhat to his displeasure, Jesus gave him no answer. His official dignity was touched;—Dost thou not recognize my authority to release thee or to crucify?

11. Jesus answered, Thou couldest have no power *at all* against me, except it were given thee from above: therefore he that delivered me unto thee hath the greater sin.

12. And from thenceforth Pilate sought to release him: but the Jews cried out, saying, If thou let this man go, thou art not Cesar's friend: whosoever maketh himself a king speaketh against Cesar.

Abating nought from his high claim of being the Son of God, but virtually assuming this sonship more distinctly than ever before in this judicial presence, Jesus intimates to Pilate that *his* power would be of no account if God from above had not permitted these proceedings for purposes far other than Roman Judge, or blinded, maddened Jew, was aware of. Judas who betrayed him to their hand knew better than they could know whence Jesus came. His sin in betraying One whom he knew to be the Son of God was fearfully damning.

These words made a yet deeper impression upon Pilate. From that point he sought more earnestly to release Jesus—so the language must imply. But he had begun to make concessions; the accusing party push their demands, returning to the attack with more desperate determination, giving Pilate to understand that it was at the peril of his place if not of his head, to let this man go. They knew they could accuse Pilate before Cæsar; he also knew they could; and this fear at last brought him to their terms. Roman Procurators in the provinces held office on a most precarious tenure. The history of those times recites numerous cases of their arraignment before the powers at Rome.

13. When Pilate therefore heard that saying, he brought Jesus forth, and sat down in the judgment seat in a place that is called the Pavement, but in the Hebrew, Gabbatha.

14. And it was the preparation of the passover, and about the sixth hour: and he saith unto the Jews, Behold your King!

15. But they cried out, Away with *him*, away with *him*, crucify him. Pilate saith unto them, Shall I crucify your

King? The chief priests answered, We have no king but Cesar.

16. Then delivered he him therefore unto them to be crucified. And they took Jesus, and led *him* away

That last remark touched Pilate in his most susceptible point. His sense of justice gave way before his personal fear of losing his place through the ill-will of these leading Jews. To bring Jesus forth from his own court-room into the open area called "the Pavement" where his accusers were standing indicated that he had at length fully yielded to their demands. Now his proclamation to them is—" Behold your King!" There he stands, surrendered to your will; what do you say?—Again, they raise their shout, Away with him; Crucify him! Shall I crucify your king? said Pilate. "We have no king," said they, "but Cæsar"—very profuse in their professions of loyalty to Cæsar. Just then it was more adroit than honest to make these flaming professions. They sought to impress Pilate, not more with the conviction of their own loyalty than of their influence at Rome, to be wielded against him if he should refuse to meet their demands. At last he delivered Jesus to their will to be crucified.

Ere we drop the case of Pilate, let us note certain points made in the other evangelists only.——Luke relates that Christ's accusers spake of his "stirring up the people, beginning from Galilee:" that thereupon Pilate inquired if he were a Galilean, and learning that he was, sent him to Herod—then in the city, and at that time tetrarch of Galilee;—glad no doubt to divide if not altogether escape the unwelcome responsibility of the case. Herod had often heard of Jesus; was curious to see him; hoped to see some miracle done by him. Jesus was reticent before him. Herod so far succumbed to the popular furor as to allow his men of war to set the prisoner at nought, and cruelly insult and abuse him;—but sent him back to Pilate as one not convicted of crime.——To this Matthew adds that in the early morning hour of the trial, Pilate's wife sent him this message: "Have thou nothing to do with that just man; for I have suffered many things this day in a dream because of him." The hand of the Lord is sometimes traceable in dreams.—This message had weight with Pilate, heightening his trouble of conscience—not to say, his superstitious fears; yet not quite saving him from his great crime.——Matthew records the final effort of Pilate to purge himself from the responsibility of this judicial murder and to transfer it to his accusers: "When Pilate saw that he could prevail nothing, but that rather a tumult was made, he took water and washed his hands before the multitude, saying—I am innocent of the blood of this just person; see ye"—or more literally, ye shall see. His meaning seems to be—Assume ye for yourselves this responsibility. They so understood it and assumed the responsibility in those memorable, awful words—"His blood be on us and on our children!"——Never were words of imprecation more fearfully visited upon their authors in the horrors of divine retribution. Ere those who were children then passed from the stage of life, Titus, at the head of the Roman legions, invested Jerusalem; laid it utterly desolate; and buried in its ruins all but the whole living generation. Particularly it is related by Josephus—personally cognizant of the facts—that an immense number of Jews, made prisoners during the siege, were tortured and crucified on the high grounds adjacent to the city walls—crucified in such numbers "that there was not room for the crosses to stand by each other; and that at last they had not wood enough to make crosses of."

Of the final earthly doom of Pilate, reliable history gives some account; doubtful tradition has said much more. It is well authenticated that the evil he so much dreaded—that of being arraigned before Cæsar for mal-administration—came upon him, and cost him his official place (about A. D. 36). "The sequel" (says Ellicott—"Life of Christ," p. 316) "is said to have been disgrace and misfortune (Eusebius), and not long afterward, death by his own hand."

On verse 15, two incidental points arise which involve critical questions. The first respects "the preparation of the Passover." Did not Jesus and his disciples "prepare" for the Passover on the day previous to this and eat the Paschal lamb on the evening previous? How then can this be the day of preparation for the Passover?——The best explanation seems to me to be this: that the Greek word for "preparation" * refers here to the Sabbath rather than to the day before the Passover began. Mark implies this (15: 42): "because it was the preparation, *i. e.* the day before the Sabbath;" and John (19: 31) supports this view: —"Because it was the *preparation*, that the bodies should not remain upon the cross on the Sabbath day (for that Sabbath day was an high day)." Referring it thus to the Sabbath, we obviate the difficulty. The Paschal lamb was eaten on Thursday evening, preparation for this having been made during the day previous; Friday in the early morning came on the judicial proceedings; then the crucifixion from about 9 A. M. to 3 P. M.; then late in the day the requisite preparation for the great Jewish Sabbath on Saturday—extra "great" when its sanctity was augmented by that of the Passover feast. In this case the day of preparation for the Sabbath was not the same as the day of preparation for the Paschal lamb, but was one day later. The preparation for the Sabbath is specially intended in this passage.

The other point is the date given here—"about the sixth hour." Was this Roman time, or Jewish? As the Romans (whom modern nations follow) reckoned from midnight, their system would make the time 6 A. M. As the Jews reckoned from the average sunrise, *i. e.* 6 A. M., their sixth hour would

---

* παρασκευή.

be 12 M. Apart from the exigencies of this passage, the Jewish system is the more probable. But so late an hour as 12 M. is impossible. For the sufferings on the cross were protracted through six hours, commencing according to Mark (15: 25) at the Jewish third hour (9 A. M.) and terminating in death at the ninth hour—3 P. M. (Mark 15: 33, 37). Moreover, the bodies remained some time on the cross after Jesus had expired, and yet were taken down before sunset of that day. The dates by Mark correspond so entirely with all the recorded circumstances and with the necessities of the case that they must be accepted as essentially accurate.——It may have been slightly later than the third hour when the crucifixion commenced; and John's statement may be taken as very general and approximative—*i. e.* the time may have been nearer the sixth hour than any other general division of the day. This explanation does not entirely remove the difficulty; yet may be the best we can suggest.—— There is some authority for reading in John "third" instead of "sixth" hour; but not sufficient to justify this change of text.

17. And he bearing his cross went forth into a place called *the place* of a skull, which is called in the Hebrew Golgotha:

18. Where they crucified him, and two others with him, on either side one, and Jesus in the midst.

On the question—By whom was the cross borne? the improved text in John (v. 17) makes it—"He, bearing the cross by himself"—implying that at least in the outset he bore the cross alone. Both Matthew and Mark say they laid hold of one Simon and compelled him to bear it; while Luke gives (perhaps) the most exact statement—"On him they laid the cross that he might bear it *after Jesus*"—*i. e.* might bear one end of it, walking behind Jesus, to relieve him in part of its burden, the whole being found to be beyond his strength.——The locality of the crucifixion can not be fixed with certainty. It was outside the city walls, yet not remote, but near a very considerable thoroughfare of travel (v. 20).

Death by crucifixion was intended to be a slow, lingering process, but one of terrible torture. The frame—one post with a transverse beam crossing it near the upper end—was first laid on the ground and the prisoner fastened to it by means of a spike ("nail") driven through the palm of each hand into the transverse beam along which the arms were stretched; and by another driven through the feet into the upright post. It is doubtful whether each foot was spiked separately, or whether the same spike was driven through both. This is a point of no special importance. In all other respects the mode is well known. After the subject had been fastened to his cross, it was raised with him upon it and fixed in an upright position, where he must hang upon these spikes till death put an end to his agony.——Under such physical torture the life-forces of our blessed Redeemer were worn away, till endurance failed him and life became extinct under the exhaustion of his agonies.

Luke, and he only, has given us the very striking scene between Jesus and the penitent thief.

19. And Pilate wrote a title, and put *it* on the cross. And the writing was, JESUS OF NAZARETH THE KING OF THE JEWS.

20. This title then read many of the Jews; for the place where Jesus was crucified was nigh to the city: and it was written in Hebrew, *and* Greek, *and* Latin.

21. Then said the chief priests of the Jews to Pilate, Write not, The King of the Jews; but that he said, I am King of the Jews.

22. Pilate answered, What I have written I have written.

On the part of Pilate, this title may have been a prudential measure—a public testimony for his own vindication to the effect that this man was executed under the charge of sedition, claiming to be the King of the Jews, and therefore in arms against the Roman power.——The emendation suggested by the Jews (v. 21) was not to Pilate's mind. Perhaps his reply tacitly signified —Ye have shown full as much of the spirit of dictation in this whole matter as I am prepared to bear. If the form in which I have put it should be a little humiliating to your nation, perhaps ye have deserved it.

23. Then the soldiers, when they had crucified Jesus, took his garments, and made four parts, to every soldier a part; and also *his* coat: now the coat was without seam, woven from the top throughout.

24. They said therefore among themselves, Let us not rend it, but cast lots for it, whose it shall be: that the Scripture might be fulfilled, which saith, They parted my raiment among them, and for my vesture they did cast lots. These things therefore the soldiers did.

Four was the number of soldiers assigned for the execution of this sentence.——The clothing of the sufferer was by usage one of the perquisites for this service.——The Scripture referred to here as fulfilled is Ps. 22: 18: "They part my garments among them, and cast lots upon my vesture." Occurring in a Psalm, the whole of which may most appositely be referred to the Messiah, this is one of the most minute among all Scripture prophecies. No wonder John should take this special notice of its precise fulfillment. These points never had any known fulfillment in the case of David. No fulfillment meets their significance except in these events here narrated. The reader is referred to my notes on Ps. 22 for the proof that the entire Psalm refers to the Messiah, and has had a definite fulfillment throughout in him and in him only.

25. Now there stood by the cross of Jesus his mother, and his mother's sister, Mary the *wife* of Cleophas, and Mary Magdalene.

26. When Jesus therefore saw his mother, and the disciple standing by, whom he loved, he saith unto his mother, Woman, behold thy Son!

27. Then saith he to the disciple, Behold thy mother! And from that hour that disciple took her unto his own *home*.

Naturally a deep interest gathers about the names and history of these women. That in this eventful hour, when not one of the eleven (apparently) save John, was near, while the Great Sufferer was passing through his last, most bitter agonies—there were women whose courage was equal to the emergency, whose sympathizing love held them to the scene; whose hearts yearned to minister in any way possible for them to his comfort or relief; and who yet, if nothing else could be done, would still stand near, waiting, weeping, loving;—such women as these command our admiration, and we may wish that we knew their history far better than we do.

Neither of the gospel historians gives the names of the whole group, each naming only the more prominent, and giving these with some diversity of name. Thus we have—(1) Mary the mother of Jesus;—(2) One described as "Mary the mother of James and Joses," and also as "the wife of Cleophas;" (3) Salome, the mother of Zebedee's sons (James and John); (4) Mary Magdalene.——Of their history as elsewhere developed it is not in place here to speak. Their presence here and the spirit they manifested are an honor to woman. We love to do them honor. There were others, in considerable number, associated with them in sympathy, in patient attendance, in devoted affection.——Apparently their presence here is alluded to by John for the purpose of stating another fact of tender interest. As Jesus saw both his mother and the disciple he specially loved standing near him and near to each other, he said to his mother, "Behold thy son;" and to the beloved disciple, "Behold thy mother." It was a delicate, tender way of committing the mother that bare him to the fostering care of this disciple for whatever years of her earthly pilgrimage might yet remain. From that hour this disciple "took her *to his own*"—as his own mother, to share with him all that his family home could supply. It was the last tribute of filial affection on the part of the Great Sufferer, and can be duly appreciated only as we think of it as said under the fearful pangs of his dying agony.

28. After this, Jesus knowing that all things were now accomplished, that the Scripture might be fulfilled, saith, I thirst.

29. Now there was set a vessel full of vinegar: and they filled a sponge with vinegar, and put *it* upon hyssop, and put *it* to his mouth.

30. When Jesus therefore had received the vinegar, he said, It is finished: and he bowed his head, and gave up the ghost.

The "all things now accomplished" would seem to be specially the sufferings he was to endure both as to kind and amount. Jesus knowing that he had drained this fearful cup to its bottom, and hence was near his end—in order to fulfill yet one more prediction, cried—"I thirst." This is supposed to refer to Ps. 69: 21: "In my thirst they gave me vinegar to drink." Great thirst is one of the effects of such extreme suffering. At an earlier hour according to Matthew (27: 34) they had offered him "vinegar mingled with gall," or as described by Mark (15: 23) "wine mingled with myrrh;" but when he tasted he would not drink. This sour wine, prepared with so-called "gall" or "myrrh" was intended to be an anesthetic, to deaden the sense of pain—which seems to have been the reason why Jesus would not drink. He was there to suffer—not to spare himself any part of the cup given him of the Father to drink. But after all the prescribed and predicted sufferings had been endured, it was proper to give expression to his dreadful thirst, and not improper to taste the vinegar presented to his lips. This done, he cried—"It is finished"—the dreadful agony is all borne; the great work is done! —and died!

At this point it can not be amiss to group together the various utterances of Jesus on the way to his cross and while suspended upon it, as recorded by the several evangelists, no one of whom has given them all.

Following the probable order of time, we arrange them thus:

(*a*) On the way to the cross, to the women who followed him, bewailing and lamenting:—"Daughters of Jerusalem, weep not for me, but weep for yourselves and for your children," etc.—a touching testimony to the unselfishness—the deep, matchless compassion of his heart; the very benevolence which bore him to the cross for guilty man.—Recorded by Luke only (23: 27).

(*b*) His prayer for his murderers—"Father, forgive them, for they know not what they do;"—most probably uttered while they were nailing him to his cross. This also comes to us in Luke only (23: 34).

(*c*) What he said to the penitent thief on the cross by his side —"To-day shalt thou be with me in Paradise." This, and indeed the entire account of the penitent thief, occurs only in Luke (23: 43).

(*d*) Next we may place that one wailing cry—which told all and more than all which the human mind can measure—that one "loud cry of unfathomable woe and uttermost desolation;" *—"My God, my God, why hast thou forsaken me?" It is vain for us to attempt the depth of meaning or of woe that lies in these words. It seems worse than puerile to say they were taken up from the lips of David (Ps. 22), and therefore may have been used by way of accommodation, not signifying really any such sense of being forsaken of God as the words from David's lips might appropriately express. In truth, that entire Psalm is Messianic, speaking prophetically of him and for him; and these first words of it give us its key-note—the ruling thought and sense of the Great Sufferer.——These words occur only in Matthew and Mark.

Next in order we may locate the three expressions recorded by John only; viz:

(*e*) The words said to his mother and to the beloved disciple.

(*f*) The exclamation, "I thirst."

(*g*) And that other, "It is finished!"

(*h*) Last of all the words given by Luke only (23: 46): "Father, into thy hands I commend my spirit."

Such, so far as the various records report them, were the utterances which fell from the Savior's lips during the scenes of his last sufferings—the only manifestations which have come down to us of his thought, his sympathies, his love, and spirit of forgiveness, of his relation to the Father, and of his immense agony, in that dark and dying hour. As last words of dear dying friends are treasured in our deepest heart, so let these testimonials of our greatest, most suffering Friend, lie embalmed in our souls, cherished in most tender remembrance—till at length we see him face to face.

Of scenes external to the suffering Jesus, Matthew has given the most full account:—that from the sixth hour there was darkness over all the land until the ninth hour; that the great vail of the temple was rent in twain from the top to the bottom (signifying that the way into the most Holy Place was open to all, and no longer to the High Priest only); that "the earth did quake, and rocks were rent, and graves were opened, and many bodies of saints which slept arose, came out of their graves, after his resurrection; went into the holy city and appeared unto many."—This last named fact, stated by Matthew only, has met with various reception. I know of no reason to discredit the record. The many questions which may be asked and can not be answered—who they were; how many; what became of them; why they were raised at all; why these rather than others; why so many and neither more nor less; what good came of it, etc., etc., may be wisely suffered to await a fuller revelation before we attempt to answer them. All we need say is that in connection

---

* Ellicott, p. 321.

with a scene so stupendous as the death of the Son of God, the Prince of life—of Him who is the Resurrection and the Life—it is by no means incongruous, unnatural, preposterous—nothing of the kind—that many bodies of sleeping saints should arise from their graves as here said. It was of course an exceptional case: the whole great transaction of the crucifixion and death of Jesus was exceptional.

The deep darkness that veiled the heavens and covered the face of the land for three hours was also exceptional; certainly supernatural, and not the result of any eclipse. The moon being then at its full, an eclipse of the sun was a natural impossibility. But this hiding of his glorious face was signally significant when the Great Maker of the heavens and earth, in his incarnate relations to our human nature, was dying in mortal agony! Man in his guilt and blindness might be reviling, insulting, torturing;—but God from his lofty throne bade his sun in the heavens to hold its light and the forces of our inner earth to give their signals of convulsion and horror!

31. The Jews therefore, because it was the preparation, that the bodies should not remain upon the cross on the sabbath day, (for that sabbath day was a high day,) besought Pilate that their legs might be broken, and *that* they might be taken away.

32. Then came the soldiers, and brake the legs of the first, and of the other which was crucified with him.

33. But when they came to Jesus, and saw that he was dead already, they brake not his legs:

34. But one of the soldiers with a spear pierced his side, and forthwith came there out blood and water.

35. And he that saw *it* bare record, and his record is true; and he knoweth that he saith true, that ye might believe.

36. For these things were done, that the Scripture should be fulfilled, A bone of him shall not be broken.

37. And again another Scripture saith, They shall look on him whom they pierced.

This entire paragraph is peculiar to John.——Upon the word "preparation," see note on v. 14.——The Mosaic law was very specific against allowing a dead or suspended body to remain over night upon the tree. (See Deut. 21 : 22, 23). These Jews seem to have deemed it doubly important to take the bodies down in this case because the following day was the Sabbath, and one of special sanctity, since it fell within the days of unleavened bread.——The custom of breaking the legs of those who suffered crucifixion had for its object to ascertain or to hasten the event of death. It seems that neither of the two thieves were found dead but that Jesus was—indicating that he was in a state of unusual exhaustion before he was nailed to the cross; or, that death was hastened by mental agonies as well as physical.——The spear piercing his side is supposed to have penetrated the pericardium—since this would account most naturally for the discharge of both blood and water. This point is important physiologically inasmuch as it proves most conclusively his actual death—upon which fact hangs that of a real resurrection from death.

It will be noticed that John certifies very specifically to the discharge of both blood and water. But whether his estimate of the importance of this fact turned on its value as proof of actual death, or upon its symbolical significance—the water, of moral cleansing; the blood, of atonement and remission of sin—is not clear. That he made account of this double symbolism appears in his first epistle (5:6): "This is he that came by water and blood; not by water only, but by water and blood."—— In each of these two facts—no bone broken, and his side pierced, John finds prophecy fulfilled. As to the former, it was forbidden to break any bone of the Paschal lamb (Ex. 12:46). In Jesus, our Paschal Lamb, this must needs be fulfilled. In Ps. 34:20, the same thing is said of the righteous:—"He [God] keepeth all his bones; not one of them is broken." But this is a prophecy as to Christ only because in his human relations he is one of God's children, cared for under the universal law.——As to the piercing of his side, see Zech. 12:10: "They shall look upon me whom they have pierced"—which occurs in a passage properly regarded as Messianic.

38. And after this Joseph of Arimathea, being a disciple of Jesus, but secretly for fear of the Jews, besought Pilate that he might take away the body of Jesus: and Pilate gave *him* leave. He came therefore, and took the body of Jesus.

39. And there came also Nicodemus, (which at the first came to Jesus by night,) and brought a mixture of myrrh and aloes, about a hundred pound *weight*.

40. Then took they the body of Jesus, and wound it in linen clothes with the spices, as the manner of the Jews is to bury.

41. Now in the place where he was crucified there was a garden; and in the garden a new sepulcher, wherein was never man yet laid.

42. There laid they Jesus therefore because of the Jews' preparation *day;* for the sepulcher was nigh at hand.

It happened that the body of Jesus was honorably cared for by two distinguished Jews—Joseph and Nicodemus—each of them a member of the Sanhedrim; each a disciple of Jesus, though not publicly known as such. Each of the four evangelists speaks in high terms of Joseph; Matthew saying of him—"A rich man of Arimathea who himself was Jesus' disciple:" Mark adding to this—"An honorable counselor who also waited for the kingdom of God, went in *boldly* unto Pilate and craved the body of Jesus;" while Luke says of him—"A counselor, a good and just man (the same had not consented to the counsel and deed of them"—*i. e.* of his fellow-members of the Great Council); "who also himself waited for the kingdom of God." John, as we see, calls him "a disciple of Jesus, but secretly for fear of the Jews."—The part borne by Nicodemus attracted less attention, no one of the gospel historians save John, having alluded to him or to his agency at all. He seems to have borne no part in obtaining the body from Pilate, but did contribute, gratefully we may hope, to furnish the necessary materials (one hundred pounds weight of myrrh and aloes) for laying out the body for interment. Remarkably, all these provisions for the interment, *i. e.* entombing of the body, were of the first class; a very large amount, we must suppose, of "myrrh and aloes;" "spices" also, applied in the folds of the linen cloth that enwrapped the body; a new sepulcher, hewn out of rock; itself in a garden of rural beauty. It is remarkable that up to the point of death, all the surroundings of the Crucified One were savage, cruel, not only disrespectful, but positively and intentionally insulting—fit only for the basest and meanest of men:—but all suddenly, from the point of actual death the scene changes utterly: every point in his surroundings betokens dignity and honor. The same sudden transition appears in that celebrated prophecy (Isa. 53), where we see him, up to the period of death, "despised and rejected of men"—but thence and onward "with the rich in his death," and passing thence to the highest honors before God;—"shall see of the travail of his soul and be satisfied;" "the pleasure of the Lord shall prosper in his hand," etc., etc. That was indeed a point of wonderful, sublimely glorious transition, where he could say of all the pain and all the shame—"It is finished;" from which onward there remained only glory and honor, dominion and power, praise and homage, through all the eternal ages.

CHAPTER XX.

The Resurrection and its Incidents.

It remains now to give somewhat fully the circumstances attending and confirming the resurrection of the Lord.——Mary Magdalene, Peter and John, find the sepulcher empty, the body of their Lord not there (vs. 1-10); Mary lingers at the sacred spot, weeping, and is greeted with the first appearance of the risen Jesus (11–18); the same day at evening Jesus appears suddenly in the midst of the assembled disciples, all being present save Thomas (19–23); Thomas is very skeptical and demands sensible proofs (24, 25); the next Lord's day evening Jesus appears similarly again and satisfies Thomas (26–29). The author states his object in this book (30, 31.)

1. The first *day* of the week came Mary Magdalene early, when it was yet dark, unto the sepulcher, and seeth the stone taken away from the sepulcher.

In this first visit made by the faithful ones to the sepulcher, Mary Magdalene was undoubtedly most prominent. Dear woman:—the love and gratitude of her heart to the Crucified One moved her to her utmost endeavors to minister to his mortal remains; brought her to the sepulcher after the Sabbath was passed ere yet it was day, and held her there watching, weeping, just in the state of mind to hear the first whispers of his voice and to be greeted with the first vision of his presence.——Remarkably, while John names the Mary of Magdala only, Matthew says the other Mary came also to see the sepulcher: Mark adds to the list the name of Salome, and moreover tells us they came, "having bought sweet spices that they might anoint him." The hasty service performed on the evening of Friday was imperfect, unfinished. They came again to complete this service of affection as soon as possible after the Sabbath is passed and the light of another day returns. ——In respect to this group of sisters, Luke names but three— compared with Mark, giving the name Joanna in place of Salome, and adds, "certain others with them." The precise number remains therefore indefinite. Obviously Mary Magdalene was the leading spirit.——They found the stone rolled away from the sepulcher, which rolling away Matthew attributes to an angel from heaven, while Mark records the anxious solicitude of the women lest this great stone should baffle their purpose of reaching and anointing the body. This angel gave them their first hint that their Lord had really risen.

2. Then she runneth, and cometh to Simon Peter, and to the other disciple, whom Jesus loved, and saith unto them, They have taken away the Lord out of the sepulcher, and we know not where they have laid him.

3. Peter therefore went forth, and that other disciple, and came to the sepulcher.

4. So they ran both together: and the other disciple did outrun Peter, and came first to the sepulcher.

5. And he stooping down, *and looking in*, saw the linen clothes lying; yet went he not in.

6. Then cometh Simon Peter following him, and went into the sepulcher, and seeth the linen clothes lie.

7. And the napkin, that was about his head, not lying with the linen clothes, but wrapped together in a place by itself.

8. Then went in also that other disciple, which came first to the sepulcher, and he saw, and believed.

9. For as yet they knew not the Scripture, that he must rise again from the dead.

10. Then the disciples went away again unto their own home.

Simon Peter is once more back among the faithful ones—a live man in the group—to whom Mary Magdalene makes report as to one who will be prompt to act in the emergency. To this Peter and to John she tells her thrilling story in those ever-memorable words: "They have taken away the Lord out of the sepulcher, and we know not where they have laid him." Who the parties were—indicated by her word "they," she did not know: all was yet in darkness—only she had found the sepulcher empty. Ah, she did not know what they had done with those hallowed remains!——The two disciples ran for the sepulcher: our author remembers the minutest circumstances of the case; how he outran his brother and reached the sepulcher first, but for some unexplained reason did not go in; how Peter came up soon, and, true to his daring, impulsive nature, dashed in; how he saw the linen which had enfolded the body carefully laid aside and the napkin which had swathed the head deposited with the utmost order by itself. These minute particulars are by no means valueless; for they testify to the writer's accurate remembrance of these points, and (what is of more value) they utterly disprove the allegation that somebody came by night and stole away the body while the guard slept. Body-snatching is not wont to be done in this quiet, delicate manner, leaving every thing arranged in perfect order; and of course, rifling a sepulcher for the sake of the valuables there would leave none of them behind.——These disciples now saw with their own eyes and "believed"—*i. e.* believed that he must have risen from the dead—a new idea in their mind, for up to this point they had not understood from the Scriptures that he was thus to rise. What Jesus had said to them of his rising from the dead on the third day (Matt. 16: 21, and 17: 22, and 20: 19) they had not well understood—at least it had not been lodged in their minds as an event fully accepted and anticipated.——After these discoveries, not seeing any thing more to be done, they returned home.

11. But Mary stood without at the sepulcher weeping: and as she wept, she stooped down, *and looked* into the sepulcher,

12. And seeth two angels in white sitting, the one at the

head, and the other at the feet, where the body of Jesus had lain.

13. And they say unto her, Woman, why weepest thou? She saith unto them, Because they have taken away my Lord, and I know not where they have laid him.

14. And when she had thus said, she turned herself back, and saw Jesus standing, and knew not that it was Jesus.

15. Jesus saith unto her, Woman, why weepest thou? whom seekest thou? She, supposing him to be the gardener, saith unto him, Sir, if thou have borne him hence, tell me where thou hast laid him, and I will take him away.

16. Jesus saith unto her, Mary. She turned herself, and saith unto him, Rabboni; which is to say, Master.

17. Jesus saith unto her, Touch me not; for I am not yet ascended to my Father: but go to my brethren, and say unto them, I ascend unto my Father, and your Father; and *to* my God, and your God.

18. Mary Magdalene came and told the disciples that she had seen the Lord, and *that* he had spoken these things unto her.

Mary's loving heart holds her to the spot. She stands by the sepulcher weeping. She knows it is empty; Peter and John had both reported it so; but still she lingers, and now, almost unconsciously she stoops down and looks in. Lo! there are two angels in white sitting one at the head and the other at the feet of the very place where the body of her Lord had lain. What ministries of love and service brought them down from their home in heaven? Had they come to attend the risen Jesus? Was it their hands that disposed in so orderly a manner both the linen clothes and the napkin?——They are present now, in the true spirit of angelic ministry, to comfort Mary. Just here, something moved her to turn and look behind—and there stood Jesus! Her weeping eyes and agitated spirit failed at first to recognize the well-known form. At first she did not even recognize that sympathizing voice, inquiring why she wept and whom she sought. Her words in reply, repeated now for the third time, show that her thoughts are still upon taking away that precious dead body in order that she and her sisters might complete their ministry of love with the sweet spices brought and ready.——At first Jesus accosted her by the term "woman;" but neither this name nor the tones of his voice secured recognition. Next, he said "Mary." Oh, how often had she heard that well-remembered voice pronouncing her own name and carrying Love's electric impulses to her heart. She could not fail to recognize those tones of love. That, said she in her thought, is my own Lord and Savior, and she instantly responds—" Rabboni "—meaning not merely " Master," but "*My* Master." No better word could have been chosen for this spontaneous response of her soul.——Why did Jesus say to her "Touch me not;" whereas on that very day (according to Matt. 28: 9) "the other women early at the sepulcher came and held him by the feet and worshiped him;" and a few days later he said to unbelieving Thomas, "Reach hither thy hand and thrust it into my side"? (v. 27).——I doubt if any conjecture of value can be made to account for the diverse attitude of Jesus in these several cases. Mary's thought, if she advanced to embrace him, was not like that of Thomas to satisfy herself of his actual resurrection. Thomas had said he should demand this sort of evidence; in great condescension to his skepticism, Jesus yielded to his demand. Why he forbade Mary's embrace is not made clear.——The construction which assumes that Mary clasped (or moved to clasp) the person of her Lord, and that he bade her not *detain* him, is not favored by the Greek word. This does not mean detain, but touch.* Whatever interpretation we adopt should at least assume that the original word said what was meant—*i. e.* it should base itself upon this text and not some other.

The words in which he would have his approaching ascension to the Father announced to his disciples must strike every reader as inimitably tender and inspiring: "I ascend unto my Father and your Father"—to one who is at once both my Father and yours; yours as truly as mine. So you may think of him—your own Father as well as the Father of your elder Brother, the Jesus whom you have followed and loved through the days of his humiliation.

19. Then the same day at evening, being the first *day* of the week, when the doors were shut where the disciples were assembled for fear of the Jews, came Jesus and stood in the midst, and saith unto them, Peace *be* unto you.

20. And when he had so said, he shewed unto them *his* hands and his side. Then were the disciples glad, when they saw the Lord.

To the disciples as a family, this was the first appearance of the risen Jesus.——As bearing upon the nature of his resurrection body there has been no little speculation upon this sudden appearance in the midst of a group sitting with closed doors. The question has been virtually put—Was his raised body so *unmaterial* that closed doors were no obstacle to his entrance?——But it were well to raise the previous question—Has John's allusion to the "closed doors" the least reference to the manner of the Lord's entrance into the room? Was it in his thought to suggest that Christ's body was of such a nature that it could and did enter despite of the shut doors? Or, was it not rather his purpose to rep-

* ἅπτου.

resent this as a private meeting of the disciples, convened in this secluded way through fear of violent persecution? The circumstance that Jesus "came and stood" certainly favors the idea of a material body. We may admit a mild form of miracle—suppose in opening the doors unobserved, or in holding the senses of the disciples that they should not perceive how he entered; but the assumption that his body was in such a sense spiritual that closed doors were no barrier to his entrance should have more evidence than this narrative affords.——That "he showed them his hands and his feet"—where the nails were driven through—was beyond all doubt designed to convince them that this was the same body which was nailed to the cross. Whatever changes it had undergone in the resurrection, it had not ceased to be a material body; it was in some vital sense the same body. Its laws of being, as to sustenance, sleep, fatigue and rest, disease, frailty, temptability, etc., etc., may have been—indeed, seem to have been—greatly changed; but the precise extent of these changes and the nature of *body after* such change—how can we know till our experience in the risen glorified body of the saints shall reveal it?

When Jesus broke thus suddenly upon their astonished vision, his words of salutation were inexpressibly cheering. What could have been more so? I am your old, your long-tried Friend. You will remember my words while yet present with you, saying, "Peace I leave with you; *my* peace I give unto you: not as the world giveth, give I unto you." I come now to reiterate the same assurances; to reaffirm the same benedictions. Oh, were they not glad when they saw the Lord, and had such proofs of his true identity—such assurances that this was verily, most certainly, their own precious Redeemer!

21. Then said Jesus to them again, Peace *be* unto you: as *my* Father hath sent me, even so send I you.

22. And when he had said this, he breathed on *them*, and saith unto them, Receive ye the Holy Ghost:

23. Whosesoever sins ye remit they are remitted unto them; *and* whosesoever *sins* ye retain, they are retained.

He repeats the tender words, his salutation of peace, adding— I send you forth on your gospel mission as my Father sent me. Ye are to take up and prosecute the same work for which the Father sent me into the world. This also was adapted at once to cheer their hearts, to brace up their courage, to inspire an undying zeal, and to impress a sense of great responsibility. But how sweetly the sense of such responsibility must have rested upon their souls accompanied with such inspiring consolations; enforced by such claims; associated with such heavenly fellowship; quickened by such assurances of final reward!

"Breathed on them, saying, Receive ye the Holy Ghost"—a symbolic act, based on the analogy between breath and spirit, and indicating that he now began to fulfill to them the great promise made so prominent in his last conversations before Gethsemane—that he would give them "another Comforter, the Spirit of truth, who should lead them into all truth."

"Whosesoever sins ye remit, they are remitted," etc. The interpretation of these words, it must be conceded, involves somewhat grave difficulties, and moreover is so important as to justify thorough and if need be extended examination.

Let it be noted, they are not introduced with the declaration—"All power is given unto you in heaven and on earth;" the administration of government and pardon under the scheme of redemption is transferred absolutely to your hands:—not in any such connection do these words stand. There is no intimation that they were designed to suspend or materially modify the doctrine—"Who can forgive sins but God only?" "The Son of man hath power on earth to forgive sins." If this view be correct, this must be one of our land-marks to guide us in the interpretation of the passage.

It may not be amiss to suggest also that in the nature of the case, the real remission of sins must assume these two antecedent conditions in the pardoning power—(1) The prerogative of supreme authority under God's moral government:—(2) A knowledge of human hearts, scarcely if at all less than omniscient—at least sufficient to determine with unerring certainty the sincerity of repentance and of gospel faith in Jesus the Savior. These qualifications are simply indispensable. It can not for a moment be supposed that God will transfer the power or the right to forgive sins to any party in heaven or on earth in whom these conditions are not met.

Advancing now to the simple question of interpretation—*What do these words mean?* let it be noted, they stand in immediate connection with the promise, or more strictly the gift of the Spirit. This gift would prepare them for the function of remitting sins, whatever this precise function as here intended might be.——It is germain therefore to our present chief inquiry to ask—Was the Spirit promised and given to enable the apostles to *administer* God's moral government; or rather, only to *publish its principles* and their bearings? Was it to give them the power to know human hearts unerringly; or simply the power to tell men how God would note their moral attitude toward himself, forgiving the penitent and the believing, but condemning to deeper woe those who under the gospel remained still impenitent and unbelieving?——Fortunately we have in the historic facts of the case the key to the interpretation we seek. When the Holy Ghost came mightily upon the apostles, Peter—very much a representative man among them—proclaimed everywhere, in the temple, and before the Great Council—not "I absolve:" not—we, apostles, are commissioned to absolve from sin, or to retain men's sins unpardoned upon their guilty souls unto their eternal damnation—but rather on this wise: "Repent ye,

for the remission of your sins" (Acts 2: 38); "Repent and be converted, that your sins may be blotted out" (Acts 3: 19); "Him [Jesus] hath God exalted with his right hand to be a Prince and a Savior, *for to give repentance* to Israel and *forgiveness of sins*, and we [apostles] are his witnesses of these things, and so is also the Holy Ghost" (Acts 5: 31, 32). Here we have it precisely. Jesus, and he only, gives repentance and forgiveness of sins. We, his apostles, are only his witnesses as to this thing. We *testify;* we *announce;* we *proclaim* this great truth and tell men how it must apply to their sinning souls. In this sense, and in this only, do we, the apostles of Jesus, remit or retain men's sins.
—— To some it may seem superfluous to press this argument from actual history. It would perhaps be so if the subject itself were not so vital, and the errors made in it so grave—if Rome had not built upon it her immense system of forgivenesses of sins past, and indulgences for sins future; and if Protestants had not labored long and immensely to find some middle ground, a little short of plenary forgiveness, administered by preacher or pope, yet quite beyond declaring, preaching, forgiveness by and through Christ alone.—— Let the argument from history then be closed by a reference to the case of Peter dealing with Simon Magus—in which Peter, holding the keys, did not, by and of himself, absolve the trembling Magus, but said—"Repent therefore of this thy wickedness, and *pray God* if perhaps the thought of thy heart may be forgiven thee" (Acts 8: 22).

But it will probably be said—These words of Jesus are perfectly plain and explicit; also that the interpretation I have suggested rather interprets their obvious sense out of them than develops the sense that must be in them.

This objection should be fairly met. I reply to it that the most obvious sense of words is not always the true sense, and that peculiar constructions are in some cases demanded by known usage. For similar usage to this above suggested I refer to an analogous case. When the Lord would commission Jeremiah as his prophet —as Jesus here commissions the disciples as his gospel preachers—Jeremiah reports the transaction thus: "The Lord put forth his hand and touched my mouth" [a symbol quite analogous to "breathing on the disciples to impart the Holy Ghost"], "and the Lord said unto me—Behold, I have put my words into thy mouth. See, I have this day set thee over the nations and over the kingdoms, to root out and to pull down, and to destroy and to throw down, to build and to plant." This, it will be noted, is perfectly plain and explicit. Jeremiah is to destroy kingdoms, and to plant and build up kingdoms. Nay, more; the Lord declares—"I have this day set thee over the nations and over the kingdoms" for this very purpose. But what is the true sense of these words? Is it that Jeremiah was really made God's vicegerent with all power on earth to *do* these things in very deed—by his own right arm? Not at all. This language means only that he was to *predict* from the mouth of the Lord what the Lord himself would do. He was only a prophet-preacher; not an executive officer armed with omnipotence.——Here let it be noted that this mode of presenting such a thought was not unfamiliar to Hebrew ears. Jesus is here speaking to Hebrew men; Old Testament-reading men; and therefore could safely follow Hebrew usage with no special liability of being misunderstood *by them*. Moreover, as said already, his words thus interpreted give us what became actual fact in their history; but if interpreted in the sense of conferring plenary power to absolve or condemn, who can show that history fulfills such a sense?

Allusion has been made to the fact that certain Protestant interpreters have sought to find some middle ground between that of the Romanist, and that, say, of Jeremiah's usage, given above. Thus Alford on this text: " By this passage authority to discern spirits and pronounce on them is reassured (see Matt. 18: 18); also (it is plain from Luke 24: 45) a discerning of the mind of the Spirit is given them."——As to the *present* meaning and application of these words he says:—" The words closely considered amount to this—that with the gift and real participation of the Holy Spirit come the conviction and therefore the knowledge of sin, of righteousness, and of judgment; and this knowledge becomes more perfect, the more men are filled with the Holy Ghost. Since this is so, they who are pre-eminently filled with his presence are pre-eminently gifted with the discernment of sin and repentance in others; and hence *by the Lord's appointment authorized to pronounce pardon of sin and the contrary*." [The Italics are his]. "The apostles had this in a special manner, and by the full indwelling of the Spirit were enabled to discern the hearts of men and to give sentence on that discernment. And this gift belongs to the church in all ages, especially to those who by legitimate appointment are set to minister in the church of Christ," etc.

Ellicott (as we should expect) has a more just sense of the difficulties of the passage. He limits himself in his text (Life of Christ, pp. 360, 361) to the remark that "the mysterious power of binding and loosing was conferred upon the inspired and anew accredited apostles;" and in his note adds—"The mysterious power now given to the apostles was an essential adjunct to their office as the ambassadors of Christ, and more especially as the rulers of his church. It had reference (as Meyer rightly observes) not merely to the general power of receiving into the church or the contrary, but to their disciplinary power over individual members of it, both in the respect to the retaining and the absolving of sins." [But let us arrest quotations and ask—Does Christ certainly save all whom the church receives into her fellowship, and *not* save whom she does not receive? Is her decision upon cases of discipline certainly ratified by Jesus, and is this the doctrine of our passage? If so, then Rome is right, and the decisions of Christian churches and ministers upon individual piety is final before the court of heaven!]

Olshausen holds that men full of the Spirit have this power of absolving and retaining; they only, and only those when so filled. He says—"With the possession of the Spirit was connected the power of forgiving sins and that of not forgiving, *i. e.* of retaining them, for in *his* nature lie the conditions through which alone such power becomes explicable and secured against abuse."

Tholuck scarcely grapples with the main question, yet says—"Only by the power of the Holy Ghost can a judgment be formed as to the moral position of men and its relations to the kingdom of God: so far the promise in v. 22 is connected with that in v. 23. This judgment of the Spirit, however, is not an indistinct emotion, but is connected with the rule of faith and life; so far the jus clavium—'the power of the keys,' is, in the later church, a right of the clergy."

Doddridge, most judicious among them all—thus: "I will soon give you the Spirit in great fullness to qualify and furnish you for your important office, in consequence of which whosesoever sins ye shall remit, or *shall declare to be forgiven*, they shall be remitted," etc.; "shall retain, or *pronounce to be unpardoned*, etc.; for ye shall have a power not only of declaring what shall be lawful or unlawful under the gospel dispensation, but also of sending or removing miraculous punishments, and discerning the spirits of men in such perfection as to be able with certainty to declare to particular persons whether they be or be not in a state of pardon and acceptance with God."

The careful reader of the above comments on this passage will see that commentators fall naturally into three classes on a rising scale, thus:—(*a.*) Those who understand the functions of the apostles to be simply *declarative*—preaching salvation for believers; condemnation for unbelievers;—tersely expressed in other form—"He that believeth shall be saved, and he that believeth not shall be damned." In yet other words they were commissioned to *proclaim to lost men the principles of the gospel system*, so that they might understand *whose* sins should be remitted and whose retained.

(*b.*) Those who would add to this function of *declaring*, the power of discerning spirits—*i. e.* of reading moral character—so as to be able to judge who is penitent and believing, and who is not; coupled with the doctrine that Jesus pledges himself to ratify and confirm their judgment.

(*c.*) Those who add one element more, viz: *authority*, acting in the place of God, to remit—absolve—men's sins; or to retain and bind—*i. e.* condemn.——This is an advance upon the next preceding, inasmuch as it is more to *pass the sentence* than it is simply to know how it should and will be passed by the Supreme Ruler.

It is noticeable that a large class of writers lay out their strength to sustain the second grade of opinions, *i. e.* to show that gospel preachers, and churches, acting officially, may be so fully taught of the Spirit as to *judge* correctly upon the question of another's personal piety.——In general this may be conceded to be true; but the further question will yet remain—Does Jesus pledge himself to indorse their decision? Does he ever promise to make those decisions infallible? And then there is the yet further question: Does he delegate to his disciples the authority to pardon or not pardon sin according to their own judgment of the case?——For plainly, if we must take the words in their most obvious sense, they will carry us quite beyond the discerning of spirits (reading men's hearts), to the higher function of applying this knowledge by really passing sentence of acquittal or of condemnation. If we recoil from the latter as abhorrent to both Scripture and reason, what do we gain by holding on to the power of judging infallibly?

In my view the only safe construction is the first above named—the responsibility of *declaring the principles* on which men's sins are forgiven or not forgiven—principles which God will indorse for evermore; upon which he will certainly act in his final judgment upon all the race according to deeds done in the body.

24. But Thomas, one of the twelve, called Didymus, was not with them when Jesus came.

25. The other disciples therefore said unto him, We have seen the Lord. But he said unto them, Except I shall see in his hands the print of the nails, and put my finger into the print of the nails, and thrust my hand into his side, I will not believe.

In that eventful meeting Thomas was absent. Probably his proclivity toward doubt occasioned this absence. He may have almost given up the hope of any thing to purpose in the future of the gospel enterprise. Jesus was dead: what could they now?——When the other disciples met him next they told him the news which had so gladdened their souls. They found him very skeptical. He would take no testimony short of the senses, and of no man's senses save his own. And he must have not only sight, but feeling—must not only see in those hands the prints of the nails, but put his very finger into those nail-prints and thrust his hand into the wounded side. This evidence would identify the risen body to his satisfaction; nothing less should. ——It was long ago said—Under God's good providence, Thomas doubted that we might *not* doubt; his skepticism suffices for all future skeptics who are really honest—should be the panacea for all subsequent doubting as to the actual resurrection of the Crucified One.

26. And after eight days again his disciples were within, and Thomas was with them: *then* came Jesus, the doors being shut, and stood in the midst, and said, Peace *be* unto you.

27. Then saith he to Thomas, Reach hither thy finger, and behold my hands; and reach hither thy hand, and thrust *it* into my side, and be not faithless, but believing.

28. And Thomas answered and said unto him, My Lord and my God.

29. Jesus saith unto him, Thomas, because thou hast seen me, thou hast believed: blessed *are* they that have not seen, and *yet* have believed.

When the prayer meeting of the next Lord's day evening came round, Thomas was there; and again, as before, Jesus came, and with the same benediction. Then he turned to Thomas. He knew what Thomas had said, and very graciously, instead of rebuking him, calls him up as near as he could wish, to see with his own eyes and to feel with finger and hand, just as he had said he must before he could believe, adding, however, this caution:—"Be not faithless, but believing." The judgment and the heart of Thomas are alike carried. He believes and he worships! "My Lord," cries he, "and my God!" Oh, my Jesus, all divine art Thou, and I adore Thee as Supreme Lord of all—my very God!——It would be a gross outrage upon believing, penitent Thomas to put these words of his into the category of profane exclamations—as if he could use such words as the mere utterance of surprise, astonishment. And it would be no less an outrage upon the purity of Jesus to assume that he would proceed forthwith to bless Thomas for profane swearing! No one can question that Jesus understood the meaning of Thomas and knew his heart—knew whether these were the solemn convictions of his soul, or the thoughtless, profane words of a loose tongue, accustomed to take the name of God in vain.

While Jesus does not rebuke Thomas directly, he gently suggests that those who believe without the evidence of their own senses will be yet more blessed.

30. And many other signs truly did Jesus in the presence of his disciples, which are not written in this book:

31. But these are written, that ye might believe that Jesus is the Christ, the Son of God; and that believing ye might have life through his name.

Several critics (German more especially) maintain very strenuously that these are the last words that John wrote in this gospel history; and that chap. 21 is spurious—written at some later period and by some unknown hand.——It can not and need not be denied that these verses have the appearance of a close, being a natural and appropriate ending. The author takes a comprehensive survey of what he has written; says there were many other incidents of like character, not included here, and gives his reasons for his selection. We may suppose that John did close here.

in precisely this way; but at a later period, for special reasons, not certainly known to us, added this chap. 21 as an appendix. His greatly prolonged life afforded him the opportunity for this. It has been suggested with some plausibility that he wrote it mainly to withstand the tradition to which he refers (v. 23) that this beloved disciple (John) "should not die." It were better to quash such a tradition by a full statement of the circumstances which gave rise to it than to let it run till his actual death should disprove it—with staggering effect upon those who had accepted it as the word of the Lord.

"Signs" in the sense of miracles—implying that miracles were the staple themes of the book. If we include, with the narratives which record the miracles, the conversations and discussions of the Lord connected therewith, we shall find that a large part of the book comes under this description.

The object of this book as here given has come under consideration already in the Introduction. It is scarcely necessary therefore to say here that his object was to set forth the Messiahship and Sonship of Jesus, and this for the twofold purpose—first, of inducing men to believe these facts, and next, that through such believing, they might find that spiritual life which such belief, honestly held and allowed to develop its legitimate influence, will assuredly give. No aim could be more noble; no results more precious. Let us be forever grateful to God for this book!

CHAPTER XXI.

This appendix details somewhat minutely a third appearance of the risen Jesus—viz. to seven of his disciples (those of the fishermen class) at the sea of Tiberias (vs. 1-14); then a conversation of Jesus with Peter (vs. 15-19); followed by a suggested conversation between the same parties respecting John (vs. 20-24); closing with the author's identification of himself and his concluding remarks as to the number of the Lord's notable deeds (vs. 24, 25).

1. After these things Jesus shewed himself again to the disciples at the sea of Tiberias; and on this wise shewed he *himself*.

2. There were together Simon Peter, and Thomas called Didymus, and Nathanael of Cana in Galilee, and the *sons* of Zebedee, and two other of his disciples.

3. Simon Peter saith unto them, I go a fishing. They say unto him, We also go with thee. They went forth, and

entered into a ship immediately; and that night they caught nothing.

4. But when the morning was now come, Jesus stood on the shore; but the disciples knew not that it was Jesus.

The impulse which moved Peter to lead off in this fishing excursion is not even hinted—whether it were recreation, pleasant reminiscences of former pursuits, subsistence, or spare time not otherwise filled. It does not appear that the Lord rebuked the movement.——One toiling night brought them no fish. In the morning Jesus stood on the shore, within speaking distance, yet not recognized. We might suggest supposable reasons for this non-recognition, but they would be only suppositions.

5. Then Jesus saith unto them, Children, have ye any meat? They answered him, No.

6. And he said unto them, Cast the net on the right side of the ship, and ye shall find. They cast therefore, and now they were not able to draw it for the multitude of fishes.

7. Therefore that disciple whom Jesus loved saith unto Peter, It is the Lord. Now when Simon Peter heard that it was the Lord, he girt *his* fisher's coat *unto him*, (for he was naked,) and did cast himself into the sea.

8. And the other disciples came in a little ship, (for they were not far from land, but as it were two hundred cubits,) dragging the net with fishes.

The precision of the Greek language appears in this question (v. 5) translated—"Have ye any meat?" In Greek the question is put by a word which is at once an interrogative and a negative—the negative referring to the thought or supposition of the questioner: thus—Children, ye have not any food here, have you? The word implies that Jesus assumes they have none.—— This immense draught of fishes served to flash it upon the mind of John that the man who told them where to find, was their own Lord Jesus. He whispers this to Peter. Quick as thought Peter girds about him his fisher's coat (in respect for the Blessed One) and dashes into the sea to meet his Lord. How like Peter! The other disciples (Peter excepted) come—not in *a* little ship, as if it might be some other little ship, coming to their help—but in *the* little ship—the same in which they had been fishing all night —dragging their burden.

9. As soon then as they were come to land, they saw a fire of coals there, and fish laid thereon, and bread.

10. Jesus saith unto them, Bring of the fish which ye have now caught.

11. Simon Peter went up, and drew the net to land full

of great fishes, a hundred and fifty and three; and for all there were so many, yet was not the net broken.

The fire of coals prepared, with fish and bread in readiness, suggest that Jesus, with his own hand, or by miracle, or by means of other helpers, had been making provision for their meal.——Simon, now on shore, was ready to lend a hand in hauling up this draught of fishes.——This great success must have been sweetly suggestive of the promise—"I will make you fishers of men." Ye shall know the difference it makes to have the presence of your Lord, and may estimate the blessedness of having him "always *with you* even to the end of the world."

12. Jesus saith unto them, Come *and* dine. And none of the disciples durst ask him, Who art thou? knowing that it was the Lord.

13. Jesus then cometh, and taketh bread, and giveth them, and fish likewise.

14. This is now the third time that Jesus shewed himself to his disciples, after that he was risen from the dead.

No one dared ask him, Who art thou? for it seemed an impertinence when they knew so well. A strange feeling of profoundest awe seems to have blended with tender affection and fascinating interest, in such a presence. If they were restrained from saying all they thought, they could at least *feel* most intensely and rejoice with exceeding great joy.——That Jesus should take his usual place at the head of the table, breaking bread and distributing to them as of old, was indeed (estimated from Oriental usage, or from the usages of any people) tenderly kind and assuring—a precious guaranty of undying affection.

At this point John closes his record of the appearances of Jesus risen, to his disciples. Let us revert, briefly as possible, to the records on this point left us by the other evangelists and by Paul.

Matthew relates two instances: (1) His appearance to Mary Magdalene and "the other Mary" as they were returning from their very early visit to the sepulcher, and hastening to tell the disciples that the body was not there (28: 9).——(2) His appearance to the eleven on a mountain in Galilee (28: 16, 17).

Mark states very definitely that Jesus appeared first to Mary Magdalene (16: 9); next to two brethren (not of the eleven) as they went into the country—the same (supposably) which Luke relates much more fully (24: 13–35); and lastly, to the eleven as they sat at meat (16: 14).

Luke narrates at some length the very early visit of the women to the empty sepulcher; how they saw two angels in human form and from them learned that Jesus had risen; but Luke does not say that they saw the Lord. The appearance of Jesus to the two brethren who went out that morning to Emmaus, Luke narrates minutely—how Jesus made himself known to them as they were breaking bread; rebuked their unbelief; "expounded in all the Scriptures the things concerning himself;" and ultimately vanished suddenly from their sight. Returning at once to Jerusalem, they found the eleven convened; learned that Jesus, during the day, had appeared to Peter, and had begun to rehearse their own story—when, lo! Jesus himself came into the midst of the group.

——Luke, therefore, as Mark also, recites three distinct appearances—of which two seem to be identical—the third in each history being omitted by the other evangelist.

John, as we have seen, specifies four several appearances.

Paul (1 Cor. 15: 5–8) makes a very well defined list.—(1) Seen by Cephas (*i. e.* Simon Peter); (2) By the twelve (perhaps identical with his appearing on the first Lord's day evening to the ten); (3) By more than five hundred brethren at once (supposed to have been in Galilee); (4) By James, not elsewhere specified; (5) By all the apostles—probably identical with the last appearance recorded by Luke; (6) Last of all, by Paul—which must have been at or after his conversion, and in either case, after Christ's ascension.

Grouping together some thoughts upon these various records, I suggest—

1. That the several narrators seem to have written altogether independently of each other. No one copies from another; no one even alludes to any other; nay more—no one seems to have had the least regard for making his statement harmonize with those of any one of his brethren. Consequently they are independent witnesses.

2. Each historian seems to have selected those cases of visible appearance which had most impressed him, or with which he was most familiar, or which seemed to him most important for the purposes of his own history. Such considerations would naturally have force upon honest minds. Every thing indicates the presence and control of such considerations in their case.

3. No one of them has made his enumeration exhaustive. The presumption is, they did not aim to. Paul's list is more full than either of the others, and presents most evidence of being drawn up to *prove the fact* of Christ's actual resurrection. Note especially the case of his being seen by more than five hundred at once—many of whom he said were living then—a strong circumstance to the point of proof. But he entirely omits the appearances to the sisters as reported by the other historians. It is obvious that his Corinthian readers would lack that deep social interest which made the manifestation of Jesus to those sisters so very precious to the disciples, and moreover would underrate the value of their testimony to the great historic fact. In Corinth Christianity had not then elevated woman as it had in Judea and Galilee.

Luke did not aim to make his enumeration exhaustive, for while his gospel history narrates in detail but two cases, alluding incidentally to a third, his reference to the subject in Acts 1:

4—"To whom he showed himself alive after his passion by many infallible proofs, being seen of them forty days, and speaking to them of the things pertaining to the kingdom of God"—implies forcibly that he knew many other cases. Indeed this statement, beyond any other we have, indicates that Jesus was often present among his followers during those forty days, and strongly suggests that all our records combined fail to be exhaustive.

4. The prominence given by the four evangelists to the cases of the sisters—Mary Magdalene and others—is manifestly due to their personal character, to their positive agency, and to the high esteem in which they were held both by Jesus and by the whole brotherhood of disciples. It is a precious tribute to the influence of Christianity upon woman, and to the services rendered by redeemed woman to that Christianity which has redeemed her. In giving so much space in their narratives to women as favored with visions of the risen Jesus, the gospel historians were thinking less of making up judicial testimony to the fact of a real resurrection, and more, of doing justice to the deep sympathy and love of Jesus for them, and to their own hearts' love for Jesus. Let us be thankful for such facts—that they existed then and have been reproduced in every age of a living Christianity—thankful also for a record so honest, so impartial, so rich in its testimony to the high appreciation in which woman's devotion to her Lord was held by the earliest Christian brotherhood.

5. It remains to say that taken in whole the recorded testimony to the fact of Christ's actual resurrection is perfectly conclusive. It is not easy to see how a fact of this nature could be more abundantly substantiated.——Of course the fact of his actual death must be established—and is so, beyond the remotest possibility of mistake. Of this point there is no occasion to treat here. The point of his actual resurrection from the dead must be proved substantially as we have seen it proved in these records—by his visible manifestations; by his bodily presence shown to mortal eyes, seen by living men and women; handled by human fingers; evinced by his living voice, by his partaking of human food with and before them, and by replacing himself in his former relations to them as their spiritual Teacher, their sympathizing Friend, their own Lord and Master.

These manifestations, we may notice, were made, not to men previously committed to make out a miracle and palm it off upon the world; not to men of easy credulity, but to men so remote from this that though it had been previously foretold repeatedly, they could not accept it in its literal sense, did not understand, believe, or expect it. As to one of their number, we are definitely told he would believe on nothing short of the fullest evidence of sight and touch. Again, these personal appearances were not made before strangers who had never or rarely seen him before, but to those who had known him best; were made not once only, but many times; not under one set of circumstances, but in almost every possible variety of circumstance—during open day and in the evening; walking by the way, and also sitting around the table at meals; in the city and in the country; in Jerusalem, on Mount Olivet, and on a mountain in Galilee; several times to one individual only; several other times to the assembled group of the eleven; again to more than five hundred brethren at once, of whom Paul, writing to the Corinthians, said—"The greater part remain unto this present [time], but some are fallen asleep." The living witnesses therefore down to that day (about A. D. 57) were still an host—*i. e.* a host for all practical purposes of competent testimony to prove a fact cognizant to their own senses. The human court that should demand more witnesses than the greater part of five hundred to a fact of personal observation, would prove itself incompetent to sit on such a question. No judge or jury—being sensible men—ever have demanded or could demand the personal testimony of so great a cloud of witnesses to prove a fact of this nature.—— Thus it appears that the actual resurrection of Jesus from the dead lacks no sort of evidence that is germain to such a question. The evidence is also abundantly ample in amount. No suspicion can attach legitimately to the transmission of this evidence in written records from that day to this. There was divine wisdom in resting this pillar of the Christian system upon such solid foundations.

We resume the narrative.

15. So when they had dined, Jesus saith to Simon Peter, Simon, *son* of Jonas, lovest thou me more than these? He saith unto him, Yea, Lord; thou knowest that I love thee. He saith unto him, Feed my lambs.

16. He saith to him again the second time, Simon, *son* of Jonas, lovest thou me? He saith unto him, Yea, Lord; thou knowest that I love thee. He saith unto him, Feed my sheep.

17. He saith unto him the third time, Simon, *son* of Jonas, lovest thou me? Peter was grieved because he said unto him the third time, Lovest thou me? And he said unto him, Lord, thou knowest all things; thou knowest that I love thee. Jesus saith unto him, Feed my sheep.

Dinner being past, Jesus has a word for Peter. Since that sad scene when Jesus stood before the high priest, and with unutterable sorrow, heard his disciple Peter, standing with the servants around the fire, deny him thrice, and since he gave him that one tender yet perhaps reproving look, it does not appear that he had alluded with either word or look to that denial. Here his mind reverts to that scene. Yet we may observe his allusions to it are rather remote than direct—rather to the antecedent cause, his excessive self-confidence, than to the dreadful sin itself:—"Simon, son of Jonas, lovest thou me more than these other disciples do?" Thou wilt perhaps remember how thou didst protest so earnestly— "Though all shall be offended because of thee, yet will I never be offended" (Matt. 26: 33, 35). Is it quite apparent that thy love toward me has been greater than that of thy brethren?—— Peter's answer prudently omits the shading of comparison; he does not care to say—*more* and better than his brethren—but his full heart prompts him to say—"Lord, thou knowest that I love thee." To which Jesus only replies—Give me long as thou livest this proof of thy love; "Feed my lambs." "When thou art converted, strengthen thy brethren." Avail thyself of all this sad experience to make thyself a better pastor, a more humble, watchful shepherd—to save other souls in their scenes of spiritual peril.——As Peter had denied his Lord three times, it was suggestive to him that his Lord puts to him this searching question three times in succession—"Lovest thou me?" The third time Peter was grieved—perhaps not merely because it reminded him so painfully of that threefold denial, but because it seemed to imply that his Lord lacked confidence in his professions. It was to the latter point only that Peter alludes in reply, appealing to his knowledge as the Searcher of hearts:—"Thou who knowest all things, knowest that I love thee."——It is wonderful how sweetly Jesus blends the faithful with the kind in this gentle reproof of the once erring but now penitent Peter. For Peter could no longer say in his heart—My Master can never love me again— never can fully and freely forgive my cruel abuse of his love:— no, verily;—for what could evince more tender love than this gentle, *very* gentle reproof for a sin so flagrant and so cruel toward his Master!

18. Verily, verily, I say unto thee, When thou wast young, thou girdest thyself, and walkedst whither thou wouldest: but when thou shalt be old, thou shalt stretch forth thy hands, and another shall gird thee, and carry *thee* whither thou wouldest not.

19. This spake he, signifying by what death he should glorify God. And when he had spoken this, he saith unto him, Follow me.

These words directly apprise Peter of his future destiny—viz. being bound and imprisoned for the Master's cause. Indirectly they imply that from this time he will be faithful to his Master even to death. By a martyr's death he will glorify God. One sad fall has marred his Christian life—but it shall be the last! For the future, having worn life away even to old age in toil for his Master, he should glorify God through a death of violence from other hands.——Then, that Jesus should add—"Follow me"—was once more to signify—I renew my call of thee into my service. Do not allow thyself to think that I can trust thee no longer!

20. Then Peter, turning about, seeth the disciple whom Jesus loved following; which also leaned on his breast at supper, and said, Lord, which is he that betrayeth thee?
21. Peter seeing him saith to Jesus, Lord, and what shall this man do?
22. Jesus saith unto him, If I will that he tarry till I come, what *is that* to thee? follow thou me.
23. Then went this saying abroad among the brethren, that that disciple should not die: yet Jesus said not unto him, He shall not die; but, If I will that he tarry till I come, what *is that* to thee?

It goes to prove that this appendix is by the same hand as the book itself (chap. 1-20); that the writer follows the same method in speaking of himself—"The disciple whom Jesus loved." He further identifies himself here by reference to the very distinctive scenes at the table—as in John 13.——This John falls into line with Peter in following Jesus. Peter, noticing this, is moved (perhaps by curiosity) to ask the Lord what *his* destiny was to be. Thou hast told me mine; please tell me his also.——It seems designed for a gentle rebuke that the Lord should say—"If I will that he tarry till I come, what is that to thee?"——Incidentally this passage may furnish light as to the sense in which Jesus used the words—"till I come;" and moreover, light as to the sense put upon these words by the disciples.——In interpreting them we must choose between the three following possible senses:—(1.) Till I come to take him to myself at his death;—(2.) Till I come for the destruction of Jerusalem;—(3.) Till I come to judge the world. The usage of this phrase in the lips of Jesus takes the range of these three senses. In one or another of them we must interpret these words.——The first is utterly inept:—If I will that he live till he dies—this is entirely inadmissible.——The third (last named) must (as it seems to me) be set aside, since it is equivalent to saying—If I will that he shall never die—for he who lives till the final judgment escapes death altogether. But this was the very misconstruction which John is laboring to obviate. This was the "saying that went abroad" as giving the meaning of Jesus in those words. John would tell his readers that this saying was a misapprehension—a mistake.——Of course there remains only the second sense—Till I come to overthrow the Jewish city and state. In fact John did live to see *this* coming of the Lord.——The passage moreover shows that, before this appendix was written, the apostles had inclined to give these words of Jesus (till I come) the third sense as put above—viz. to apply them to his great coming to the final judgment, and apparently, to look for this event as then not far remote. In this they were mistaken. Little by little Jesus and his teaching Spirit sought to correct this erroneous view as to Christ's then future coming.

24. This is the disciple which testifieth of these things, and wrote these things: and we know that his testimony is true.

The person spoken of above without name, and very indefinitely, is here purposely identified with the author of the book.——The plural, "*we* know," has given certain critics occasion to say that this verse must have come from some other hand than John's because John could not claim to be "we." But what if John intended to say that there were other witnesses beside himself to the truth of his statements? The word "we" might include with himself an indefinite number of his Christian brethren, cognizant like himself of the verity of the transactions he has here recorded. The first person in the phrase (v. 25)—"*I* suppose"—goes as far to prove that some one man (*e. g.* John) wrote these verses, as "*we* know" does to prove that two or more men were the authors.

25. And there are also many other things which Jesus did, the which, if they should be written every one, I suppose that even the world itself could not contain the books that should be written. Amen.

"Things which Jesus did"—should in strictness refer to his works rather than to his words; yet the phrase "other things" suggests that words are included here no less than acts. This gospel history is made up of both, and the matters omitted were of the same character as the matters recorded.——In the writer's view it were vain to attempt an exhaustive history of all the precious words of Jesus, or of all his blessed deeds.——That "the world could not contain the books," etc., is of course hyperbole, and probably is a proverbial phrase—of the same class with a "camel going through the eye of a needle." It is simple folly to discuss the literal truthfulness of such phrases. Men have always taken the liberty to speak in proverbs, and more or less, with the exaggerations of hyperbole. Sensible readers are not often stumbled by such liberties of language.——In what sense "could not contain" is to be taken, it is scarcely worth our while to debate. Obviously he thinks of their reception and utility *as books* rather than of storing them in warehouses as merchandise. Even the Bible might have been made too large, too copious, for its own practical purposes.——It will be noticed that this remark is not out of place at the close of this appendix to John's gospel. He would say—At first I closed this history with an allusion to its leading purpose (as ye may see in 20: 30, 31), but subsequently circumstances occurred which called for this brief addition. A great many more things are yet unwritten, but enough for all practical purposes is recorded; too much would be an evil. My history therefore closes here.——If we may suppose him aware of what his brethren, Matthew, Mark, and Luke, had long before written, we shall have a deeper sense of the wisdom which guided him in the selection of what he has recorded. As to the wisdom of omitting what is nowhere recorded, it is ours to trust, not to judge.

FIRST EPISTLE OF JOHN.

GENERAL INTRODUCTION.

The preliminary questions useful to introduce the reader to this Epistle are—
  I. *Who was the author?*
  II. *When, where,* and *for whom* originally, was it written?
  III. What were its *immediate specific objects?* What then present wants in the churches did it aim to supply?
  IV. What are its relations (if any) to the *gospel* of John?

I. The question of authorship has never been deemed difficult. By most if not all good critics, the author of this Epistle is held to be the same John who wrote the gospel. Some quite decisive historic testimonies have come down to us from the early Christian Fathers, with one voice to this effect. The names of the witnesses are of the best; Polycarp and Papias who knew John personally; Irenæus, a disciple of Polycarp, and hence but one remove from John; Origen and Clement, both of Alexandria, but of world-wide learning and personal knowledge of their times.*

But foreign historic testimony that John wrote this Epistle is rendered practically needless by the decisive indications found in the Epistle itself—its striking similarity to the gospel in style, in spirit, in themes of discourse, in the choice of staple terms and phrases—in short, in every prominent quality which gives character to a literary production. Let the reader note how much this writer speaks of "*life;*"

---

* More is said of the personal history of these witnesses in my General Introduction to the Gospel of John.

"*eternal life;*" " light," " darkness ; " of walking in light and of walking in darkness; of love to God and love of the brethren; of faith and its moral power; of Jesus as the Propitiation for our sins. Recurring to the gospel he will find that these thoughts, these themes, and these staple forms of expression, are its prominent characteristics. No reader can place these two books side by side, examining each with care, without being impressed with their remarkable similarity in all vital respects. To read and compare them is to see and feel the proof that they come from the same literary hand and from the same Christian heart.

II. *When, where,* and *for whom* originally, was it written?

As to the *date* of this Epistle, nothing decisive has come down to us from sources external to the books of the New Testament. Testimony from this book itself is only approximate, not specific. The writer speaks as a patriarch—an aged father to his little children; indicating therefore his own advanced age. His allusion to " the last time " (2: 18) is by no means definite as to date, since the phrase might refer to a period shortly before the fall of Jerusalem; or if to a point subsequent to that fall, it is quite impossible to say how long subsequent.

Very probably it was written *after the gospel*. In the order of nature it comes after, for it presupposes the facts of the gospel history. Its object could scarcely be accomplished, nor could a sensible writer expect to accomplish it, except as it rested on a general knowledge of the facts of that gospel history. In other words, with such an object in view as this Epistle manifests, the author would certainly write his gospel history first and this Epistle subsequently, based upon those historic facts. Since nothing forbids us to date the Epistle *after* the gospel, and the considerations above named favor it, we may safely rest in this conclusion.

As to the *locality* of the author at his writing, it may be said—

(*a.*) That by general consent of the Christian Fathers, John removed from Jerusalem to Ephesus shortly before Jerusalem fell; and passed the remaining years of his life in that city, or in its vicinity.

(*b.*) In John's gospel we noticed the frequent explanation of Jewish customs and of Hebrew words and phrases—implying that he wrote with his eye on other than Jewish readers, for men residing elsewhere than in Palestine, and supposably for the churches of Asia Minor. These circumstances support the theory that this Epistle also was written from Ephesus, and for the same original readers as his gospel.

(c.) The fact that in his Apocalypse John sent letters to the seven churches of Asia adds still further corroboration. Moreover, those brief letters show that false teachers were even then imperiling the purity of those churches, and that, as usual, immoral practices accompanied (or followed) departures from the faith in Jesus. Correspondingly, in this Epistle also we find allusions to doctrinal errors and to degeneracy in morals. These coincidences strongly favor the theory that this Epistle had in view the same churches, and the same prevalent or threatening evils within them.

III. What were its *immediate objects?* What then present wants in the churches did it aim to supply?

To these inquiries the Epistle itself gives no uncertain answer. Its one comprehensive object is put distinctly (2: 1) in the words—"These things I write unto you *that ye sin not.*" The whole Epistle opposes sin; urges personal holiness. Every thing looks toward a truer, stronger love, and a purer life.

To accomplish these objects required effort in two directions: (1.) To withstand errors in doctrine, especially those which dried up the very fountains of gospel life and power —e. g. denying that Jesus Christ had come in the flesh.— (2.) To show that the great facts of the gospel—such as the provisions made for pardon and victory over sin; the great love of God for lost men, revealed in Jesus Christ—demand of believers a loving heart and a blameless life.

Hence, to maintain the fundamental truths of the gospel scheme, and to show the natural legitimate connection between faith in these truths and a really Christian life, are the main objects sought in this Epistle.

IV. *What, if any, are its relations to the gospel of John?*

Briefly said, its relations to the gospel are supplemental. It aims to secure more thoroughly the declared objects of the gospel; viz. " that ye may believe that Jesus is the Christ, and that, believing, ye may have life through his name." He would give men more just views of the Sonship of Jesus and of the atoning virtue of his death; would exhort them to a more intelligent and steadfast faith in these truths; would admonish them against those perversions and abuses of the gospel which would emasculate its moral power toward the spiritual life of faith and love and the moral life of practical godliness. He saw that in both directions—poisoning the fountains of gospel truth, and diverting its streams from their place of power and blessing in the Christian heart and life—there was need of vigorous effort. So he sent forth this brief but vigorous Epistle for the joint purposes of working a purer doctrinal faith and of promoting a better Christian life.——How he made and sustained his points, we shall see as we bring his words under special consideration. His object was thoroughly practical; his points made are exquisitely simple, yet sublimely grand; his logic, none can gainsay; the love of his heart, manifested richly throughout the Epistle, should endear these messages to the church of every age. Truly we have cause of gratitude to the Inspiring Mind for raising up such a witness in behalf of gospel truth and for bequeathing to the Christian world this last legacy from his pen.

FIRST EPISTLE OF JOHN.

CHAPTER 1.

With no formal introduction; with no hint as to the people or churches specially addressed; the writer enters at once upon his work, giving first the subject matter—the great theme of which he is to speak, viz. *the incarnate Son of God* (vs. 1-3); then the purpose or object in view (vs. 3, 4); the substance of his message (v. 5); the personal application of the truth conveyed in this message and its fruits (vs. 6, 7); and especially that it is a salvation from sin provided for men who are sinners (vs. 8-10).

1. That which was from the beginning, which we have heard, which we have seen with our eyes, which we have looked upon, and our hands have handled, of the Word of life;

2. (For the life was manifested, and we have seen *it*, and bear witness, and shew unto you that eternal life, which was with the Father, and was manifested unto us;)

3. That which we have seen and heard declare we unto you, that ye also may have fellowship with us: and truly our fellowship *is* with the Father, and with his Son Jesus Christ.

No reader can fail to note the striking similarity between the opening of this epistle and the opening of John's gospel. Alike they discard all preliminaries; alike they call our thought at once to the person of the eternal Word, made manifest in human flesh —the incarnate Son of God. Most of the same descriptive terms are here which are there, this Great Personage being set forth as "the Word of life," who was "from the beginning;" was "with the Father;" and was "made manifest to us." Remarkably, this last point—his manifestation to us (his disciples)—is expanded with great fullness:—"which we have heard," *i. e.* whose human voice our mortal ears have heard; whom we have seen with our own eyes as human eyes see fellow-men in the flesh; "whom we have looked upon," giving yet another but analogous Greek verb of seeing which superadds the idea of attentive contemplation;—and whom our hands have handled—or better, whom we have touched with our hands as in the familiar intercourse of human life, and perhaps with some allusion to unbelieving Thomas, permitted to put his hand into the print of the nails and into the wounds in his side. We can not fail to notice that this repetition and reiteration were intended for strong testimony to the actual appearance of the divine Word in human flesh, in a real personal body, like other human bodies—very possibly to bear against the notion that the body of Jesus was not material but spiritual; was a body in appearance only, not in fact; a mere phantom, unsubstantial and unreal.

Thus John labors to emphasize and expand the true idea of his cardinal word *"manifest;"* the human body of Jesus brought before our very senses; his voice entering our ears; his form present to our mortal eyes under every variety of condition; his material body subjected to our touch. He lived with us; talked, walked, toiled, rested, slept, waked, ate and drank before and with us as man with man, as friend with friend. What more or better evidence of a true and real human nature could we desire?

What we have thus seen and heard we now declare to you. Our desire in this writing is that ye may be brought into full fellowship with us, that is to say—that ye may come to know the Father and the Son Jesus Christ as we have learned to know them, and that ye may enjoy the communion of love with the Father and the Son as we do; so shall we have fellowship with each other. For we would have you understand fully that we enjoy the fellowship of love and friendship with the Father and with his Son.

Fellowship! How shall we fathom the depth of meaning in this precious word?——Going down into the essential idea of the original word * we find it signifies *somewhat in common* between two parties, having for its basis a more or less intimate knowledge of each other, upon which is founded a common interest, a common sympathy, a common mutual love. Such is fellowship between one human being and another; such in its nature must be the fellowship of man with his Maker and Redeemer.

In yet another line of search into the deep significance of this word, we might follow the thread of John's personal history, asking how it came to pass that *he* reached this conscious sense of fellowship with the Father and with his Son Jesus Christ.——The gospel history from his pen gives us the first utterances of this precious testimony. The opening verses of this epistle echo the same voice. John seems to have been a relative, perhaps a cousin, to the child Jesus, born of Mary. Having been a disciple of John the Baptist, he was early pre-

---

* κοινωνια.

pared to become one of the first disciples and followers of Jesus. Among the chosen twelve, he was brought nearest to the loving heart of the Master; sat by his side at the last supper, and leaned on his bosom there; was one of the three chosen to witness the transfiguration, and to be nearest the Great Sufferer during his agony in the garden. Among the eleven, he only seems to have been near the cross during the dread agonies borne by Jesus there. Who first gave him the distinctive title, "The disciple whom Jesus loved," we are not told; but we may think of him as knowing the heart of Jesus beyond most of his brethren—as having entered most deeply into his sympathies —as giving to him the purest love of his own heart. It was John who testified of Jesus that, "having loved his own that were in the world, he loved them to the end" (John 13: 1); John who remembered and recorded the precious words:—"He that hath my commandments and keepeth them, he it is that loveth me: and he that loveth me shall be loved of my Father, and I will love him, and will manifest myself unto him."— Also:—"If a man love me he will keep my words, and my Father will love him, and we will come unto him, and make our abode with him" (John 14: 21, 23). We must suppose that John had a lively and deep sense of the meaning of these words and a precious experience of the communion they promise. Moreover, it was through knowing Jesus so well that he came into similar communion and fellowship with the Father. John above any other sacred writer has unfolded this great idea—that to *know Jesus is to know the Father*. "Have I been so long time with you, and yet hast thou not known me, Philip? He that hath seen me hath seen the Father" (John 14: 9).

Thus pushing our inquiries historically, we may get somewhat definite conceptions of what John means by "fellowship with the Father and with his Son." First in the order of time, he came to know and to love the incarnate Son. Through the intimacies of close acquaintance and of confidential friendship; through the perpetual manifestations of loving sympathy; through the profoundest appreciation and admiration of the character of Jesus, and by means of shaping his own character more and more into the same image, there sprung up the sweet confidence of mutual friendship and fellowship. The two friends became one in heart and sympathy; one in the purposes and aims of life.

From this point we have only to advance one short step further and note that the human Jesus as thus seen and studied, known and loved in the flesh, brought John to know Jesus as divine—as the Logos whose glories shone forth and were manifested in the sinless man. And then, through the manifestations of him who was at once the Son of man and the Son of God, John came to know the Father and to have fellowship with him. The incarnation was the stepping-stone for the ascent upward from man to God. Thus the disciple John was introduced to the Logos as revealed through the man Jesus, and through Him, to the Eternal

Father.——Essentially what was true of John becomes true of all disciples of Jesus. By faith and love they enter into the same deep communion and fellowship with the Father and with his Son Jesus Christ.

And now as to the essential blessedness of this fellowship with the Father and the Son as possible to be enjoyed even here and now by mortals of our race, I have no words—I know of none—adequate to set it forth. To know a God, so pure, so good, so glorious; to love such a God with undivided, supreme affection, and devotion; to come into the fellowship of humble trust, unqualified submission, grateful and devout adoration on the human side—over against which on the divine shall be the manifestation of God's forgiving love, sympathy, and care; to feel a deep consciousness that this union of fellowship and friendship is real, is sure, is growing, is promised of God to endure forever—what shall we—what can we say that will adequately set forth its blessedness!

Corresponding to the glory and worth of this blessedness possible to human souls is the value of those revelations of God to men through his incarnate Son, and through his indwelling Spirit, by means of which it has been gained and realized, and is surely made possible to redeemed sinners. When "the disciple whom Jesus loved" pours out before us the fullness of his heart in such heaven-inspired words as we find in this epistle, let us accept them as warmed with the deepest love of his soul, and as witnessing to the ripe and blessed experience of one who felt that he had "fellowship with the Father and with his Son Jesus Christ."

4. **And these things write we unto you, that your joy may be full.**

The improved text reads this verse—"These things we write that *our* (not "your") joy may be full." Assuming this to be what John wrote, we must interpret him to mean—Our burdened heart must have relief by pouring out these words of love and sympathy. We so long to see you all sharing in common with us this deep and true fellowship with the Father and with his Son —how can we forbear to write you these testimonies to the truth as it is in Jesus?

5. **This then is the message which we have heard of him, and declare unto you, that God is light, and in him is no darkness at all.**

"This is the message"—the great central truth, comprehensive above any other—which we have heard from him (*i. e.* Jesus as manifesting God to men); and "declare unto you," not in this epistle only, but in the gospel history which I wrote to you as well—"*that God is light*"—pure light, with no darkness whatever. "Light," then, is the vital word in the message.

What is the precise and full idea in this word when applied as here to describe or interpret to us God?——Perhaps our best conception of it is a blending of the two ideas—*truth* and *purity*; truth as related to the intelligence; purity or holiness as related to the moral nature. Truth is a better word than knowledge only in so far as it better gives the notion of what is absolutely reliable—certainly in harmony with facts as they are; and also because it has been associated with knowledge concerning God, and knowledge coming from God concerning his creatures. Knowledge is to the mind what light is to the eye, so that the word "light," borrowed from the material world, gives us a very happy conception of that true knowledge which emanates from God even as heaven's light beams on our eyes from God's sun in the heavens. Then, moreover, the related idea of moral purity inheres in the word light, as darkness and sin are kindred ideas. All deeds of sin and shame love darkness, and can not bear the light. So we get the full and true sense of this richly comprehensive word "light" as said of God when we combine the two great ideas—truth, and purity or holiness. Precious ideas they are indeed:—God, the infinite fountain of truth—of all that knowledge which illumines the mind and blesses the souls of all intelligent beings in heaven and in earth: who is also the fountain of holiness, moral purity; its best model and exemplar, and forever giving forth influences and agencies to beget corresponding holiness in creatures as they come under the impression of his perfect, blessed character. God truthful; God sinless;—God the fountain of all truth; God the Author and Giver of all holiness to his creatures—these are the great ideas which lie in the word *Light* as it stands here descriptive of God.

6. If we say that we have fellowship with him, and walk in darkness, we lie, and do not the truth:

7. But if we walk in the light, as he is in the light, we have fellowship one with another, and the blood of Jesus Christ his Son cleanseth us from all sin.

Let no one suppose that to call God *light* is so abstract and metaphysical as to be almost unmeaning and void of practical bearing upon human souls. Nothing could be farther from the facts of the case. For, observe: this great abstract idea of God is brought to view here for the very purpose of its practical bearings. Does any man say, "I have fellowship with God," while yet he walks in darkness, *i. e.* sin, he certainly says what is not true, and what in his case can not possibly be true. Light and darkness have nothing in common—have no communion with each other. To have fellowship with God is to see and to love all that we know to be true of him; is to have in good degree his purity; implies certainly that one loves holiness, seeks it, longs for it, cherishes and cultivates it as the heart's richest treasure. But this is utterly inconsistent with walking in darkness. Men do not walk in the darkness of night when the sun shines full in the heavens above them; so neither do men walk in the ways of sin while the light of God shines full on their souls, and they are in hearty sympathy and fellowship with God. The incompatibility is as absolute in the one case as in the other.——To "do not the truth" is to be wholly out of harmony with it, living in constant violation of its spirit and of its moral demands. The man who lives so and yet claims to be in fellowship with God is either trying to deceive others, or is deceived as to himself.

On the other hand, if we walk in the light as God is in the light—walk according to his truth as made known to us, meeting every call of duty, yielding sweetly to every honest moral conviction, seeking supremely to know God's will and to do it, then "we have fellowship one with another;" a kindred spirit animates all hearts that are in this common moral attitude toward God and his truth. This walking in the light of God is so nearly the same thing in all human souls and produces so fully the same spiritual results that there will surely be a cordial fellowship and sympathy between all who stand in this common relation to the Great Father of light and of love.

To show how the light (truth) that comes from God is brought to bear practically upon those who receive and love it, the writer comes down from abstract, general forms of statement to the specific and concrete—to tell us how our sin is taken away and we are restored to the pure moral image of God: viz. thus:—"*The blood of Jesus Christ his Son cleanseth us from all sin.*"

Upon this very rich and expressive passage, all thoughtful readers will naturally raise two main questions:

(1.) How is it that *blood*, naturally defiling, should be said here to "*cleanse*"?

(2.) Does this cleansing refer to forgiveness or to sanctification; which, if either alone, or may it include both?

(1.) That blood should *cleanse*—a result so foreign from its nature and from the current ideas of mankind—must be due to some very special quality—some fact quite aside from the common course of things. No other explanation can be given except that which comes from the *bloody sacrifices* of the early ages of the race, unfolded fully in the Mosaic sacrificial system. There the great idea stands forth in the light of God's own institution—that "without the shedding of blood, there is no remission of sin;" yet that with it, under it, by means of it—atonement is made and God forgives the penitent offerer. The voice of God speaks in those bloody sacrifices—Let the innocent lamb be offered in sacrifice on mine altar; so his blood shall make atonement for your souls. He shall die that ye may live. Thus and thus only did blood under the old economy become an emblem of moral cleansing. Forgiveness of sin came through the shedding of blood. The death of Jesus as "the Lamb of God" fills out the prophetic (or typical) idea of the ancient lamb of sacrifice and has availed to "take away the sin of the world." (John 1 : 29.)

(2.) As to the second main question—the sense of the term "cleanse," I accept it as comprehending both forgiveness and sanctification. When the sacred writers aim at the utmost brevity in speaking of the great work of Christ for men, they bring to view the moral cleansing;—*e. g.* "Shalt call his name Jesus, for he shall save his people from their sins;" "Behold the Lamb of God who taketh away the sin of the world;" "The blood of Jesus cleanses from all sin." Yet they understood as fully as we do that there are really two quite distinct parts of this one great work; viz. the forgiveness of past sin, and the recovery of the soul from the spirit of sinning—its restoration to moral purity. We may see in v. 9 below that John has both these ideas in his mind: "He is faithful and just"—first to forgive us our sins; secondly—to cleanse us from all unrighteousness. Hence we must comprise under the words—"cleanseth us from sin"—both forgiveness and moral purification; both the blotting out of sins past, and the taking away from the heart the love and the indulgence of sin.——It is the more admissible—nay, more than that—the more appropriate to group these two ideas, forgiveness and moral transformation, under the one word "*cleanse*"—(1.) because moral transforming always presupposes forgiveness, inasmuch as forgiveness naturally comes first in order: no one becomes pure in heart till first forgiven:—and (2.) because the method of God's own providing for the pardon of sin, through the atoning death of Jesus, itself develops a mighty power of truth and love, bearing toward the cleansing of human souls from sin. "For the love of Christ constraineth us." How can we sin against him who has loved us even unto dying for us that we may live?——Thus the taking away of sins past by pardon and of the sinning heart present, by moral cleansing, are naturally linked together, both in the divine agencies that work them out in human souls, and in the experience of all saved men. Hence we may know that when moral cleansing is named, forgiveness is certainly presupposed and implied.

These verses (7-9) have sometimes been pressed to make them bear upon the question of sinless perfection in the present life. It can never be well to force any passage of Scripture to testify on a point irrelevant to its true design. In this passage there is no apparent indication that John had this particular question in his mind at all. What he would say on this question he has not told us here—certainly not in direct, explicit terms. How the things he does say bear legitimately on this question can be reached only by inference. For plainly the two opposite characters present to his thought in this passage are—(*a*) The man who walks in darkness—who, if he says he has fellowship with God, lies, and does not the truth—the open, manifest sinner on the one hand; (*b*) And on the other hand the honest, sincere believer, who walks in the light of God, has fellowship of soul with all the Christian brotherhood, and really with the Father and the Son. These are the two opposite characters of whom he speaks. The former class stand utterly aloof from Jesus as a Savior, declaring—" we have no sin" (v. 8); "we have not sinned" (v. 10); we have no need of such help as your system of so-called salvation in Christ professes to provide.——The other class confess themselves sinners: "God is faithful and just to forgive their sins, and to cleanse them from all unrighteousness."—— These are the two classes, morally considered, of whom he speaks, and this is what he says of them respectively. Upon the new and quite distinct question whether this moral cleansing becomes absolutely perfect on earth, we can not assume that he intended to express an opinion. Indeed, if we make him speak directly to this point, I do not see how we can defend him from self-contradiction; for on the one hand we should make him say —" The blood of Jesus cleanses us from all sin "—absolutely, perfectly from *all*—even here and now;—but on the other hand, in the next breath we make him declare that " if we say we have no sin at all, we deceive ourselves, and the truth is not in us "— all which would amount to saying that salvation by Christ is an impossible experience; that nobody is cleansed from sin by the blood of Christ.——Such results come of forcing a man's words beyond his intent, and applying them to questions entirely foreign from his thought. Hence I have ventured to call the application of John's words here to this modern question " a side issue," quite remote from his purpose and intent.

8. If we say that we have no sin, we deceive ourselves, and the truth is not in us.

9. If we confess our sins, he is faithful and just to forgive us *our* sins, and to cleanse us from all unrighteousness.

10. If we say that we have not sinned, we make him a liar, and his word is not in us.

On these verses the first question exegetically will be whether the same class are in John's thought in both v. 8 and v. 10,—in the former, saying—" we have no sin;" in the latter, saying— " we have not sinned."

That these slightly differing descriptive phrases do refer to the same class of men, is rendered more than probable—nearly or quite certain—by these facts:——(*a*) That John affirms of them both the same things—in the former verse "they deceive themselves;" in the latter they "make him (God) a liar;" in the former verse, " the truth is not in them;" in the latter, "his word is not in them;"——(*b*) By the further fact that in both these verses the characters described are put in contrast with those who confess their sins, and whom God "is faithful and just to forgive and to cleanse from all unrighteousness;"—and again (*c*) By the fact that a fair construction of the words in v. 8 gives essentially the same sense as the words of v. 10 bear. "If we say that we have no sin," *i. e.* no sin that needs to be forgiven and cleansed; if we take the ground that we have no occasion for such a Savior as Jesus—a Savior provided for sinners—we virtually say that "we *have not sinned*." "They that are whole have no need of a physician." In both verses (8, 10) the men who have no sense of being personal sinners—who refuse to see any sin, wrong, guilt, in themselves—are described and their case put. We may conclude therefore that in each of these verses John describes the same moral class of men.

Such men never come to Jesus for pardon, cleansing, and life. They rule themselves out from the range of gospel blessings.—— But alas! they utterly deceive themselves; the truth is not in them. They represent God to be a liar, for God declares all men to be in sin. The giving of his Son to die for men is his own declaration before the worlds and the ages of this broad universal fact as to the race. Conceived of as responsible moral agents, they are sinners.

In this point of view we readily see why "confessing our sin" is the first condition of being saved through Christ. If we say —"I have no sin;" "I have not sinned;" we charge God with slandering our moral character; and what is more still, with throwing away the life and blood of his Son needlessly, for a thing of nought—for no worthy consideration—for nothing better than a vain display of uncalled-for and falsely professed benevolence! Do those who will not confess themselves sinners consider how cruelly they insult God, and how fearfully they abuse his love and outrage his patience!

As to those who "confess their sins"—implying not the confessing of the *fact* only, but of the wrong and guilt of it also— God is both "faithful and just to forgive."——In what sense "both faithful and just"? "Faithful" as having promised, and therefore as in good faith fulfilling; "just," as doing a righteous thing—a thing which he can righteously do by reason of the provisions made in the atoning death of Christ.

Is there perhaps a slight antithesis between these words, "faithful" and "just," of this sort? He can in good faith forgive and *yet be just* to himself and to the demands of a perfectly holy law —a wonderful achievement—to make forgiveness consistent with justice; the blotting out of sin and the free pardon of the sinner, consistent with a law which declares—"The soul that sinneth, it shall die." This is what God does when in both faithfulness and justice he forgives the penitent who confesses his sin.—— By such a system of forgiveness and moral cleansing through the blood of Christ, God has prepared the way for pardoned sinners to come into fellowship with the Father and with his Son Jesus Christ.

CHAPTER II.

Much in the usual style of epistolary writing, John passes from one subject to another as new thoughts come to his mind, all however converging to the one great endeavor—"*that ye sin not*"—and particularly that ye may not be self-deceived as to really knowing God; that ye may love the brethren and not love the world, nor be misled by those who deny Christ, etc.

1. My little children, these things write I unto you, that ye sin not. And if any man sin, we have an advocate with the Father, Jesus Christ the righteous:
2. And he is the propitiation for our sins: and not for ours only, but also for *the sins of* the whole world.

"Little children"—not young in years absolutely, but only relatively to the writer, that very aged patriarch who belonged to a past generation.——The great purpose which lay ever warm upon his heart is here put in simplest, fewest words—"*that ye sin not.*" If he might only preserve them all from sin—sin that worst evil that could befall them—that worst thing they could do—that fountain of all the ills and woes of mortals! How should it be resisted, repelled, watched against, hated, avoided—with utmost endeavor and with ever wakeful solicitude!

But if under subtle or overmastering temptation, or through some outburst of passion, any man should sin, let me hasten to his relief with the message—"We have an Advocate with the Father, Jesus Christ the Righteous One." Through Him ye may find salvation. He pleads for penitent sinners before the Father, so that sin can be forgiven. No man need sink in despair under a sense of unforgiven sin.

"Advocate" (Gr. Paracletos) is the same word which Jesus applied to the "Holy Spirit of truth"—the "Comforter" (John 14: 16, 17). As our Advocate with the Father, Jesus is most truly and richly a Comforter to guilt-burdened souls. With blended pity and love, he pleads for our pardon before the Father's throne. Oh, the blessedness of such a Friend—an Advocate so kind to us and so prevalent in intercession before the Father!

"Jesus the *Righteous* One"—to be taken in the sense of the sinless, in harmony with Heb. 7: 26: "For such an High Priest became us—holy, harmless, undefiled, separate from sinners;"—one who had no sins of his own to preclude him from audience before Infinite Purity. To the same purport also are the words of Peter (1 Peter 3: 18)—"Christ once suffered for sins, the *just* for the unjust, that he might bring us to God."

"He is the propitiation," *i. e.* the Propitiator—one who makes propitiation; who propitiates in the sense of making pardon possible to a righteous God consistently with all due regard to the law which sin has broken and the sacredness of the penalty which the transgressor has both incurred and deserved. Strictly the idea is not that Jesus works upon the pity and love of the Father to bring him over from wrath to mercy; but rather that he obviates the otherwise stern necessity of executing the penalty of death for sin; and thus opens the way for the safe exercise of the pardoning power. The way being thus opened, the infinite love of God flows out naturally and mightily in the freest forgiveness of the penitent who accepts for himself the atonement made by Jesus. In this sense the blood of Jesus Christ, the Righteous One, makes propitiation for our sins. He prepares the way for the Supreme Ruler to forgive with honor to himself, with safety to his throne, with joy eternal to his own heart.——Such a propitiation is in its nature, "not for our sins only" (the "our" including Christians), "but for the sins of the whole world." In its relations to law, to government, to pardon, the atonement made by the blood of Christ is complete in itself before any sinner receives pardon through it, and whether the number ever forgiven under it be less or greater. It would have been an atonement ample for all the world even if no sinner ever accepted it. In its nature it was large enough, broad enough, for the race; and therefore really made salvation possible for *all* sinners in the same sense in which it made salvation possible for *one* sinner. Hence this atonement is properly called "universal," "unlimited"—not meaning or implying by these words that it saves all mankind, for in itself, considered as made by the death of Christ, it saves no man. The salvation comes only upon the sinner's believing. Its practical results of real salvation reach never a soul till that soul accepts it for himself with penitence for sin and humble faith in this atoning blood as his ground of hope for pardon.

Every thoughtful reader will see that it is *because* Christ's atonement is really made for all and offered to all, that the guilt of every sinner who refuses it becomes so great, and withal, so necessarily and so justly fatal to all possibility of salvation. Because sinners "deny the Lord who bought *them*," they bring on themselves swift and sure destruction. They need not die—if only they would come to Jesus and take the offered life; but oh, if they *will not have life*, then what but destruction, with no remedy!

3. And hereby we do know that we know him, if we keep his commandments.

4. He that saith, I know him, and keepeth not his commandments, is a liar, and the truth is not in him.

5. But whoso keepeth his word, in him verily is the love of God perfected: hereby know we that we are in him.

6. He that saith he abideth in him ought himself also so to walk, even as he walked.

We need some reliable test of true piety that we may judge

safely either of ourselves or of others. The Christian state, the being a Christian, John puts in two forms of statement: they "*know God;*" they are "*in God.*" But the test of the true Christian is one—*keeping God's commandments.* Nothing avails without this; with this, nothing more is needful. According to John therefore, this is the sovereign, certain, and only necessary test.——We may remember that Jesus taught the same: "My sheep hear my voice; they follow me." "If any man serve me, let him follow me." "He that hath my commandments and keepeth them, he it is that loveth me." "If a man love me he will keep my words," etc., etc.

We shall the better understand the meaning of John and appreciate the value of his test if we turn for a moment to consider his notion of what true piety is.——He speaks of it as *knowing God.* As reported to us in John's gospel, Jesus used this word "*know*" in the same deep, comprehensive sense: "This is life eternal, that they might *know* Thee, the only true God, and Jesus Christ whom Thou hast sent" (17: 3).——Beginning at the bottom of the subject we must note that true religion pertains to *intelligent beings.* It assumes first of all capacities for knowledge, and not least, for an actual *knowledge of God.* Next, it assumes that this knowledge is in some good degree according to truth:—it is knowing some things truly of God.——A yet more vital element is, that the human soul *adjusts itself to this knowledge;* receives it approvingly, joyfully; makes it welcome; and voluntarily puts itself into harmony with the legitimate demands which such knowledge of God makes upon his intelligent offspring. For, to know God truly is to know him as to his relations to ourselves: *i. e.* to know him as Creator, Father, Ruler. To adjust ourselves to a God so known —known as standing in such relations to us—is to bow our will lovingly to his will; is to render to him the homage of humble adoration, praise, and especially, or perhaps we should say *comprehensively,* of simple obedience to all his revealed will.

But some one will ask—Are there not thousands in Christian lands who *know* much about God and yet this knowledge lies in their souls only as a cold abstraction of truth—a speculation, a theory which is admitted as true by the intelligence, but its moral demands are resisted by the will, or, if not consciously resisted, are at least ignored—practically disowned and set at nought?——Manifestly and most sadly, this must be admitted. If it be still inquired—Why then did not John allow for this very large exception to his general law and forbear to assume without qualification that "knowing God" well defines true piety because it means and implies it—this may be said in explanation and defense of his usage of words.——(1.) Ordinarily, men do not learn much about God unless they love him and love to learn of him.——(2.) Legitimately, knowing God begets —at least tends powerfully to produce—true love to God. Hence an effect so natural may be embraced under the same word used for the cause, *i. e.* knowing God carries with it both the knowledge (intellectually considered), and its natural fruits—the love and obedience it begets.——(3.) This closely connected result—love following upon knowledge—will be the more sure if the external surroundings, the forces of the times, are such as to rule out all inducement to get the theory of God unless the heart is ready to yield to his moral demands. A somewhat vigorous persecution of those who know God—who study and obey him—will tend to sift out the ranks of his pupils and exclude from his school all save those who listen to the moral demands of such knowledge, and therefore study God for the sake of loving and obeying him.——Note now that such were the external circumstances when Jesus lived and John wrote. Hence in their use of language they might naturally assume what was then ordinarily the fact—that those who knew God intellectually gave him their heart's love morally.

Let us be careful to consider that in the sense of Jesus and of John, to "*know God*" is to open one's heart to this knowledge, to bow one's will sweetly to its moral demands, to bring the soul voluntarily and with earnest endeavor into fullest harmony with all we learn of God. Thus the crucial test of really knowing God is that we honestly obey his commandments. This test we can apply (if so we will) to ourselves: we can also with a fair measure of certainty apply it to other men.

Recurring to our passage let us note that in v. 3 the Greek tense requires—"Hereby we know that we *have known* him"—though probably this aorist tense should include the present also;—*have known and still know.* "If we keep his commandments" involves both a previous conversion and a present Christian life.——According to v. 5, keeping God's word develops the love of God in human souls to its perfection. It is the way to reach this great and glorious attainment—perfect love. The simple spirit of obedience, diligently cultivated, steadfastly maintained, made supreme over all the moral activities of the soul—this brings up the love of God to its highest development.——The law of the Christian life therefore is—"He that saith he abideth in him ought himself so to walk as Jesus walked." To be *in Christ* as branches in their parent vine is to drink only at the fountains of his life—to be fed from the springs of influence and vital moral force which flow forth from him to his people. Of course this implies that we live and walk according to the model left us in his earthly life.——Let it then be deemed forever futile and vain for a man to say he abides in Christ unless the fruits of his heart in the outward life show it.

7. Brethren, I write no new commandment unto you, but an old commandment which ye had from the beginning. The old commandment is the word which ye have heard from the beginning.

8. Again, a new commandment I write unto you, which thing is true in him and in you: because the darkness is past, and the true light now shineth.

What I have written here of "keeping his commandments," and accounting this the only evidence of knowing God and of being in him, is nothing new, but is rather the old doctrine of my gospel history, well known to you from the beginning of your Christian life, or of the gospel age. But again I write to you what may be regarded as a new commandment only inasmuch as it presents this old truth in new aspects and new applications; for with the march of time, truth receives new developments; the old darkness disappears and clearer light shines.——This antithesis between the old command and the new seems somewhat obscure; yet probably the new aspects referred to are those which appear in vs. 9–11—and perhaps onward; *e. g.* that hatred to one's brother nullifies all proof of piety, for hatred is a sure characteristic of moral darkness—the ungodly state, as love is of light—the really Christian life.*

9. He that saith he is in the light, and hateth his brother, is in darkness even until now.

10. He that loveth his brother abideth in the light, and there is none occasion of stumbling in him.

11. But he that hateth his brother is in darkness, and walketh in darkness, and knoweth not whither he goeth, because that darkness hath blinded his eyes.

Probably there were asperities and alienations of feeling among professed brethren against which John intended these verses should bear. Let such unloving professors of religion understand that their spirit is of earthly darkness, and not of gospel light; is of the world, not of Christ; that they know not the true light, but abide still in the old darkness of their ungodly life. Doubtless if such men suppose themselves Christians, they are blind and self-deceived.——He who walks in love abides in the light, and will not make either himself or his fellow-men stumble in the Christian life.

12. I write unto you, little children, because your sins are forgiven you for his name's sake.

13. I write unto you, fathers, because ye have known him *that is* from the beginning. I write unto you, young men, because ye have overcome the wicked one. I write unto you, little children, because ye have known the Father.

14. I have written unto you, fathers, because ye have known him *that is* from the beginning. I have written unto

---

* The corrected text at the close of v. 7 omits "from the beginning"—a change which leaves the sense the same.

you, young men, because ye are strong, and the word of God abideth in you, and ye have overcome the wicked one.

To three classes distinguished by age, viz. children, fathers, and young men, he writes now and has written before. In these verses he gives the special reasons why he has written. The reasons for both the present and the former writing seem to be substantially the same, the slightly varied expressions amounting to much the same in thought:—to little children because they are forgiven through Christ, or otherwise put—"have known the Father;" to the fathers in the church because they had "known him who is from the beginning," of whom in his gospel John had said—"In the beginning was the Word;" to young men because they had overcome Satan; were strong in the vigor of youth and in the freshness of their Christian life through having God's word abiding in their hearts. He assumes it to be a glorious achievement for young men at the age when the world, the flesh, and the devil are perhaps most seductive and powerful, to have overcome the devil and to put all their youthful vigor into Christian work and the Christian life.

In the last clause of v. 13 (the second address to little children) the corrected text gives, not "I write," but "I have written"—a change which makes the order complete—each of the three classes being named twice; once as addressed now; and again, as having been written to previously.——Whether the former writing refers to his gospel; to some other epistle; or to the preceding part of this—is neither very certain nor very important.

15. Love not the world, neither the things *that are* in the world. If any man love the world, the love of the Father is not in him.

16. For all that *is* in the world, the lust of the flesh, and the lust of the eyes, and the pride of life, is not of the Father, but is of the world.

17. And the world passeth away, and the lust thereof: but he that doeth the will of God abideth forever.

Naturally John's allusion to the moral victory achieved by young men suggested these words of admonition as to the chief dangers of the Christian life.——The love of the Father and the love of the world are naturally incompatible because both say, "Give me thy heart," and "no man can serve two masters"—especially two so antagonistic as God and Mammon.——The analysis and classification of the different forms of worldly good (as in v. 16)—"the lust of the flesh, the lust of the eyes, and the pride of life"—are exceedingly useful as indicating in general what is meant by "the world" and by "loving the world," while at the same time it is not wise to regard this classification as exhaustive. There may be yet other forms of worldly good not less hostile to loving God; not less ensnaring therefore and ruinous. The love of money is not named here. Let no one forget that Jesus put Mammon among the chief enemies of human souls, and that Paul said, "The love of money is the root of all evil"—(1 Tim. 6: 10). John may have had reasons for placing the points named here in the foreground—supposably because these were then the forms of worldly pleasure which most imperiled the young. But John would justly rebuke us if we should infer from his not naming the love of money that he made no account of that form of world-loving.

Of every form of worldly good he would say—It is short-lived, fleeting, sure to pass swiftly away. While yet one is saying to himself—"I have gained it; behold what a treasure!" lo, it is gone! Or, what is equally fatal, the pleasure-lover himself passes away, and is no more!—That John had this in mind may be indicated by his contrast: "He that doeth the will of God abideth forever." In a very precious sense he never dies. Never is he torn away from all he loves. It is only the miserable worldling who "is driven away in his wickedness." Oh, how does the portion of the righteous rise in its preciousness and brighten in glory as the years roll away and as the end of human life draws near!

18. Little children, it is the last time: and as ye have heard that antichrist shall come, even now are there many antichrists; whereby we know that it is the last time.

"The last time"—in the Greek, "the last *hour*." The question will arise—Did John suppose the days then passing to be the *last hours* of time? Could he have been so much mistaken, and yet be writing letters under inspiration?

To meet these questions fundamentally, let us group together the parallel passages of the New Testament which will give us the current ideas of the age and the then current usage of these and kindred terms. "Hath *in these last days* spoken to us by his Son" (Heb. 1: 2);—"Christ was manifested *in these last times* for you" (1 Pet. 1: 20);—"It shall come to pass *in the last days*, saith God, I will pour out my Spirit" (Acts 2: 17)—supposed to be fulfilled at the Great Pentecost;—"Now the Spirit speaketh expressly that *in the latter times* some shall depart from the faith" (1 Tim. 4: 1); "*In the last days* perilous times shall come" (2 Tim. 3: 1);—"Remember the words spoken before by the apostles . . . how they told you there should be mockers *in the last time*" (Jude 17, 18);—"These things are written for our admonition *upon whom the ends of the world are come*"—*i. e.* upon whom the two ends of the ages meet—the former age coming to its close and the latter age beginning (1 Cor. 10: 11);—"Now once *in the end of the world* hath Christ appeared to put away sin by the sacrifice of himself" (Heb. 9: 26).

The careful reader of these passages will see that the italicised phrases describe the Messianic age, the period commencing with his incarnation and including all that was to be subsequent. The Jews divided all time into two ages ("*worlds*" they sometimes call them)—the age before Christ and the age after—much as the Christian world make the birth of Christ the dividing line of time, reckoning what preceded in one table, and all that follows in another. In dividing time thus into two great ages, neither the Jewish world nor the Christian express any opinion as to the length of the last age. We agree to call it the last days, the last age, committing ourselves to no theory as to its duration. Any further consideration of questions in reference to the views of the apostles respecting Christ's future comings, will come fitly into my Excursus on this subject in the Appendix.

The word "antichrist" is peculiar to John and occurs only in these Epistles (2: 18, 22, and 4: 3, and 2 Eps. 7). The reference to antichrist in the verse before us seems to contemplate some definite individual; but in v. 22 *any one* who denies the Father and the Son is an antichrist.——"Ye have heard that antichrist shall come"—for Jesus had forewarned his people (Matt. 24: 11, 24) of the coming of "false Christs and false prophets," and so also had Paul in speaking to the elders of the Ephesian church (Acts 20: 29, 30) (where John was writing) and also in writing to Timothy, then at Ephesus (1 Tim. 4: 1, and 2 Tim. 3: 1). These forewarnings designated the time as in the latter days. Jesus placed false Christs and prophets, in time, shortly before the destruction of Jerusalem.

19. They went out from us, but they were not of us; for if they had been of us, they would *no doubt* have continued with us: but *they went out*, that they might be made manifest that they were not all of us.

Some of these antichrists were apostates from the Christian faith. John thinks it important to show how men once supposed to be real Christians might become apostate. He explains it thus: They *never were true Christians*. If they had been they would have remained true to Christ; but they went out, not because *they* wished to show that they never belonged there, but because *God* sought to show it. We may assume that John remembered what Jesus had said so very strongly and what himself had recorded so fully (John 10: 26-29): "My sheep hear my voice, and I know them, and they follow me: I give them eternal life; they shall never perish; none shall ever pluck them from my hand," etc. It is not strange therefore that he should pause at this point to explain how the case of these apostates can be harmonized with those strong words of Jesus as to keeping all his sheep safely unto eternal life.

20. But ye have an unction from the Holy One, and ye know all things.

In the best manuscripts the last clause of this verse stands—not "ye know all things," but "*ye all* know"—the word "all" qualifying the persons—not the things. Ye all have Christian knowledge.

"Unction," *i. e.* chrism, or the anointing, may be a tacit allusion to the name Christ—the anointed One; but more probably rests on the ancient Hebrew usage of anointing priests and kings for their sacred functions—which anointing became an emblem of divine illumination for their work. The word passed down into the Christian age to signify the teaching of the Spirit as promised by Jesus—"He shall teach you all things," etc. Thus taught by the Spirit they had such Christian knowledge that they could detect these antichrists and withstand their seductions.

21. I have not written unto you because ye know not the truth, but because ye know it, and that no lie is of the truth.

22. Who is a liar but he that denieth that Jesus is the Christ? He is antichrist, that denieth the Father and the Son.

Fortunately, John could have confidence in the brethren to whom he wrote that their knowledge of gospel truth would be equal to this emergency. They must see that to deny the Messiahship of Jesus would be fatal to the whole gospel scheme. This being denied, nothing remains. For, to deny this denies both the Father and the Son. We have no God left to love and to worship, for God the Father has most fully indorsed the mission of Jesus his Son. If this is not reliable, we have lost God, and virtually have no God—Father, Son, or Spirit—on whom we can rely.

23. Whosoever denieth the Son, the same hath not the Father: [*but*] *he that acknowledgeth the Son hath the Father also.*

In our English version the last clause of this verse is put in Italics, indicating doubt of its being genuine. There seems to be not the least occasion for this doubt. The best manuscripts contain it, and the course of thought with this clause included is entirely in harmony with John's habit. To deny the Son is to lose the Father; to confess the Son retains to us the Father—two propositions mutually correlated to each other. Men must hold to the Father and to the Son both and equally, or must lose both. It is impossible to retain the Father after having rejected the Son.

24. Let that therefore abide in you, which ye have heard from the beginning. If that which ye have heard from the beginning shall remain in you, ye also shall continue in the Son, and in the Father.

25. And this is the promise that he hath promised us, *even eternal life.*

Hold fast, therefore, to the doctrine of Christ which ye have heard from the first. So doing, ye will continue in the Son and in the Father; and the promised blessings of this gospel—that eternal life in which all culminate—shall be your portion.

26. *These things have I written unto you concerning them that seduce you.*
27. *But the anointing which ye have received of him abideth in you, and ye need not that any man teach you: but as the same anointing teacheth you of all things, and is truth, and is no lie, and even as it hath taught you, ye shall abide in him.*

All these things I have written to warn you against being seduced from the truth as to Christ.——"Anointing" (v. 27) (Greek) is the word translated " unction" (v. 20), and refers here as there to the truth taught them by the Spirit. In this teaching John has unlimited confidence—that they have it; that it is pure truth; and will be all they need to know concerning Jesus.

28. *And now, little children, abide in him; that, when he shall appear, we may have confidence, and not be ashamed before him at his coming.*

"That *if* he shall appear"—"if" being a more accurate translation than "when."——"Not be ashamed," should rather be—not be *put to shame;* for in that august and glorious hour, it is not supposable that perishing mortals will be ashamed of Jesus, coming in his glory. The one only thing they have to fear is that Jesus may be ashamed of them, and they be put to shame before him.

But what shall be said of this supposition—that Jesus may possibly appear?——This at least—that such a supposition is *always in order*—never can be out of place.——Also this farther:—that if the *time when* lay in a sense uncertain before John's mind, and he could not be sure but it might be really near, there would be the greater propriety in making this supposition. As to the opinions of the apostles on this time-question, my views have been expressed and referred to sufficiently.——As to the moral bearings of this coming, nothing could be more fearful than to be found out of Christ—not abiding in him—when that august day shall break upon the world.

29. *If ye know that he is righteous, ye know that every one that doeth righteousness is born of him.*

"He is righteous"—but who is meant by "*he*"? The nearest expressed antecedent is "*he*" who is to appear—Jesus. Yet in the subsequent context, "born of him" should refer to God, the more so because sons so born are in the next verse spoken of as "sons of God." But the sense is essentially the same whether "he" refers to Christ or to God.

If ye know that God is righteous ye know that the righteous ones among men are his children, born of him. Nothing short of such a new birth insures the fruits of intrinsic righteousness of character and life. It is perfectly safe to assume and affirm this, for, apart from the grace that regenerates human souls, there is no essential righteousness in human character.

CHAPTER III.

The central doctrine in this precious chapter is that being born of God reveals itself in an unsinning, loving life in this world, and in the consummation of purity and blessedness in the next.

1. *Behold, what manner of love the Father hath bestowed upon us, that we should be called the sons of God: therefore the world knoweth us not, because it knew him not.*

It will aid the reader toward the full sense of this verse to consider its close connection with the verse immediately preceding, and also the bearing of the words which the best authorities introduce after the clause—" the sons of God "—viz. "*and we are.*" These words suggest that the marvel of God's love is not merely that we should be *called* the sons of God, but that we should really *be* such;—" and we are."——Connecting this verse with the one next preceding, we have this line of thought: Inasmuch as the glory of God's character is its infinite righteousness, it follows that every one who practices righteousness, being in heart and life really righteous, shows that he has been born of God. He has become what he is through the new birth by the Spirit.——Then John breaks forth in this expression of admiring wonder: "Behold what manner of love the Father hath bestowed on us that we should be called sons of God!" Yet let us not put too much emphasis on the word "*called,*" as if John thought more of the honor of the name than of the value of the thing which the name indicates. Let us recall the fact that Hebrew usage—most marked in Isaiah—employs the verb "call" to signify not so much the name as the reality. Such must be John's meaning here not only because of this ancient Hebrew usage, but because the improved text manifestly gives this sense. Behold this love of God—that he should not only call us sons, but that we should really be sons! The great love shines forth in the new birth which makes us sons in spirit and in life, rather than in the gift of a name and the honor of a public adoption into the family of God. The intrinsic righteousness which makes us like our Heavenly Father is more than the honor of the recognized parentage, though the latter be truly great and wonderful. Oh, the ineffable love manifested from God in that work of his Spirit which transforms human hearts from enmity to love—from all iniquity into the spirit of intrinsic righteousness like that of God himself! In what fitting words shall we celebrate and set it forth! That we—such as we were by nature and such as we had made ourselves by sin—should not only be *called* but should in fact *become* sons of God by being transformed into his moral image—what less can we say of this than to exclaim—Behold what manner of love in God does this reveal! Was such love ever known elsewhere in all the universe?

John proceeds to say—No wonder that men of the world know not us, for they know not God. When Jesus came among men revealing God, their eyes were blind, their souls dark as to this light of God. Therefore it were vain to expect they will recognize us as God's sons, born into his moral image. They have no eyes (morally speaking) to discern such moral qualities. Hating such light, the power of a bad heart to darken the human intelligence takes fearful effect and dooms them to the guilt and ruin of moral blindness. Hence Christians may walk in the light and the love of Christ through life, heirs of a heavenly kingdom and yet unknown; nay more, with heart and life attuned to the intrinsic righteousness of God, yet as really unrecognized of the world as Jesus himself was when he lived before human eyes unknown.

2. Beloved, now are we the sons of God, and it doth not yet appear what we shall be : but we know that, when he shall appear, we shall be like him; for we shall see him as he is.

3. And every man that hath this hope in him purifieth himself, even as he is pure.

Beloved, so much we know of our prerogatives and blessings; but of the far more glorious future—ah, indeed, we know but little! What we shall be, who can tell? Yet let it suffice us to know that whenever Jesus shall appear, coming in the clouds of heaven to take his risen saints into their promised glory with himself, then we shall be *like him*—all-glorious and all-pure even as he—"for we shall see him as he is." The moral transformation of our souls into his image will be made absolutely perfect then, effected under the normal law of all such moral changes, viz. to see, to study, to behold admiringly, lovingly, itself begets the transformation. Such a character as that of Jesus—so sweet, so charming, so enrapturing—impresses itself perfectly into the souls of his people. It molds, transforms, new creates; and we become like him, for we see him, not dimly, not remotely, not imperfectly, not with the least false shading; but perfectly *as he is;* so that the impression taken up by our own willing, loving souls will be perfect as the image that we behold.

It was a wise hand that framed and hung the curtain that shades the glories of the heavenly world somewhat from the curious upturned eyes on this hither side. No doubt it is well—none can yet say how well—that "it doth not yet appear what we shall be." Too much for the imagination to play upon might divert us dangerously from the rougher work and the sterner realities of our earthly Christian life. Of the wisdom of hiding the things kept behind this curtain we can not perhaps speak altogether positively; but of the wisdom of revealing what is suffered to shine through we can speak somewhat intelligently, and surely ought to speak with profoundest admiration. Oh how glorious and yet how safe to be assured that we shall be *like Him!* Like Him whose moral image is infinite beauty and unspeakable glory; like Him whom above all others we love, revere and adore. How should this satisfy us, though we were to know nothing else whatever of heaven! Satisfy? nay more—how should it ravish our souls with ineffable delight; how should it breathe through our whole being the deep repose of a perfect consummation! Surely the Christian who has thrown his whole heart into earnest endeavor to become like Christ, with watchfulness and prayer and manifold recastings, laboriously eliminating the evil and giving fresh culture to the good—will know how to appreciate this one blessed assurance: "We shall be like him, for we shall see him as he is."

In this very line of thought John himself would lead us;—"Every man that hath this hope in Him (Christ) purifieth himself even as he (Christ) is pure." Such a hope of being in the better world perfectly like Jesus puts the soul upon its utmost endeavors to reach even here the highest attainable conformity to his pure character. By one of the highest and best laws of our being, we labor spontaneously to prepare ourselves for the future responsibilities, dignities, labors and trusts that lie before us in anticipation. Adjusting his revelations of the heavenly world to this law of our being, God puts in the foreground of the revealed heaven these two great facts—that we are to see Jesus as he is; and that we are to become perfectly like him. Now let this revealed knowledge have its free play of action and reaction upon our souls, and how mightily must it inspire us to the utmost endeavor to perfect this maturity of Christian character even here!

The sort of influence we shall receive from the heaven we think of will be as that heaven itself. A fancied sensual paradise will feed sensuality. A heaven of scientific pursuits and acquisitions might very naturally stimulate scientific culture. Too much place given to the social side of our nature as to be developed among our fellow-men would be in danger of toning down the grand aspirations which John contemplates. But to put the vision of Jesus as he is, and the becoming verily like him, not only into the foreground but over the whole ground of our view—this is at once wholesome in its perfect safety, and in its very nature is grandly sublime!

If our ideal heaven were such a heaven as this, and if all our hopes of heaven were these hopes of seeing Jesus as he is, and of being absolutely like him, the mistaken hopes and the failures of the hoping, to reach heaven, would be indefinitely less, and the moral power of anticipating heaven would be indefinitely greater and purer.

4. Whosoever committeth sin transgresseth also the law: for sin is the transgression of the law.

5. And ye know that he was manifested to take away our sins: and in him is no sin.

6. Whosoever abideth in him sinneth not: whosoever sinneth hath not seen him, neither known him.

The connection of these verses with those which precede should be carefully noted—viz. that the spirit of the Christian life, his sonship, his intrinsic righteousness, his aspirations to be like Jesus—are all fundamentally *anti-sin*—there being no sympathy whatever but the most repellant contrariety between such a Christian and the sinner whom he here contemplates.

The noticeable thing in v. 4 is the prominence given to the fact that sin is *against law*. It would seem that these propositions—the doer of sin practices law-breaking: for sin is breaking law—must allude to some heresy then current, supposably one which ignored the moral law, perhaps denied its binding force, and thus virtually broke down God's standard of human duty and obligation. Of this, however, we can not speak positively.

It deserves consideration whether the word John uses, translated "transgression of the law" * should not be taken in the sense of lawlessness—the lawless spirit—in which sense he would affirm that the doer of sin manifests lawlessness; that the chief element of guilt in all sin is the lawless spirit which it involves—the reckless disregard of God's authority; the deliberate repelling of God's standard of human duty. This would evince a heart in hostile and even disdainful attitude toward God. In this aspect of sin, the difficulties of the passage mainly if not wholly disappear. For, with such a spirit of sin, the Christian life is utterly contrasted. There can be no difficulty in maintaining that such sin must be unknown in the true Christian life, and is utterly inconsistent with it. His deficiencies and short-comings never reach the point of defiant lawlessness. He may sin inadvertently, or through sudden impulses of temptation, or in falling short of the highest and purest possible devotion to Christ; but his sin is not lawlessness.

Jesus was made manifest in human flesh (as ye all know) for

---

* Anomia.

the great purpose of taking away sin,* and was himself sinless. Hence his example bears with its solid force against sinning. The great aim of his mission to earth bears in the same direction. Let his people remember all this forever.——Consequently whosoever abideth in him, as the branch in its parent vine, drawing his life-forces from Jesus himself, does not sin. Such ministrations of spiritual life-power, beget the fruit of holiness, not of sin. The man who sins makes it plain that he has no just spiritual apprehensions of Jesus—surely does not in the gospel sense, "abide in him." The same doctrine is put in v. 9 below in terms somewhat differing, but in sense the same.

The only really difficult question involved in these passages respects the sort of sins of which some, not to say many who give unquestioned proof of piety, confess themselves from time to time—or perhaps all the time, guilty. Not that they confess to a lawless spirit; not that they disown obligation or deny Christ; not that they make up their mind to forsake his service and sell themselves to work iniquity: no; but they confess to falling below their own standard of duty; to inadvertent transgressions; to deficient zeal and love. What shall be said of such confessed sin in the case of men apparently true followers of Christ?

Shall we say that John uses the words "*sin*" and "sinner" in the strong emphatic sense which is so common in the gospel histories, a sense involving open, flagrant immoralities—*e. g.* "Behold a woman in the city who was a sinner" etc. (Luke 7: 37, 39); "He was gone to be a guest with a man that is a sinner" (Luke 19: 7); "Publican and sinners"—often; "How can a man who is a sinner do such miracles?" . . "We know that this man is a sinner." (John 9: 16, 24).—This usage, being both common and strong, must be conceded (it would seem) to have weight in the interpretation of these words of John.—According to this usage he who practices sin is a positive character—a real *sinner*, whose spirit and life fix and stamp him as a known law-breaker, even if not in every case a man of lawless spirit.

But it behooves us to beware lest we push this supposed sense of his words too far, and so let a bad class of sins, such as should distress any Christian heart, escape condemnation as not included under the word "sin." For, beyond all doubt, John is here laboring to show that Jesus, our Exemplar, had no sin; that he came to take away all sin, and that the pure life of the Heavenly One should inspire all his friends with aspirations for the same purity even here.

What then is John's doctrine, here, in regard to those imperfections of which many apparently true Christians confess themselves guilty?

With a deep undisguised sense of the great delicacy and real difficulty involved in this question, I yet venture the following

---

* The best textual authorities omit the word "our," making the affirmation general.

suggestions:——(1.) There is nothing here which indicates that John had these consciously imperfect yet upward struggling Christians definitely in his mind, and meant his statements to bear specially upon them.——(2.) Consequently the utmost caution should be used in applying these words to cases which seem to have been foreign from his thought.——(3.) Yet all his statements and reasonings bear against every form and degree of sin of which men can be intelligently conscious, and toward the attainment here in time of Christ-like purity.

On this passage Luccke remarks—"John speaks not of the different degrees of perfection which struggling Christians have reached, but of the ideal and absolute difference between Christian virtue and piety, and sin in general."——Neander (Epistle of John, p. 194) speaking of the really Christian spirit and of its possible imperfections, remarks: "That the determining tendencies of the Christian, of the will in the Christian, can be no other than holy and averse to sin: that only the after workings of the former relations of sin, of the old man, oppose themselves to what is now his determining and controlling tendency."

7. Little children, let no man deceive you: he that doeth righteousness is righteous, even as he is righteous.

8. He that committeth sin is of the devil; for the devil sinneth from the beginning. For this purpose the Son of God was manifested, that he might destroy the works of the devil.

Manifestly John was not beating the air, but levelling his blows against teachers of false doctrine, then abroad, infesting the churches. Under what pretenses they sought to defend iniquity, and perhaps immorality, it is not of special importance that we should know. No doubt John met them, squarely confronting their doctrine when he said—None save the doer of righteousness is a righteous man, like Jesus Christ. Profession of righteousness without the real practice of it is worse than worthless. Sin is of the devil, and he who commits it works under his master and in his service. The Son of God became manifest among men to war upon the devil, to counteract and destroy his works. No antagonists were ever more squarely confronted than they or in more deadly hostility to each other.

9. Whosoever is born of God doth not commit sin; for his seed remaineth in him: and he cannot sin, because he is born of God.

Beyond question, being "born of God" here is the new birth, regeneration; and the figure of the human birth is still carried out in the allusion to "his seed" as remaining in him. As we might say, one born of royal parentage carries ever in his veins his royal blood.——But when we pass from the material to the spiritual and ask—What is that in the human soul which, being introduced in regeneration, remains in him, by virtue of which he can not sin, what shall we say? Does Peter express it accurately (1 Peter 1: 23)—"Being born again, not of corruptible seed, but of incorruptible, *by the word of God* which liveth and abideth forever"? This turns our mind to God's revealed truth as the corresponding spiritual reality. Yet does not the nature of the case suggest also a certain receptivity to this truth and a certain moral attitude of will and purpose, due influentially to the Spirit of God, which give cast and tone to all subsequent moral activities? Metaphysically considered, the philosophy of the new birth is deep. It is more easy, perhaps more common, to talk about it superficially than profoundly. As interpreters we may reasonably be satisfied with saying that according to John's philosophy of mind the new birth brought into the soul an element at once morally powerful and permanent, which quite forbids any relapse into utter, fatal antagonism to God. In the strong emphatic sense of sinning, the new-born soul can not sin.

10. In this the children of God are manifest, and the children of the devil: whosoever doeth not righteousness is not of God, neither he that loveth not his brother.

In the sense common in the gospel of John (*e. g.* 8: 37–44), according to which Jesus admitted that the Jews were Abraham's progeny but denied that they were his children, the being children here implies that they have the spirit of their father. In this sense the children of God and the children of the devil may be readily tested and proved: The former practice righteousness; the latter wickedness: the former loveth his brother; the latter hateth.

11. For this is the message that ye heard from the beginning, that we should love one another.

12. Not as Cain, *who* was of that wicked one, and slew his brother. And wherefore slew he him? Because his own works were evil, and his brother's righteous.

From the beginning of the gospel age—perhaps John would say—in my gospel history—ye had the message which commanded that we "love one another" (John 13: 34, 35). An example in point—put in contrast—will make it plain and give it force: "Not as Cain who was of Satan" (impelled by his instigations) "and slew his brother." But note with what masterly ease and accuracy John puts his finger on the impelling motive. Cain could not bear to see his virtuous brother accepted of God, and himself, consciously guilty, rejected. "His own works were evil and his brother's righteous," and worst of all, God knew it and saw fit to testify his views of them both. It was too much for the wicked brother to bear. So envy and jealousy work unto murder.——But is every body's envy and hate of a brother of the same sort and of like guilt with that of Cain? So John implies.

13. Marvel not, my brethren, if the world hate you.

14. We know that we have passed from death unto life, because we love the brethren. He that loveth not *his* brother abideth in death.

15. Whosoever hateth his brother is a murderer: and ye know that no murderer hath eternal life abiding in him.

That the world should hate you should surprise no one. The case of Cain explains it all. When we truly love the brethren with love like Christ's, we may safely infer from it that we have passed from death in sin unto life in God. A loving heart toward Christian brethren is one of the surest tests of piety and one most easily applied.——On the opposite hand, to hate one's brother is the spirit of murder as ye saw in Cain; and how can a murderer have eternal life abiding in him?——Note the pith and force of the phrase "eternal life" to signify true godliness—such a character as ripens for immortal blessedness and is indeed a heaven already begun in the soul. The pungency and force of the phrase lie in the obvious incompatibility of murder and love dwelling in the same bosom.

If we take love to the brethren as an infallible test of piety, it becomes vitally important that we make no mistake as to its genuineness. On this point there may be fatal mistakes. For example; there is a social good feeling that falls far short of Christian love of the brethren: there may be a common sympathy in church work and religious service which has little to do with love to Christ or to the souls of men. Even worship may be congenial for its esthetic taste and surroundings rather than for its adaptations to the broken and contrite spirit.——Then moreover, what is thought to be brotherly love may go not beyond complacency in really lovable social qualities, and may have in it none of that outgoing benevolence which loves and seeks the highest spiritual good of the brethren and gives itself spontaneously to prayer and labor in their behalf. Only that love of brethren is genuine, and, as a test of piety reliable, which *presupposes love to God*—as John expresses it; loving him that begat, we love his begotten; loving God, we love his children, for they become (we may say) *lineal* brothers—brethren not in name but in blood—in spirit; in character.

16. Hereby perceive we the love *of God*, because he laid down his life for us: and we ought to lay down *our* lives for the brethren.

The reader will notice the words "of God" in Italics, indicating that the Greek has no words corresponding. These Italic words are not at all necessary to the sense. They rather mislead than lead well, for the thought is rather upon Christ than God. Herein have we known [*i. e.* have had the means of fully appreciating] what real love means; viz. by this—That he [Jesus Christ] laid down his life for us. This is the crowning illustration of real love. We need go no further for one more expressive.——Note the striking contrast which suggested this allusion to the death of Christ—viz. between the murderer who takes another's life because he hates, and Jesus who lays down his own because he loves.——From this example of Jesus the writer advances to the Christian duty. We ought to be ready to follow Christ, even to the laying down of our lives for the brethren. Why not? This could not be more than Jesus has done for us.

17. But whoso hath this world's good, and seeth his brother have need, and shutteth up his bowels *of compassion* from him, how dwelleth the love of God in him?

18. My little children, let us not love in word, neither in tongue; but in deed and in truth.

The service of love is often withheld at a point far short of laying down our life for the brethren. Consider this case in point:—A man has this world's good—literally, the *life* of this world, in the sense of the means of supporting life; and sees his brother in want and shuts up his bowels of compassion—hardens his heart against sympathy and shuts his hand from help;—How can the love of God be in him? Can it be possible that he loves God and yet manifests no love for God's children? His love can not reach God in the way of beneficence; such love is cheap in the sense that it costs him no outlay of labor or sacrifice. If he had any real love for God's children, he might readily show it—but he shows it not! Let him not deceive himself with the delusion that he loves God!——Mark how pungently John puts his admonition—Let us not love in word neither in tongue; word-love, tongue-love, is odious, disgusting, hateful to God as it is worthless and abusive to the suffering poor. Let your love be that of deeds and realities, a love that evinces its sincerity by its legitimate fruits of beneficence.

This opens the great subject of charity to the poor; not indeed presenting all its nice questions as to helping the indolent, the improvident, the wasteful, the dishonest, the vicious; but putting the subject forward in its simple elements—compassion for the needy. It was not in place for John to raise questions as to the wisdom of one method of relief compared with another, nor to show how to forestall abuses of charity. He must be expected to speak for his own times. Then, some Christians lost all by confiscation; some were imprisoned; some banished; some slain—for their fidelity to Christ. Shall pinching want occasioned by such fidelity to Christ be unrelieved by their well-fed brethren? The principle of loving one's Christian brother at the cost of some sacrifice of worldly good to meet their greater need, John ought to present in strong light, and has done it. Let us beware lest we dishonor this principle, disown this duty, and fail of the blessings of obedience because in our times Christian charity is sometimes selfishly abused, and numberless questions as to the wisest method are sprung upon us. It were better to fall below perfect wisdom than to mar the beauty and miss the blessedness of real love.

19. And hereby we know that we are of the truth, and shall assure our hearts before him.

20. For if our heart condemn us, God is greater than our heart, and knoweth all things.

21. Beloved, if our heart condemn us not, *then* have we confidence toward God.

By such tests as this, proving our love by really *doing good*, making sacrifices for our more needy brethren, we may know that we are of the truth, and are entitled to have confidence of soul before him. "Assure our hearts before him" in the sense of allaying conscientious fears and taking encouragement from a consciousness of real honesty before God.——"Being of the truth" looks toward "loving in deed and in truth." To have this proof that our love is genuine will justify a quiet non-accusing conscience. The word "heart" is applied here to what is commonly known as the *conscience*—the moral sense, considered as taking cognizance of our own moral states and acts. God has given us this capacity of self-inspection and self-judgment. John manifestly assumes that in general its decisions are to be obeyed as in harmony with God's, and that we may expect God to sustain and endorse them. If our own conscience condemns us—*e. g.* as to the point here in hand—for withholding our sympathy and aid from our more needy and suffering brother, we may be very sure that God—greater than our heart and knowing all things more perfectly than we can—will condemn us also. But if our conscience condemn us not, we may at least have confidence toward God that he does not condemn us. John does not say—It is therefore certain that God will not condemn us, but only, that we may have a quiet trust, free from painful solicitude.

22. And whatsoever we ask, we receive of him, because we keep his commandments, and do those things that are pleasing in his sight.

This calm, non-accusing, really approving conscience, sustains most vital relations to prayer. We do not come before God already self-condemned for our dishonesty, insincerity, hypocrisy: no, but rather with confidence that we honestly aim to keep his commandments and do evermore what we suppose and believe to be pleasing in his sight. John says that, coming before God in this moral attitude, we receive of him whatever we ask.——Let it be carefully observed here that John does not rest our prevalence in prayer upon the basis of our personal merit; does not say that having *deserved blessings*, we may be sure of receiving; but merely says that a consciousness of honesty toward God and of a steadfast aim to do his commandments legitimately begets confidence before him, and that God will respond with favoring answer to our prayer—of course only for Christ's sake. Well does Neander remark on this passage—"As sons, whose filial relation has suffered no interruption, can with child-like trust and confidence ask all from their father; so believers whose life is of the truth, who are conscious of no disturbance of their filial relation to God through unfaithfulness on their part, can ask all with child-like confidence from God their Father."

23. And this is his commandment, That we should believe on the name of his Son Jesus Christ, and love one another, as he gave us commandment.

24. And he that keepeth his commandments dwelleth in him, and he in him. And hereby we know that he abideth in us, by the Spirit which he hath given us.

Altogether like John are these comprehensive words expressing the elementary principles of gospel requirement. If you ask what are the central commandments in the gospel scheme, he answers—*Believe in Jesus; love one another.* Keeping his commandments ye come into most intimate mutual relations to him; ye dwell in him; he dwells in you; and of this indwelling his Spirit, present to your soul, is the witness. We may know that Christ dwells in us by the self-conscious testimony which his Spirit bears to our inmost heart.——This witnessing of the Spirit, taught plainly here by John (see 4: 13), and also by Paul (*e. g.* Rom. 8: 16), is doubtless liable to abuse (what point of gospel truth or grace is not?), yet is none the less a thing of fact and of conscious experience. If the mission of the Spirit be a reality, and his presence in Christian souls, a fact, why should it be thought a thing incredible that he should make his presence manifest in the temple where he dwells? Why should not his voice be heard—nay more, be sometimes *identified*—made so definite, so clear, so emphatic, so precious, that the human soul may hear and may verily know that this *is* his own voice and none other than his?

———oo;o;oo———

CHAPTER IV.

To expose false spirits; to prove their false character by decisive tests; to give tests of real piety for each one's own self-judgment; to give prominence to love as the cardinal element of Christian character—these are the leading themes in this chapter.

1. Beloved, believe not every spirit, but try the spirits whether they are of God: because many false prophets are gone out into the world.
2. Hereby know ye the Spirit of God: Every spirit that confesseth that Jesus Christ is come in the flesh is of God:
3. And every spirit that confesseth not that Jesus Christ is come in the flesh is not of God: and this is that *spirit* of antichrist, whereof ye have heard that it should come; and even now already is it in the world.

Other spirits than those from God have infested the church more or less in all ages. The law of Moses contemplated their presence and provided tests for their detection (Deut. 13: 1–5)— these tests being not the miracles they claimed to work but the doctrines they taught. In the age of Jeremiah, they were a terrible curse upon Israel. Jesus forewarned his disciples against them (Matt. 24: 11, 24)—not without reason, as their own subsequent writings show. It was therefore the dictate of wisdom to enjoin—"Believe not every spirit, but try the spirits whether they are of God." Not all who profess to be led by the Spirit of God are to be accepted. Try them by what they teach; receive them not till ye know that their message is in accordance with God's revealed truth.——At the time and place where John lived and wrote, the touch-stone was the question whether "Jesus Christ had come in the flesh"—the denial of his true humanity, involving of course the denial of the incarnation of the Son of God.

It deserves more careful attention than is sometimes given to it that these words of John—"Believe not *every spirit*, but try the *spirits* whether they are of God"—imply that these "spirits" claimed to come with inspiration from God. We must suppose that they imitated the true prophets of that age; put on the airs of ecstasy, rapture, strong mental excitement, so that the utmost vigilance and the application of searching tests became a necessity for the protection of the churches. Furthermore, coupling these representations of John with the teachings of Paul it becomes clear that in the view of the apostles, these false prophets were really instigated by the devil. Their inspiration came from him. Paul said—"We wrestle not against flesh and blood [only] but against principalities, against powers, against the rulers of the darkness of this world, against wicked spirits in high places (Eph. 6: 12). So the apostles held and taught. Were they mistaken? Was this notion a mere superstition of the age? Has the progress of human thought lifted this notion as an incubus of superstition from the heart of the intelligent, scientific world of our days? Or is it not rather the case that the last of Satan's devices is to beguile men into ignoring his agencies, not to say also his very existence?

4. Ye are of God, little children, and have overcome them: because greater is he that is in you, than he that is in the world.

5. They are of the world: therefore speak they of the world, and the world heareth them.

6. We are of God: he that knoweth God heareth us; he that is not of God heareth not us. Hereby know we the spirit of truth, and the spirit of error.

"Have overcome them"—the "false prophets and lying spirits." Notice, John says—"*Have* overcome," although the battle was yet mostly to be fought still. Their victory could be anticipated with the utmost certainty; for to have God on our side is always certain victory. The opposing parties have tried their relative strength on many a field of struggle—God always the conqueror. To have "God on our side"—we are wont to say; but John puts this fact more forcibly—"*God in you;*" "Greater is He that is *in you* than he that is in the world." When God is *in us*, he can not suffer *us* to be overcome.——Matching God against Satan, God is evermore the greater and the mightier, so that even "little children," Christians in the infancy of the religious life, are already more than conquerors when they fully admit the mighty God into their trusting souls. "They that wait on the Lord shall renew their strength."——Those false prophets "are of the world;" are not sent of God, but come forth from the world, possessed by the spirit of the world, in sympathy with the world only and altogether. Hence their speech and doctrine are of the world. No marvel then if men of the world hear them. Of course they will. "But we are of God," in the same sense in which they are "of the world." Therefore the men who know God will hear us; men not of God will not hear us. This test will enable you to discriminate the spirit of truth from the spirit of error. Godly men are in sympathy with the former; ungodly men with the latter. Men of God hear and love the truth; godless men receive and love falsehood—the errors and lies that claim to be Christian doctrine.

7. Beloved, let us love one another: for love is of God; and every one that loveth is born of God, and knoweth God.

8. He that loveth not, knoweth not God; for God is love.

9. In this was manifested the love of God toward us, because that God sent his only begotten Son into the world, that we might live through him.

10. Herein is love, not that we loved God, but that he loved us, and sent his Son *to be* the propitiation for our sins.

Again and again the author enjoins—Let us love one another—as if in his regard this was the most sacred of Christian obligations, the first of Christian duties. Was it because in his time this duty was grievously violated; or because his own fatherly, loving heart was full of this spirit to constant overflowing; or was it due to his intelligent conviction of the relative place of this in the glorious group of Christian graces? Probably, if we saw the whole heart of this patriarch we should find that not some one alone but all these causes combined lent their force to impress his deep sense of the worth of brotherly love in the household of faith.

Let us observe the logic of the precept; "Let us love one another, *for* love is *of God;*" the inbreathing of his Spirit brings it down from his own infinite fullness of love. When God gives us of his Spirit, what can it be less or other than love? The loving human heart has been born of God, for such love comes not of man; is not born of the flesh; is in no sense congenial to man's selfish nature. Therefore the presence of such pure love to one another testifies to the new birth from God and to a spiritual knowledge and apprehension of him.——Hence the converse of this should also be true; he that loveth not his brethren can not possibly know God—in the sense of an experimental apprehension of his character and a true sympathy with his nature—*for God is love.* Therefore to know God as he is means that we know his love and experience the inbreathings of that love through our own moral nature.

"For God is love." The same truth is reaffirmed (v. 16). Let us give it our thoughtful attention.

In form, the statement seems abstract, metaphysical; for observe, it is not that God is kind, affectionate, evermore manifesting his good will; but that he is *love itself*—the very impersonation of love; all love, and nothing else but love. It is of course comprehensive, all-embracing. It means that there can never be any thing in him, nothing coming forth from him, that is not loving—an outgoing of his love.

But some one will say—Does this statement really include and cover every element of his being? Is it not of his nature that he should fill the universe with his presence so that there shall be never a point of space, in heaven, earth, or hell, where God is not? How can this quality of his nature be conceived of as falling under this definition—God is love?——So of his *power*, which, since he is God, must be simply infinite—equal to any results which power can produce. But how can this infinite power be brought within the definition—"God is love"?

We must answer these and analogous questions by admitting the broad distinction between God's *natural* attributes and his *moral.* The natural are so irrelevant to John's line of thought that he seems not to notice them at all. Really, as compared with the moral, they have only a slight importance. Yet perhaps it is more to our purpose to say that John might reasonably leave out of account the whole group of God's natural attributes because they can never very greatly need either proof or illustration. They are self-affirmed so vigorously in every man's sober reason; they become such a necessity to our idea of God, that they prove themselves. The man who can not intuitively see and know that God must be every-where present, and infinite in power and all-searching in knowledge, has not yet begun to think to purpose—has too little mind to be profited by any logic of reasoning or force of facts.——Not so in the great realm of God's *moral nature*. Here it is not so clear to every man's strong intuitions that "God is love." For do we not see suffering, calamity, among his creatures? Do not human nerves, made by his own hand, sometimes quiver with pain and seem to be nothing else but inlets of agony? Do not these sufferings sometimes fall upon guileless infancy and upon sinless animals, and fall, it may be, with no apparent graduation to human guilt? To allude to these seeming irregularities, not to say mysteries, under God's government may suffice to show that this definition of God is by no means gratuitous and uncalled for. If it be certainly true, and if in very deed all the apparent irregularities, mysteries, and seeming contradictions to it which appear in the history of our world are reducible within this definition; if the entire sufferings in the universe be not inconsistent with God's perfect love, but come legitimately under it—permitted in wisdom and limited to what they are by love—how sublime must be the revelation that shall prove it! How glorious the outshining of truth that shall disclose the love that lay behind every apparently dark dispensation—underneath every mysterious law of human existence!

But some one's troubled heart will ask—Can it be possible that John meant all this when he said, "God is love"? Are we not overstraining his words when we give them so broad a sweep of application?

Let us see. The subject is too grave to be passed upon without attentive and candid consideration.

How does John know that God is love? What made him think so?

Some devout minds will expect me to answer this question by falling back upon his inspiration and saying—He wrote so under the dictation of the inditing Spirit.——This is doubtless one way to answer the question, but not the only way. This epistle of his (it so happens) does not leave us there, but suggests very distinctly that John did not so much take this statement upon trust as see the truth of it in the great revelation which God had made of his love. The next verse gives us the light we need. We shall see there how the great love of God had been manifested before his eyes. He tells us how his mind became established upon this everlasting rock of truth as to the loving heart of God. One great fact was proof enough:—"Because God sent his only begotten Son into the world that we might live through him." This means real love. If you ask for some demonstration of God's love, here it is. I do not mean, he would say, love in our heart toward God, but love in God's heart toward us. It was this love that made him "send his Son to be the propitiation for our sins."——Do we take in the full significance of this great gift and sacrifice from God, considered as a demonstration of his love?——Reflect;—"Propitiation for our sins"—"that we might *live* through him." Consider; sin is rebellion against God, with its root in causeless hatred, enmity. It is not only guilt, but meanness. Such sin makes the sinning character odious, disgusting. It seems to take out of man almost every quality that God could regard as noble or attractive. And yet God so loved this debased, hateful, guilty world of sinners that he sent his only begotten Son to die a sacrifice for them that they might live! Was not this *love, all* love, one vast outpouring of love, one sublime and resistless demonstration of an infinite heart of love? How can it be conceived possible that God should give up his only Son to such a doom if his heart were not pure and perfect love?

Thus the Apostle John reached the conclusion—or shall we rather say—felt the conviction—that God is love. It forced itself upon his soul. He *felt* the proof of it as it came upon him with overwhelming richness and fullness. Herein is love. Do ye ask, What does love mean, and where can perfect love be found? Here it is! Who shall ever doubt that God is perfect love after such a demonstration?

11. Beloved, if God so loved us, we ought also to love one another.

"If God so loved us"—if God, so pure, could love us, so vile; if God to whom sin is so revolting and sinners are so unlovable, and whose love, to reach us, must condescend so low and bear so much abuse;—oh, if under such circumstances, God can so love us, "*we ought to love one another*." What infinite force lies in this logic! The heart, broken for sin, sensible of the great compassion of God toward one so vile, will surely feel that *for me* to love my brother, each being alike objects of God's infinite love, is a duty to be done—a claim to be met—with all the heart.

12. No man hath seen God at any time. If we love one another, God dwelleth in us, and his love is perfected in us.

13. Hereby know we that we dwell in him, and he in us, because he hath given us of his Spirit.

To our mortal eyes God is invisible; not a man has ever seen him: but what has this to do with the Apostle's thought here? Perhaps this:—I have been speaking to you freely of God and of his love for us, *as if* we could really know much of him. But how is it that we know him?——Usually we get our best knowledge of other beings by seeing them; but none of us have in this sense seen God; we do not pretend to have seen him with these mortal eyes. But if we love one another, God comes nearer to us than merely being present to our eye of sense;—aye indeed, if we love one another, *God dwelleth in us.* He is not a God simply *outside* of us, to be apprehended by the sense of sight; but He lives within us, and thus his love reaches its full and proper development in our souls. We know that we dwell in him and he in us by means of the witnessing testimony of his Spirit. This Spirit brings a sense of God's presence, and with it, fullness of joy, and so inspires a sweet confidence in his love. The Spirit dwelling in our hearts *is* the presence of God there. No longer is God far away, but inexpressibly, delightfully near.

14. And we have seen and do testify that the Father sent the Son *to be* the Savior of the world.

15. Whosoever shall confess that Jesus is the Son of God, God dwelleth in him, and he in God.

Under such revelations of a present God, inspiring in our hearts pure love to our brethren, impressing us with a perpetual sense of his own perfect love, we are richly prepared to see and to testify that the Father sent the Son to be the Savior of the world. Nothing less could bring such an experience of love into our inmost heart. In such experience we have the proof of this mission of Christ, outgrowing from the love of the Father.—— Conversely, this confessing that Jesus is the Son of God certifies that God dwells in us and that we dwell in him. Of course John means indefinitely more than a confession with the lips only. He means a confession that wells up from the depths of human hearts—from hearts that have accepted this truth in love and have felt its transforming spiritual power.

16. And we have known and believed the love that God hath to us. God is love; and he that dwelleth in love dwelleth in God, and God in him.

This is one vital point in our experience; we have known and believed the love that God bears toward us. We accept it as true— indeed, as a most blessed truth.——On the words, "God is love," see Notes on v. 8.——The words—"He that dwelleth in love"— should be construed in keeping with the strain of this chapter, and indeed, of this whole epistle. So construed, they refer especially to *love of the brethren,* (considered as having its root in love to God)—the deep mutual affection which reigns in the hearts of those who are born to God and are brought under the full influence of the love God hath toward all his children. Loving the Father supremely, we shall surely love all his children. One who dwells in the atmosphere of such love to the brethren dwells in God and God in him.

17. Herein is our love made perfect, that we may have boldness in the day of judgment: because as he is, so are we in this world.

This verse is somewhat obscure, and has been interpreted variously by good critics.——I understand "our love" (Gr. love with us) to refer particularly to mutual Christian love of the brethren: the "day of judgment" to be (as usual in the N. T.) the final judgment of the race: "boldness" I take in the sense of an unrestrained, joyful confidence, as toward one with whom we are on terms of intimacy and may speak freely. In the phrase—"Because as he is"—"he" must refer specially to Christ and the clause, to his earthly life, which we follow in close imitation while we walk in love to God and love to the brethren.——The entire verse may be paraphrased thus:—By thus dwelling in supreme love to God and consequent love of God's children, and by thus having God dwelling in us (v. 16), our mutual Christian love for each other is developed to its due perfection, so that we may be without fear as to the day of final judgment; for as Jesus lived in this world, walking in supreme love to the Father and in mutual love to his people, so do we live in this world, and are therefore exempt from slavish fear and full of the sweet confidence of peace with God through Christ.

18. There is no fear in love; but perfect love casteth out fear: because fear hath torment. He that feareth is not made perfect in love.

19. We love him, because he first loved us.

Such love expels fear, in the sense of anxiety, the spirit of restless apprehension. Fear of this sort is tormenting; its presence testifies that the soul is not yet perfect in love, for love surely begets confidence. Spontaneously a sweet confidence will spring up in the soul, and you can not be afraid of the God whom you honestly, deeply love.

In v. 19—the reasoning underlying the word "*because*" may be understood in either of two somewhat different senses; one comparatively narrow; the other more broad and general. The narrow makes it the mere love of gratitude, as I gratefully love one who gives me favors, and because of those favors. The more broad relation puts the manifested love of God for men, in the order of nature and causation, *before* the love we bear to God. While we were yet enemies Christ died for us. "We have known and believed the love that God hath to us" (v. 16) and this love has subdued the enmity of our hearts toward him; laid the foundation in the sacrifice of his Son for our pardon and peace with God, and hence for all the love of human souls toward their loving Father.——Thus all our love for him has *followed his*—comes after it in the order of nature; is wholly indebted to God's love for the provisions which have made pardon possible and for the influences which have subdued our enmity, melted our hardness, and molded us to responsive love.——This broad view of the relation of God's prior love to our posterior love seems to me most in harmony with the scope of this chapter.

20. If a man say, I love God, and hateth his brother, he is a liar: for he that loveth not his brother whom he hath seen, how can he love God whom he hath not seen?

21. And this commandment have we from him, That he who loveth God love his brother also.

The doctrine of John is that love of the brethren is one of the most decisive and most easily applied *tests* of true love to God. In this view of it he said (3: 14), "We *know* that we have passed from death unto life because we love the brethren." The same doctrine underlies the argument in 3: 18–21; If we love the brethren in deed and in truth, "we know that we are of the truth, and shall assure our hearts before him" (God); "for if our heart condemn us not" in this thing (a point determined with comparative ease and certainty), "then have we confidence toward God." Hence in view of this great and decisive test, "if a man say, I love God, and hateth his brother, he is a liar"—he ought to know better; probably, in so plain a case, he does, and therefore purposely affirms what he knows can not be true—not so much self-deceived as a real deceiver.

In the last clause of v. 20, John's philosophy seems to be that *seeing* in the order of nature precedes loving, since seeing represents the most perfect knowledge of character possible to us in our present state, and all true love rests on such knowledge of character. If then, having seen his brother, he yet hates him, how can he pretend to love God whom he has never seen? If your heart were tuned to love; if the Spirit of loving were there, ye would certainly love your Christian brother. Not loving him, it is more than vain to pretend you love God whom of course you know less perfectly than your brother.——Hence the pith and force of the great commandment: If ye love God, love also your brother who is one of God's children.

CHAPTER V.

Following the same general line of thought as in the previous chapter, John would show Christians how they may *know* they love God;—in his own words (v. 13)—" that ye may *know* that ye have eternal life, and that ye may believe on the name of the Son of God." Incidentally, he speaks also of the blessedness of being sons of God, and of this assured confidence as to our relationship to him.

1. Whosoever believeth that Jesus is the Christ is born of God: and every one that loveth him that begat loveth him also that is begotten of him.

Real faith in Jesus as the Christ is proof of the new birth; none but the new-born have it. Such souls, new-born to God, naturally love their divine Father, and consequently love all his spiritual children. Loving God as their Father, they love all who stand in like relation to this loving Father. This is the well-known law of the human family through all ages. The love of father and mother begets love to the brothers and sisters, standing in the same common relation, and born into the fellowship of the same mutual love.

2. By this we know that we love the children of God, when we love God, and keep his commandments.
3. For this is the love of God, that we keep his commandments: and his commandments are not grievous.

Noticeably the usual order is here reversed; for whereas John has been wont to make love of brethren the proof of true love to God, here he makes love to God and the keeping of his commandments the proof for the genuineness of our love to the brethren.——As usual, keeping God's commandments is accounted the evidence of love to God. Jesus had taught this most fully and repeatedly (*e. g.* John 14: 15, 21, 23, 24, and 15: 10, 14).

"His commandments are not grievous"—can not be, coming from such a source, for they come from the kindest and most loving of Fathers;—are not in their nature, for they enjoin only love and good-will, which, the heart being right, are of all things most delightful;—are not therefore in the conscious experience of the obedient, for they find all true obedience supremely joyous—a burden (if it may be called such) delightfully borne. The service of love is a perpetual charm to the loving heart. "It is more blessed to give than to receive." Blessed are they who try it, for they shall know it, as no theorizing can set it forth.

4. For whatsoever is born of God overcometh the world: and this is the victory that overcometh the world, *even* our faith.
5. Who is he that overcometh the world, but he that believeth that Jesus is the Son of God?

Note in these verses the logic of their connection, introduced by "*for*" in the sense of *because*. The reason why we keep his commandments and do not find them "grievous," is that every thing born of God conquers the world. Observe next the use of *whatso*ever instead of *whoso*ever—the neuter pronoun in place of the more usual and natural masculine. The same usage appears in the gospel of John (6: 39, and 17: 2); "This is the will of him that sent me, that of every *thing* which he has given me, I should lose nothing." "Thou hast given him power as to all flesh that every *thing* thou hast given him he should give eternal life to them." The neuter seems to be chosen as bearing more decisively the sense of universality—absolutely *all* in its totality.

"Overcometh," translates the common Greek word for being victorious, gaining the victory, which has the ring of war, battle, triumph. John has used it in this epistle before, *e. g.* of his Christian young men (2: 13, 14) who had conquered ("overcome") the Evil One; also of his converts—"little children," he calls them—as withstanding successfully the lying spirits, false prophets, who had assailed them (4: 4).

What, then, does John affirm here? That every soul, really new-born to God, becomes victorious over the world; and, being thus victorious, keeps God's commandments and finds them not "grievous." When the power of the world over the heart is broken, we obey God's commandments with ease and delight—find them no burden.

How is this victory over the world achieved? John has but one answer—*by faith*, which he explains to be "believing that Jesus is the Son of God," and of course taking hold of his strength as such. *Ye can conquer the world* because Jesus *can give* you this victory, and will, if ye trust him by faith for the help ye need. First, John affirms this; then boldly challenges every opponent to show a case of such victory over the world achieved by any other force than this. Let all the human philosophies be invoked, or all the educational forces, or all the social powers; can they produce one human soul lifted by their training, and by their boasted forces, into real victory over the world? Such I take to be a fair exposition of these precious words.——Will the reader accept the suggestion that this truth is in the best sense intensely, gloriously, *practical?* It comes to us in our moral weakness; finds us encompassed with temptations from without; weakened perhaps by moral defeats from within; put to hard conflicts against many a subtle, stubborn foe, and sometimes not a little discouraged;—yet what does it say? Its words are not many, but they are wonderfully pregnant with meaning:—"*victory over the world*"; "*victory through faith in the Son of God*"*!* The truth put into these few words meets our case perfectly. Let it scatter our fears to the winds, and lift our souls into the calm assurance of trust, peace, victory!

Some readers will ask how these verses bear upon the question of a sinless Christian experience in this life.——To meet this question briefly, I suggest—(1) The passage must be treated in the same way as the analogous passages (that above 3: 4, and that below 5: 18): "Whosoever is born of God doth not commit sin," etc. Much if not all that was said in exposition of those words is pertinent here.——(2) Whatever John means by "overcoming the world," he declares to be the experience, not of a few only of God's children, but of all. He seems to have no thought of two classes of real Christians—one sanctified, and the other not sanctified. All that he embraces under the words—"overcome the world"—he represents as the common experience of all those who are truly new-born to God.——(3) It is supposable that in his age professed Christians were more positive in character than in our times; that the class unfortunately but too well known to us, who are so world-loving, so much conformed to its spirit and usages as to involve their piety in grave doubt, may have been in his time mostly unknown; or perhaps John would say of them as Paul of Demas—"hath forsaken me, having loved this present world," and therefore would not take them at all into account as having been born of God. Be this as it may, John does not seem to provide any place in the Christian fold for those who did not in some very positive sense gain the victory over the world. What he would say as to the imperfections in love and in service, in spirit and in life, among those who in the main were conquerors of the world, the flesh, and the devil, perhaps he has not told us. It does not appear that he had this point definitely in his mind, and it behooves us not to press his words too severely in our efforts to apply them to points which he may not have contemplated. Yet I am sure we may assume that very glaring imperfections; that very manifest sins; that positive, open conformity to the world in spirit and life, must not be forced into harmony with his words, "overcometh the world."

6. This is he that came by water and blood, *even* Jesus Christ; not by water only, but by water and blood. And it is the Spirit that beareth witness, because the Spirit is truth.

Water as related to the spiritual life is universally the symbol of moral cleansing; blood, of the propitiation wrought by Christ's atoning death. No other interpretation of these words can be thought of. The usage of the Scriptures—the Old Testament and the New alike—goes solid in support of this simple construction and application of these words. The reader may refer to my notes of John 3: 5 for the usage of the word "water."——The Spirit of truth bears witness to these great facts as to the work of Christ. It is his mission to teach these truths and to impress them in their living power on human hearts. His special witnessing agency came after Christ's ascension, in and after the scenes of the great Pentecost.

7. For there are three that bare record [*in heaven, the Father, the Word, and the Holy Ghost: and these three are one.*

8. *And there are three that bear witness in earth*] the Spirit, and the water, and the blood: and these three agree in one.

The words here put in italics and included within brackets are unquestionably spurious. No important manuscript contains them; none of the really ancient versions have them. They utterly lack the authorities requisite to entitle them to a place in the sacred text. No modern critic, versed in such questions, defends them as genuine.*

These words not only lack external (historical) authority; they are also entirely out of place in the Apostle's argument. He is here producing the testimonies for Christ which are brought out *on the earth*, before human eyes; not those which supposably might be brought forth *in heaven*. For, it may well be asked, What have his readers to do with the latter? And how can it be pertinent to ask them to believe in Jesus on the strength of witnessing testimonies to him which are seen or heard only in heaven?

9. If we receive the witness of men, the witness of God is greater: for this is the witness of God which he hath testified of his Son.

Following the course of thought in the antecedent context (vs. 6, 8) this "witness of God" must be specially that of the "Spirit" as borne emphatically after Christ's ascension. That God's testimony to his Son through the Spirit should be accounted greater than that of any man or even of all men is most obvious, and its weight ought to be resistless.

10. He that believeth on the Son of God hath the witness in himself: he that believeth not God hath made him a liar; because he believeth not the record that God gave of his Son.

To every believing soul there is a form of testimony unknown to the ungodly; peculiar to the believer; viz. that which he has *in himself.* He knows there is a joy and peace in believing which no delusion could ever give; he knows that through Jesus he has communion with God; he knows that for Jesus' sake God hears his prayer. He is deeply conscious of a spiritual

---

* According to Luecke (Eps. John, page 267-8), these words are found only in two Greek manuscripts, and those quite insignificant —one dating only from the sixteenth century, and the other without any weight of critical antiquity.——See also Neander on this Epistle, page 289.

power of the Holy Ghost, of which he can say (with Dr. Thomas Scott): "I could as soon believe there is no Holy Ghost as to doubt his personal presence in my heart" in connection with certain truths of God's word to which he referred.

In this self-conscious, witnessing testimony, he who is a stranger to God intermeddleth not. It lies wholly outside the pale of his conscious experience. He will know what it is only when, in the honest sincerity of his heart, he too believes on the Son of God.

The last clause of this verse looks toward external testimonies only. He who believes not makes God a liar, inasmuch as he virtually charges him with giving false testimony as to his Son. God's record as to his Son has been clear, explicit, and in point of significance, unmistakable. He therefore who will not believe this record, virtually arraigns the witness on the charge of falsehood.

11. And this is the record, that God hath given to us eternal life, and this life is in his Son.

12. He that hath the Son hath life; *and* he that hath not the Son of God hath not life.

All the exposition these plain words can need will be found in John's gospel in such passages as 17: 3, and 3: 36, and 5: 24–26. Our author borrows them substantially from his Master.

13. These things have I written unto you that believe on the name of the Son of God; that ye may know that ye have eternal life, and that ye may believe on the name of the Son of God.

John is a writer of definite aims. He knows what results he wishes to secure. He stated his object in his gospel history (20: 30, 31); he does the same as to this epistle here.

The most reliable authorities omit from this verse the last clause—"and that ye may believe on the name of the Son of God." This being omitted, the declared object of this epistle (if the statement refers to it in whole) is one—"that ye may know that ye have eternal life."——Under this knowing are two supposably distinct points, viz. (*a*) Knowing that this salvation through Christ means eternal life, provides for it, secures it; and (*b*) Knowing each for himself that he has a personal interest in this salvation. We have seen that this epistle brings out these personal proofs or tests of piety with remarkable fullness. No other portion of God's word makes this point so prominent. "Hereby we *know* that we dwell in him and he in us" (4: 13); "By this we *know* that we love the children of God," etc. (5: 2); "We *know* that we have passed from death unto life, because we love the brethren" (3: 14). Such is the strain of this epistle.

14. And this is the confidence that we have in him, that, if we ask any thing according to his will, he heareth us:

15. And if we know that he hear us, whatsoever we ask, we know that we have the petitions that we desired of him.

"Confidence"—yet the Greek word is more suggestive than this for the case of prayer, signifying the *freedom of speech* which is felt toward an intimate friend—the talking familiarly *with* one as when we know and can fully trust him. In Heb. 4: 16 our version puts it—"come with *boldness*"—but this should be taken in the good sense—a free utterance with no restraint of fear.

In the conditional clause—"If we ask any thing according to his will"—we need to inquire—Is it the *manner* of asking, or the *sort of thing asked*, that must be "according to his will"? The words *might* refer to either—*i. e.* as to the manner—whether in the name of Jesus or in our own; as to motive—whether for the glory of God or for our own; for the interests of God's kingdom, or to consume upon our lusts. Or on the other hand, it may refer specially to the thing asked—the blessing sought. The next verse, pursuing the same subject, saying—"If we know that he hear us, *whatsoever* we ask"—indicates that the latter is the sense intended. The thing we ask must be according to his will.

In its practical bearings, the question of unsurpassed interest as to prayer is that of its *limitations*. As put here the limitation is—"*according to his will*"—it must be for things in harmony with the will of God.——Now this limitation can never disturb or embarrass any true child of God in the least. For he will always say—I can desire nothing, can ask nothing save what is agreeable to my Father's will. I have unbounded confidence in both his love and his wisdom. I know his love will give me any thing I need if he can do it wisely, and I know his wisdom never can misjudge.——Moreover, if what seems to be my interest clashes with other greater interests, I withdraw my request. Let God be the judge; let him favor the more important interests, whatever may befall me and mine.——Yet further: In this passage John seems not aware that these words —"any thing according to his will"—amount to any limitation whatever. For, mark how he speaks in the next verse: "If we know that he hear us *whatever we ask*"—be it what it may. Observe, he does not say—Since the promise includes only things according to his will, we must be studiously careful to limit our requests to such things, and also our expectation of success;— this he does not say. Apparently it had escaped him that he had said any thing about this limitation. Really he does not seem to think it amounts to any restriction upon prayer. Probably as it lay in his mind, it was no restriction at all. Things out of harmony with the will of God have no place in prayer. We would neither ask them, nor have them if we might. Hence we come unembarrassed to the broad, magnificent, glorious conclusion—"We may know that we have the petitions that we desired of him." This is our confidence toward God in the matter of prayer. He hears us whatsoever we ask. We can not wish for any thing other than what is according to his will. Those things that are outside of his will—out of harmony with his wisdom and love—are not what we desire. If we were to ask for them it would be our mistake—made through misapprehension of his will; and we shall thank him forever for withholding these things. If we err in wisdom of judgment, we rejoice that he can never err, but will certainly set the matter right by withholding whatever it would be unwise to give.

16. If any man see his brother sin a sin *which is* not unto death, he shall ask, and he shall give him life for them that sin not unto death. There is a sin unto death: I do not say that he shall pray for it.

17. All unrighteousness is sin: and there is a sin not unto death.

These verses must be put in their natural connection with the two next preceding. John would say—Observe how this doctrine of prayer applies in reference to prayer for a sinning brother in the church. There are certain possible limitations here that should be understood. All classes of sinners can not be reached and saved by prayer. There are some sins that are naturally "*unto death;*" for such, no prayer can avail.——This case is described in terms so general, that no small difference of opinion has existed as to its true interpretation.——Some points however are made clear, *e. g.* that this sin is that of "a brother," doubtless a brother in the Christian fraternity. One who thought so much as John did of love for the brethren would have the deepest sorrow of his soul moved by the sin of a Christian brother, especially if it were of such sort as must greatly imperil his salvation.——Note also that this must be a sin, not of the secret thought merely, but of the visible life, for the "man" is supposed to "see" it. Further, the doctrine is that some sins are "unto death," while other sins are "not unto death;" and also, that this distinction is one which the praying brother can make. Christians are assumed to be able to classify the sins they may see in their brethren as to this point. If one sees the sin to be "not unto death," he shall pray, and life shall come in answer to his prayer. But if he judge it to be a sin "unto death," John says—"I do not say that he shall pray for it." I could not enjoin it as his duty. Perhaps this negative statement purposely leaves the praying brother to be governed by his own inward sense of the case, by the impulses of the Spirit within his own soul. But no inspired direction enjoins prayer in such a case, though possibly John implies—does not peremptorily forbid it. This latitude however can be at best only hypothetical.

Are we competent to go into this discrimination and draw the line, even proximately, between sins "unto death" and sins "not unto death"? The subject is too momentous to be left under any darkness if it be possible to get light upon it. If some sins are really "unto death," so manifestly mortal that no prayer for the sinner can be even advisable, much less available, then surely it were well to know what they are—and let all men take warning!

All light on this point—that *is* light—must come from God's word.——We readily recall the awfully solemn words of Jesus respecting the sin of blasphemy against the Holy Ghost (Matt. 12: 31, 32, and Mark 3: 28–30, and Luke 12: 10). They show that sinners *may* insult, traduce, malign, resist, the Holy Ghost, beyond possible forgiveness. That sin must surely be "unto death"!

The writer to the Hebrews (10: 26–29) defines a sin of similar sort in the words—"For if we sin willfully after we have received the knowledge of the truth, there remaineth no more sacrifice for sins, but a certain fearful looking for of judgment and fiery indignation." . . this sinner "having trodden under foot the Son of God and counted the blood of the covenant an unholy thing, and *done despite to the Spirit of grace.*"——Probably the same sin is in his eye in 6: 4–6; "For it is impossible for those who were once enlightened, etc., . . . if they shall fall away to renew them again unto repentance, seeing they crucify unto themselves the Son of God afresh, and put him to an open shame."——Peter held the same views of a certain class of apostates (2 Epis. 2: 20–22): "If after they have escaped the pollutions of the world through the knowledge of the Lord and Savior Jesus Christ, they are again entangled therein and overcome, the latter end is worse with them than the beginning," etc. We may remember that Paul recognizes a fearful "peradventure" on the point whether God will give certain opposers repentance (2 Tim. 2: 25, 26), and Peter expresses a similar doubt in the case of Simon Magus whether, even if he were to pray himself, this wicked thought of his heart could be forgiven;—"Pray God" (said he) "if, perhaps, it may be."

Underlying all these passages is the doctrine that some sinners, especially apostates once greatly enlightened, are past recovery. Their sins are "unto death." So far as appears from the descriptive points given of these cases the fatal elements are—the *degree of light sinned against*, and the *bearing of the sin against the Spirit of God*. The work of the Spirit in this world is so delicate, so vital, so sacred, and so much depends on his being treated with due honor, that God must and will shield him from insult and his work from dishonor, though it cost the eternal damnation of every blasphemer and contemner of his name!——Hence Christians are to judge what sins are unto death, mainly, I apprehend, by these tests—The light sinned against; and the abuse of the Spirit of God.

We ought to note that one object of John in these verses is the relief of praying Christians. For if they were to pray without regard to this discrimination, it might become terribly agonizing, perplexing, and even stumbling, to find that their prayer availed nothing, and not to understand the reason of this failure.

18. We know that whosoever is born of God sinneth not; but he that is begotten of God keepeth himself, and that wicked one toucheth him not.

19. *And* we know that we are of God, and the whole world lieth in wickedness.

Are these verses related in thought to the two next preceding? Usually, this should be assumed unless the nature of the case forbid. Being assumed here, we may put the logic of the connection thus:—Those, who "sin unto death" are not of those who have been "born of God." We know that those thus born to God do not sin fatally—"unto death." Every such new-born soul keepeth himself through grace, and that wicked one—the devil—toucheth him not. Wide as the poles apart are these two classes; we, Christians, are of God, made his sons by his regenerating grace: the whole world lieth in wickedness. The one class are under God's protecting hand; the other are under Satan.

20. And we know that the Son of God is come, and hath given us an understanding, that we may know him that is true; and we are in him that is true, *even* in his Son Jesus Christ. This is the true God, and eternal life.

21. Little children, keep yourselves from idols. Amen.

The great points of truth which "we *know*," and which have wrought these transformations of character and state in us—briefly put here—are—that the Son of God is come into our world; has given us an understanding of the true God; and has brought us into relations to God, best expressed by the words, "we are *in him.*"——Moreover, we are in him, the true God, by being in his Son Jesus Christ. First knowing and receiving his Son, we have come to know, receive, and love the Father. Being in the Father comes of first being in the Son. So intimate and so peculiar is the relation of the Father to the Son that we can scarcely distinguish even in thought the being in the Son from being in the Father who sent him.

On the clause—"This is the true God and eternal life," we meet the nice critical question whether the pronoun "this" refers to the Father, spoken of before as "him that is true," or to the Son.

In favor of referring it to the Son are these considerations:—(*a.*) That Son is the nearest antecedent. Usually this fact is decisive.——(*b.*) The Son is known in the writings of John as "the life;" (John 1: 4) "The *life* is the light of men;" and (1 John 1: 2) "The *life* was manifested;" "We show unto you the eternal life who was with the Father," etc. Thus we see that the Son is called not only "*the life*," but explicitly—"the eternal life."——(*c.*) A third consideration of great force is, that John having twice already in this one verse spoken of the Father as "the true One," *i. e.* of course—the true God, and having said this in most explicit, emphatic terms, there is not the least occasion to repeat it again. To do so adds nothing to the thought, but really weakens his statement.——Bear in mind John has said—The Son of God has come; he has made known to us the true One—the really true God. We have come to be in this true God—*i. e.* by first being in his Son. Having said all this, is it even supposable that John should close with saying—This personage whom I have called "the true One is the true God? Rather is not this his thought? This Jesus the Son who has thus revealed God to us and brought us into fellowship with him, is also himself really God and the Eternal Life.

The objections made to this construction are chiefly doctrinal: *i. e.* of this sort; This passage can not be construed to say that the Son is "the true God" because he *is* not and can not be. There is but one true God; and to make Jesus one is to make two.——John has not told us definitely how he would meet this objection, but has left us the fact with no attempt at metaphysical explanation.—From his silence on this point it is probably safe to infer that we shall need the light of a brighter world and perhaps the power of more acute, discriminating, comprehensive thought ere we shall "know the Almighty to perfection."

The closing words are—"Little children, keep yourselves from idols." Is this warning connected in thought with the subject then in hand? Perhaps so; perhaps not. In that age—idolatry being every-where about them—it could never be amiss to give this warning. Yet a certain connection is supposable—say with v. 19; "The whole world lieth in wickedness;" we who are of God must needs withstand idolatry on every side.——Or possibly with v. 20; We worship the Father as God; the Son also as the true God; beyond these, none. Beware of being drawn to the worship of idols.

INTRODUCTION

TO THE

SECOND AND THIRD EPISTLES OF JOHN.

These two short private letters are supposed to have been written by the aged Apostle John. One is addressed to a sister in the church whose proper name I take to have been Cyria [Gr. Kuria]; and the other to a brother (apparently a layman) whose name is given—Gaius. The residence of neither is given. We can only assume that both resided within what we may call John's diocese—within the circle of churches under his apostolic supervision, for with each he manifestly had some personal acquaintance; had seen them both before and hoped to again. Neither were poor in this world's goods, for both letters assume that they were exercising a somewhat large hospitality, receiving Christian strangers to their houses. Indeed, the special purpose of each letter assumed this—in the case of Cyria suggesting the danger and unwisdom of receiving into her house and to her hospitality men who brought some other doctrine than the truth in Jesus; and in the case of Gaius, that he should receive to his house, to his confidence and sympathy, certain traveling missionaries—perhaps self-sent—yet laboring for Christ's name and taking nothing of the Gentiles toward their support. Virtually therefore this was an apostolic certificate of Christian character and of recommendation to the confidence and aid of this hospitable and worthy lay brother.

Thus the object of these private letters is made quite plain from their contents.

As to the author of these letters—supposed to have been John the Apostle, let us inquire *on what grounds* they are ascribed to him.

His name is not here. The writer only calls himself

"the elder" (presbuteros), which may mean either an old man or an elder [officer] in the church. John lived to a great age; at the date of this writing was probably better known through all the churches of Asia Minor as *the aged one*, than by any other appellation. For some unknown reason John was always remarkably reserved in the use of his own name. He never gives it in his own writings. In a number of passages his gospel refers to himself, but never even whispers his own name John. The first epistle is entirely written without name. It would therefore be aside from his habit to give his name in these epistles.

The *historical evidence* that John wrote these epistles is peculiar;—I can not say defective or suspicious. By some of the early Fathers they were classed among what were technically called "*the antilegomena*," *i. e.* the disputed books. They did not from the very first obtain universal reception among the writings of Apostolic men.

But under the circumstances this fact does not in the least disparage their inspired authority. It is only what should be expected. For consider—They were merely private letters. They belonged to John's private correspondence with individual parties. If they had been written to a church, *e. g.* the Church of Ephesus, they would have come into notoriety at once. First read in the religious assemblies of that church and of course endorsed by them; then copied and sent to other churches, they would soon find their way into general confidence and use. But both these were *private* letters. Cyria and Gaius knew the writer; each welcomed John's letter, and doubtless kept it as a family treasure. But probably at first there was no demand on them to send their private correspondence to be read in public church assemblies. In fact the letters were not only private in their address but personal rather than public in their character. How they ever became known to the Christian public does not appear; doubtless it was a work of time. Not that they lacked merit, for they were indeed treasures, and by and by good men abroad came to know and appreciate them.——Most of the epistles in our New Testament were public in nature and intent, and consequently were introduced at once to public notice and confidence. Paul wrote four letters to individuals; but three of these were to young ministers (Timothy and Titus) in responsible positions, under every inducement to bring these letters before their churches. His letter to Philemon is the only one analogous to these two from John. But Philemon was in a prominent position, for there was a "church in his house" (v. 2), and he was personally known to a considerable circle of Paul's fellow-laborers (vs. 23, 24).——Hence that these two private letters from John should be rather slow in obtaining a general reception among inspired epistles is precisely what should be expected. Any different result would be *prima facie* suspicious.——The fact that their general reception took time testifies to the watchful care of those early churches in regard to admitting written documents into their canon of inspired writings.

Ultimately the historical evidence in favor of these epistles became abundant and most satisfactory. The church and school at Alexandria (Egypt) indorsed them strongly. Clement, Origen, Dyonisius—successively at the head of that great Theological School—received them. There is a certain life-likeness in the indorsement given by "Bishop Alexander of Alexandria" who, in a letter missive to the bishops of his diocese, justifies the excommunication of Arius and his adherents by a direct appeal to 2 John 10.* So also in a synod held at Carthage under Cyprian, on the then important question of baptizing heretics, one Aurelius, Bishop of Chullabi, gave his vote in the words of 2 John 9, saying—"John in his own epistle lays down this doctrine, saying," etc. †——The testimony of Irenæus, whose early residence was in Asia Minor, is emphatic and decisive;—"For John, a disciple of the Lord, hurls his condemnation ['damnationem'] against these [heretics], nor would he allow a God-speed ['ave'] to be said to them," etc.

Much more testimony might be adduced: let this suffice.

Of the internal evidence that these letters were from the same John who wrote the gospel and the first epistle, it can scarcely be necessary to say a word. Every reader will see the sentiments, the phrases, and the loving heart of the same John. No other Apostle wrote so; indeed, no other man.

* Luecke, pg. 298. † Luecke, pg. 299.

SECOND EPISTLE OF JOHN.

1. The elder unto the elect lady and her children, whom I love in the truth; and not I only, but also all they that have known the truth;

2. For the truth's sake, which dwelleth in us, and shall be with us for ever.

3. Grace be with you, mercy, *and* peace, from God the Father, and from the Lord Jesus Christ, the Son of the Father, in truth and love.

As said in the introduction, I take the word translated "lady" to be a proper and not a common noun—the personal name of this Christian sister, Cyria.——"Elect" in the Christian sense—one of God's chosen, beloved. The same word is used of her sister (v. 13), some of whose children were then with the apostle.——"Love *in the truth*"—might in some connections be taken adverbially in the sense of *truly*. But here the emphatic repetition of the word "truth"—"all who have known *the truth;*" "for the *truth's* sake;" and at the close of the salutation—"*in truth* and love," and in v. 4, "walking *in the truth*"—strongly support another construction—substantially of this sort;—love in the interests of truth; in the fellowship of the truth; for the truth's sake.——Throughout John's writing we are impressed by the prominence given to *love*—love to Christ, love to the Father, love to the brethren. How wonderfully does this sentiment live and glow in his soul and this word distill in fragrance from his lips! But here we see a like prominence given to *truth*. Certainly in his thought "*truth is in order to goodness*"—a necessary means to that end; at the very foundation of all intelligent love. The love he thinks of is not sentimentalism; is not a mere emotional good nature; but is an intelligent benevolence, which seeks for all men the good that is seen to be the highest and best possible; which intelligently sees a perfect God at the head of the universe, and giving him the supreme love of the heart, loves all his creatures for his sake, following his high example, obeying his perfect will. Thus love in creatures, being at once intelligent and moral, rests on the *basis of truth*. What we know and believe of the Infinite God—Father, Son and Spirit—inspires and directs all rational love of man to man; and pre-eminently of Christian man to his fellow-Christians.——John wrote this epistle under a quickened sense of the priceless value of Christian truth, this sense being wrought into intense feeling by the dangerous influence of men who were undermining the foundations of the gospel system. What would become of love if men were to deny that Jesus Christ is come in the flesh? What can that love be good for which knows no Jesus—which has dishonored his name—which has stricken down all the moral forces toward pure benevolence, which have come to us in the revelation of God's great love to lost men in giving his only Son? When the vital truths of the gospel, and indeed of all revealed religion, are thus slaughtered, what can be left us? What are men's professions of love worth after they have stricken down and blotted out all the great love-inspiring truths of Christianity?

4. I rejoiced greatly that I found of thy children walking in truth, as we have received a commandment from the Father.

5. And now I beseech thee, lady, not as though I wrote a new commandment unto thee, but that which we had from the beginning, that we love one another.

6. And this is love, that we walk after his commandments. This is the commandment, That, as ye have heard from the beginning, ye should walk in it.

This Christian sister had children. John had learned that they were walking in truth according to the Father's commandment, and rejoiced in this exceedingly. Such a mother does a glorious service for God, for the church, for mankind. We may notice that John has not fallen in with the notions sadly prevalent in the early church, of a superior sanctity in celibacy, virginity, and the monastic life. He believes in virtuous mothers and in truth-loving, truth-abiding children.——We notice the same staple Christian graces put forward here as in John's gospel and first epistle:—Christian love of the brethren, and obeying God's commandments—the essence, proof, and manifestation of true love.

7. For many deceivers are entered into the world, who confess not that Jesus Christ is come in the flesh. This is a deceiver and an antichrist.

8. Look to yourselves, that we lose not those things which we have wrought, but that we receive a full reward.

9. Whosoever transgresseth, and abideth not in the doctrine of Christ, hath not God. He that abideth in the doctrine of Christ, he hath both the Father and the Son.

The truth of God was vigorously assailed; false prophets and teachers were abroad in force. Their doctrines are sufficiently defined; they denied the real incarnation of the Son of God. Whether so intended by themselves or not, this was equivalent to renouncing the whole gospel scheme. There was no Jesus, no Savior for lost men if Christ had not come in the flesh.——These deceivers did not hold but rejected the true doctrine of Christ (v. 9). Of course there was no God of truth left to their system, for they had made the true God a liar by not believing his testimony as to his Son. Take care now (John would say) lest, seduced into these fatal errors of doctrine, ye lose all that ye have wrought through years of gospel labor, and fail utterly of any reward.

10. If there come any unto you, and bring not this doctrine, receive him not into *your* house, neither bid him God speed:

11. For he that biddeth him God speed is partaker of his evil deeds.

John understood that Oriental rights of hospitality were held most dear—not to say sacred; that it would be a hard thing—a stern test of principle, to turn from your door any well-appearing stranger who might present himself as your friend; but John is inflexible; the bottom truths of the gospel are more to him than the demands of hospitality. Therefore, he enjoins—If any man come to your door, seeking admittance to your hospitality, and begging your good offices in his behalf, yet if he bring not this true doctrine of Christ but discard it—receive him not into your house; give him not even the common friendly salutation (God speed and bless you), for to do even this is to make yourself responsible for his mischief—is to assume a share with him in all the evil he may do. For this some may disown you; but I implore you be true to Christ and to the cause of heavenly truth, however much this firmness may displease men who have no gospel truth in their souls, or however it may seem to dishonor the claims of hospitality.

12. Having many things to write unto you, I would not *write* with paper and ink: but I trust to come unto you, and speak face to face, that our joy may be full.

13. The children of thy elect sister greet thee. Amen.

I have much to say—more than I can write; but these things are too vital to be postponed;—so much must be said.——The burden then pressing on the heart of this noble patriarch is lifted when he has admonished this sister, tenderly, solemnly, to stand firm against those deceivers and antichrists who were discarding the true faith of Christ.

THIRD EPISTLE OF JOHN.

1. The elder unto the well beloved Gaius, whom I love in the truth.

2. Beloved, I wish above all things that thou mayest prosper and be in health, even as thy soul prospereth.

"Love in the truth," as in 2 John 1—love in the common bonds of the gospel of truth, in behalf of the truth and in its precious sympathies.——Frail of body, but strong and noble of soul, Gaius was a rare man. The men are few in our world for whom this chief prayer of John for Gaius would be appropriate —that their body might be as vigorous as their souls are healthy, thriving and strong. In the case of most men this prayer needs to be reversed, and put thus:—I wish above all things that thy soul may thrive in piety as thy body does in its healthful vigor.

3. For I rejoiced greatly, when the brethren came and testified of the truth that is in thee, even as thou walkest in the truth.

4. I have no greater joy than to hear that my children walk in truth.

Gaius seems to have been one of John's spiritual children. Full of love for Jesus and his truth as John's heart was, it should not surprise us to hear him say—"I have no greater joy than to hear that my children walk in the truth."——To walk in the truth is to put gospel truth to its proper use by making it govern all the commonest deeds of life, even all human activities—by fundamentally controlling the whole heart, *i. e.* the will. A blessed earthly life is this which is shaped evermore by the behests of the truth as it is in Jesus.

5. Beloved, thou doest faithfully whatsoever thou doest to the brethren, and to strangers;

6. Which have borne witness of thy charity before the

(369)

church: whom if thou bring forward on their journey after a godly sort, thou shalt do well:

7. Because that for his name's sake they went forth, taking nothing of the Gentiles.

8. We therefore ought to receive such, that we might be fellow helpers to the truth.

Testifying warmly to the noble hospitality and hearty good will of Gaius to his Christian brethren and even to those who were personally strangers, John now commends to his confidence and aid certain missionary brethren going forth for the work of Christ, and in so far at their own charge that they "took nothing of the Gentiles." To help such men was to be fellow-helpers to the truth—a consideration which such a man as Gaius would surely appreciate.——In v. 6 our translators have expressed the Greek word which every where means *love* by the word "charity." Neither they nor we should restrict the sense to almsgiving. It is here rather that full-souled love which may indeed develop itself in giving alms, yet not in this way only, but in every other way possible.

9. I wrote unto the church: but Diotrephes, who loveth to have the pre-eminence among them, receiveth us not.

10. Wherefore, if I come, I will remember his deeds which he doeth, prating against us with malicious words: and not content therewith, neither doth he himself receive the brethren, and forbiddeth them that would, and casteth *them* out of the church.

Even the venerable John encountered opposition in his own churches. The spirit of this opponent John puts in one Greek word which it may be hard to match perfectly in our tongue; yet we might call him a *power-loving* man, whose master passion was to *be first* every-where. Consequently he must needs oppose whatever counter-worked his ruling passion. This Diotrephes would not receive those whom John commended to the church by letter. They not being *his* men, nor working under his control, he was bound to oppose. Worse still, he slandered the aged apostle; would neither receive the brethren he sent nor let the church receive them, and seems to have had power enough to expel them. John writes:—"If I should come, I will remember his deeds"—said apparently with reference to some infliction of physical evil—judgment from God—a form of miraculous power which seems to have been lodged in the hands of the apostles to meet cases of this sort.

11. Beloved, follow not that which is evil, but that which is good. He that doeth good is of God: but he that doeth evil hath not seen God.

This is the general rule or law for the Christian life, resting on eternal foundations. Doing good is godlike; the doer of evil has not known God. There is nothing godlike in his work; no influence from God has moved him that way. It is worse than vain for him to pretend (as Diotrephes had doubtless done) that he was serving God.

12. Demetrius hath good report of all *men*, and of the truth itself: yea, and we *also* bear record; and ye know that our record is true.

Why Demetrius is spoken of here does not appear clearly. Probably he had had trouble with Diotrephes; perhaps had been expelled from the church by his means. If so, this would account for John's indorsing his character so decidedly.

13. I had many things to write, but I will not with ink and pen write unto thee:

14. But I trust I shall shortly see thee, and we shall speak face to face. Peace *be* to thee. *Our* friends salute thee. Greet the friends by name.

The full heart of the aged apostle finds but meager and tame expression through ink and pen. He hopes to see this dear brother soon, and therefore closes here with heartiest Christian salutations.

Dear old man! It may have been a slow and painful labor for that trembling hand of thine to put on paper so many blessed words as have come to us in thy gospel history and in these three letters. We thank thee for them all! A heavenly fragrance breathes forth through them from thy warm, loving heart. Precious witnesses for the true doctrine of Jesus are they, which the Christian world could never afford to spare. Most and best of all —they give us the words, the spirit, the life and the love of Jesus Christ as manifest in the flesh, making it seem to the thoughtful readers thereof all along the ages that they have been introduced and made personally acquainted with Jesus himself. Such written words are a precious legacy, a heavenly benediction to mankind.

EXCURSUS I.

On the Divinity of Christ as related to the Trinity and Unity of God.

The very opening of John's gospel springs this great question upon us. The term Logos ["Word"], beyond all controversy, designates that pre-existent Personage who became incarnate in the human Jesus. John affirms of this Logos these several facts: That he existed from eternity; that in that eternal state he existed *with* God; and that he *was* God. Also that all things were made by him, and yet, that this truly divine Personage "became *flesh*," *i. e.* in the sense of entering into mysterious union with man; and so "dwelt among us," revealing the glory of the only-begotten Son of God.

In the outset let it be premised that I use the terms *person* or *personage* to avoid circumlocution, and moreover as being the nearest approximation to the true idea, yet not thereby implying that absolute and perfect distinction which the term indicates when used of men as related to each other.*

---

*The question often arises—Inasmuch as the word "person" is admitted to be defective and sometimes misleading, why not use some better word? Why not get a perfectly descriptive term—one which will give the exact sense with no liability to misapprehension?

The answer is—No human language can furnish such a word. This impossibility rests mainly on the fact that neither our own human nature nor any other created nature fully known to us furnishes any analogy to this triune relationship. Therefore human speech furnishes no word to express it, or the parties to it.——All human language is of necessity built on known human relations, experiences, knowledges; and therefore supplies us with no words for things that have no human analogy.

I have said—"rests mainly" on the absence of analogy in human nature. Let me add that immense difficulties embarrass all our attempts to define this triune relationship by any circumlocutions of speech, because the light from revelation on this point comes in the form of statements which *assume* and *imply* rather than *define* and *affirm* metaphysically what it is. For example: "The glory which I had with thee before the world was" (John 17: 5) assumes and implies some distinction between "I" and "thee," but does not define it metaphysically.

A certain undefined distinction, expressed by this qualified use of the word "person" exists between Father, Son, and Spirit. As we shall see in the progress of the discussion, each is manifestly represented as being truly divine, and yet as in some sense distinct from the others.

How can these facts be reconciled with the unity of God? How, on any laws of being known to us, can the Logos be himself God and be also "*with* God" as John most clearly affirms, and yet there be but one God? How shall the Bible doctrine of the Trinity of persons in the Godhead be adjusted to the Bible doctrine of the unity of God?

It is vital to any practical good from this investigation that we hold firmly in mind that it is the *Bible doctrine* of the Trinity and nothing else or other than this, that we have occasion to explain and defend. If we are to have any theory at all as to this triune distinction of persons, we need one which will apply to the language of the Scriptures—to the modes of expression found in them touching the relations of the Father to the Son and of the Son to the Father, and of either or both to the Spirit. For we can know nothing of Christ's real divinity save from the Scriptures; or, more comprehensively stated, we can know nothing of a Trinity of any sort in the Godhead except what comes to us in this written revelation. It is therefore most appropriate to begin with the inquiry: *How do the Scriptures present this subject?* What words and statements do we find here which seem to assume and imply that special distinction in the Godhead which we indicate by the term "person"?

Let us then group together at least the more important passages which involve this distinction.

Obviously we should omit from this group all those passages in which the human nature of Jesus is made prominent. For, plainly, it might be suppposed that a divine effluence, analogous to that of the Holy Ghost upon all Christians, might have dwelt in the man Jesus, and yet this indwelling of the Spirit would fall entirely short of implying real divinity. It would involve nothing like distinct personality in the being of God.

Foremost in our group of test passages we may fitly place the opening verses of John's gospel—already brought before the reader. The Logos—the same who was made flesh by a human birth of the virgin Mary—existed from eternity; is declared to have been *with God;* and to be really God. Of this last named point, the highest sort of proof is given in the fact that "all things were made by him" as the absolute and universal Creator.

Again: "The Father loveth the Son, and hath given all things into his hand" (John 3: 35). This "giving of all things into his hand" is nothing less than the investiture with supreme dominion (See Matt. 28: 18), such as no merely human being could hold and wield; such as must imply attributes perfectly divine.——
Let it be noted here that this gift of all power made by the Father to the Son involves the very distinction which we call per-

sonal. For the meaning can not be that the Father gives all things into *his own* hands; but rather that he gives them to another than himself—even to the Son. So also the love of the Father for the Son—apparently put here as a reason for investing him with supreme dominion—involves some sort of distinction of person. Such language is often used of human fathers giving property or dominion to their sons—a fact which must be held to interpret these inspired words.

Analogous to this is the passage (John 5: 22, 23): "The Father hath committed all judgment unto the Son"—a responsibility which requires divine attributes and a conveyance of prerogative which assumes distinct personality—both points being made the stronger by the declared purpose or object in view; viz. "that all should honor the Son even as they honor the Father. He that honoreth not the Son, honoreth not the Father who hath sent him."——Also John 7: 62: "What if ye see the Son of man ascend up where he was before?"—in which words the speaker thinks of himself as being in heaven before his manifestation in human flesh, his ruling consciousness being that of his divine nature. The same ruling consciousness—the divine eclipsing the human—appears often in the words of Christ; *e. g.* John 17: 5: "The glory which I had with thee before the world was;" the ego [I] being none other than the pre-existent divine Personage—unquestionably thought of as distinct from the Father—"which I had with Thee."——See also John 17: 24: "For thou lovedst me before the foundation of the world."——Also John 8: 58: To the question put by the Jews; "Hast thou—being not yet fifty years old—seen Abraham?" Jesus answered; "Before Abraham was, I am"—"am" in the sense which assumes perpetual and changeless existence, being borrowed apparently from the passage in Moses (Ex. 3: 14): "*I am* hath sent me," etc.——Here also the "I" must contemplate his pre-existent personality.

Note also the numerous passages in which Christ claims to have seen and known the Father (*e. g.* John 6: 46, and 1: 18, and Matt. 11: 27); also to be the only Personage capable of revealing the Father, and moreover, really revealing him: "No man hath seen God at any time; the only begotten Son who is in the bosom of the Father, he hath declared him" (1: 18). Also this statement;—"I came forth from the Father, and am come into the world: again, I leave the world and go to the Father" (John 16: 28). In the first clause here the divine is the ruling consciousness; in speaking thus of himself, his thought is upon the divine in his nature rather than the human. He speaks not as man but as God; yet certainly of himself as God, not in any such sense as would comprehend *the whole of God* and ignore all distinction of Father from Son.

Note also how the Son classes himself with the Father (as in John 14: 23): "If a man love me he will keep my words; and my Father will love him, and *we will come* unto him and make our abode with him"—language which assumes virtual equality with God, and which also involves some sort of real distinction of personality.

A similar implication appears in the different methods in which Christ promises the gift of the Spirit: "I will pray the Father and *he* will give you another Comforter" (John 14: 16); compared with this: "When the Comforter is come whom *I* will send unto you from the Father" (John 15: 26). Here the agents—"I," "he" or "the Father," appear as distinct persons, yet each as really divine; each interchangeably thought of as doing the same thing, and therefore as really exercising divine prerogatives.

In John's first epistle we have similar expressions: "That which was from the beginning . . . which we have looked upon and our hands have handled of the Word of life"; . . . "We show unto you the Eternal Life who was *with the Father*, and was manifested to us," etc. (1 John 1: 1, 2).——Also this: "We are in him that is true, even in his Son Jesus Christ. This is the true God and eternal life" (1 John 5: 20).

Turning from John to Paul, I adduce first a passage in which the Christian doctrine is put in contrast with heathen polytheism (1 Cor. 8: 4–6): "We know that an idol is nothing in the world, and that there is no other God but one. For though there be that are called gods, whether in heaven or in earth (as there be gods many and lords many); But unto us there is but one God, the Father, of whom are all things and we in him; and one Lord Jesus Christ, by whom are all things, and we by him." Here a broad line of distinction is drawn between the Father and the Lord Jesus Christ; yet not such a distinction in Paul's view as precluded him from affirming that while heathen idolaters have "gods many," Christians have but one God. The relation of all things that exist, to the Father on the one hand, and to the Lord Jesus Christ on the other—expressed here by "of" ($\varepsilon\xi$) as to the Father, and by the preposition "by" (dia) as to the Lord Jesus Christ, suggests the Father as the infinite original Source of all created being, and the Son as mediately the Agent by whom this creation is wrought. Yet this mediate agency must involve the attributes of real divinity. Paul does not tell us how he harmonizes the doctrine of but one God with this manifestly distinct personality of the Father from the Lord Jesus Christ, coupled with the actual creatorship of the latter, carrying with it, as it must, his real and true divinity.

Let us also note some passages in which Paul seems to indicate his conception of a Trinity in God (*e. g.* 1. Cor. 12: 4–6): "Now there are diversities of gifts but the same Spirit; and there are differences of administration but the same Lord; and there are diversities of operations but it is the same God who worketh all in all." Here "the Spirit," "the Lord," and "God" are each thought of as doing essentially the same thing; prosecuting the same work; each and all conveying spiritual gifts to the people of God.——Most fully in harmony with this is his form of what is known as "the Apostolic benediction" (2 Cor.

13: 14): "The grace of the Lord Jesus Christ and the love of God and the communion of the Holy Ghost be with you all." The reader will have a sufficient comment on this passage if he will suppose another of Paul's epistles to close thus: "The grace of the one God, and the good will of the angel Gabriel, and the blessing of the Holy Virgin (or of the great Apostle Peter) be with you all."

It deserves remark that the doctrine of distinct personality in the Godhead, coupled with the true divinity of the Son, is not based on certain isolated passages, wrested out of their connection and so misinterpreted. For in some instances the doctrine is found wrought into the entire scope of the context, and elaborately argued as the very point to be proved. See for example the entire first chapter to the Hebrews: "God . . . hath in these last days spoken unto us by his Son, whom he hath appointed heir of all things; by whom also he made the worlds; who being the brightness of his glory, and the express image of his person, and upholding all things by the word of his power, when he had by himself purged our sins, sat down on the right hand of the Majesty on high;" all which involves distinct personality and also real divinity. Then the writer places this exalted Son in contrast with the angels, and labors to prove not only that he is greater than they, but that he is really divine and they are not; that he is called God (vs. 8, 9) as they are not; that he laid the foundations of the earth—a work never done by them; and that angels are required to worship the Son, obviously with such worship as is appropriate to no being lower than God.

This group of passages (and such as these) present the conditions that must be met by any theory proposed for the purpose of harmonizing distinct personality as between the Father, the Logos, and the Holy Ghost, with the doctrine of one God only.

Let it now be carefully observed:

(1) That this personality is put, not in modified, qualified terms, as if the speakers were consciously using language in some other than its ordinary sense; but in plain, unqualified phrase—such as, if used, of various men, would by no means suggest anything less than entirely distinct persons.

(2) That these persons are represented as performing distinct works, exercising diverse functions and each his own—functions moreover that are truly divine; *e. g.* the Father usually as originating the great scheme of redemption—("God so loved the world that he sent his Son," etc.; "We have one God *of* whom are all things," etc.); the Son as creating all things; becoming heir of all things; as being the universal Lord and final Judge; and the Holy Ghost as a spiritual force, wielding a power of truth for moral regeneration in human souls.——[As bearing upon the precise question now before us, it is not pertinent to introduce the special functions of the Son *considered as incarnate*. His human nature, his sufferings unto death, the atonement thus

made—all that rests upon the incarnation proper—should logically be omitted.]

(3) These persons are represented as having a distinct moral character—to such an extent distinct as to become objects of mutual love to each other; *e. g.* "For thou lovedst me before the foundation of the world" (John 17: 24). In this passage, the "me" can be no other than the Logos, for "before the world was," the incarnation had not taken place. There was no human nature included under "*me*," but only the divine.——Either loving or being loved involves the possession of all the grand elements of a moral being. Moreover it can scarcely be necessary to suggest that the words—"*Thou* lovedst *me*"—express distinct personality in terms most clear and decisive. Who can express personality in stronger and less ambiguous phrase?

Now obviously, any theory proposed for the purpose of harmonizing these scriptural representations with the unity of God must meet these conditions; otherwise it is valueless.

At this point, and before we proceed to name and discuss the various theories which look toward this harmony, it seems important to bring under brief review a sample at least of the passages which teach or imply the unity of God. It behooves us to inquire *how* this unity is affirmed; to what extent it is put in contrast with polytheism, and how far (if at all) it may seem to be affirmed in such connections and relations as bear upon [or if it be so *against*] distinct and equal personality.

Passages from the Old Testament come first in order; *e. g.* Deut. 4: 35, 39, and 6: 4, 5, 14. "The Lord, he is God; there is none else beside him," etc. "Hear, O Israel, the Lord our God *is one Lord*," etc. "Ye shall not go after other gods," etc. Compare also Isa. 44: 8, and 42: 8, and Ps. 86: 8, 10, and 89: 6, and Jer. 10: 6.——It is the less important to cite and expound these passages, inasmuch as they do not appear to bear purposely against or even upon the tripersonality of God; but are leveled against the giant delusion of the ages—viz. polytheism—the indefinite multiplication of gods, in diversified grades, in various spheres of activity, of countless nationalities and basest morals.

Turning to the prominent New Testament passages, note first John 17: 3: "This is life eternal, that they may know *Thee, the only true God*, and Jesus Christ whom thou hast sent."——The noticeable thing in this passage, and in the prayer of which it forms a part, is that while it seems to affirm the absolute unity of God in most explicit terms, it yet equally seems to imply and therefore to hold the true divinity of the Logos, and also his distinct personality. For the knowledge of Jesus Christ as that in which eternal life consists is put on the same footing with the knowledge of "*Thee*, the only true God." We find also among the words of this prayer, these: "The glory which I had with thee before the world was" (v. 5); "They have known surely that I came forth from Thee" (v. 8); "Thou lovedst me before the foundation of the world" (v. 24); "The world hath not known Thee, but I have known Thee" (v. 25); "I have declared unto them thy name," etc. (v. 26). In the same prayer, therefore, Christ seems to affirm the unity (shall we say *absolute* unity) of God, and also to imply for himself an eternal pre-existence; the coming forth from God into the world; the being loved of the Father before the foundation of the world; and the perfect knowledge of God—each and all of these facts being such as can be affirmed or implied of no one who is less than divine. Must we not therefore infer that his conception of the unity of God did not in his mind conflict with his own assumption of these divine attributes and relations?

The passage (1 Cor. 8: 4–6) has been referred to above. It is remarkable for its very explicit antithesis with polytheism ("though there be that are called gods, as there are gods many, and lords many"); also for the somewhat close definition of the Christian doctrine—"the one God, the Father, of whom are all things and we in him; and one Lord Jesus Christ, by whom are all things and we by him."——It is not easy to see how a somewhat distinct personality—personality of some sort—could be more definitely expressed than it is here. The only real question upon this passage is whether the creatorship, attributed here to the Lord Jesus Christ, involves true divinity. Did the Logos create by means of a derived and delegated power, of such sort as might be exercised by a being of derived existence and of attributes less than divine?——Bearing against such a supposition, we have the uniform strain of the Scriptures which in numerous passages appeal to creatorship as the highest proof of true divinity. See Heb. 3: 4: "He that built all things is God." Jer. 10: 11, 12: "Thus shall ye say to them" (idolatrous heathen)—"The gods that have *not* made the heavens and the earth, even they shall perish from the earth and from under these heavens." "He" (the true God) "hath made the earth by his power," etc. Ps. 96: 5: "For all the gods of the nations are idols; but the Lord made the heavens." See also Isa. 42: 5, and 44: 24.

It seems therefore undeniable that our finite minds are expected to accord the attributes of true divinity to him who is revealed to us in the Scriptures as universal creator.

In Eph. 4: 5, 6, occurs an exhortation to Christian unity, based on the oneness of all the vital elements of the gospel scheme—there being in it but one Lord [Jesus]; one sort of saving faith; "one God and Father of all" Christians (Jew or Gentile), "who is above all, through all, in all." If there were many gods, there might be as much foundation for many diverse sects or sorts of worshipers as there would be for any one sect. Perfect *moral* unity between the Lord Jesus and the Father is vital to Paul's argument in this passage: such a unity is every-where implied; often affirmed.——Over against this, Jesus is never represented to be Lord [of all] in any such sense as conflicts with these affirmations as to "one God and Father of all."

In 1 Thess. 1: 9, Paul wrote—"Ye turned to God from idols to serve the living and true God, and to wait for his Son from heaven," etc.—a passage of importance as showing how naturally the inspired minds of that age put in contrast the serving of idols and the serving of the one living and true God. But the unity of God as opposed to polytheism is not necessarily a unity inconsistent with tripersonality.

Let it be noted also that "waiting for his Son from heaven" as explained in the New Testament involves and implies the real divinity of the Son, so that "turning to God from idols" does not exclude divine homage to the Son. To regard the Son as divine is *not* idolatry. Yet it would be if God's unity were of such a sort as must rule out the real divinity of the Son.

Twice in Paul's first epistle to Timothy, he brings out strongly the doctrine of the divine unity, viz. in 1 Tim. 1: 17, and 6: 15, 16: "Now unto the King eternal, immortal, invisible—the only wise God, be honor and glory forever and ever; amen." The best manuscripts omit the word "wise;" the best critics decide against its authority. The omission improves the sense—the thought being manifestly, not that the eternal King is the only God who has wisdom, but the only real God who exists at all. We must accept this passage as an explicit affirmation that there is but one God; yet nothing in the context indicates that the inspired apostle, either by implication or otherwise, meant to deny that the Son is also divine. The passage has no apparent reference of any sort to the Son or to the Holy Ghost.——The other passage runs thus: "Which in his times he shall show" [*i. e.* which appearing of the Lord Jesus he shall exhibit—cause to be seen—in its due time]—"even he who is the Blessed and only Potentate; the King of kings and Lord of lords; who only hath immortality, dwelling in the light which no man can approach unto; whom no man hath seen or can see: to whom be honor and power everlasting. Amen."——Thus in most sublime strains this passage bears human thought back of him who reveals God to created minds, to the Great Unseen and Unapproachable—the deathless One of whom immortality is a prime attribute, and whose power over his universe is simply supreme and eternal—"King of kings and Lord of lords." Yet these epithets which express supreme power are elsewhere applied with unabated fullness and force to the Lord Jesus. He too is "King of kings and Lord of lords" (Rev. 17: 14, and 19: 16)—as indeed we might expect from his own declaration:—"All power is given unto me in heaven and in earth" (Matt. 28: 18).——If to any one these words—"all power *given*"—should seem to indicate that the very nature of the Son is inferior—of lower grade as to divinity than that of the Father—"the Blessed and only Potentate"—it deserves special consideration that this apparent inferiority may be *only* apparent—not real; due to the subordinate part he acts in the great scheme of human redemption, and not to any intrinsic inferiority of nature. It certainly does not appear that these lofty terms of majesty are applied to the Father for the purpose of proving the natural inferiority of the Son and of the Spirit. Apparently the Son is before the eye of Paul *as seen in his incarnation*—coming back from heaven to the final judgment of the race—which fact of itself implies a position of relative subordination to the Father, yet without by any means assuming in the pre-existent Son a lower grade of divinity—(or better expressed) a grade of attributes less than really divine.

Last, we notice the extraordinary passage with which John closes his first epistle (1 John 5: 20): "We know that the Son of God is come and hath given us an understanding that we may know Him that is true" (the true *One*, and not as some copies have it, the true doctrine or thing); and we are in him that is true—in his Son Jesus Christ. "This [one] is the true God and eternal life."——This passage deserves to be studied with the utmost care. A paraphrase will help to present my view of it—thus: We know that we have attained the knowledge of the true God (the great world around us have not); for we are certain that the Son of God has come and has revealed to us such truth and hath given us such apprehension of it that we *know*—not merely *may* know, but (according to the best manuscripts) *do* know Him who is the true God. We not only know him but we are *in* him—that is to say, we are in his Son Jesus Christ. To be *in* the true God is to be *in* his Son; and to be *in* the Son is to be *in* the true God, for *this one*, Jesus Christ his Son, *is* the true God and eternal life.——The clause which in our English version commences with the word "even" in Italics must stand in grammatical apposition and therefore be identified in thought with the clause next preceding. We are in him who is the true God, the Father, by being in his Son Jesus Christ. To be in Christ is equivalent to being in the Father—carries with it the same relation toward the Father—because his Son Jesus Christ *is* the true God and is the fountain of eternal life.

Beyond these statements as to the metaphysical relations of the divine Father and the divine Son, John does not carry us. Was this exposition of it satisfactory to his own mind? It would be very difficult to prove that it was not. He drops no word which even suggests that he saw in these statements any conflict with the unity of God.

It is now in place to bring under special consideration some of the leading theories which have been proposed and more or less extensively held as harmonizing the unity of God with the scriptural representations of his tripersonality. Do they, any of them, meet the required conditions?

I arrange them as follows:

1. That the Logos is a created being; the first-born and the highest, but yet really deriving his existence from the Father, who is the one God only.——It does not essentially improve this theory to say that the Son came into being by "emanation" from the Father; nor to say [with Lessing] that "to think, to will, and

to create, are with God one," and that so, God projected his thought of himself into an existent person, "wanting in no perfection which he himself possessed." No matter what the mode of putting forth creative power may have been. The vital point is a derived existence, which necessarily carries with it the denial of his eternal being, and indeed the denial of all truly divine attributes. A created being may be very great; but no created being can be God. No created being can be worthy of worship as God. No created being can sit at the right hand of the Father on the throne of universal dominion, enjoying equal honors and praises with the Father. To admit this at all is to subvert the eternal and necessary distinction between the Infinite and the finite; is to annihilate all just notions of the worship due to the Infinite God and to him only.

2. That, ontologically considered, there is no original, essential distinction to which the term "person" can apply. The language of the Scriptures is to be explained as simply bold personification, there being at bottom nothing beyond distinct manifestation. God unrevealed is Father; but God considered as revealing himself to his intelligent creatures, whether before or after the incarnation, is the Logos: considered as energizing morally in the hearts of moral creatures for their regeneration and holiness, he is called the Spirit. It is only the one God, working in these diverse forms—much as the same one man may be a son to his parents; a father to his children; a husband to his wife; a magistrate to the civil community; a physician in professional business.

This theory might relieve the philosophical difficulties quite satisfactorily if only it could be made to meet sensibly the conditions of the scriptural representations. But to meet these conditions is entirely vital; and is indefinitely more important than to relieve our mundane philosophy. If we accept the Scriptures as a revelation from God, we must at least give them a fair, common sense interpretation.

Let this theory be tested by applying it to the Scriptures in question. Let "Father" be the name for the first manifestation; Son, for the second; Spirit, for the third.——The first manifestation loves the second and has given all power unto it: the second manifestation addresses the first, speaks of the glory enjoyed with it before the world was, and aspires to return and enjoy again the same glory. The second manifestation was from eternity with the first and was really God. Sometimes the first is represented as sending forth the third, and sometimes the second does the same thing.——It seems therefore that if we fall back to the facts affirmed in Scripture in reference to the things said and done by these several manifestations toward each other and toward our lost world for its redemption, we find these manifestations to be really persons, despite of our new and improved philosophical nomenclature. They fulfill the functions of personality. They have the mutual affections characteristic of personality, and bear to each other and to the universe the mutual relations of distinct persons.

It will perhaps be replied that these words of Scripture are bold personification, and nothing more: that the first manifestation is personified as Father; the second as Logos, etc. The reply to this would be that high bold personification has its proper atmosphere and home in the realms of fancy and imagination, and is entirely inadmissible elsewhere. The cool, good sense of mankind rebels utterly against its introduction in prosaic, matter-of-fact narration. The style and tone of John's gospel are altogether of this latter sort. To make this gospel history an allegory, after the model of Bunyan's "Christian Pilgrim" or Hannah More's "Parley the Porter," would shock the common sense of honest readers. The theory of manifestations in place of personality or as its philosophical explanation, does violence to all fair principles of interpretation and is therefore inadmissible.

3. A third theory assumes that the entire group of mental attributes or powers requisite to constitute a moral agent (classified well into intelligence, sensibility and free will), when existing in combination, constitute the one God. These mental attributes, broken up and rearranged or distributed, constitute severally the respective persons who appear in Scripture as Father, Son and Holy Ghost. No one of the several persons possesses the entire group. Thus, it would seem, we must understand Alford, his language being this (Com. p. 615): "The Son *never works of himself*, but always as the revelation of the Father;" "his work is the Father's *will*, and the Father has no Will except the Son *who is all* his will." "The Christian Fathers rightly rejected the Semi-Arian formula:—'The Son was begotten by an act of the Father's will'—*for he is that Will himself.*"——The statements of Athenagoras (one of the Fathers in the second century) seem to assume this theory: "The Son being in the Father and the Father in the Son, in oneness and power of Spirit, the understanding and reason [nous and logos] of the Father *is* the Son of God. If you inquire what is meant by the Son, I will state briefly that he is the first product of the Father, not as having been brought into existence (for from the beginning God who is the Eternal Mind [nous] had the Logos in himself, being from eternity instinct with Logos ['logikos']); but inasmuch as he came forth to be the idea and the energizing power of all material things which lay like a nature without attributes and an inactive earth, the grosser particles being mixed up with the lighter" (p. 385).——Again: "For we acknowledge a God, and a Son, his Logos, and a Holy Spirit, united in essence—the Father, Son and Spirit, because the Son is the Intelligence, Reason, Wisdom of the Father; and the Spirit an effluence, as light from fire" (p. 405).

In examining this theory the reader should be cautioned to keep it distinct from the one immediately preceding—viz. the theory of personification, or simply diverse manifestation.

The theory now under discussion must be carefully analyzed. What does it mean and imply? Does it mean that the Logos, going forth from God as the Will, took from the Godhead all there was of the *Will-power*, leaving none to the Father and none to the Spirit: *i. e.* leaving to the Father and to the Spirit only intelligence and sensibility; and, moreover, does it mean that the Logos, going forth thus as the Will-power, took from the Godhead *this power only*, and no intelligence—no sensibility? If so, then we must ask—How mere Will-power is to act to purpose without intelligence and without sensibility? What moral quality could there be in the exercises of such Will-power? How can such exercises be supposed to be worthy of love and of honor and glory from the Father?——And, moreover, how utterly inert must the Father and the Spirit be—all Will-power being abstracted? How does this theory help us conceive of Father, Logos and Spirit as each working severally in his respective sphere or function, *e. g.* in the scheme of human redemption?

Returning to the theory in question, we ask again—Does it allow to the Logos a *moderate amount* of intelligence and sensibility, but an extra amount—a very special development—of the will-power? And, as to the Father and the Spirit, does it in a corresponding manner accord to them a diminished will-force, but intelligence and sensibility in full divine measure?
——Then we must ask—What is gained by this reapportionment of the respective elements requisite to mental and moral action? Is it supposable that the Son acts with more energy of will than the Father, or than the Spirit? Or that he acts with somewhat less intelligence, or with less of the sensibility of emotion, desire, affection? What is the proof of either of these points? Does this theory bring any help whatever to the proper understanding of the scriptural representations on this subject?

Yet again; may we suppose this to be theory—viz. that God, considered as putting forth the energy of his will, is the Logos; that God, considered as loving the well-being of creatures and consulting with himself in wisdom and forming the great plans of creation and redemption, is the Father; and, moreover, considered as carrying out the scheme in the appliances of moral power [truth, persuasion], is the Spirit?——Then we have these problems to solve: how the will-power *in repose* during the past eternity can be said to have been "with God" and to "be God;" how the will-power, *going forth* in time for its activities in human redemption, can be said to be God; also, how God, considered as doing the work of the Logos, can be an object of love to God considered as *not* doing this work, but simply as giving up his Logos to do it?

Thus if we carry out this theory in its actual application to the words and to the apparent sense of Scripture, we shall find that we either have (despite of our theory) the distinct personality which we are seeking to escape because of its philosophical difficulties; or we slide into the theory of no distinction save in simple manifestation; or we abstract all sense and make nonsense of the scriptural conceptions and representations as to the mutual work and relations of Father, Son and Spirit.

4. Yet another theory labors to construct a Trinity by first making out a duality in all moral beings, resting upon the capacity of self-knowledge. This capacity, we shall readily see, belongs necessarily to all moral agents—human or divine—because without this power of knowing one's self, there could be no self-culture and no conscience; no compunction for wrong-doing; no intelligent self-approval for doing right.

Now in making up a duality of persons (suppose in either God or man) these speculative philosophers reason thus: "I know myself." I who have this knowledge am one; self, the object of this knowledge, is another, counting two—the knower and the known. Thus, say they, we certainly have a duality in all morally acting minds; and we need but one more to make up a trinity.

There are at least two fatal objections to this theory.——(1.) That two is not there, but lacks one of it. This difficulty, being mathematical, is thoroughly stubborn. Moreover, there is no room for the third in this category. A third party—standing on the same footing, of the same sort—is a natural impossibility. The great fact of a capacity for self-knowledge provides for an *apparent* duality (only apparent, however, not real), but can never provide for even an *apparent* Trinity. There can be no third party springing up out of this capacity for self-knowledge.

(2.) A second objection equally fatal is that this apparent duality is restricted to self-knowledge and disappears the moment we pass beyond it. As to all other activities and functions of mind even this duality has no existence.——This will be seen if we lay side by side the following propositions.——(*a.*) God knows himself—an apparent duality; God and self.——(*b.*) God knows man:—two entirely distinct parties. The proposition makes not the least approach toward a duality in God. God and himself here coalesce in one, with no conceivable distinction.——(*c.*) Again, God creates matter. Here is no shadow of distinction between God and himself. This distinction which was supposed to appear when the point affirmed was self-knowledge, disappears at once and universally when we step beyond the realm of self-knowledge. Therefore, for the point now in question—a duality or trinity to be developed in the work of human redemption, this theory is utterly valueless. The functions requisite in this great scheme have no affinity with self-knowledge. They call for outgoing activities altogether foreign to the study or conception of one's own mental states or acts, and therefore by their very nature shut off all aid from this apparent duality of persons.

5. Yet another theory which has found favor perhaps more extensively than any other among evangelical Christians, rests on an assumed distinction between essence or substance, and its attributes.

Commencing our analysis with matter, we naturally, perhaps

necessarily, think of a basis or substratum, underlying its qualities. A lump of matter has form, color, weight, etc., etc.—qualities, we call them; but we are wont to assume a basis of simple matter in which these diverse qualities inhere, albeit it might puzzle us to say what basis would remain if all these qualities, attributes, were taken out of it.

From this stepping-stone we ascend to our conception of spirit. Here too we seem compelled to think of some substratum, some basis which men are wont to call essence or substance. In this essence there exist the various spiritual faculties or powers which are called attributes. Now a theory to explain the trinity of persons in the Godhead has been built on this assumed distinction between essence and attributes. The three persons are said to be in essence one, but in grouping of attributes three. It is said that although in the subject *man* there can be but one group of attributes in any one spiritual essence or substance, yet we know too little of God to deny the possibility of a triune distinction in his nature—*i. e.* a threefold grouping of attributes in one divine essence.

Of this theory we may at least say, it is impossible to disprove it. It may possibly be the true solution of the mystery. It makes entirely in its favor that it does not build on any supposed analogy in the nature of man. Most obviously there *is no such analogy*. Man has no trinity in his being analogous to that which the Scriptures assume as to God; and the assumption that he has can never subserve any other end than to perplex, confound, and mislead.——In candor I must also express it as my opinion that, while this theory can not be disproved, so also it can not be proved. The elements of the problem lie beyond our depth—in the mysteries of the Infinite Mind.

In conclusion I call special attention to the following points:

1. The sacred writers (John and Paul) make no attempt to harmonize the trinity of God with his unity. Indeed they write as if they were entirely unconscious of any discrepancy between them. They seem to have no thought of any incompatibility between their conception of one only Supreme God, and the equal divinity of the Father, and of the Son, and of the Holy Ghost. I find no allusion to this subject as one involving mystery; much less any attempt to explain it as if it demanded explanation in order to its intelligent reception and practical utility. Paul does seem to speak of the incarnation as a great mystery: " Without controversy great is the mystery of godliness; God was manifest in the flesh; justified in the Spirit; seen of angels; preached unto the Gentiles; believed on in the world; received up into glory" (I Tim. 3: 16). On the face of it this passage seems to refer to the incarnation, and to this only: not at all, to the relations of the trinity to the unity of God. No similar utterance as to the trinity appears in either Paul or John. May we assume that they had no sense of mystery in these relations? Shall we conclude that they had a theory which relieved the subject of all

its otherwise apparent mystery, or that they accepted it as a mystery beyond the comprehension of human thought in this earthly state, and therefore wisely passed it in utter silence?—— A few words from their lips or pen might have helped us to decide between these two alternatives; but for such words we look in vain. Probably it is well left where it is. If we may suppose that the teaching Spirit determined in their case what *not* to say as well as what to say, we must rest in this conclusion.

This course of remark applies not only to passages in which John or Paul express their own thought (under inspiration of course), but also to those in which John (in particular) records the spoken words of Jesus; *e. g.* in his discussions with the Jews, and in his prayer (John 17) with his disciples. Jesus assumes his pre-existent divinity; his eternal existence with the Father in superlative glory—yet with no intimation that this might seem incomprehensible to human thought, or might so stagger our human conception as to justify repellent skepticism. He neither suggests that these things involve mystery too deep to be fathomed, nor does he volunteer any metaphysical explanation to relieve supposed incompatibility.

EXCURSUS II.

What is said by Jesus himself as to his then future comings, considered with reference to modern pre-millennial theories.

In the gospel of John we have met this prolific word in several passages.* In the other evangelists also it occurs in various senses.† Many minds are confused by the various meanings and various applications of this word. Some (as I believe) have radically misapprehended Christ's meaning, and have built upon their misconceptions a system at variance with the real doctrines of Scripture—especially this:—That Jesus has promised to come in his human body, long prior to the final resurrection and general judgment, to set up a sort of kingdom unknown before, reigning visibly over his people and virtually superseding the present dispensation of the Spirit.——Some hold this modified view—that the Scriptures are not clear on this point; that this visible coming and new kingdom *may* be the true sense of Scripture;—may therefore become real, but that as they understand the Scriptures, the question is left open and unsettled.

It is entirely vital to any useful discussion of this subject that we have definite views of the system built upon the supposed visible coming and personal reign of Christ.

Is it (*a*.) That the righteous dead are to be raised to live and reign with Christ in immortal bodies? This is generally if not universally held as a part of the system.

Is it (*b*.) That when Jesus shall visibly come, all living saints will be changed from mortal to immortal?——I suppose this also is the current opinion of those who hold to this visible coming and earthly reign.

Is it (*c*.) That the wicked, living on the earth at the supposed coming are to be destroyed by judgments; and if so, is this destruction universal, and are no more wicked men to live on the earth, and is probation to cease? Then the outcome of the system is—an end to probation in this world; an end to labor for

---

* *E. g.* 14: 2, 3, 16–18, 23, 28, and 21: 22, 23.
† Matt. 16: 27, 28, and its parallels (which are, Mark 9: 1, and Luke 9: 27); Matt. 24: 29–34, and its parallels (viz. Mark 13: 24–30, and Luke 21: 27, 31, 32); also Matt. 26: 64, and Luke 18: 8.

the salvation of sinners; a real transition into a state of universal retribution.——In regard to this scheme, we must ask—What is the benefit of cutting off all further labor for the salvation of men? What business have we to be longing and praying that gospel work may cease? And what is gained by having the future paradise of the saints located on this planet rather than in heaven?

But perhaps the more common view is that a *part only* of the wicked found on the earth are to be cut off; that a part survive and will continue as before under the normal laws of the present life; that gospel work will still go on among them, and with greater success than ever before.

Of the system in this form we may ask—Does it honor the Divine Spirit to assume that the bodily presence of Jesus will be more efficient toward the salvation of sinners or toward the spiritual life and joy of believers than the Spirit's invisible power? Does this correspond with the opinion expressed by Jesus himself:—"It is expedient for you that I go away" (as to my visible person), "and the Comforter come"?

Again: the doctrine being (supposably) that gospel agencies in this new reign are to be wielded, not by mortals but by immortals, then how about "having this treasure in earthen vessels that the excellency of the power may be of God and not of man"? Will it any longer be God's plan "by the foolishness of preaching to save them that believe"? How are immortals to come down to mortals in the sympathy of fellow-sufferers and reach them as standing with them on the common level of earthly frailty and suffering? Who can be very sure that this change would be a real improvement upon the present system of labor for the salvation of sons and daughters, of neighbors and fellow-sufferers?——It may seem to be very nice to be lifted at once out of all earthly frailty, but the further question will be—Ought we to be ready to forego the facilities which our kinship with sinners gives us in labor for their salvation? If men are tired of earthly toil and suffering even in the Master's service, for the salvation of the souls he died to save, and are absolutely impatient to get out of it, then they have the question to settle with their Master whether he will modify the system for their special convenience, relieving them from all burdens—from all hard work—from all liability to the infirmities common to a world of probation.

But some may say—You misapprehend the system. Only the raised saints are immortal; the living are to remain under the normal laws of our present life; and the wicked also.——Then these questions will arise: Who is to do the gospel work—the mortals, or the immortals? If there is to be co-operation, then under what laws? How are the immortals to work for the salvation of mortal men?——And yet again: How are the living saints all along the future ages of this new system, to have the real presence of Christ? Who and how many among the millions of them are to be favored with the special privilege of seeing his transfigured form and of hearing his celestial voice? With organs of sight limited to a few hundred feet, more or less, and of hearing yet more restricted as to space, who shall hear and who shall see the Son of man in this new form of his manifestation? To make the case plain, suppose that when Jesus trod the hills and valleys of Judea and of Galilee, instead of one hundred and twenty disciples in and about Jerusalem and five hundred who could be gathered in one spot in Galilee, there had been as many hundred thousands as at this moment, located in every country on the face of the earth, how many of them could have set their eyes on his glorious form, or bent their ears to his inspiring voice? How many of them all could have sat around the same table with him or wet his blessed feet with their penitent tears? Is there not a vast amount of careless thinking and thoughtless wishing when men compare the possible communion of saints with Jesus, spiritually manifested under the present system, with their privileges under this imagined visible reign of Christ on earth, themselves being still subjected to their present limitations of sense?

Not to push further at present either our search for the exact system of those who are enamored with the idea of Christ's personal reign on earth, or the difficulties we should find in its adoption, let us rather inquire:

Did Jesus promise such a coming and such a reign on earth? Has this system of views any scriptural bottom whatever?

To answer this inquiry satisfactorily, we must bring under consideration all the important passages in which Jesus spake of his own then future coming. What are they, and what do they legitimately mean?——Of course, their meaning must be ascertained from the connection in which they severally stand, and from whatever else is said as to those comings. A classification based on these principles will exceedingly facilitate a just and clear apprehension of the whole subject.

The passages in which Christ spake of his then future comings may be brought into four classes, arranged according to the various senses, or perhaps rather *purposes*, of the coming.

1. He comes for the purpose of taking his people to himself at their death.

2. He comes in the sense of manifesting his presence in the hearts of his people through the Divine Spirit, "the Comforter."

3. He comes in power (or in his kingdom) in the sense of bringing sore judgments on Jerusalem and the Jewish nation, contemplated as a great, hostile, persecuting power.

4. He comes at the end of the world to raise all the dead, and to judge all mankind.——His coming in judgments on Jerusalem (No. 3) is in several passages regarded as a type and pledge of this final coming, and consequently the two are brought into specially close connection.

1. Following out this classification, I place in the first class John 14: 2, 3: "In my Father's house are many mansions: I go

to prepare a place for you. And if I go and prepare a place for you, I WILL COME AGAIN and *receive you to myself*: that where I am, there ye may be also."——It seems too obvious to admit of rational doubt that these words refer to Christ's coming in the event of death to take each believer home to himself in heaven. This construction is in harmony with the course of thought in this connection, as manifested for example in Christ's words to Peter (13: 36)—"Whither I go thou canst not follow me now, but thou shalt follow me afterwards"—*i. e.* at thy death.—— Moreover, the only alternative construction which seems at all supposable (viz. that this coming is at the end of the world, and the taking of them to himself is only after the final judgment) is set aside by the doctrine of the entire New Testament—that Jesus does in fact take his people to himself immediately at their death: "This day shalt thou be with me in Paradise" (Luke 23: 43). The beggar (Lazarus) "was carried by angels into Abraham's bosom" and "was comforted" (Luke 16: 22, 25); "To depart" (in Paul's view) was "to be with Christ" (Phil. 1: 23), etc., etc. The Revelation of John every-where locates departed saints with Jesus even then. Hence scripturally the idea that this coming and receiving his people to himself refers to the final judgment is untenable. It must therefore refer to his coming at the death of each individual saint.

2. In a second sense of "coming," Jesus comes to his people in the manifestations of his presence by and through the Holy Spirit. Thus we must explain John 14: 16-18, 23, and perhaps v. 28: "I will pray the Father, and he will give you another Comforter, that he may abide with you forever, even the Spirit of truth: . . Ye know him, for he dwelleth with you, and shall be in you. I will not leave you comfortless; *I will come to you*"— *i. e.* come in the person of this "other Comforter" "who shall receive of mine, and shall show it unto you" (16: 14).——This construction is most abundantly confirmed throughout this context, the next verse declaring—"Yet a little while and the world seeth me no more" (his body being removed from earth), "but *ye see me*"—*i. e.* through the manifestations made of me to your souls by the Spirit.——Again, (v. 23): "If a man love me he will keep my words and my Father will love him, and *we will come unto him* and make our abode with him"—this coming being expressed (v. 21) by the word "manifest." See also v. 28: "Ye have heard how I said unto you, I go away and *come again unto you*"—probably in the sense of spiritual manifestations through the Holy Ghost, though possibly this may refer to John 14: 3—coming again to receive them to himself. To one or the other of these classes this passage must refer.——The reader may compare also Rev. 3: 20: "I will come in unto him and sup with him, and he with me."

3. In the third class Jesus speaks of himself as "coming in power" or "in his kingdom," in the sense of bringing desolating judgments on Jerusalem, and makes this fearful visitation of

retributive justice a type and pledge of his final judgment of the whole race.

The standard passages are—Matt. 16: 27, 28, with its parallels (Mark 8: 38, and 9: 1, and Luke 9: 26, 27); also Matt. 24: 29-34, with its parallels (Mark 13: 24-30, and Luke 21: 31, 32).—— That these passages have one reference to the final judgment is unquestionable :—"The Son of man shall come in the glory of his Father with his angels; and then shall he *reward every man according to his works*"—nothing less than the final judgment; but Jesus adds—"Verily I say unto you, There be some standing here who shall not taste of death till they see the Son of man coming in his kingdom,"—which with equal certainty must be a long anterior coming, of somewhat similar character, for similar purposes of retributive justice—yet, falling within the life-time of that generation, must refer to his judgments on Jerusalem. We are shut up to the same construction of Matt. 24 and its parallels.

It may in some cases be doubtful in which class (No. 3 or No. 4) we shall locate such passages as Matt. 26: 64: "Hereafter ye shall see the Son of man sitting on the right hand of power and coming in the clouds of heaven." It would be true in both senses of his coming—in the nearer future by terrible judgments on themselves, their city, temple and nation; in the more remote future, on his "great white throne" before which "should be gathered all nations." For our present purpose it is of no special consequence in which class we place this passage. It must certainly fall into one or the other. Its descriptive terms favor the latter—the final coming to judgment.——Of Luke 18: 8—"When the Son of man cometh, shall he find faith on the earth?"—it need only be said—there is nothing in the connection which serves to locate it at all. It seems to have been left indefinite purposely. If *at any time* the Son of man should come to see (as the Lord looked down upon the world in Noah's time to see what men were doing) would he find faith there? There is not here the least intimation of a visible, personal coming, nor the least hint of setting up a personal reign on the earth.

The passage (John 21: 22, 23) has been discussed in its place in the commentary.

4. Of passages in the fourth class, the standard one is Matt. 25: 31-46. The others of most importance have been noticed incidentally in speaking of the third class. The purposes and results of this coming are so entirely definite, so unlike the supposed personal coming for a visible reign on the earth, that there need be no difficulty in referring them to the final judgment.

Upon these passages thus classified, I remark—

1. Only the last of the four classes contemplates a visible, personal coming. The first may be by angelic ministration; the second is spiritual—through the agency of the Holy Ghost; the third is wrought through providential agencies; the fourth and this only, is a coming *in person*, visibly manifest before the universe.

2. None of these passages can by any fair construction be re-

moved from the class in which it is here arranged. [This must be taken as the author's personal conviction.]

3. Substantially, I think, they are exhaustive as to the subject, comprising all the passages in which Jesus speaks of himself as yet to come. No passage of any conceivable importance has been omitted intentionally.

4. Consequently, none of these passages can be fairly interpreted to promise and prove a visible coming yet future but long prior to the general judgment, for the purpose of inaugurating a visible reign on the earth. They do not mean such a coming.

5. Hence this doctrine of a visible, personal coming and reign on the earth has *no foundation in the recorded words of Christ*. So far as his words are concerned, it is a theory without a bottom. Nothing that Jesus has said contains the doctrine, or gives it the least support.

These facts might seem to constitute a sufficient refutation of this theory; yet somewhat more may be said—thus:—

(*a.*) This theory of a personal reign of Christ, superseding the present dispensation of the Spirit, is debarred *by its unwisdom*. Jesus himself has declared the present system—the spiritual dispensation of the Spirit—to be better: "It is expedient for you that I go away" (personally)—withdrawing my bodily presence—"that the Comforter may come." "If I go not away he will not come; if I go, I will send him unto you." The joint presence of both (Jesus in the body and the Spirit in his spiritual power) is not contemplated as falling within the divine plan. One or the other separately, but never both present and combined—is manifestly assumed and implied as the plan of God. Jesus affirms the dispensation of the Spirit to be the better and the more efficient.

——The same superiority in point of effective power is implied also in those words of Christ (John 14: 12): "He that believeth on me, the works that I do shall he do also; and *greater works than these* shall he do, because I go to the Father"—because Jesus, having gone to the Father, will send upon them the Spirit of power.

[On the alternative—either Jesus bodily, or the Spirit spiritually—but not both—see the commentary under John 16: 14, 15, p. 238-240.]

(*b.*) This theory of Christ's personal reign instead of the Spirit's agency is debarred by the expressed and implied *perpetuity of the Spirit's dispensation*, till the end of the world. "That he may abide with you forever" (John 14: 16). "Lo, I am with you alway" (as from that day forward *by the manifestation of the Spirit*) "even to the end of the world." In the same sense in which he was "*with them*" in the scenes of the first Christian Pentecost and onward, he would be to the end of time. What his presence *was* and what it *signified* then, it was to be to the end.

(*c.*) This theory of a personal reign is ruled out by the fact that the definite points it makes as to the nature, the surroundings, the laws and workings of this supposed personal reign are altogether imaginary—are simply and only speculation—there being not a word from Jesus himself which throws any light upon the assumed points in this theory. All there is of it comes from other sources than the words of Jesus. Most of the points which make up this ideal coming and reign seem to be the invention of human fancy; the rest is obtained from words of apostles and prophets misinterpreted. It ought to beget the gravest doubts as to the soundness of the whole scheme that *Jesus himself said absolutely nothing about such a visible reign in this world of probation and mercy and of gospel work for the salvation of men.*

(*d.*) Nay, more; during his public ministry Jesus persistently *contended against* the notion then current that his reign was to be visible, earthly, like that of human kings dependent on his visible presence. This notion was a deeply rooted error of the Jews of his generation, strongly imbedded moreover in the ideas of his own disciples—so strongly that it embarrassed and retarded their just conceptions of the nature of his kingdom, and for some time (we know not how long) tinged with more or less of error their notions of this kingdom.

This theory of Christ's visible coming and personal reign on earth is therefore the old error of worldly Jews revived, reproduced, and (sad to say) pushed, despite of the life-long opposition made against it by the teachings and life of Jesus.

(*e.*) If it be still insisted that Jesus has promised to "come in his kingdom;" to set up a kingdom, and that "the kingdom of heaven was near at hand," etc., etc.; and that, as this has not been done yet, it must be still future and may be now very near at hand—I reply:—The testimony of Jesus and of his apostles is perfectly decisive to the point that this kingdom was set up at the very beginning of the gospel age. Both he and they began their preaching with the declaration: "The kingdom of God [or of heaven] is at hand." As reported by Mark (1: 15) Jesus began with declaring—"The *time is fulfilled* and the kingdom of God is at hand." When questioned before Pilate, he avowed himself to be a king even then—but said: "My kingdom is not of this world"—not of earthly sort—but is an empire of truth—truth ruling and swaying the hearts of men.——When he had ascended to the Father, Peter proclaimed (Acts 2: 36)—"Let all the house of Israel know assuredly that God *hath made* that same Jesus whom ye have crucified *both Lord and Christ*"—"Lord" in the sense of Monarch, and Christ in the sense of Anointed King. What can this be but his inauguration as King in his long promised kingdom?——No less decisive is this (Acts 5: 31): "Him hath God exalted with his right hand to be a Prince and a Savior"—*hath* exalted already; "exalted to be a Prince"—a King on his gospel throne.——Proofs might be multiplied almost indefinitely to the same purport—that the Scriptures represent Jesus as exalted and enthroned *at his ascension*, to be universal King and Lord—precisely fulfilling all the promises made respecting his coming in his gospel kingdom. As illustrative cases (not exhaustive) see Phil. 2: 9-11, and 1 Pet. 3: 22. [Other senses of the word "*coming*" as used by Jesus, see treated above].

(*f.*) As a last argument for the near personal coming and personal reign of Christ, it may perhaps be said (it has been) that even if the words of Jesus do not teach this doctrine, the words of his disciples do teach it, for they supposed this coming even then near at hand. This lies outside of the words of Jesus, and therefore outside the limits of this essay; yet still very briefly I answer, If they did so suppose they were mistaken. The facts of the case have shown their mistake. Such a personal coming and visible reign on the earth *was not* then near at hand. Almost two thousand years have passed, and still Christ's reign is only spiritual, invisible, "not of this world;" and the visible, personal coming has not appeared. If the apostles, under the perverting influence of their early Jewish training, were expecting such a coming and such a reign soon—within their own life-time or shortly after, it was a mistake. That is the best that can be said of it. It does not become *us* to make this mistake because they did. But let us carefully make a broad discrimination between what they thought during the earthly life-time of Jesus, before they were enlightened by the Spirit; and what they held and taught when under inspiration they wrote their epistles. The former is of comparatively small moment to us; the latter is worthy of careful consideration.

Yet again: if it be claimed that their epistles teach and imply the *near visible coming* of Christ to set up a kingdom of this world, then it must still be said—on that construction of their words they were mistaken. If it be retorted that this way of speaking of the apostles is damaging to their inspiration, my reply is—Let those who put this construction upon their words see to that. The responsibility is theirs. For myself I do not believe that Paul and James and Peter (at the point when they wrote for us inspired epistles) did believe at all in Christ's personal, visible coming to reign on the earth; and of course they did not believe that such a coming for such a reign was then near at hand. My construction of their words does not at all imply that at the time of writing their epistles they held erroneous views on this point. They do seem to have been under somewhat grave misapprehensions on this subject up to and at the time of Christ's death. Immediately before his ascension, they put the question—"Wilt thou at this time restore again the kingdom to Israel?" (Acts 1: 6). How soon the teaching Spirit eliminated from their minds whatever was erroneous on this subject, is not revealed—perhaps can not be certainly known. But to hang a whole system of faith in a visible and personal reign of Christ on this earth upon their early misconceptions would be superlatively unfortunate, not to say unwise.

LECTURE-ROOM NOTES.

VAN DOREN'S SUGGESTIVE COMMENTARY.

D. APPLETON & CO., Broadway, New York; R. DICKINSON, 73 Farringdon St., London.

The following Scholars are interested in the Series:

GENESIS.—Professor BEECHER, Auburn Theological Seminary.
BOOK OF JOB.—THOS. ROBINSON, D. D., England.
PSALMS.—Professor I. MURPHY, D. D., Belfast Theological Seminary.
ECCLESIASTES AND PROVERBS.—L. YOUNG, D. D., Virginia.
ISAIAH.—Professor SMYTHE, D. D., Londonderry Theological Seminary.
MATTHEW.—Professor J. VERNAHAN, Ph. D., London.
LUKE.—W. H. VAN DOREN, D. D., Chicago. 2 vols. (*Now ready.*)
JOHN.—W. H. VAN DOREN, D. D., Chicago. 2 vols. (*Now ready.*)
ACTS.—W. R. GORDON, D. D., New Jersey.
ROMANS.—THOMAS ROBINSON, D. D., Morpeth, England. 2 vols. (*Now ready.*)
GALATIANS.—Professor T. CROSKEY, Londonderry.
HEBREWS.—Rev. THOMAS DOGGETT, Niagara.
CATHOLIC EPISTLES.—J. DEMAREST, D. D., New Jersey.

Rev. Dr. **FAUSSET**, *York, England, the Commentator.*
"I know no exposition of Scripture so terse, so suggestive, and yet so full and so clear."

DEAN **ALFORD**, *the Commentator.*
After a long, friendly letter, he apologizes thus: "I have had time only to read sixty pages. It will be a most useful work."

Rev. **CHAS. LEE**, *Havestock Hill.*
"The work of Dr. Van Doren contains the maximum of thought in the minimum of space."

THE HOMILIST, *London.*
"The idea of this series is an unusually happy one. It is preëminently suggestive."

THE FREEMAN, *London.*
"This work is much after our own heart. These volumes are among our best helps."

THE CHURCHMAN, *London.*
"This work contains under each sentence a few brief, well-chosen notes, which will be found of great value."

SWORD AND TROWEL, *Spurgeon, Editor.*
"This commentary is novel in its arrangement, and well sustains its title of suggestive."

CHRISTIAN WORLD, *London.*

"Dr. Van Doren's work is more condensed than Lange's, containing the pith and marrow of criticism. It will be prized by all who love the doctrines of the Reformation."

MORNING STAR, *London.*

"In this work are condensed the thought and criticism of many volumes. We shall hail with delight a complete work on this admirable plan."

J. C. RYLE, D. D., *Commentator.*

"A curious and original work. It succeeds in supplying an astonishing amount of thought and criticism in very few lines."

Rev. JAMES HAMILTON, D.D.

"I am sure Dr. Van Doren will have the gratitude of all whose books are few and whose time is precious."

Rev. J. JONES, *of Belfast.*

"To ministers and school-teachers I would say, that they will here find an amount of knowledge, in my judgment, not to be found in the same space anywhere else."

W. L. ALEXANDER, D. D., *Edinburgh.*

"I am much pleased with the plan, and with the success with which it has been carried out."

THE FORWARD, *London.*

"This work is cheap, compact, and suited to this hard-working age. The plan is new and useful."

BAPTIST MESSENGER, *London.*

"In ordinary cases we do not consult commentators in two cases out of ten with real advantage. But in the 'Suggestive Commentary' we have not in a single instance been disappointed."

BRITISH QUARTERLY, *London.*

"Dr. Van Doren, in the form of short sentences, brings together the gist of all previous commentators, and supplies abundance of hints to those who have but little leisure."

ENGLISH PRESBYTERIAN, *London.*

"To clergymen and students this work is invaluable. We have brought the work under the special notice of our friends in private."

WESLEYAN TIMES, *London.*

"An excellent idea, admirably worked out. We have tested the work on the Lord's Prayer, and we cordially commend it."

WESLEYAN METHODIST TIMES.

"It is a work to make men think, and not save them from thinking. These volumes will be welcome to many a student of the Scriptures. Hard-worked ministers and Bible-class teachers will be well repaid by studying them."

THE INDEPENDENT, *London.*

"This is a remarkable work, and valuable as well. If there ever was *multum in parvo*, it is here found. The labor in preparing it must have been immense. The work is eminently suggestive, and will save an enormous amount of time."

L. HALSEY, D. D., *Professor Theological Seminary, Chicago.*

"Every page bears marks of thorough and accurate scholarship, and of patient, careful study. It is the most *readable* commentary we have ever met. It is impossible to say things in quicker time or narrower space than he has said them."

G. B. CHEEVER, D. D.

"It is admirable. The best *multum in parvo* I have ever seen."

PRINCETON REVIEW.

"This work has been highly recommended by the journals of Great Britain. It certainly evinces thought, labor, and learning."

Cowles's Notes on the Old Testament

I. THE MINOR PROPHETS.
1 vol., 12mo. $2.00.

II. EZEKIEL AND DANIEL.
1 vol., 12mo. $2.25.

III. ISAIAH.
1 vol., 12mo. $2.25.

IV. PROVERBS, ECCLESIASTES, AND THE SONG OF SOLOMON.
1 vol., 12mo. $2.00.

V. NOTES ON JEREMIAH.
1 vol., 12mo. $2.25.

By Rev. HENRY COWLES, D. D.

From The Christian Intelligencer, N. Y.

"These works are designed for both pastor and people. They embody the results of much research, and elucidate the text of sacred Scripture with admirable force and simplicity. The learned professor, having devoted many years to the close and devout study of the Bible, seems to have become thoroughly furnished with all needful materials to produce a useful and trustworthy commentary."

From Dr. Leonard Bacon, of Yale College.

"There is, within my knowledge, no other work on the same portions of the Bible, combining so much of the results of accurate scholarship with so much common-sense and so much of a practical and devotional spirit."

From Rev. Dr. S. Wolcott, of Cleveland, Ohio.

"The author, who ranks as a scholar with the most eminent graduates of Yale College, has devoted years to the study of the Sacred Scriptures in the original tongues, and the fruits of careful and independent research appear in this work. With sound scholarship the writer combines the unction of deep religious experience, an earnest love of the truth, with a remarkable freedom from all fanciful speculation, a candid judgment, and the faculty of expressing his thoughts clearly and forcibly."

From President E. B. Fairfield, of Hillsdale College.

"I am very much pleased with your Commentary. It meets a want which has long been felt. For various reasons, the writings of the prophets have constituted a sealed book to a large part of the ministry as well as most of the common people. They are not sufficiently understood to make them appreciated. Your brief notes relieve them of all their want of interest to common readers. I think you have said just enough."

INTERNATIONAL SCIENTIFIC SERIES.

NOW READY.

No. 1. **FORMS OF WATER,** in Clouds, Rain, Rivers, Ice, and Glaciers. By Prof. JOHN TYNDALL, LL. D., F. R. S. 1 vol. Cloth. Price, $1.50.

No. 2. **PHYSICS AND POLITICS;** or, Thoughts on the Application of the Principles of "Natural Selection" and "Inheritance" to Political Society. By WALTER BAGEHOT, Esq., author of "The English Constitution." 1 vol. Cloth. Price, $1.50.

No. 3. **FOODS.** By EDWARD SMITH, M. D., LL. B., F. R. S. 1 vol. Cloth. Price, $1.75.

No. 4. **MIND AND BODY.** The Theories of their Relation. By ALEX. BAIN, LL. D., Professor of Logic in the University of Aberdeen. 1 vol., 12mo. Cloth. Price, $1.50.

No. 5. **THE STUDY OF SOCIOLOGY.** By HERBERT SPENCER. Price, $1.50.

No. 6. **THE NEW CHEMISTRY.** By Prof. JOSIAH P. COOKE, Jr., of Harvard University. 1 vol., 12mo. Cloth. Price, $2.00.

No. 7. **THE CONSERVATION OF ENERGY.** By Prof. BALFOUR STEWART, LL. D., F. R. S. 1 vol., 12mo. Cloth. Price, $1.50.

No. 8. **ANIMAL LOCOMOTION;** or, Walking, Swimming, and Flying, with a Dissertation on Aëronautics. By J. BELL PETTIGREW, M. D., F. R. S., F. R. S. E., F. R. C. P. E. 1 vol., 12mo. Fully illustrated. Price, $1.75.

No. 9. **RESPONSIBILITY IN MENTAL DISEASE.** By HENRY MAUDSLEY, M. D. 1 vol., 12mo. Cloth. Price, $1.50.

No. 10. **THE SCIENCE OF LAW.** By Prof. SHELDON AMOS. 1 vol., 12mo. Cloth. Price, $1.75.

No. 11. **ANIMAL MECHANISM.** A Treatise on Terrestrial and Aërial Locomotion. By E. J. MAREY. With 117 Illustrations. Price, $1.75.

No. 12. **THE HISTORY OF THE CONFLICT BETWEEN RELIGION AND SCIENCE.** By JOHN WM. DRAPER, M. D., LL. D., author of "The Intellectual Development of Europe." Price, $1.75.

No. 13. **THE DOCTRINE OF DESCENT AND DARWINISM.** By Prof. OSCAR SCHMIDT, Strasburg University. Price, $1.50.

No. 14. **THE CHEMISTRY OF LIGHT AND PHOTOGRAPHY.** In its Application to Art, Science, and Industry. By Dr. HERMANN VOGEL. 100 Illustrations. Price, $2.00.

No. 15. **FUNGI;** their Nature, Influence, and Uses. By M. C. COOKE, M. A., LL. D. Edited by Rev. M. J. BERKELEY, M. A., F. L. S. With 109 Illustrations. Price, $1.50.

No. 16. **THE LIFE AND GROWTH OF LANGUAGE.** By Prof. W. D. WHITNEY, of Yale College. Price, $1.50.

No. 17. **MONEY AND THE MECHANISM OF EXCHANGE.** By W. STANLEY JEVONS, M. A., F. R. S., Professor of Logic and Political Economy in the Owens College, Manchester. Price, $1.75.

No. 18. **THE NATURE OF LIGHT,** with a General Account of Physical Optics. By Dr. EUGENE LOMMEL, Professor of Physics in the University of Erlangen. With 188 Illustrations and a Plate of Spectra in Chromolithography. Price, $2.00.

No. 19. **ANIMAL PARASITES AND MESSMATES.** By Monsieur VAN BENEDEN, Professor of the University of Louvain, Correspondent of the Institute of France. With 83 Illustrations. (*In press.*)

D. APPLETON & CO., PUBLISHERS, 549 & 551 Broadway, N. Y.

A SUPERB NEW WORK BY LACROIX.

THE EIGHTEENTH CENTURY.

THE MANNERS, CUSTOMS, AND COSTUMES OF THE EIGHTEENTH CENTURY, IN FRANCE, 1700–1789.

Illustrated with twenty-one magnificent Chromo-lithographs (art-gems in themselves), and *three hundred and fifty* highly-finished Wood-Engravings after Watteau, Vanloo, Rigaud, Boucher, Lancret, J. Vernet, Chardin, Jeaurat, Beauchardon, Saint-Aubin, Eisen, Gravelot, Moreau, Cochin, Wille, Debucourt, etc. The designs, lithographs, and engravings, all executed by eminent artists, under the direction of M. Racinet, the well-known author of "Polychromatic Ornament." In one sumptuous volume, imperial 8vo, cloth, emblematic gilt sides, and gilt edges, $15; half calf, $18; calf, $21; tree calf, $28; morocco, extra, $24.

The comprehensive character of this work will be appreciated more fully by noting contents, embracing, as they do, the social ranks and customs, the public occupations, amusements, etc., of "La Belle France," as follows, viz.:

1. The King and the Court.	8. The Finances.	14. Fêtes and Pleasures of Paris.
2. The Nobles.	9. Commerce.	
3. The Bourgeoisie.	10. Education.	15. The Cuisine and Table.
4. The People.	11. Charities.	16. The Theatres.
5. The Army and Navy.	12. Justice and Police.	17. The Salons.
6. The Clergy.	13. Aspect of Paris.	18. Voyages, etc.
7. The Parliament.		19. Costumes and Modes.

*** The splendid success of the various works of M. Lacroix, on the "Manners, Customs, and Dress, during the Middle Ages, and during the Renaissance," suggested the preparation of a work of a similar character, on the "Institutions, Manners, and Dress, in France, during the Eighteenth Century." This sumptuous volume is a brilliant exhibition of every grade of life and society in France, from 1700 to 1789. The work is illustrated with 21 full-page Chromo-lithographs, richly colored, and 350 beautiful Engravings on Wood. These illustrations are copied with the utmost care from the original paintings of the best and most esteemed artists of the eighteenth century, and in beauty of design, exquisite finish, and the real interest of their subjects, far surpass any similar productions. The typographical excellence, and elaborate and appropriate binding, combined with its intrinsic literary and artistic value, render it one of the richest volumes ever published.

OTHER WORKS BY THE SAME AUTHOR.

THE ARTS IN THE MIDDLE AGES, and at the Period of the Renaissance. By PAUL LACROIX, Curator of the Imperial Library of the Arsenal, Paris. Illustrated with 19 Chromo-lithographic Prints by Kellerhoven, and upward of 400 Engravings on Wood. 1 vol., imperial 8vo, cloth, gilt sides and back. 520 pages. Price, $12; half calf, $15; half morocco, $15; full calf, $18; full morocco, $25.

MANNERS, CUSTOMS, AND DRESS, DURING THE MIDDLE AGES, and during the Renaissance Period. By PAUL LACROIX. Illustrated with 15 Chromo-lithographic Prints by F. Kellerhoven, and upward of 400 Engravings on Wood. 1 vol., royal 8vo. Half morocco, price, $12; half morocco, extra, $15; half calf, $15; calf, $18; tree calf, $25; morocco, extra, $21; morocco, super extra, $25.

MILITARY AND RELIGIOUS LIFE IN THE MIDDLE AGES, and at the Period of the Renaissance. By PAUL LACROIX. Illustrated with 14 Chromo-lithographic Prints by J. Kellerhoven, Réjamey, and L. Allard, and upward of 400 Engravings on Wood. 1 vol., royal 8vo. Half bound, $12; half calf and morocco, $15; calf, $18; tree calf, $25; morocco, extra, $21; super extra, $25.

D. APPLETON & CO., PUBLISHERS,
549 & 551 *Broadway, New York.*

MEMOIRS OF GENERAL WILLIAM T. SHERMAN,

WRITTEN BY HIMSELF. Complete in Two Volumes. With a Military Map showing the Marches of the Armies under General Sherman's Command, inserted in a pocket at the end of the second volume; size, 30 by 47 inches. Small 8vo, 400 pages each. Price, in Blue Cloth, $5.50; Sheep, $7.00; Half Morocco, $8.50; Full Morocco, $12.00.

"These memoirs are by far the most interesting and important contribution yet made to the military history of the Rebellion by any of the leading actors in the great struggle. The staggering blows which General Sherman dealt to the Confederacy have secured him the undying gratitude of his countrymen, while the brilliancy which he displayed as a strategist, and the surpassing ability which he developed as a commander, entitle him to rank among the most distinguished leaders that the world has produced. The personal history of so marked a man must always possess extraordinary interest. When it is related by the man himself, and in that peculiarly racy style which General Sherman's letters and speeches have made familiar to the public, it becomes not only absorbing but fascinating. The march from Atlanta began on the morning of November 15th. General Sherman's narrative of this whole movement is of romantic interest. Some of his descriptions are not only picturesque but thrilling in their eloquence. And interspersed are well-told incidents, many of them full of genuine humor, which give unusual vivacity to the story. In military annals the narrative is unique, but it must be read in its entirety to be appreciated. The terse, clear, vigorous English in which the memoirs are written is one of their greatest charms. This fitly reflects the intense personality of the man. The straightforward, spirited narrative will enable a grateful country better to appreciate the immense value of the services which General Sherman rendered it in the critical period through which he helped guide it, and it will also aid others than Americans in forming a clearer estimate of the tremendous struggle in which the author of these memoirs bore so distinguished a part."—*N. Y. Times.*

"An autobiography so unreserved as this of General Sherman, printed during the lifetime of the writer, would certainly be an unsafe procedure for one who had the least need of any assistance from humbug. The author of these memoirs is a man who can afford to be seen as he is. Strip him of his epaulets, his brass buttons, and his cocked hat, and he still appears a valiant, able, and distinguished person. Indeed, it is quite necessary that he should be stripped of these accoutrements. We need to see him amid the camp-fires of Georgia, or on the march with his wagon-trains and foraging-bummers. So much for the picturesque and external man. But there is no need that he should conceal the mind behind all this. General Sherman has told his story with the most entire unreserve, and the story is one which Americans will be proud to read. We cannot help a feeling of satisfaction in being of the same race and the same country with such a man. We have here a picture of a person, resolute yet cautious, bold yet prudent, confident yet modest; a man of action to his finger-ends, yet withal something of a poet; we see all through the book the evidences of a chivalrous mind and of an intellect of singular force and precision. . . . We have spoken of Sherman as, in some sort, a poet. All through these great campaigns, while his whole mind is absorbed with the events he is conducting, he nevertheless appears to take a poet's joy in the spectacle of his battle-fields and moving armies. His enthusiasm will be shared by his readers. That passage in which he speaks of his last look on Atlanta, and tells us how it brought to his mind 'many a thought of desperate battle, of hope and fear,' has an eloquence which no mere writer of books can reach. The skill to write in that way is not taught in Blair or Whately."—*N. Y. Evening Post.*

"Sherman shows that he can wield the pen as well as the sword. His style is as much his own as that of Cæsar or Napoleon. It is a winning style. We see a gifted man telling his life in a plain, artless fashion, but with a trenchant rhetoric. Whenever an opinion is demanded he gives it. His picture of the early days in California is as graphic as a chapter from Sir Walter Scott. Now and then there are criticisms upon his contemporaries which will provoke comment; but, plainly enough, Sherman means what he says. This is the value of the work. We are glad the General has written it. In many cases it throws new light upon the Rebellion. Only by such light can the full measure of that momentous time be taken. And, whatever criticisms may be made upon the book, we honor the General for having given us so graphic and just a history of events in which he himself was so illustrious and successful an actor."—*N. Y. Herald.*

D. APPLETON & CO., *Publishers*, 549 & 551 Broadway, N. Y

"A rich list of fruitful topics."
BOSTON COMMONWEALTH.

HEALTH AND EDUCATION,

By the REV. CHARLES KINGSLEY, F. L. S., F. G. S.,
CANON OF WESTMINSTER.

12mo. Cloth. . . . . . . Price, $1.75.

"It is most refreshing to meet an earnest soul, and such, preëminently, is Charles Kingsley, and he has shown himself such in every thing he has written, from 'Alton Locke' and 'Village Sermons,' a quarter of a century since, to the present volume, which is no exception. Here are fifteen Essays and Lectures, excellent and interesting in different degrees, but all exhibiting the author's peculiar characteristics of thought and style, and some of them blending most valuable instruction with entertainment, as few living writers can."—*Hartford Post.*

"That the title of this book is not expressive of its actual contents, is made manifest by a mere glance at its pages; it is, in fact, a collection of Essays and Lectures, written and delivered upon various occasions by its distinguished author; as such it cannot be otherwise than readable, and no intelligent mind needs to be assured that Charles Kingsley is fascinating, whether he treats of Gothic Architecture, Natural History, or the Education of Women. The lecture on Thrift, which was intended for the women of England, may be read with profit and pleasure by the women of everywhere."—*St. Louis Democrat.*

"The book contains exactly what every one needs to know, and in a form which every one can understand."—*Boston Journal.*

"This volume no doubt contains his best thoughts on all the most important topics of the day."—*Detroit Post.*

"Nothing could be better or more entertaining for the family library."—*Zion's Herald.*

"For the style alone, and for the vivid pictures frequently presented, this latest production of Mr. Kingsley commends itself to readers. The topics treated are mostly practical, but the manner is always the manner of a master in composition. Whether discussing the abstract science of health, the subject of ventilation, the education of the different classes that form English society, natural history, geology, heroic aspiration, superstitious fears, or personal communication with Nature, we find the same freshness of treatment, and the same eloquence and affluence of language that distinguish the productions in other fields of this gifted author."—*Boston Gazette.*

D. APPLETON & CO., Publishers,
549 & 551 BROADWAY, N. Y.

THE EXPANSE OF HEAVEN;

A Series of Essays on the Wonders of the Firmament.

By R. A. PROCTOR, B. A.

1 vol., 12mo. Cloth. . . . . . Price, $2.00.

"It is Mr. Proctor's good fortune that not only is he one of the greatest of living astronomers, but that he has a power of imparting knowledge that is not equaled by any living astronomer. His style is as lucid as the light with which he deals so largely, and the plainest of readers can go along with him with entire ease, and comprehend all that he says on the grandest subject ever discussed by mortal intelligence. Most scientific writers either cannot or will not so use the pen as to make themselves understood by the many; not so with Mr. Proctor: he both can and does so write as to command the attention of the million, and this too without in the least derogating from the real dignity of his sublime theme. Few of us can study astronomy, because that implies a concentrated devotion to an inexhaustible matter, but we all can read astronomical works to our great advantage if astronomers who write will but write plainly; and in that way, without having the slightest claim to be spoken of as "scientists," we can acquire no ordinary amount of knowledge concerning things that are of the loftiest nature, and the effect of which must be to elevate the mind. Such a book as 'The Expanse of Heaven' cannot fail to be of immense use in forwarding the work of education even when it is read only for amusement, so forcible is the impression it makes on the mind from the importance of the subjects treated of, while the manner of treatment is so good."—*Boston Traveller.*

"Since the appearance of Ennis's book on 'The Origin of the Stars,' we have not read a more attractive work on astronomy than this. It is learned enough to be instructive, and light enough to be very entertaining."—*Alta California.*

"It reads like a work of fiction, so smooth and consecutive is it; but it inspires the worthiest thoughts and the highest aspirations."—*Boston Commonwealth.*

"Perfectly adapted to their purposes, namely, to awaken a love for science, and at the same time to convey, in a pleasant manner, some elementary facts."—*Church Herald.*

"This is not a technically scientific work, but an expression of a true scholar's conception of the vastness and grandeur of the heavens. There is no dry detail, but blended with the scholar's discoveries are the poet's thoughts, and a true recognition of the Almighty's power."—*Troy Times.*

D. APPLETON & CO., Publishers,

549 & 551 BROADWAY, N. Y.

A thoughtful and valuable contribution to the best religious literature of the day.

RELIGION AND SCIENCE.

A Series of Sunday Lectures on the Relation of Natural and Revealed Religion, or the Truths revealed in Nature and Scripture.

By JOSEPH LE CONTE,
PROFESSOR OF GEOLOGY AND NATURAL HISTORY IN THE UNIVERSITY OF CALIFORNIA.

12mo, cloth. *Price*, $1.50.

OPINIONS OF THE PRESS.

"This work is chiefly remarkable as a conscientious effort to reconcile the revelations of Science with those of Scripture, and will be very useful to teachers of the different Sunday-schools."—*Detroit Union.*

"It will be seen, by this *résumé* of the topics, that Prof. Le Conte grapples with some of the gravest questions which agitate the thinking world. He treats of them all with dignity and fairness, and in a manner so clear, persuasive, and eloquent, as to engage the undivided attention of the reader. We commend the book cordially to the regard of all who are interested in whatever pertains to the discussion of these grave questions, and especially to those who desire to examine closely the strong foundations on which the Christian faith is reared."—*Boston Journal.*

"A reverent student of Nature and religion is the best-qualified man to instruct others in their harmony. The author at first intended his work for a Bible-class, but, as it grew under his hands, it seemed well to give it form in a neat volume. The lectures are from a decidedly religious stand-point, and as such present a new method of treatment."—*Philadelphia Age.*

"This volume is made up of lectures delivered to his pupils, and is written with much clearness of thought and unusual clearness of expression, although the author's English is not always above reproach. It is partly a treatise on natural theology and partly a defense of the Bible against the assaults of modern science. In the latter aspect the author's method is an eminently wise one. He accepts whatever science has proved, and he also accepts the divine origin of the Bible. Where the two seem to conflict he prefers to await the reconciliation, which is inevitable if both are true, rather than to waste time and words in inventing ingenious and doubtful theories to force them into seeming accord. Both as a theologian and a man of science, Prof. Le Conte's opinions are entitled to respectful attention, and there are few who will not recognize his book as a thoughtful and valuable contribution to the best religious literature of the day."—*New York World.*

D. APPLETON & CO., Publishers, 549 & 551 Broadway, N. Y.

The Recovery of Jerusalem.

BY

Capt. WILSON, R. E., and Capt. WARREN, R. E.,
Etc., Etc.

1 *vol.*, 8*vo.* Cloth. *With Maps and Illustrations.*

Price, $3.50.

"This is a narrative of exploration and discovery in the City of Jerusalem and the Holy Land. It is a volume of unusual interest to the student of antiquities, and throws much light upon what was already partially known about the Holy City, and opens up many curious speculations and suggestions about things that were entirely unknown until the excavations and explorations commenced which the book faithfully records. The maps and illustrations much enhance the interest, and aid in a thorough understanding of the things described. It is a volume of over 400 pages, 8vo., bound in cloth, and altogether beautifully presented."—*Springfield Republican.*

Christ in Modern Life.

SERMONS PREACHED AT ST. JAMES'S CHAPEL.

By Rev. STOPFORD A. BROOKE.

1 vol., 12mo, Cloth....................Price, $2.00.

The main thought which underlies this volume is, that the ideas which Christ made manifest on earth are capable of endless expansion, to suit the wants of men in every age; and that they do expand, developing into new forms of larger import and wider application, in a direct proportion to that progress of mankind, of which they are both root and sap. If we look long and earnestly enough, we shall find in them the explanation and solution not only of our religious, but even of our political and social problems. All that is herein said is rested upon the truth that in Christ was Life, and that this Life, in the thoughts and acts which flowed from it, was, and is, and always will be, the light of the race of man.

D. APPLETON & CO., Publishers, New York.

www.ingramcontent.com/pod-product-compliance
Lightning Source LLC
Chambersburg PA
CBHW022118290426
44112CB00008B/727